EXTRA TIME
THE FINAL CHAPTER

Willie Maddren

The Official Biography

Updated by Hilary Maddren

with Dave Allan

kindly sponsored by
Bakers Tailoring

All profits from sales of this book will be donated to the Willie Maddren MND Fund in support of research into Motor Neurone Disease.

Willie Maddren

Copyright 2005 Willie Maddren MND Fund

All rights reserved

The moral right of the author has been asserted

Extra Time first published in Great Britain in 1998.
Extra Time – The Final Chapter first published in Great Britain in 2005 by
The Willie Maddren MND Fund
83 Junction Road, Norton, Stockton-on-Tees, TS20 1PU

ISBN 0-9533687-1-8

No part of this book may be reproduced or transmitted in any form or by any means without written permission from the publisher, except by a reviewer who wishes to quote brief passages in connection with a review written for insertion in a magazine, newspaper, internet website or broadcast.

Designed and printed by Hillprint Media, Prime House,
Heighington Lane Business Park, Newton Aycliffe, County Durham.
Tel 01325 245555. www.hillprintmedia.com

Photo Credits

The authors and pubishers are grateful to the following for permission to use photographs in this book: Colorsport, North Eastern Evening Gazette, North of England Newspapers, Highland Studios, Middlesbrough Football Club, Newcastle Evening Chronicle, North News & Pictures, Gary Walsh Photography.

Extra Time – The Final Chapter

If you enjoy reading this book, please don't lend it out.
Recommend it to your friends but ask them to buy another copy.
That extra sale may one day help to save someone's life by
helping to find a cure for Motor Neurone Disease.

Willie & Hilary Maddren

BAKERS
TAILORING

Bakers Tailoring has been suiting the people of Middlesbrough since 1911. Starting off life as a merchant naval outfitter, Bakers have always been renowned for quality, service and style. Bakers Tailoring was relaunched on Middlesbrough's Linthorpe Road in March this year, opened by Middlesbrough's footballing legend Juninho. The interior has a 60s retro feel giving the ultimate shopping environment, a modern day gentleman's outfitters, carrying some of Europe's top quality collections, including Alfred Dunhill, Canali, Aquascutum, Cerruti 1881 and Pringle.

CUSTOM MADE TAILORING SPECIALISTS

CASUALWEAR

CONTEMPORARY CLASSICS

HOME & OFFICE VISITS AVAILABLE

FREE CUSTOMER PARKING

TEL: 01642 226358

194 LINTHORPE ROAD
MIDDLESBROUGH
TS1 3RF

www.bakerstailoring.com

EXTRA TIME
THE FINAL CHAPTER

CONTENTS

		Page
	Foreword by Graeme Souness	1
	Foreword by David Mills	3
	Prologue by Hilary Maddren	5
	Introduction	9
	To My Hero	17
1	Shankly was Wrong	18
2	When I was a Lad	23
3	Reserve Recollections	44
4	Joy...and Pain	59
5	The Case for the Defence	66
6	When Stan was the Man	80
7	Up the Boro!	94
8	The Team that Jack Built	121
9	Tales from Down Under	140
10	Boring Boro?	153
11	Game Over	172
12	In Retrospect	197
13	It's a Funny Old Game	212
14	On the Coaching Ladder	228
15	Back at the Boro	237
16	Just about Managing	250
17	Building Boro's Future	284
18	Mission: Impossible	310
19	Shop till I Drop	323
20	The Day that Changed My Life	339
	All I Require	360
21	A Game I Can't Win	361
22	Hilary's Story	387
	My Kid Brother	393
23	The Last "I Love You"	394
24	The Final Chapter?	405
	I Am Not There	415
	Father, Confidant and Entertainer – by Lucy Maddren	416
	Putting Life in Perspective – by Steven Maddren	419
	My Dad, My Hero – by Laura Maddren	422
	Proud to be his Son – by David Maddren	424
	Motor Neurone Disease: An Introduction	426

Acknowledgements

LOOKING back over my life, there are so many people I would like to thank for the love, friendship, experience and knowledge they shared with me.

Of course, I must mention my parents, for the loving, caring way in which they brought me up to have good morals and standards, and for the way they have shaped my life in so many other positive ways.

As I progressed in professional football, Middlesbrough manager Stan Anderson and coach Jimmy Greenhalgh taught me good habits and how to be a good pro. Another major influence was Jack Charlton, who gave the club and its supporters those magnificent days in the mid-1970s. More recently, Jack has shown me much warmth and understanding of my illness. For his lifelong friendship and loyalty, I would also like to thank Steve Smelt, my physio during those difficult days as Middlesbrough's manager.

I have received so much support and understanding since contracting Motor Neurone Disease, not least from all those involved with the Cleveland branch of the MND Association. My neurologist, Dr Peter Newman, and his staff have given me much reassurance. To my friend Geoff Stoker, who has always been there for me.

I am fortunate to have enjoyed a truly special relationship with the People of Teesside, who have shown me love and warmth throughout my life.

Members of my family have been pillars of strength. My brothers, Dave and Chris, and sister, Claire, all gave me love and understanding all my life and especially in these last few testing years. My devoted in-laws have played their part too, while my children, Lucy, Steven, Laura and David, have displayed untold bravery and undying love.

Most of all, my wonderful wife, Hilary, who has given me unbending support, the strength to carry on when I am at my lowest ebb and the sort of love that few in the world shall ever know.

Willie Maddren

Extra Time – The Final Chapter

I HAVE been grateful for the support of so many friends, from Bill and Judith Gates, for lending a listening and understanding ear when I was down, to George and Maureen Smith, for their continued friendship and fundraising in Willie's name.

To Marjorie and Trevor Cook during the latter stages of Willie's illness, not only for being good neighbours but for helping to keep our family social life alive. To my group of Hartlepool girl friends, who have helped me laugh, lunch and shown me how to shop once more.

Special thanks to Kendra, Vicky, Jackie, Pat and all my staff from the shop, who in the final years kept things running like clockwork without me, so that I could spend that special time at home with Willie.

I have been touched, too, that it is not only the Maddren family that takes time out to remember Willie, but others do so, often quietly, without pomp or ceremony. Two such people are our friends, Ann and John Johnson, who I know have often laid flowers at Willie's graveside, in memory of the many New Years we spent together.

And, finally, to all those who have helped keep alive Willie's name either by purchasing this or the original book, and by taking part or attending the numerous fundraising events for the MND cause.

Hilary Maddren

Willie Maddren

Acknowledgements

WORKING on this book reawakened my admiration for both Willie and Hilary. Quite simply, Willie was an inspiration and I was privileged to spend so much time with him while writing the original book. The knowledge that he was such a special man must only serve to heighten the sense of loss felt by Hilary and all of his family. The saying goes that behind every great man there's a great woman. This great woman, Hilary, always stood right alongside her great man with a strength and dignity that defies belief. Since his passing, she has been as good as her word to him in carrying on the fight to try to find a cure to Motor Neurone Disease. Recalling those painful memories after all these years was an emotional journey for her to make, but I know sales of this book will mean it was worth it.

Thanks to my true friend Mike McGeary for spending time proofreading the book's manuscript and rightly pointing out my numerous grammatical errors. I also remain grateful to Mark Hooper for carrying out a similar role on the original book. Father Paul Farrer's technical skills were also much appreciated this time around. A special mention too, to Peter Groves, Richard Mortimer and all at Hillprint Media for their support for this project a second time. The service they have offered has always gone beyond the call of duty. The support of Adil Ditta in ensuring that Bakers Tailoring sponsored the book was much appreciated.

The biggest thanks to my beautiful wife, Bernie, who once again forfeited our quality time together while, night after night, my fingers pounded the keyboard until the early hours. Her support was invaluable. So too was the encouragement to write I always received until his passing of my much-missed Dad. After Hilary and I, Bernie was the first to read *The Final Chapter*. If, like her, you read it with tears in your eyes, I would ask you to recommend to your friends and family that they too buy the book to further boost the Willie Maddren MND Fund.

Dave Allan

Dedication

To my devoted wife Hilary
and my adoring children
Lucy, Steven, Laura and David

Willie Maddren

Extra Time – The Final Chapter

A Shining Beacon
Foreword by Graeme Souness

It is a privilege to have this opportunity to pay tribute to my great friend, Willie Maddren. Quite simply, Willie was an outstanding man, a true gentleman whose personality, attitude and character stood out like a shining beacon in the world of professional football. The biggest tribute I can pay him is that he displayed attributes every human being, let alone top sportsmen, could wish for.

I first met Willie when I joined Middlesbrough from Tottenham in 1972. I was the 19-year-old new kid on the block who was grateful for Willie, two years my senior, taking me under his wing. We soon became firm friends, and it is no exaggeration to say that, in pointing me in the right direction whilst I was still trying to find my way in the game, he was an enormous influence on my career.

The publication of the original version of *Extra Time* rekindled many special memories of our five years together at Middlesbrough. Willie was always great fun to be around, displaying an almost childlike sense of humour that made him hugely popular in the Ayresome Park dressing room. At the same time, he always commanded great respect among his teammates. He was a true professional, who really loved his sport – always first on to the training pitch and last off it.

Unfortunately, the serious knee injury he suffered denied Willie the opportunity to fulfil his enormous potential, but I have no hesitation in saying that he would otherwise have established himself as one of most high profile footballers in the country. Whilst he achieved great success on a regional basis, I have no doubt that he would have been an England regular for many years but for injury forcing him into a premature retirement from the game.

Willie Maddren

Those who were lucky enough to have known Willie will appreciate what a special man he was. I wasn't in the least bit surprised when he retained his unique sense of humour right until the end of his life. Even now, he still has the ability to bring a smile to my face whenever I see his name or picture in the media.

Willie was one of a rare breed and I, for one, was privileged to stand alongside him. His memory is one I truly cherish.

Graeme Souness

Extra Time – The Final Chapter

An Unassuming Hero
Foreword by David Mills

There can have been few more popular men in the history of football than Willie Maddren. Football supporters recognised his ability as a player, but perhaps only family and friends could appreciate his personality away from the game. He was always immensely popular with team-mates. In fact, I didn't know of anyone, inside or outside the game, who didn't like him. He was humble and unassuming, and yet he possessed a toughness about him too. He was someone that you would gladly have alongside you if ever you were 'in the trenches'. Those many qualities naturally ensured that Willie gained great respect from all who met him.

As a young boy, I would listen to people talking about players from previous generations, many of whom I didn't actually see play in person. One of those players was John Charles. I had an image of Willie being a modern day John Charles, equally capable of playing centre-forward or centre-half, though he would have been comfortable playing in any position. Willie had virtually every quality that a manager could wish for in a player – pace, two good feet, passing ability over any distance, aerial power, the ability to read the game, physical and mental strength plus immense courage. How he would rely on those last two qualities later in his life.

Willie and I grew up together at Middlesbrough Football Club, although our first meeting came as opponents for our respective schools in the Stockton & District Under-15 League. It followed that we would both be selected to represent the district team, and that was where our enduring friendship began. Although we were similar ages, Willie was actually a school year ahead, so he joined Boro slightly in advance of myself. After I signed, we found ourselves playing together for the club's under-19s in the Northern Intermediate League, progressing into the

Willie Maddren

reserves, the first team and finally England's under-23 side.

One of Willie's greatest qualities was his sense of humour. He was naturally able to laugh at situations and at other people, but more significantly he had that wonderful gift of being able to laugh at himself. It was a quality that he retained until he could laugh no more. As his illness took its toll on his health, I witnessed his physical decline during my regular visits to his home, but his positive attitude remained the same. He was always full of mischief. Tears of laughter frequently resulted in our reminiscing as we recounted tales from our playing days.

Knowing as I do the love and affection Willie had for Hilary and his children, I am sure that he must have endured moments of incredible mental torture. And yet never once on my many visits did his positive approach alter. He always retained a grin on his face, never revealing even an ounce of self-pity.

There were occasions when on answering the door to me, Hilary would politely ask if I could reduce the amount of frivolous conversation, as Willie had endured an uncomfortable period. I understood perfectly and would promise to be on my best behaviour, but she and I both knew that it wouldn't necessarily be something that I had total control over. Sure enough, it wouldn't be long before there were howls of laughter from Willie and I. I would protest my innocence to Hilary, blaming Willie's infectious laugh. Eventually I would depart, leaving Hilary with the task of restoring some semblance of sanity back to her household.

A combination of hysterical laughter and deep emotion would result in tears rolling down my face as I climbed into my car and pulled off the driveway. I would travel only a few yards along the road before having to stop to take a few minutes to compose myself.

The word "hero" has been used on many occasions to describe the exploits and achievements of many men. You can add Willie Maddren's name to the top of the list.

David Mills

Prologue
By Hilary Maddren

It is better to have loved and lost than to have never loved at all. I believe passionately in that statement. How could I possibly think otherwise when I loved, and was loved, by someone as special as Willie? Most reading these words will have known him as a wonderful footballer, a short-time football manager and an inspiring campaigner and fund-raiser who fought terminal illness with a bravery that went far beyond the call of duty. To me, he was all those things and so much more.

He was my husband and my best friend, who treated me with such love, respect and affection. People always tell me – whether they were close to him or met him only fleetingly many years ago – what a "nice guy" Willie was. It's true, he was a nice guy. But he was a special nice guy. Special, not because he was a talented footballer, which I am reliably told he most certainly was. And not because he showered me with expensive and thoughtful gifts. Sad to say, I rarely got any of those. In fact, many of his gifts were at the other end of the scale, the worst being an Easter egg from the children for Mother's Day because he had forgotten and that was what was on special offer at the off licence. No, Willie was special because he cared – not just for those he loved but for everyone he came in contact with. His public persona was his private persona. He was interested in everything people had to say, even if he didn't agree with them or understand the topic. He showed a genuine interest in other people's lives, problems and feelings. He had an opinion on everything but would only air it when he felt it appropriate. He would never intentionally offend or hurt anyone. Quite simply, he was a true gentleman.

Willie Maddren

Precious few people in this world boast that special talent for inspiring those around them. The ability to inspire and make a difference to other people's lives is such a rare gift. But to do so not only in your own lifetime but five years after your death, as Willie continues to do, is the mark of a truly remarkable man. It is that unique commodity – the one that made the ordinary man that Willie was, stand out like a beacon as an extraordinary human being - that ensured that I was moved to write this eulogy and you were inspired to buy it.

Occasionally, in moments of reflection, I look through the books of remembrance that people completed after his death. So many people, most of whom probably didn't really know Willie but who felt like they did, wrote the most wonderful things. Willie was that kind of man. He made a lasting impression on the lives of the people he met, no matter how briefly.

When Willie was alive, we were frequently surprised and delighted at just how many individuals and groups were inspired into fundraising action in his name, some of them time and time again. When he finally lost his brave fight against Motor Neurone Disease in August 2000, I thought that the charitable activities would stop. How wrong could I have been? Instead, they just continued on. Christmas concerts, raffles, sponsored walks, sponsored runs, sponsored bicycle rides, sponsored motorbike rides, sponsored football tournaments and even sponsored leg waxes. Willie would have been proud as punch. He would have been proud too of his sister Claire's wonderful effort in writing a fundraising book about their early life in Haverton Hill.

Even in his dying days, Willie took much joy and satisfaction from the fact that the MND fundraising campaign we set up in his name had brought in such fabulous amounts of money. Of course, it would have been far easier – and very understandable – had he chosen to sit at home and live what remained of his life in private. But, almost from the outset, he was determined to use his name and profile to spearhead a campaign that would go on to raise both cash for research into MND and more awareness of this awful disease. But even Willie could never have imagined how the campaign would snowball. The fund has now topped £250,000 and continues to grow. It has supported numerous research projects into the illness and, just as importantly, given MND a public profile within the region that had never previously seemed possible. Indeed, the name of Willie Maddren is now as every bit synonymous with Motor Neurone Disease as it is with football and Middlesbrough FC.

Extra Time – The Final Chapter

And yet, of all of those wonderful fundraising efforts, the one closest to Willie's heart was the great success of his autobiography, *Extra Time*. The sale of its 8,000 print-run produced a marvellous profit in excess of £40,000. Oh, how it made me smile when, after his death, I read in the *Evening Gazette* that his book was the number one best seller in the town. I knew Willie would be laughing his socks off at the thought, for he had asked that on his death there be no memorial flowers. As a florist with her own shop, that was like a shot in the foot. But he had rightly insisted that the best tribute anyone could pay him was to either make a donation to the MND Association or buy the book.

Willie thoroughly enjoyed working on *Extra Time*, spending endless hours reminiscing about his football career and a life he knew he had been fortunate to lead. It is fair to say that publishing his autobiography was a journey that he had to make to be at peace. He took great pride in the way the book touched so many. People who didn't even know him wrote to say how it had moved them to tears. Each of them revealed that as much as they had enjoyed reading about his football memories, the final chapters had most struck a chord that made them reassess what was important in life. Unlike many men, Willie was always comfortable with his own emotions and felt no embarrassment at describing his innermost feelings about the dreadful predicament in which he found himself.

When it was suggested I write *The Final Chapter* to Willie's story, my initial response was to ask what there was left to tell. Willie had covered his life story from start to finish. There were more facts and figures in the original *Extra Time* than there are in *The Guinness Book of Records*. He was always wonderful at remembering information like statistics and dates – except, perhaps, when it came to my birthday! But then, when I started to think back, it struck me just how much more there was to tell. As I recalled the many sad times and the equally frequent magical moments I spent with Willie, the memories came flooding back.

Of those halcyon days of our early married life, spending time together with the children and enjoying a 'normal' married life. Those distant days when Motor Neurone Disease was nothing more to us than an awful disease that *other* people contracted. Memories of his time as Middlesbrough's manager when the football club was at its lowest ebb. And of my delight – yes, delight! – that he had finally been sacked. Dark memories of the day my loving husband came home to tell me he had a terminal illness. Of trying to continue leading a relatively normal life until it became impossible. Of the endless hospital visits, of sleepless nights, of his bravery in the face of such pain and discomfort, of his relentless spirit in the face of adversity, of the way he would smile through it all. And of his final hours, his funeral and the months after his death when life sometimes seemed so meaningless. All of those memories I recall in the final chapters of this book. I would not swap them for anything. We said all the things we wanted to say to one another and did most of things we wanted to do together.

So here it is, *The Final Chapter*. Wherever he is, Willie will be so proud to know he is still making a difference after all this time. By purchasing this book, you have already shown that his inspiration goes on and on. But maybe, as a result of reading it, you might just reassess what's important in your life. Whatever your feelings, enjoy the book and thank you for your support.

Introduction

I THOUGHT Jack Charlton was a friend of mine. Until two minutes earlier I was sure of it. Now he had given me reason to question that belief. As we stood at the bar of a hotel on the outskirts of Swansea, Jack gave me the hard facts, the brutal truth of a once proud football club's dire financial situation. He did not beat about the bush.

"Willie, the club is £1.3 million in debt, the ground is in a state of absolute decay and desperately needs the sort of money spending on it that this football club does not possess, the size of the wage bill and playing staff will have to be halved and at least two of our best players must be sold to keep the bank happy.

"It's an impossible job." Jack paused for a second and smiled, eyes twinkling, before adding: "Oh, and by the way, I've recommended you for it..."

Brilliant. He had just presented me with a long list of reasons why anyone in their right mind should run a million miles away from Middlesbrough Football Club. Then he tries to tell me that it's just the job for me. Or rather I was just the man for the job. But that was Jack for you.

Or rather that was the new, relaxed Jack who I had come to know over the previous couple of months. Now, in addition to the respect and admiration I had always held for him, I felt a warmth and for the first time had begun to think "Hey, I really like this guy." Gone was the cold arrogance and aloof nature I had come to know and frequently scorn during my years as a player under his successful four-year regime as Middlesbrough's manager. In those days, as much as I admired his coaching and tactical know-how and respected all that he had achieved in football, I hadn't always liked the guy. But that blunt, couldn't-give-a-damn-what-you-think nature had now been replaced by a less abrasive, laid-back manner. Jack had mellowed and I had come to enjoy working with him and learning from him.

It seemed a sabbatical away from football had done him a world of good. He had used those months wisely, whiling away the hours following his first love - fishing. But Jack had not been completely out of the limelight. A highly talented angler, he had even had his own fishing show on television while he was in regular demand for after-dinner speaking and as an expert football analyst for the BBC. Eventually he would return to football management and surpass all of his previous exploits in the game as the man who would transform a mediocre Republic of Ireland into a force in world football. But that night in Swansea he was not yet ready to return to the hassles of running a soccer team.

He had returned to Middlesbrough four weeks earlier as a favour to the club's chairman, Mike McCullagh. They had been friends for many years so, when Mike - desperate to halt the club's slide towards the Third Division - contacted Jack and asked him to help out, he had felt duty-bound to help a friend in need. Jack's spell in charge of the club was still fresh in the memory of most Middlesbrough fans and they had welcomed him back with open arms - the return of the prodigal son, here to save the day. I had been part of the Boro team Jack had managed and there was little question that he had built the best side the club had boasted in more than 20 years. With that in mind, there were few who doubted his ability to pull out the stops and avert disaster. I, for one, had been ready to give his appointment, albeit temporary, my full backing. Now, it seemed, he was ready to re-pay the "favour" by recommending me to be his successor.

"Why don't you take the job?" I asked him. It wasn't really a question. Deep down, I knew the answer and Jack's reply did not surprise me.

"It's a far different situation to the one I inherited 11 years ago and I don't need the aggravation of it at this time in my career," he explained. "I can do without all that. I don't need the money, I've got commitments away from football, I'm enjoying my fishing and I've got plenty of TV work. No, this job needs a young, ambitious man who is prepared to give it the necessary drive, energy and enthusiasm. Someone who has passion for the club - but most importantly someone who is prepared to do the job for bugger all!"

He wasn't joking about the pay. Middlesbrough were facing financial ruin and did not have the resources to pay the sort of money a top manager would expect. But Jack knew, just as I did, that I wanted this job like life itself. We were talking about the chance to manage the club I loved at the sport I loved. How could I be anything other than positive about the idea? And yet the following months would confirm to me that Jack was a wise man to turn down the chance to manage Middlesbrough.

It was the end of April 1984. The miners' strike was raging and the names of Margeret Thatcher and Arthur Scargill were rarely out of the news, Libyan diplomats were expelled from the UK after the shooting of WPC Yvonne Fletcher outside their embassy, Ronald Reagan became the first American President to visit China and Middlesbrough were facing relegation to the Third Division for only the second time in the club's long history. I cared little for the former items of news. My own little world revolved only around the success or failure of Middlesbrough Football Club. Little did I know that for the next 18 months I would suffer untold stress and pressure, much of it of my own making. I have always thought of myself as a winner and find it hard to accept failure of any sort. That proud belief was about to be tested to the full as I undertook the biggest challenge of my career.

The struggles and strains of management, often battling against ridiculous odds, were to take me to the limit, both physically and mentally. Indeed, it is my own belief that more than a decade later, through my own failing health, I am paying the dire consequences of the stress and trauma I put myself through during my time as manager of Middlesbrough Football Club. But back in 1984 I was brimming with a combination of excitement and trepidation about the challenge ahead. I had full confidence in my own ability to manage the club. I knew I had a good understanding of tactics and was eager to try out my own ideas. I knew too that I had an ability to analyse the strengths and weaknesses of opposition teams. On hanging up their boots, many footballers do not care to go into the coaching or management side of the game. I, however, always believed I had the skills and know-how to make a good manager.

That my first chance to manage a football club had come at my beloved Boro made the opportunity all the more exciting. I had grown up on Teesside alongside the people who were now the very lifeblood of the club through their support. Being one of them myself, I knew just how much football meant to the people of Teesside and wanted desperately to give them the successful team they craved for. At 33, I was young for such a responsible role, perhaps even the youngest manager in the Football League. But I was far from overawed with the prospect and looked forward to pitting my wits against other more experienced managers, just as I had enjoyed taking on the best of the best in my playing days.

****

Willie Maddren

AS I settled into my seat at Middlesbrough's fabulous Cellnet Riverside Stadium in August 1996, I could not help but wonder about how times had changed at the club in the decade which separated the managerial spells of Bryan Robson and myself. Making his home debut for Boro that day, as the pride of Teesside took on Italian giants Inter Milan in a benefit match for me and my family, was £7 million signing Fabrizio Ravanelli. If press speculation was to be believed, Middlesbrough had agreed to pay the striker an incredible salary of £42,000 a week.

It was all so different to my first months in charge of the club 12 years earlier. Then, in my first meeting with Chairman Mike McCullagh, he had outlined to me that not only would I be limited to making free transfer signings but that the maximum wage I could offer any potential new players would be just £250 a week - "£300 if you really have to go that far," he added as a meagre gesture of flexibility.

Of course, I was fully aware of the club's grave financial situation. Or so I believed. What Jack Charlton had told me in Swansea had only confirmed and embellished on what I already knew. The club was in big trouble and not only would I have to sell the star players to keep the wolves from the door but I would have no cash to spend in the transfer market as I sought replacements.

Unshaken by such limitations, I believed that I could add to the players already at the club with a number of free transfer signings. I had taken a look at the players freed by their clubs and felt there were several good players among the list who would add considerably to the playing squad I already had. How naive I was.

Contacting the better players among that list of free transfers and whetting their appetites for Middlesbrough Football Club was easy enough. What I had not prepared myself for was the fact that the club's new maximum wage had been set so low that players would be financially better off at clubs I had previously classed as being among the game's minnows. Now those so-called minnows could offer better wages than Middlesbrough and, not surprisingly, I was to find it almost impossible trying to persuade the better players to move to Teesside when they could earn more elsewhere.

The club's previous regime had installed many of the players I had inherited - several of whom I neither rated nor liked - on to unrealistically high salaries. Those salaries were now like a noose around the club's neck, tightening by the day as players with limited ability or commitment took home salaries the club could not afford to pay. Of course, this was long before the days of £42,000 a week salaries.

Extra Time – The Final Chapter

There were, however, several players on wages in excess of £550 per week plus bonuses. Quite an amount in those days. Meanwhile, I would be limited to just £300 in attempting to attract players of greater ability than those I already had. It was a frustrating, embarrassing and often impossible situation.

It resulted in a player released by little Grimsby Town turning down Middlesbrough because he had earned more at Blundell Park. It resulted too in another player, faced with a choice between Middlesbrough and Oxford United, choosing the latter purely for the financial rewards. I found it almost beyond belief that these two small "family" clubs now boasted more financial clout than Boro. At that moment, I could not help but ponder how far the club had fallen in such a short space of time since I had played my last game for Boro just seven years earlier.

And yet that pitiful salary ceiling was not the only sign that the club was truly crippled by debt. In that first meeting with my Chairman, I had been told that a trouble-shooter had been appointed to act as the club's financial controller for at least the first three months of my time in charge of team affairs. David Gaster's responsibility was to keep a tight rein over the club's finances but he often seemed more like a pair of shackles on me. In our first meeting, soon after my appointment as manager, Gaster put me under pressure to keep travel costs and other team-related expenses to an absolute minimum. His words resulted in me agreeing that no away games within a 180-mile radius - as far as Birmingham City to the south - would involve overnight stays. Instead, the team would travel there and back by coach on the day of the match. I fully realised, as no doubt did Gaster, that sitting on a cramped coach for up to four hours at a time was hardly ideal preparation for playing professional football and I emphasised to him that I would not be held responsible should the team bus be caught in traffic, causing our late arrival at any away fixtures.

If I thought that was bad, however, I hadn't seen anything yet.

During my time as a player under Jack Charlton, Boro had traditionally spent a few days during the pre-season build-up at Largs in Scotland. Naturally, I felt that a similar trip now would be good for morale and team spirit and put the idea to David Gaster.

I was not prepared for his reply. "Not a cat in hell's chance," he told me. "There's no way we can spare the cash for the travel expenses, let alone the cost of staying at hotels."

I was taken aback by such an abrupt response but I was not about to accept that as the end of the idea. I was determined to get the lads there come hell or high water and personally contacted three Scottish clubs, Hibernian, Morton and Motherwell. I asked them to guarantee enough money in return for us playing pre-season friendlies at their grounds and eventually secured guarantees worth some £2,000.

That, however, was enough only to cover our hotel expenses. The week's travel costs would be another £1,000 and it irritated me immensely that the club could not find the money to cover such a meagre sum. Eventually, I personally approached Appleyard's, the local van hire specialists, who agreed to supply a 12-seater coach free of charge on the condition that the club covered the insurance costs.

A few days later, a small squad of players set off for Scotland in surprisingly high spirits given our primitive mode of transport which was made up of our free-of-charge mini-bus and two cars. The cars were an absolute necessity as half of the coach was packed full of our kit. When I think back now, it was pure farce.

Unable to hire a driver for the tour, we had our own personal chauffeur in David Mills, the club's first choice striker. Anyone seeing us would have thought we were a Sunday League team rather than the representatives of a Second Division club from one of the largest towns in the north of England. David and I made light of it but we couldn't help but ponder the incredible downward spiral Middlesbrough Football Club had hit since the relative glory days of the previous decade.

****

THE Middlesbrough Football Club of the mid-'70s was like a different world to the cash-starved organisation it was to become a decade later. Those were the days when Boro were recognised as one of the biggest clubs in the business and when the idea of star players doubling up as chauffeurs would have been laughed off the pitch.

Welcome to the world of close season tours around the world.

Never mind scraping a few quid together for a few days in Scotland. This was a time when money was no object - except when it came to buying new players - and trips to the other side of the earth were no more than perks of the job. Norway, India, Hong Kong and Australia were all visited just a couple of years after a

Extra Time – The Final Chapter

similar trip to Norway, Denmark, Russia, Hong Kong, Singapore, Australia, New Zealand and Tahiti.

Those were the days when Middlesbrough boasted an outstanding team with players of the quality of Bobby Murdoch, Stuart Boam, John Hickton, Terry Cooper and David Armstrong. But there was only one who could really be called the star of that Boro side - and his name was Graeme Souness.

It was on our second world tour, in 1977, that Souey went AWOL in a style which would have made even Emerson blush. My old mate simply went missing as the rest of the team prepared to leave Hong Kong for Australia. It could have cost him a hefty fine or even his career with Middlesbrough - and it was all for a woman.

As it turned out, he was let off the hook completely as the club were desperately trying to persuade him to sign an extension to his contract at the time. It didn't work and Souey joined Liverpool just a few months later, helping them to lift the European Cup in his first season at Anfield. But by then he had made a disappearance more legendary than any appearance he could ever make.

Souey, along with several team-mates, had spent much of our last night in Hong Kong, chatting up the local ladies in our hotel bar. He was stopped in full flow, however, when we were ordered to go up to our rooms and collect our suitcases. Our 'plane was due to leave in two hours and the club coach would depart the hotel in 15 minutes.

I was sharing a room with Graeme at the time and there was no suggestion that he was about to do anything untoward as we made our way upstairs to collect our luggage. As we climbed back into the lift and began our descent, my mind was on the flight ahead. Graeme was about to take flight, too - but not on any aeroplane.

As the lift descended to the second floor, the doors opened and eyes agog I could only watch Souey step out into the corridor and smile: "I'll see you in Australia in three days, Buff - I'm fixed up with one of the dancers!" With that, the doors shut and I was left to contemplate what I had just witnessed.

In case you're wondering why he called me Buff, his nickname for me was Buffalo Bill. On this occasion, however, he had thoroughly earned his future sobriquet of Hong Kong Souey!

Moments later, after a brief search for our star player, the team bus left the hotel Sounessless for Hong Kong airport. I next saw him, as he had promised I would, three days later in Melbourne. "Now then, Buff!" he grinned as he made himself at home in another hotel room after arriving in the early hours. He appeared unconcerned by my warning that he was set to be deported back to England on the next available flight. But that was Souey for you - totally laid back and always ready to put having a good time top of his priorities.

His other nickname was certainly well deserved. For he truly was Champagne Charlie!

Extra Time – The Final Chapter

To My Hero

You're in my thoughts constantly and I pray so hard for you
You've said you don't want sympathy and I don't know what to do
I want to help you all I can and share your doubts and fears
You are my special brother who I've loved for all your years
You've been inflicted with this illness or is it just a test?
They say God works in strange ways and often tests the best
Prove to Him you will not quit, put up a fight and win
You never did like losing and I know you'll never give in
There will be days when you think life is cruel, feeling dismayed and sad
Console yourself thinking of the pleasurable times you've had
You've entertained and thrilled the crowds, earning honour and respect
Your qualities to be an achiever can often get complexed
I know you're putting on a show, hiding all your fears
Not wishing to burden others and not wanting pity or tears
You will deal with every setback as it comes along
Looking forward, thinking positive, acting brave, gallant and strong
Attempting every hurdle no matter how hard it may seem
Saying "The best is never over" and you will fulfil your dream
Just think of all the good you're doing for research for MND
It's because you are so popular people are donating generously
There's new cures coming every day and I'm sure there's one for you
So stick out your chin, do not give in, and you will relive your life anew
You will prove to God you have taken his test, fought it hard and won
You are my heroic brother - loved and admired by everyone

by Claire
(Willie's Sister)

1

Shankly was Wrong

BILL Shankly was wrong. The legendary Liverpool manager is famously quoted as saying: "Some people think football is a matter of life and death - I can assure you it is much more serious than that."

At times during my playing career and later as manager of Middlesbrough Football Club I would not have hesitated in agreeing that football sometimes meant as much to me as life itself. In the light of what has happened to me in more recent times, however, I know now that those much repeated words were painfully wide of the mark. Football is not life and death. It is a sport. For others, like myself for many years, it is also an income and a way of life. But to confuse it with the value of life itself is a naive mistake. Alas, it is a mistake which all too many of us make.

No doubt Shanks' words were said tongue-in-cheek. As passionate as he was about the national game, even he could not have truly believed such an outlandish statement. But to thousands upon thousands of players, managers and supporters the world over, football's importance in their everyday life is taken to such an extreme as to be unhealthy. It is an all-consuming passion which too often distorts the true value of other far more important aspects of our lives.

Consequently, on the eve of the 1992 FA Cup final between Liverpool and Sunderland, I reminded my old pal Graeme Souness of the folly of believing Shankly's famous quote. Just days earlier Graeme had undergone heart by-pass surgery but had insisted that he would sit on the bench at Wembley as the team he managed attempted to win its first major honour under his leadership. Knowing the stresses and strains of football management all too well, I was concerned that Graeme might put himself under too much pressure so shortly after a major heart operation and that his will to win might actually cost him his life. With this in

Extra Time – The Final Chapter

mind, I sent Graeme a telegram which read simply: "Shanks got it wrong, you know. Whatever the result tomorrow, look after yourself." Fortunately, Graeme suffered no negative effects from his day on the bench though I'd like to think he took on board my advice.

I know full well the way the outcome of a single football match can shape the moods and even the lives of those who love the game as I do. And yet, looked upon through my eyes today, the significance of a bad result - be it championship decider, cup final or relegation crunch match - is immaterial. The hard truth my family and I have had to face every day for the past three years has put the relatively inconsequential matter of football scores into painful perspective. 'Heart-breaking' is a phrase which is both abused and over-used. I often hear or read about the so-called 'heart-break' caused by a football match or a failed business deal and think to myself so what?

People spend so much time, such huge chunks of their lives worrying about trivia. Just as I once did, they worry about money and about their jobs. And yet I know just how easy it is to get wrapped up in your own little world with its peculiar stresses and strains. For almost two decades I became immersed in the complexities of football. As a player, my whole life revolved around the next match and too often little else seemed to matter. When that life was taken away from me at the tender age of 27, I thought my whole world had collapsed. And yet the loss, as painful and frustrating as it was, was nothing compared to the cruel torment I now live with every day - of knowing that I will die long before my time.

The onset and steady progression of Motor Neurone Disease throughout my body has slowly eaten away at the quality of my life to the point where, as I write this book, I am now wheelchair-bound, unable to feed, dress or wash myself and struggling even to talk for long periods. I have the look and voice of a man who has just supped 10 pints of best bitter, though I have been cheated of the pleasure and sensation that goes with such indulgence. On both hands my fingers have curled like autumn leaves. Perhaps that is a fitting metaphor as at the relatively young age of 47 I am in the autumn of my life with the winter, it feels, fast approaching.

Living like this and knowing that, ultimately, the illness will claim my life long before I reach old age is a reality which I and my loved ones often find hard to accept. I occasionally fall into periods of depression where I ask why me? Why has this cruel disease gripped me and those who share my life within its vice-like and ever-tightening grip? The questions remain unanswered. What answer can anyone give?

And yet amid all the hurt, despair and tears, I have discovered a new and even fulfiling side to life which I very much doubt I would ever have come across had I not suffered the misfortune to contract a terminal illness. If through this book I can help even one person alter their thinking and realise that there is so much more to be taken from life than the hustle and bustle, stresses and strains of material gain and achievement in their job, then the time it has taken to write these pages will have been well worthwhile.

For many, many years I spent every waking hour of the day worrying about how to do things better in my work. First in football management and then as the owner of my own sports retail business, I subjected myself to enormous pressure that must not only have been to the detriment of my health but to my family life too. How wrong I was. I realise now, thankfully not before it is too late, that I had my values and priorities completely mixed up. I know now that good health and enjoying every possible moment with my loved ones is what life is all about. Material things no longer mean anything to me. I admit that I am wealthy enough to have a lovely home, nice car and all the trimmings of a middle class lifestyle and it may therefore sound easy to say that money is not important to me. But I speak from the heart when I tell you that I would give all that up right now in exchange for my health. Providing I had my family and good health, I would be just as happy living in a small terraced accommodation without any obvious means of income.

The real value of life is good health and the love you share with your partner, children, family and friends. I only wish it had not taken the loss of one of those joys, my health, for me to realise the truth.

For far too long I misguidedly believed that the path to a successful and fulfiling life was putting my all into my working day. During my time as manager of Middlesbrough F.C., football was everything, the be all and end all. I simply didn't have a family life. My four children grew up almost without me noticing. Only during my illness have I realised just how little time I spent with my wife Hilary both in mind and body. I was far too concerned with work to be accompanying her on shopping trips or showing interest in the family home. Even on Sunday afternoons when Hilary and I would take the kids for a day out, all too often my mind would be elsewhere - usually planning tactics for the next match or new lines of stock for the shop.

After enduring untold pressure, much of it self-inflicted, as manager of a struggling football club existing on a shoestring budget, I leaped out of the frying pan and into the fire. Initially, I owned only a small sports retail outlet but as the business grew, I put myself under ever-increasing pressure. I look back on that period now and wonder why I suffered it for so long. I worked endless hours, often from eight in the morning to nine in the evening, only to get home and suffer sleepless nights worrying about cashflow. Whatever I did, I refused to settle for being second best and dedicated long hours in pursuit of perfection. But it was at the expense of my wife, children and even my own health. When I ask myself if it was worth it, if I am truthful I have got to answer no.

If I have a message to all the business people out there, subjecting themselves to all the stresses and worries of the rat race that is the working week, it is to tell them that it just isn't worth it. We all get caught up in this hurly burly lifestyle where everything is done at 100 miles per hour but I'd ask those following that route just to stop for half an hour and ask themselves if that is what they really want from life. Is job satisfaction, promotion, monetary or material gain truly what is important to you? There is a choice - though it might just mean jumping off that treadmill!

If I had my time over again, I would at least release my weekends to enjoy a family life and take a closer interest as my children matured into young adults. Perhaps if I had made more effort to switch off I might have been able to look at my job more objectively too. Of course, in times of despair I am comforted by the knowledge that I achieved much in football that most can only ever dream about but I would have no hesitation in swapping it all for a long and healthy life.

I am now totally focused on enjoying those things in my life which are truly important. Prior to contracting Motor Neurone Disease, I never devoted enough time to Hilary and the kids but I have been fortunate enough to be handed the chance to make up for lost time. When my failing health permits, Hilary and I use our time together wisely. We drive to the seaside or into the country and simply enjoy one another's company. Over the last three years, we have enjoyed more quality time together than most couples do in 20 years. Where once we would have been working all hours, we now ensure we enjoy every last moment with each other. It is an experience which has proved more fulfiling than anything I could have achieved either in football or business. In a sense, I have tried to look on it as an early retirement.

Many people are never fortunate enough to find the perfect partner, one with whom they are totally compatible. I have much to be thankful for that, in Hilary, I have a wonderful wife with whom I have shared the joy of love and affection.

But I look back too and wonder why I didn't take more time to stop and observe the simple pleasures of life. As my illness has deprived me of an ability to take part in activities I previously took for granted, I have learned to take enormous pleasure from more simplistic things. I will often sit in the garden and take time to look at and enjoy the beauty of the flowers and trees. They have always been there, of course. I had simply never taken the time to appreciate them. I look at the colour of the garden in bloom, how the changing light of the day reflects in the trees. It gives me a tremendous feeling just to see the way the light catches the ripples in my garden pond. Before my illness, I never sat down long enough to enjoy life's beauty. If I wasn't at work, I would no doubt be watching TV or out on the golf course. Now, though time is running out for me, I have much of it on my hands and my physical inability to be active has given me this wonderful opportunity to appreciate the beauty of the world around me.

Of course, it is no substitute for being the active adult most guys in their late 40's would expect to be. How I wish I could leap out of my wheelchair and kick a football about with my young son David or help my daughter Laura out with her netball practice. So as you read through my life story and my many wonderful experiences as a professional footballer, I hope you will put it into context with what I have experienced since. Just as my playing career was cut short in its prime, so too will my life. For that reason I cannot escape from an overriding feeling that I have been cheated.

But this is not a time to be morose or to dwell too long on the future but perhaps better to reflect on what has gone before and the many happy memories of my life and career as a professional footballer that stimulate me in my moments of depression. Magic moments that saw me progress from naive schoolboy to playing alongside my boyhood heroes, receiving player of the year awards with my hometown club, winning representative honours for my country and playing alongside and against some of the greatest players of the 1970's.

2

When I was a Lad

MY LIFE wasn't always full of the glamour which football brought my way. Indeed I'm proud to say that my achievements in football and life in general were founded on an upbringing which, although loving and enjoyable, could hardly be described as privileged. Haverton Hill, the area of industrial Teesside in which I spent the first five years of my life, was never likely to have encouraged passers-by to stop off for a look around. Situated midway between the working class towns of Hartlepool to the north and Middlesbrough to the south, Haverton Hill was a small estate of terraced council houses in the shadow of the nearby ICI chemical works at Billingham.

One of my mother's daily chores was to clean the windows of the grime which emanated from the plumes of choking yellow-tinged smog which bellowed out from ICI's sulphuric acid plant. The fumes hung in the air and filled our lungs but I very much doubt that my parents or our neighbours even once considered complaining. To do so would have been to bite the hand that fed us. For, like many of Haverton Hill's male adult residents, my father earned his living there, as a process worker on the factory's plasterboard plant. Those who did not earn their crust with ICI would invariably work at the local Furnace shipyard whilst their wives, my mother included, stayed at home to bring up their families.

In my testimonial programme many years later, Daily Mirror football writer Charlie Summerbell described nearby Port Clarence, which he mistakenly attributed to be my birthplace, as a God-forsaken place. I have little doubt that others would have described Haverton Hill in a similar vein. But to me and the rest of the Maddren family it was home.

Number 12 Young Street, midway along one of Haverton's many rows of terraced houses, was home to our family of six. The youngest of four children, I grew up with my two brothers, Dave and Chris, and my sister, Claire. All were some years older than me - Claire 11 years older - so I think it is probably fair to say I wasn't exactly planned. But my parents, Vince and Mary Maddren, treated us all equally and I have nothing but fond memories of my formative years. Mam seemed to spend most of her days cooking food. Dad, having finished his shift at ten o'clock in the evening, would arrive home after three or four pints in the local pub and expect to see his dinner on the table. Keeping discipline was a job Dad left to Mam, though we knew he would intervene if we took advantage of her loving nature. Having said that, he hardly ever raised a hand to us as his towering physical presence meant one word was usually enough to bring us into line.

Dad supplemented his weekly wage from ICI in a joint venture with my Grandad who lived round the corner on Cowpen Bewley Road. Father and son hired out handcarts to locals who would sometimes carry all of their household possessions on them when moving home. Dad earned a further income from selling pigs at the local market having reared them on his small allotments at the end of our street, where he also grew vegetables for the Maddren household. Indeed, I vividly remember squealing with delight as a young boy as I rode on the back of one of Dad's sows. Occasionally, when the sow had tired of suckling large litters, it would either kill its own offspring or ignore them with the result that Mam would be left to rear the occasional wreckling in the house, making the piglets a bed out of a cabinet drawer. One of those piglets became so much a part of the family, we treated it almost like a pet and gave it the name "Titch". Titch would follow Mam around like an obedient dog, much to the amusement of the neighbours.

Of course, holidays abroad were not even on the agenda in the mid-1950s. Apart from occasional stays with our uncle in Doncaster, the nearest thing to a holiday for the Maddren siblings would be a visit to Seaton Carew, the local seaside resort, as part of the annual day trip organised by the local workingmen's club. On board one of maybe eight double-decker buses, we would wait in anticipation as we turned each of three long bends before sending up a huge cheer as the sea-front amusement arcades came into view. On the beach, races would be organised with the princely sum of half a crown being the reward for winning. Such was my success on one occasion that I ended the day with seven shillings and six pence. Coming in the days before pocket money was ever heard of, this was like a small fortune to me.

Extra Time – The Final Chapter

Although it was only seven miles away, getting to Seaton Carew at any other time in the summer holidays would take up to two-and-a-half hours and involve catching the number two bus from Haverton to Teesside's landmark Transporter Bridge. Such were the queues, however, that it would often be another hour-and-a-half before we could catch a second bus to Seaton Carew. To this day, Dad often recites a tale of taking us all on one of those endless journeys only to have our stay cut short. Within five minutes of setting up on the beach with our deckchairs, buckets and spades, Claire cut her foot on a sharp piece of glass with the consequence that the Maddren family spent the rest of the day at Middlesbrough General Hospital - much to Dad's sorrow as he had already paid for the hire of the deckchairs!

In those days, those very few residents of Haverton Hill who were fortunate enough to own cars were looked on almost as royalty. Indeed, I still recall thinking I was the bee's knees the day as a young boy I got a lift to Seaton in the back of a car owned by my friend 'Wakker' Tindall's father. And I was probably aged three, when at the house of another friend, Peter Best, I watched television for the first time on a 14 inch black and white screen surrounded by 20 or so friends who had descended on the house to witness this wonder of technology.

Having two older brothers - Dave was my elder by five years, Chris by four - also had the tendency to lead me into my fair share of mischief. I'm sure our parents' hearts would have missed a beat had they known that we often whiled away the hours at the nearby Haverton Hill Marsh on a boy-made raft which would invariably submerge about two inches as we held on to its sides and paddled across the water. When I think back now, it is frightening to think what might have happened had our makeshift raft ever turned over, given the fact that neither the three-year-old William Maddren, nor either of his elder brothers, had yet learned to swim.

Me and my big brothers: Dave (left) and Chris ready for a game of football on Seaton Carew beach when I was four years old.

By the age of four I would frequently hitch a ride around the streets on the back of wagon trailers owned by a local haulier, Bobby Durham. The trailers would travel from their depot along the top of our street to refuel, trundling along slowly enough to allow me the luxury of hanging on the back. The weekly visit of the local fishmonger to Young Street, with his horse and cart, also offered me the chance to cadge a lift along the back streets, sitting under the cart on the wagon's back axle.

At one stage Mam spent several weeks desperately trying to avoid the fishmonger after an incident with Nigger, our black labrador dog. As the

My brothers, Chris (left) and Dave, pictured with Dad and his handcart at the end of Young Street, Haverton Hill, during the mid-50's.

fishmonger carried out his business one morning, Nigger saw a golden opportunity to grab himself a tasty meal and duly leaped on to the cart, swiped a large piece of smoked fillet and raced away with the fish hanging from his jaw before the fishmonger had the chance to move. For weeks afterwards, Mam, unable to pay for the expensive piece of fish, had to pretend she wasn't in when the monger came knocking on our door seeking compensation. Eventually, he did catch up with her, however, and Mam was forced to pay him half a crown for his troubles.

While Dad did his best to make ends meet with the help of vegetables from his allotments, food was obviously in the family as my grandparents earned their living through a fruit shop on Hope Street while Uncle Dixon also ran a fruit and veg business. His sales were carried out from the back of a horse and cart he trailed for long hours around the streets of Haverton Hill and Billingham. Such an occupation inevitably meant an early morning start for Uncle Dix and all too often a pre-dawn wake up call for Dad shortly after putting head on pillow after an energy-sapping night shift at the factory. The horse Uncle Dix owned was an elusive individual, especially when it knew work was on the cards, and would often give him the run-around while he chased it around the field along by the marshes. Looking like a reject from a Western film, Uncle Dix would attempt to lasso the horse with a rope which he slung over his shoulder. When he tired of this, however, he would call on the help of Dad to catch the horse and ensure the day's fruit and veg was delivered to the waiting customers. When he wasn't busy selling fruit and veg, or catching that damned horse, Uncle Dix would occasionally take us and all of his own family - sometimes as many as 16 people - on the long journey to Seaton Carew on the back of his cart.

My Grandad, a powerfully built man of good morals, died when I was just three years old. I am reliably informed, however, that he still holds the record for hand hewed ironstone from Boosbeck Mine.

It was with my brothers that I first got into football, enjoying a kick about on an area of wasteland opposite the end of Young Street. I would have been maybe four years old and seem to remember spending most of the timing chasing my elder brothers and their mates in an attempt to get a kick of the ball. Like Chris and Dave, I was soon hooked on the game and each year our Christmas presents would include a leather football, a pair of footy boots and a pair of boxing gloves, all bought on a rare visit to Middlesbrough where Jack Hatfield's shop was the only place to buy sporting goods. The gloves were Dad's idea as he was a strong believer in ensuring we were capable of looking after ourselves, though he always insisted that violence was only acceptable in self-defence and should never be used to bully those less fortunate than ourselves.

Then, when I was aged four-and-a-half, we left Haverton Hill for the fast-developing new housing estates of Billingham some three miles away. In those early days, 85 Braemar Road often seemed like the coldest place on earth. With no central heating and only one small fire, our new house offered little protection against the harsh winters and I would often sneak into bed between my brothers to try to keep warm.

Soon after our move to Billingham came my first day at school, an ordeal in itself for such a shy young lad. On my first morning at Roseberry Primary School, I walked the mile and a half from home hand-in-hand with Mam and soon settled into the day's lessons. However, I later mistook the ringing of the lunchtime bell as my signal to head home. Walking across the playground and out of the school gates, I was followed by the cries of older children who raced after me, signalling for me to come back. Believing them to be chasing me, I simply upped my pace until their voices disappeared into the distance. With no idea how to get home, I simply ran down Marsh House Avenue until I recognised Braemar Road. However, there must have been 200 houses in Braemar Road and I had no idea what the number of our new house was. Indeed, after looking into almost every garden along the way, I eventually only recognised home by the sight of a large pig trough Dad had converted into a planter for his blooms.

I will never forget the horrified look on Mam's face as I walked through the door. "What are you doing here? And how on earth did you get here?" she demanded to know. I tried to explain that my schoolmates had chased me but she was hearing none of it and gave me a quick about-turn and marched me back to school.

Away from school, the young Maddren brothers were usually to be found playing on farmland at the back of our house. It was there that we hit upon a great way to supplement our meagre pocket money. Stalking the farmland with our pet ferret, we caught many a rabbit which we duly sold to McDowell's butchers in the nearby Wolviston Village. For a rabbit of a reasonable size we could make as much as five shillings. This little earner came to an abrupt halt, however, on the outset of the rabbit disease myxsomatosis. No longer would the butcher even entertain the thought of buying a wild rabbit caught locally.

Another way in which we would seek amusement was at a place called Norburn Beck, on Lord Londonderry's estate, now owned by Sir John Hall, the man who has done so much to build Newcastle United's empire in recent years. One day, I was accompanied in a spot of beck jumping by Chris, my neighbour Wilf Lawrence and two friends, Geoff Salmon and Brian Peckitt. As we dared one another to attempt to jump ever wider parts of the beck, one of us inevitably fell in. The unlucky fall guy was Wilf, who ended up soaked through. Knowing we would all have hell to pay if we let Wilf return home in such a state, we hit upon what seemed a great idea of building a fire to dry out his clothes and underwear. That wasn't a bad idea in itself. Where it fell down was that we lit the fire at the foot of a hollow tree. Chris and Brian were high up the tree collecting branches to put on the fire when the flames began to get out of control and reached probably 12 feet in height. Chris and Brian were forced to leap fully 15 feet to the ground to escape the flames which were engulfing the tree. As we stood wondering what on earth to do, the decision was taken out of our hands with the sound of a barking dog nearby. It was the game-keeper and his canine companion. Needless to say, we made a sharp exit and his cries for us to return to the scene of our "crime" only resulted in us running faster until we were back in the comparative safety of

Extra Time – The Final Chapter

Wolviston Village.

Despite my rather embarrassing start to school life, I soon became accustomed to my new surroundings and faired reasonably well academically. However, it wasn't long before I turned my attentions from the classroom to the school football pitch. By the time I was eight I was playing in the school's 'B' team alongside boys who were two years older me. When I wasn't playing in organised games, I would spend time developing my skills with my brothers and Geoff Salmon on nearby playing fields known as John Whitehead Park, usually wearing wellies and playing with an old punctured ball which would bruise your toe ends. Two football crazy friends, Geoff and I would kick the ball back and forth in all weathers under a street lamp until it was either too dark to play on or we were chased by residents sick of the thump-thump sound of the ball. With such hi-tech distractions as videos and computers, kids nowadays don't play football as we did then but it was on the streets of Billingham that I learnt my early skills.

Being younger than most of my team-mates, I wasn't particularly outstanding in my first couple of years in the school team but by the time I was a fourth year junior I was starting to shine and was both captain and star of a team under the leadership of Mr Archer, the PE teacher. Mr Archer, a middle-aged guy with long grey hair and a lovely manner, looked after the team (although I held him in high esteem, it would be misleading to say he was our coach for I can never remember him talking tactics) without ever bothering to change from his trademark grey suit into a tracksuit. However, he did make one long-lasting mark on my life. For it was he who first called me Willie. Until then I had been simply William -or Maddy to my friends. But the Willie label stuck and it has been with me ever since. I've never been Bill, only Willie.

The Maddren males with Mam and Dad on Scarborough beach during a rare family holiday.

It was in my fourth year of juniors that Roseberry achieved a league and cup

When I was a Lad

double, beating the usual winners Billingham North School in the cup final. I had a powerful shot for my age, probably a result of playing with a full-size football with older boys, and I remember actually hitting the crossbar direct from a corner early in the game. Noting how close I'd come to giving us the lead, I tried the same trick again some minutes later and this time bent the ball into the net to put us one up.

Then, midway through the second half, we won a penalty which I stepped up to take. Before I had chance to strike the ball, however, dozens of kids had raced round the pitch and took their place directly behind the goal for a bird's eye view of my spot-kick. To add further pressure to the situation, I remember my brother Dave shaking his fist and yelling in encouragement "C'mon young un!" Thankfully, I scored the goal to clinch a 2-0 win and for the first time in my young life I was the hero of the hour.

And yet I very nearly missed the final as a result of a freak accident a couple of days earlier. During a game of cricket in the park, one of my school team-mates, John Dunne, bowled a cork ball which spun off the top of the bat and hit me on the cheekbone, which duly swelled to an awful size. It was initially suspected that I had cracked the bone, making me doubtful for our big game. The following day at school, John was in danger of being lynched by our fellow team-mates. "If Maddy doesn't play, you're going to get it," they threatened.

Thankfully, I only had bad bruising and we celebrated our win together over a bottle of pop at Smith & Jacque's Dance Club, just up the road from our school. It would be wrong of me to suggest I was the only good player in that team, however. Two more who stood out were Peter Bolton, a big, physical lad who I

I look on whilst my sister Claire tries to keep a straight face as a monkey bites her finger!

Extra Time – The Final Chapter

remember on the team photograph was holding up his shorts with a snakebelt, and the school's head boy John Hugill, a skillful player who was distracted from football by his academic achievements and I believe went on to become an accountant.

Away from football, I was always a fairly shy, quiet lad. But when it came to football, I was brimming with confidence and felt I could take on the world. Fortunately I had my elder brothers to keep my feet on the ground. Dave in particular, although proud of my achievements in the game, always made sure I did not become big headed. After each game I would always ask Dave how he thought I had played and, whatever my performance, his stock answer would be "You could have done better." A good footballer himself, Dave never had the opportunity to develop his raw talent as, after passing his scholarship, he attended a grammar school where they played only rugby. I was always given plenty of encouragement by my parents but Dad's shifts meant he rarely got to see me in action. Dave and Chris, however, were always on the sidelines shouting me on. Although a keen footballer, Chris excelled in his boyhood as the ultimate climber of tall trees.

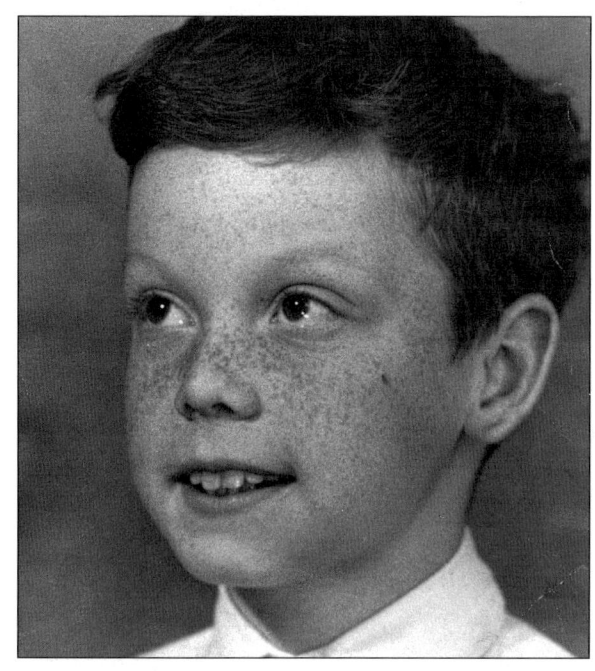

It was around that time that for the first time I went to see Middlesbrough, the local professional football team, in action at Ayresome Park. I had heard countless tales from Dave and Chris about Boro's star centre-forward, Brian Clough - a player Dave likened to God. But, as a result of my own playing aspirations, the nearest I had come to the professional game was watching Northern League side Billingham Synthonia training under floodlights. Clough had departed the Second Division club some

William Maddren, aged seven.

months earlier but Boro still boasted two England internationals in forward Alan Peacock and winger Eddie Holliday.

As I climbed the last step to reach the Boys' End with my brothers, I struggled to take in the atmosphere created by 24,000 supporters. As the teams ran out to a huge roar from the crowd, I had only one thought - Wow! Mouth open and eyes agog, I spent most of the match in awe of the surroundings - even the stripes on the pitch impressed me - and I consequently remember very little of the game. Two own goals gave Boro a straightforward win over Liverpool but I went home more excited by the theatre itself than the actors who had performed within it.

Following that first visit to Ayresome Park, dreams of one day playing for Billingham Synthonia were forgotten and I began to raise my horizons to pulling on the red and white shirt of Middlesbrough Football Club. From that day on, I became a regular on the Ayresome stands, usually accompanied by Dad, Chris and Dave. Occasionally, I would get what was known as "a squeeze" with Dad, whereby the turnstile operator would allow the two of us to squeeze in for the price of one.

On one occasion, an evening match against Derby County in torrential rain, I agreed to meet Dad in the ground's East Stand after first climbing over a wall out of the Boys' End. In doing so, I ran the gauntlet of getting past a policeman but I eventually joined Dad in the more expensive East Stand. But, on joining him, I wondered why I had even made the effort as I was forced to watch the match on tiptoes stretching to see the action over the heads of the adults in front of me. One thing which struck me, however, was the absence of bad language and anyone who did make a rude remark in the earshot of a young boy like myself would quickly be pulled back into line.

Brian Clough's successor as Middlesbrough's goal machine, Alan Peacock, would go on to play for England in the following summer's World Cup finals and was naturally the recognised star of the team during my early years as a Boro fan. He was not, however, the player the young Willie Maddren pretended to be when kicking a ball about with his mates. That distinction belonged to Ian Gibson, the club's young midfield playmaker. Gibson always seemed to be a yard ahead of others in terms of his thinking ability and passing.

The male members of the Maddren family became regulars in the Bob End and our matchday routine involved catching the number 64 bus, a red double-decker which would invariably be filled with choking cigarette smoke which made it difficult to see the seat in front. A 20-minute ride would take us from Billingham to Newport Bridge in Middlesbrough, from where we would walk in excited anticipation the remaining mile to Ayresome Park.

Middlesbrough would win the vast majority of their home games though perhaps the match which stands out most in my memory was a 3-3 draw with our deadly rivals Sunderland shortly before Christmas 1962. A Sunderland side inspired by Teesside's former hero Brian Clough looked to be on for an easy win until an exhilarating fightback gave Boro a share of the spoils, with Billy Horner scoring a 35-yard belter. I remember too being honoured to have the opportunity to see goalscoring legend Arthur Rowley in action, though a long distance gem in the opening five seconds from Bill Harris - another player I admired - helped send Rowley's Shrewsbury side crashing to a 5-1 FA Cup defeat.

Meanwhile, I moved on to secondary school, attending a complex of three new schools known as Billingham Campus. After just a year at Stephenson Hall, I was transferred to Farraday Hall where I quickly established myself in the school's under-13's team. However, competition between the three schools and the local grammar school, Bede Hall, was not limited to the football pitch. Pupils from the three comprehensives would gang up against the brighter kids from the grammar school. Against such odds, opportunity for revenge was rare but I will never forget the retribution a gang of the Bede Hall lads took out on me and my friends after cornering us on our way to the school's swimming baths during my solitary year at Stephenson Hall. We always ran the gauntlet against Bede's fifth formers but on that one occasion had the living daylights beaten out of us.

It was during that same year, when snow was on the ground, that I hit a Bede Hall fifth former, David Young, known as Big Uggy, smack on the side of his head with a measured throw of a snowball. A chase ensued along Marsh House Avenue and I seemed certain to pay for my insolence until, panic-stricken, I took a detour into the front garden of one the houses and began pounding against the front door. I have rarely been so thankful as I was when my desperate pleas were answered swiftly by the lady of the house. She issued a stern warning to Big Uggy not to be a bully and to tittle off home. To add injury to insult, Uggy later suffered at the hands of Dave who, having heard of my close escape, clipped him one and told him never to go anywhere near his kid brother again. It would take Big Uggy many years to gain revenge but gain it he did. He later became a policeman and booked Dave for having two bald tyres on his car!

When I was a Lad

While I was never the brightest academically at school, I was in the top class in most subjects and was proud to be named as Head Boy in fourth year. However, while I was just an average pupil in the classroom, I excelled on the sports field. At 15, I was a regular in the Cleveland & Teesside Men's Cricket League, scoring two centuries in Sunday league matches and a 92 in a Saturday afternoon match when the standard was higher. At school level, my class-mates simply could not bowl me out and, together with another talented cricketer called Trevor Atkinson, I would inevitably bowl right through the innings. Another lad, John Johnson, who would go on to bowl for County Durham, would often ask me if he could have a turn at bowling, to which I would always respond: "No, John, you might be too expensive." I wasn't being big-headed, it was simply a reflection of the belief I had in my own ability though it does embarrass me now when I think what John went on to achieve as a professional cricketer.

A natural athlete, I also represented the district basketball team and was even asked to represent the district at the high jump despite never having attempted the discipline - and promptly won the competition to qualify as county representative. It was a similar story with the javelin. Never having thrown a javelin in my life, I won a district tournament. In fact, I turned down the opportunity to represent the county at both the high jump and the javelin as I preferred to play cricket in the Cleveland & Teesside League. Cricket was my first love after football and I honestly believe that with the right coaching I could have made it as a professional batsman.

Ironically, I never progressed beyond district level on the football pitch. It was a great disappointment to me that although I was regularly chosen to represent Stockton and Billingham, I was never even offered so much as a trial for Durham County Boys. In fact, I couldn't help but wonder if the selectors were biased towards youngsters from Stockton as five boys from the town - one of them being David Mills, who I would later play alongside at Middlesbrough - were picked for the county and not one from Billingham.

Despite failing to catch the eye of the county scouts, I knew I was progressing and developing my game as part of Faraday Hall's school team. A goalscoring midfielder, I was a fine dribbler, had a strong shot but also had a natural tendency to defend and would instinctively pick up the runs of opponents, a skill which doesn't come naturally to most young footballers who are drawn to the attraction of attacking. Ironically, that defensive instinct would later be to my detriment when playing at centre-forward for Middlesbrough's first team when I would

Extra Time – The Final Chapter

frequently frustrate the manager by chasing after the full-back instead of holding my position.

Though Faraday weren't the best team in the league, we always did reasonably well and with the enthusiastic support of Geography teacher Alan Medd as team coach there was plenty of opportunity to take part in organised training sessions after school. Indeed I would rarely be home before seven o'clock in the evening.

One of my Faraday team-mates was a lad called Micky Walters who even at 13 years of age was exceptionally tall and had hair covering his back and chest, giving him the look of a man many years his senior. Opposing players would frequently walk on to the pitch before a match, take one look at Micky and complain: "Hey sir, he's never 13!" Many a time I would leave Micky waiting for a bus to his home in Port Clarence, only to see him instead take a detour into the local pub, the Telstar, for a couple of pints. I doubt very much that he had any trouble getting served either.

I had Micky to thank for giving me the opportunity to join Port Clarence Juniors. At the time I was very pally with a lad called Dave Jeffs, whose father Bill won FA Amateur Cup winners medals with Crook Town and Bishop Auckland. Bill was the manager of Whitby Town who I trained with from the age of 13. Their squad included a prolific goalscorer called Jimmy Mulvaney, who later died prematurely, I believe suffering from Motor Neurone Disease. I was still training with Whitby when they reached the Amateur Cup final at Wembley. Despite Whitby's defeat to Hendon, the whole day was a wonderful personal experience.

By the time I was 15 I had developed enough for Dave to ask me to play for Stockton and Billingham Technical College for whom he was also a regular player. Several days later, however, Micky asked me which club I intended to join and I told him that I planned to accept Dave's invitation to play for Billingham Tech. Expressing his surprise at my decision, he explained that he was set to join Port Clarence Juniors in the Cleveland Junior League - a local league for those aged up to 18 - and impressed upon me that it would be a far better league for me to play in, especially as games were often watched by Football League scouts. Of course, I could see the sense in Micky's words and duly agreed to attend a trial match.

The following Thursday I attended a training session for a trial, where I was introduced to the guys who ran the Port Clarence Juniors team, Harry Holmes, Dick Fisher and Bob Tennant. Within 20 minutes I had impressed enough for the

When I was a Lad

Port Clarence coaching team to pick me for the following Saturday's fixture against Middlesbrough Juniors. I can remember quite vividly pulling on a black and white striped shirt before the game and finding that most of the team's kit was riddled with holes. Meanwhile, our opponents, the cream of Middlesbrough, were kitted out immaculately. But as if to prove that the strip does not maketh the man, Port Clarence took a 2-0 lead through two goals from a guy called Peter Seaman, who was one of the most prolific scorers in the junior league. We still had that two-goal lead with perhaps only 25 minutes remaining but ultimately the supreme fitness of the Middlesbrough lads told and they ran out 3-2 winners. Nevertheless, I was happy with my own performance and was delighted to have played at a standard of football that I knew could only be of benefit to me.

Port Clarence duly became my number one team, though I continued to represent my school and would often play for Faraday Hall on a Saturday morning and Port Clarence in the afternoon. Boasting sides representing ICI Wilton, Billingham Synthonia, Cargo Fleet and South Bank, the Cleveland Junior League was of a standard which demanded a lot of a 15-year-old like myself.

However, I quickly established myself as one of the key members of the team and it was not long before I was offered the opportunity to go to Leeds United on trial. I was excited though somewhat nervous about the prospect of joining one of football's true giants but I need not have lost any sleep over it, for I was never to get that trial at Elland Road. Just two days before I was due to attend, I broke my ankle in a bizarre accident which had nothing to do with football. I was mooching about a local brick yard with friends when we were spotted by a security man who took chase. In my rush to escape, I leaped probably 12 feet off the end of a slag heap and landed on the side of my ankle. After the initial agony, I proceeded to walk home in some pain where I explained my predicament to Mam. In hospital later, X-rays confirmed my ankle was broken and my dream of a trial at Elland Road was in tatters.

It took my ankle more than two months to recover from the break, most of that time spent in plaster. By the time I was back on my feet, the opportunity of a trial with Leeds had long since disappeared, never to arise again. I was heart-broken at the time, of course. With hindsight, however, I can't help thinking that breaking my ankle was a blessing in disguise. For if that trial had resulted in me joining Leeds, it's quite possible I may never have enjoyed a break into their first team in the way that I was to do so at Middlesbrough. At the time when I was established in the Middlesbrough team as a central defender, Leeds boasted a host of top class

Extra Time – The Final Chapter

players in that very position, including my future manager Jack Charlton and England international Norman Hunter.

At the end of that season, with yours truly back in the side, Port Clarence Juniors reached the league's cup final where we met Billingham Synthonia, a side packed full of good young players. I eagerly awaited the final as it was my first opportunity to play under Synthonia's floodlights. As it turned out, we lost the match 5-1 though I knew I had played well. What I didn't know was that while Dad watched the game from the stand he had been approached by a Mr Powell, a guy from the local town of Thornaby who was scouting for Everton. Only when we got home did my father tell me that he had told Mr Powell that I was too young to consider signing associate schoolboy forms, especially with a club from the other side of the country. As we were later to discover, Mr Powell had his own concerns as he described Dad as a "firebrand". Deep down, I think Dad always hoped that Middlesbrough, the club we supported, would eventually come in for me.

The following season, with our best players a year older, Port Clarence began to do well in the league and advanced to the quarter-finals of the North Riding Junior Cup. We were due to play St Pius Youth Club, who played on the wilderness ground where Teesside Park stands today. Arriving early for the game, I and two team-mates, Peter Horan and Paul Smith, asked a group of boys where the pitch was, only to be told that we were nowhere near, that St Pius played near Joe Walton's Boys Club in Grangetown. Panicking, we jumped on the next available bus to travel the seven miles or so to Grangetown. When we arrived three quarters of an hour later, we asked once again where St Pius played, to which we were informed that they played near Cleveland Park dog track on the very wilderness ground we had originally been to.

When we finally got to the wilderness ground, the match had reached the half-time interval - and Port Clarence, with only eight players on the pitch, were already 4-1 down. Harry and Dick were, of course, horrified that we had arrived so late but were relieved that the team was back to full strength for the second half. Within five minutes of the re-start we pulled a goal back to start an amazing comeback which saw us run out 6-5 winners - much to the relief of us three boys.

The semi-final saw us drawn once again to play Middlesbrough Juniors. There was confusion before the kick-off, however, when the match official failed to turn up. In his absence, the game was refereed by one of Port Clarence's senior players who perhaps displayed a slight bias towards his team. His name was Keith Lamb, more recently known for his role as the Chief Executive of Middlesbrough Football Club. A Peter Seaman hat-trick inspired us to a 4-1 lead only for Middlesbrough's superior fitness to haul them back into the game and we eventually fell to a highly disappointing 6-5 defeat. Nevertheless, playing against Boro's under-18 side had given me a good measure of my own ability and I recognised that I was as good, if not better, than many of their players.

Soon afterwards I was tipped off that I was to be watched by a scout for Middlesbrough. The match in question saw me score twice in a 5-1 win over ICI Wilton. After the match, I felt I had played well but there was no approach from anyone on the touchlines to either Harry, Dick or myself. However, I did not have to wait long for the approach to come - though it was not in the circumstances I had anticipated. Trailing 2-0 to Stockton Juniors in our following match, we were forced to re-shape the team when centre-back Peter Horan was sent off for kicking Stockton striker Peter Blowman - a guy who had already played several times for Hartlepool's first team. With just 20 minutes left, I was pushed into the centre of defence for the first time in my life and hardly gave Blowman a kick of the ball. I can still remember thinking at the end of the game how easy it was to play in that position.

As I walked from the pitch after the final whistle, I was greeted by a stocky, square-faced but pleasant guy who turned out to be Middlesbrough's scout, Freddie Barnes. He told me he would like to come and see my father to discuss the possibility of me signing schoolboy forms for Boro and he duly visited my parents' house a few evenings later. Realising what was dear to my Dad's heart, Freddie took him to the Billingham Arms Hotel and, I believe, clinched a deal for my signature over a couple of pints. Once my father had given Freddie the thumbs up, I had no hesitation in signing associate schoolboy forms.

The truth is that we both knew this was the first step to realising our shared dream of me playing for the team we loved, Middlesbrough.

My own enthusiasm was, however, tinged with self-doubt as I wondered whether I would be good enough to step up to the intermediate level of under-19 football. As a teenager, I was still quite a shy lad who lacked confidence whenever I found myself in a different environment away from my friends. That lack of confidence followed me from junior football through to my first call-up for the full England squad some years later. Nevertheless, it had been my boyhood dream to play for the Boro and I was determined to overcome my shyness and, following

Extra Time – The Final Chapter

three sleepless nights, I arrived at Hutton Road with my father one nasty Saturday morning to play for Boro's junior side against Sheffield Wednesday.

It had been raining for two days and the pitch was extremely wet as I approached the door of an old wooden changing room. Dad, who was probably as nervous as I was, whispered good luck before I left him. I knocked on the door of the hut and entered the changing room. There I was met by the club's intermediate team coach George Wardle who greeted me with a firm handshake and introduced me to the rest of the team. That small room of young hopefuls included two lads with whom I would go on to become good friends as our young careers developed, Joe Laidlaw and Alan Murray. However, the only other triallist that day was a boy from Hartlepool called Steve Smelt who later became a great friend through his role as club physiotherapist for both Middlesbrough and Hartlepool. I can remember looking at Steve's face during the pre-match team talk and thinking that he looked just about as petrified as I felt. The only thing I can remember from George's talk that day was that he said Sheffield Wednesday's centre-half had already played three or four games in the first team. "Wow!" I thought. "I really am in big company today."

The first 10 minutes of the match were quite a culture shock. I had never before played in a game where the ball had whizzed around with such speed and accuracy and I found it very hard to come to terms with the pace of the match. As the team's rather naive debutant, playing in the old inside forward position, I was easy meat in the opening minutes for several crunching tackles from the opposition defenders. However, after about 20 minutes the penny dropped and I realised that I needed to knock the ball off first touch. Although I didn't pull up any trees that day, when the final whistle blew a close to a 3-0 Boro win, I felt I had done myself justice. Coming off the field, feeling completely drained after a traumatic 90 minutes, I could see from the look on Dad's face that he thought so too.

A few moments later as we climbed into his Austin A40, Dad asked me if I had enjoyed myself, to which I rather sheepishly replied in the positive. When he asked me how I had got on with the rest of the lads, however, I had to admit to him: "I don't know, Dad, nobody spoke to me." The truth was that apart from my fellow triallist Steve Smelt not one of my team-mates had uttered a word to me before or after the match. In those days it was rare for a newcomer like myself to be accepted until they could prove that they were a footballer worthy to be welcomed into the dressing room. What I didn't realise at the time was that to the five or six apprentices in the team my arrival was a potential threat to their own hopes of a

When I was a Lad

career in professional football.

A fortnight later, I received a letter from the club requesting me to take part in an evening fixture in Newcastle. Of course, I had to seek permission from my school headmaster to take the afternoon off to enable me to make my way to Middlesbrough before continuing on to Hunter's Moor where Newcastle intermediates would host their counterparts from Middlesbrough. As United needed to win the game to clinch the league title, I was far from sure whether I would be picked for the team in such an important match. The Middlesbrough squad included four of the club's most promising junior players in Peter Wilson, Michael Allen, Joe Laidlaw and Alan Moody together with a few of the more experienced reserve team players. In turn, United's side included Alan Foggon and Geoff Allen, two players I knew had already experienced first team football at St James' Park. So it was with great surprise and a huge gulp of air that I found myself named in the starting line-up when George read out the Boro team. Boro's assistant manager Harold Shepherdson had accompanied the team that night and I can remember him saying to the other players to look after me and give me plenty of encouragement as I looked frightened to death. How right he was!

Not long after the team had been called out, George stared down at my footwear. I was wearing an old pair of what I would call the old low-back "continental" boots - Slazenger, if I recall rightly - which I had bought for one pound from a pal of mine, Peter Robertson. In my haste to have my own pair of football boots, however, I hadn't bothered discussing with 'Fatty Robbo' such an unimportant detail as their size and consequently now found my boots turning up at the toes as they were a size too big for me. To make matters worse, only a quarter of an inch remained on the boots' worn plastic studs where the metal seats were protruding through.

George gave me a piercing look and asked me how I felt I could do myself justice in such antiquated footwear on a rain-sodden pitch. He enquired whether my father was coming up to watch the game, to which I told him that yes, he would probably be outside waiting for the kick-off. At that, I followed George out of the door as he proceeded to give Dad a rollicking, knowing full well that I would have done well even to stand up on the waterlogged pitch, let alone make any impact in the game. Like myself, I don't think Dad had even given the subject a thought but I then realised I was now in the professional world and my equipment had to be spot-on. Rather red-faced, my father agreed with George and promised to buy me a better pair in time for my next match.

Extra Time – The Final Chapter

For the time being, I borrowed a pair of boots from Bobby Lake, one of the apprentices who had not been selected that night. Inserted in the base of the boots were inch-long leather studs and on the wooden floor of the dressing room I felt almost as if I was on stilts. Again, there was a fast and physical start to the game but after 10 minutes I got just what I needed to calm my nerves. When Newcastle conceded a free-kick about 25 yards out, Joe Laidlaw quickly grabbed the ball and rolled a pass across to yours truly. Almost without thinking, I struck the ball violently with my left foot and was delighted to see the ball fly into the far corner of the net. As I was mobbed by my team-mates, I remember thinking that this was a significant step towards being accepted by my playing colleagues. As I ran back to the halfway line, I glanced over to my left to see a rather stout gentleman joyously leaping up and down in celebration of my goal and, somewhat embarrassed, I looked away from my proud father. The game ended 2-2 but from a personal point of view the result was insignificant. I was simply pleased to have again done myself justice, especially in a game littered with more experienced players.

The following week, I was to discover there was a class system among the club's intermediates - and I was clearly looked on as second class. Steve Smelt and I were given chitties to visit Jack Hatfield Sports shop to purchase some new boots. George Wardle had obviously informed the club that my footwear was something that Arthur Neagus would have been proud of. Told I could spend up to five pounds, I departed Hatfield's feeling thrilled to be the proud new owner of a pair of Mitre boots which had cost four pounds and 10 shillings. A smile as wide as my face remained until I saw the pair of Adidas boots Smelty had exchanged for his 10 pound chitty. As a Catholic schools international, he had been allowed to spend twice as much as I had on his footwear.

Playing more times for the intermediates during the following weeks, I quickly realised that the standard of young professionals at the club was very high. One of my intermediate team-mates, Joe Laidlaw, was already a regular with the reserves and had on occasions travelled to away games with the first team. But others - Alan Moody, David Mills and Pat Cuff - were schoolboy internationals. And the list didn't end there. Don Burluraux was showing great promise, winger Alan Murray looked particularly confident while Michael Allen and Stan Webb were also regulars in the second team. In comparison, I - without even a county trial to my name - was shy and lacking in confidence when surrounded by such high calibre team-mates. Still, I was determined to show the club's coaching staff that despite my less lofty background I could more than match the players already on Boro's books.

But my growing confidence was shattered after a game against Wolves Juniors at Hutton Road. With the temperature in the high 70's, it was a tough day for football, especially for a lad still building up his fitness, and I was tripping over my tongue during the final 20 minutes. I was so tired during the final minutes that I could not have done anything with the ball had I even had the chance so I was not prepared for the verbal onslaught I received during the post-match teamtalk. In front of my new team-mates, George Wardle accused me of hiding and cheating on the rest of the lads. He demanded 100 per cent effort and nothing less than that would do. I was far too shy to even consider pointing out that I had been on my last legs out there and left Hutton Road feeling highly deflated.

I spent the week praying that, having rollicked me, George would put his criticism behind. But those hopes were shattered within minutes of my arrival at Hutton Road for the following Saturday's fixture. George began his pre-match talk by reminding everyone how I had "hidden" when the going got tough. He made me feel so small that I felt I could have left the room under the three inch gap at the bottom of the dressing room door. Lacking the confidence to simply shrug off such criticism, the quality of my performances dipped to a new low during the following weeks. Quite simply, I was scared stiff of George and was a mouse in his company. Whether he was testing my character, I don't know, but I believe that coaches should make their players feel 10 feet tall before they walk on to the field of play, not humiliate them in front of their colleagues. Thankfully, I eventually got used to George but his harsh attitude caused several promising players to buckle under the pressure and they never fulfilled their potential.

When the school holidays came around, I was invited along with the other lads to a day's training at Ayresome Park and was told to report on a Friday morning at 9.30 prompt. My brother Dave offered to accompany me to the ground - and but for him perhaps I would not have even had the courage to go. When the clock alarm woke me from my slumber at 7.30am, I was frozen with nerves and may well have stayed in bed had it not been for Dave ordering me to get ready. Later, as we approached the imposing iron gates of Ayresome Park along the cobbled street which led to the ground, I spotted Bill Gates, one of the club's most experienced players, and nervously enquired: "Excuse me, can you tell me where I'm supposed to report for a trial?" Bill ushered me through the gates and, to my astonishment, took me through the first team dressing room. I was overawed to walk past players

Extra Time – The Final Chapter

like top scorer John Hickton and club captain Gordon Jones - stars I normally hero-worshipped from the stands. I couldn't help but wonder what on earth someone like me was doing among such great players. Bill eventually pointed me in the direction of the reserve team dressing room to get changed. Having done so, I was greeted by the club physio Jimmy Headridge who enquired if I would like to train with the club's first teamers and reserves. Without hesitation, but with more than a little trepidation, I told Jimmy I would quite happily do so and quickly found myself sharing a light training session on the Ayresome Park pitch with many of my boyhood heroes.

Upon meeting my brother at Rea's coffee bar later, Dave was visibly trembling as he asked me how training had gone. He could hardly believe his ears as I told him that I had trained with the club's first team players. I went on to explain how wonderful it was just to see the dressing room, boot room and showers. To me, smelling the linament in the dressing room was almost to taste the club's tradition and history. I had shared the very same dressing room that the club's legends had used many times before - great players like Wilf Mannion, George Hardwick, Brian Clough and Alan Peacock.

By the May of 1967, decision time was drawing near. Middlesbrough hadn't been forthcoming in offering me an apprenticeship and I knew I had to make a decision on whether to stay on for further education or join ICI, having recently passed exams to qualify for an apprenticeship with the chemical giant. Both of my brothers and my sister Claire already worked in the ICI while my father was still an employee, though he had by now switched from the plasterboard plant to the machine shop. Without the offer of an apprenticeship with the football club, I made my mind up that I would follow in the long line of tradition and join ICI where, so I was told, I would have a job for life.

But Dad was not ready to leave it at that. He was irritated by the fact that Middlesbrough had not made a decision on my future and proceeded to try to force their hand. One day he rang Harold Shepherdson, and told him: "Listen Harold, I think it's only fair to tell you that Leeds United have enquired about our Willie again. If Middlesbrough don't offer him terms in the near future, then I think it will be only common sense for Willie to join United." His story was complete fabrication, of course, but it did the trick.

Two days later, Dad and I were invited to Ayresome Park where the club asked me to sign apprenticeship forms with them. Father and son were over the moon and I signed on the dotted line for my boyhood heroes.

3

Reserve Recollections

MY FIRST weekly wage with Middlesbrough F.C. was the princely sum of five pounds - and I felt like the Sultan of Brunei. My new salary was a considerable step up on my normal pocket money of five shillings. I took great delight at the end of my first week of work at being able to give my mother two pounds and ten shillings for my upkeep.

At the back of my mind, however - even on the day I signed terms with the team I loved - was a nagging doubt that I would ever be good enough to make the grade at a professional level. I continued to suffer from that overwhelming lack of confidence throughout my first months with the club and, to a lesser extent, throughout my career.

Playing for the intermediate team as a member of the club's groundstaff rather than just as a triallist put more pressure on me and I found life increasingly difficult in my early months. I was not initially an automatic choice for the side and George Wardle may well have been justified in leaving me on the sidelines, preferring to choose the likes of Alan Murray, David Mills, Michael Allen and the one looked on as the brightest prospect among us, Joe Laidlaw. Quite why the club's coaching staff had switched me to inside-forward from midfield I am not sure but they must have seen something in me that suggested I might be able to score goals at a good rate. I was quite happy to play at inside-forward though Dad, who watched all my games, would often criticize me for not being selfish enough. "You're spoon-feeding Laidlaw and Murray, Willie," he would tell me as he drove me home afterwards. "You've got to be more selfish and get your name in the headlines."

Perhaps the truth was that I was a little bit overawed at the time but there is no doubt my biggest drawback was the fact that I was already carrying the knee injury that was to ultimately finish my career a decade later. An operation to remove the cartilage in my left knee duly followed, though for a while it seemed my career might be over before it had even begun. It took far longer than expected to return to full training but when I did finally get back on the football pitch I was a different player. From that moment my performances for the club's intermediates improved dramatically. Perhaps I felt I had nothing to lose. The pressure was off and I no longer felt such a weight of expectation on my shoulders. I became more relaxed in my play and improved in leaps and bounds. At the same time my strength and fitness was also coming on and my confidence hit new heights as I began to make a name for myself as the intermediates' regular goalscorer playing at centre forward.

The intermediates' coach on a day-to-day basis was Jimmy Headridge, a Scottish cross-country champion who was also employed as one of the club's two physiotherapists, George Wright being the other. With Jimmy taking care of the first team's knocks and strains, George Wardle was the part-time coach in charge of our Saturday morning fixtures. The two physios were renowned for their Micky-taking antics as the club's youngsters carried out their daily chores around the ground.

"Maddren!" George Wright would scream at the top of his voice. "Come here!"

As I made my way towards him I would wonder to myself: "Bloody hell, what have I done now?" When I got there, however, he would simply ask in a friendly tone: "Are you OK, son?" I would be thinking to myself that this guy was a complete weirdo.

The next time George yelled my name across the ground, I marched across to him, cocky as you like. "Yes, George?" - to which he loudly lambasted me: "Why aren't those bloody baths washed out?" He would always do the unorthodox just to catch out me and the other lads.

Jimmy Headridge had a wonderful sense of humour though my first impression was that he was a bit strange. I first came into contact with Jimmy on the team coach travelling to a fixture at Carlisle United. I spent much of the journey staring out of the window but after a while couldn't help noticing that every time I glanced around he would be peeping between the seats in front. He would smile, wink at me and turn away. This was repeated every five minutes or so throughout the journey and even continued in the Penrith hotel we stopped off at for a bite to eat on the way. As the rather quiet newcomer to the team, I wondered to myself:

"Hell, what have we got here?" Whether this was all part of some sort of initiation ceremony by Jimmy, I don't know but it certainly left me wondering. But that, I soon discovered, was Jimmy for you - daft as you like!

He used that wicked sense of humour on us boys many times. On one hot pre-season afternoon, he spotted a young triallist helping himself to one of the salt tablets that professionals traditionally took at the time in the belief that it would help to replace the salt they had sweated from their bodies during training. "What have you just taken?" he bellowed out accusingly at the boy. The triallist pointed at the tablets that remained before responding nervously: "One of them." With that, Jimmy ordered the hapless youngster into a small room adjoining the physiotherapy room. "Close the door, put the light out and lie on the treatment bench," he yelled. "And don't move until I come back!"

It was fully an hour and a half before Jimmy finally returned, bursting in and flicking the light switch. There was the nervous youngster prostrate on the bench, not daring to move. "What the bloody hell are you doing in here?" shouted Jimmy. "Out you go and don't waste my time!"

In my early days at the club I was often disappointed that I didn't see more of a football. After all, it was football that I was there to learn, I thought to myself. Mondays after a Saturday home game were the worst. Then it was the traditional duty of all the apprentices to sweep the Ayresome Park stands of litter left behind by the supporters. It was a boring and thankless task made all the worse by the fact that several fellow apprentices were awarded professional contracts which alleviated them of their chores. That left only three apprentices, myself included, to clean up the whole ground. On one occasion I swept the whole of the South Stand myself. The sight of me arriving home that evening prompted Mam to ask: "What's all that dust on you? I thought you were meant to be a professional footballer, not a chimney sweep!" Even so, I was always careful to ensure those stands were swept immaculately - not only because I have always been a great believer in doing a job well but just in case one of the club coaches checked my work and made me do it all again.

Another job as an apprentice was cleaning out the individual slipper baths together with the bigger plunge bath every lunchtime and again at about four o'clock if the first team had trained morning and afternoon. I don't think I need to explain just how little I enjoyed that particular task. Another daily chore, on a rota basis, was cleaning the boots of the first team players and collecting their kit and

Extra Time – The Final Chapter

hanging it up on their pegs in the dressing room. Each player had two pieces of kit which was expected to last the full week, with the consequence that shorts and shirts would often be caked in mud by Friday when the kit would be sent in baskets to a laundry on the town's main high street, Linthorpe Road. I didn't appreciate it at the time, of course, but one thing each of those rather arduous tasks gave me was a sense of discipline, something for which I later became very thankful.

Even the end of the season did not bring a respite as it was then that we would be enlisted as groundsmen and painters, forking the pitch in preparation for re-seeding and painting coats of red paint on to the Ayresome Park seats and black on to the ground's toilet walls. Unlike the professionals, who would enjoy a long break over the summer months, we were thankful for the two or three weeks we were allowed as holiday during the close season.

In between all the chores, however, we did play plenty of football. Daily coaching sessions took place at the club's training ground on Hutton Road, about a mile from Ayresome Park. At the time the Ayresome pitch was considered to be second only to the turf of the national stadium at Wembley and yet the the Hutton Road pitch wasn't too far behind Ayresome's and playing a cup final there was often the highlight of the season for many local teams. Hutton Road's changing facilities were somewhat less impressive, comprising solely of a wooden shed. Consequently, our daily routine involved getting changed into our kit at Ayresome Park before making our way to the training ground, either hitching a lift from one of the senior players - if we were lucky - or making our way there on foot. However, we were all aware that training always started right on time and that there would be hell to pay if we were late. With that in mind, my fellow apprentices and I would frequently arrive at Hutton Road completely knackered, having ran the majority of the way in a desperate attempt to keep to the strict time-keeping.

With training over, there was only one place for the players to be. The hang-out for several of the senior pro's was Rea's Cafe, just a stone's throw from Ayresome Park. The son of Mr and Mrs Rea would go on to become far more famous than perhaps any Middlesbrough footballer as rock star Chris Rea. If we finished our chores early enough, us young lads considered it something of a privilege to join senior pro's like Arthur Horsfield, Willie Whigham and Johnny Crossan in Rea's for a mince pie or a toasted ham and cheese sandwich, perhaps followed by a blob of Rea's own ice cream.

At the end of my first season as an apprentice, I joined a group of my teenage team-mates on a near disastrous holiday on the Costa del Sol that could so easily have ended our football careers before they had really begun. As with the majority of the other lads, it was my first experience of a holiday abroad and I set off feeling excited about the fortnight ahead, accompanied by Joe Laidlaw, Alan Moody, Alan Murray, Brian Myton and Steve Howie. Within minutes of our arrival at our Calalla de Costa hotel, we were in one of the numerous local bars as I ordered the first of 10 Bacardi and Cokes I was to consume over the next hour-and-a-half. We were all extremely merry as we snaked our way back to the hotel through the town's narrow streets at the end of an enjoyable night's drinking. I thought nothing of it when Alan Murray banged a metal garage door as we walked by - but Alan had made a mistake that turned our night on the bars into the sobering reality of a night behind bars.

Paul Gascoigne, eat your heart out! More than two decades before Gazza hit the headlines with his version of the Dentist's Chair, here I am swigging back the sangria during my first holiday abroad - a near disastrous visit to Calalla in Spain.

Within minutes, the local police arrived. On spotting them, Messrs Murray, Myton and Howie made a sharp exit and disappeared down one of the many dark streets. But Alan Moody, Joe Laidlaw and I were slower to react. We were arrested for disturbing the peace and were briskly escorted to the local nick where our hosts fell some way short of providing the hospitality promised in our holiday brochure. After relieving us of our belts - presumably to ensure we did not hang ourselves - we were shown to our accommodation for the evening. The only feature in our cold, small cell - measuring no more than three feet by six feet - was a concrete slab jutting out from the wall. This was bed for all three of us with a hole in the floor as our toilet. My attempts to plead our innocence to the Spanish jailer in broken

Extra Time – The Final Chapter

French failed dismally. The cell's solid door was slammed shut and, with a huge sigh, we prepared to settle down for the night as best we could.

In our drunken stupor, we quickly agreed our sleeping arrangements. Joe and I would share the slab while Alan would curl up on the floor in the corner of the cell. However, Joe made the unfortunate decision to sleep on the outside of the slab. Midway through the night, I told him to move out of the way as I was going to be sick. Sadly, his reactions weren't quick enough and he was given a pebble-dashed design to his clothing, compliments of yours truly. Justice was done, however, when half an hour later Joe returned the compliment.

Our ordeal only ended at half past five in the morning when we were released after paying a 60 peseta fine. Still very much under the influence of drink, I and my two fellow future professional footballers staggered our way back to the hotel in the early morning gloom. Given that this was my first taste of alcohol, it will come as no surprise that not a single drop of Bacardi and Coke passed my lips for over 25 years after that harsh lesson.

Together once again, the six of us promised each other that our brush with the law would remain a secret on our return to the football club. But we were about to unwittingly embark on an escapade that we would find somewhat harder to hide. We made the mistake of informing the waiters at our hotel that we were young professionals with an English football team and quickly found ourselves challenged to what we understood to be a kick-about two days later. As we enjoyed the sun the following day, we were horrified, therefore, to see a car driving through town announcing over a loud speaker that a football match would be held the following day at 3pm between Calalla and Middlesbrough F.C. On making further enquiries, we realised things had got way out of hand as tickets were being sold in advance of the big game at 50 pesetas each. However, there was now great pressure on us to play and we felt our only option was to get things over and done with.

The following day Calalla's little ground was packed with nearly 2,000 locals and holiday-makers as "Middlesbrough F.C." lined up on a dustbowl of a pitch represented by six naive teenagers, four fellow guests from our hotel and a Dutch holiday-maker who reckoned he was reserve team goalkeeper for Feyenoord. I quickly developed doubts about the Dutch guy's boasts that he was a professional 'keeper as he ducked his head at the first violent shot that came his way! But this was serious stuff - at least as far as the Spaniards were concerned. We had seen

Reserve Recollections

Calalla lose only 3-0 to Barcelona reserves the previous week and knew they would be no push-over. We undoubtedly risked injury as players on both sides kicked lumps out of one other for the next 90 extremely physical, energy sapping minutes which ended in a 4-3 win for the home side.

Afterwards, we simply hoped beyond hope that word would not get back to Teesside of our unofficial friendly on behalf of the club. But we had reckoned without former Blackpool goalkeeper Tony Waiters who had watched the entire escapade from the stands. Waiters must have been on the phone sharpish on his return to England because our arrival back at Ayresome Park was greeted almost immediately by a summons to the office of assistant manager, Harold Shepherdson. He was furious and wasn't interested in our attempts to explain. "Do you realise the seriousness of what you have done?" he yelled. "You're all bloody lucky not to be dismissed right here." Indeed, I honestly believe the only reason we weren't shown the door was directly related to the fact that both Joe Laidlaw and Alan Moody were regarded as potential stars of the future.

To have lost my big chance over such farce would have been a huge body blow to me. Playing football and being paid for it was a wonderful life and I knew far greater things awaited me if I could continue to listen, learn and develop my game. After a year as an apprentice, I knew the time was approaching when I would discover if I was to be taken on as a full professional or released. But it was not through the carefully chosen words of a club coach that young players would discover the outcome of this make or break decision on their future careers but by the brand of footwear they were allowed to purchase. The close season was traditionally the time when the club's retained list would be made public but most players knew long before then simply by asking for a chit to buy new training shoes to replace the pair they had worn out during the previous months. Adidas Samba and prepare yourself for a crack at professional football. Dunlop Green Flash and prepare yourself for soccer's scrapheap. It really was that straight forward. Imagine my joy, not to mention relief, therefore, on the sunny July morning when I received a chit to take to Jack Hatfield sports shop to buy a new pair of Adidas Samba training shoes. Sadly, it was also a time to bid farewell to friends. Several lads I had trained with on a daily basis for more than 12 months were released by the club, including Steve Fenton, Dave Dixon, Peter Wilson, Bobby Lake and one of my fellow holiday-makers, Steve Howie. None of them made it in professional football, though Peter and Dave later emigrated Down Under and the former actually captained Australia during the 1974 World Cup.

Extra Time – The Final Chapter

Having climbed another rung on the ladder of success, I knew I would now be expected to step up my workrate to justify my weekly wage packet of twelve pounds. In 1968, that was an enormous wage for a 17-year-old and I was well aware that I was earning probably four times what many of my old school-mates were taking home as apprentice instrument artificers or fitters at ICI. Indeed, as I sat on the top deck of the number 64 bus on my daily journey from Billingham to Newport Bridge on my way to Ayresome Park I would occasionally chuckle to myself as I glanced at the smog bellowing out from the factories. That's not meant to sound disrespectful to the thousands of guys who earned a living through the local industry. Even then, I knew just how lucky I was to be enjoying such a wonderful life thanks to my talent with a football at my feet.

And yet the life I led away from Ayresome Park was hardly distinguishable from that of most other lads of the same age. It simply was not in my nature to be flashy. Indeed, half of my weekly wage would be handed straight over to Mum on my arrival home on pay day. Much of the rest would go towards savings for my next holiday. A few rounds on the 'Chip & Putt' golf course at Eston with Alan Moody and Don Burluraux was about as glamourous as it got and yet before long I found myself at the centre of some rather malicious gossip. As an alternative to

Yours truly is pictured (back row, third right) with the successful Boro juniors side I played in. Pictured are (back row, from left): Burluraux, Smith, Allen, Cuff, Maddren, Myton, Fenton. Front row (from left): Brine, Murray, Moody, Stonehouse, Mills and Charlton.

our regular night out at the pictures, my girlfriend Diane and I would occasionally join my family at the Low Grange Club, just a few minutes' walk from my parents' house. Those visits to the club came to an abrupt end the day I learned I had been reported to Harold Shepherdson for being seen drunk on several pints of Guinness. Quite who had felt the need to spread such gossip about me, I don't know but it hurt to be the target of such talk. The simple truth was that I would never drink anything more than a couple of pints of Coca-Cola so the suggestion that I had been drunk mystified me. Even so, at that early age, I made the decision to stay away from the boozers if socialising there with friends produced such results. It was sad that I no longer felt at ease mixing with the people I had grown up with and worse still when talk spread among the gossip-mongers - "Oh, Willie Maddren, he considers himself too good to come in here now that he's a professional footballer."

Such things served to encourage a special bond among the club's young professionals and I became firm friends with David Mills, Alan Moody, Don Burluraux and Stan Webb. However, eating out at Uptons' cafe or at Parker's Grill on Linthorpe Road could hardly be described as living it up. Don, who lived out of town in North Skelton, was a particularly close friend. He was so laid back that he made Perry Como look nervous and never took offence when I teasingly called him Woolly Back. I would often visit Don to see the canaries he reared for competition and I always felt a close affinity to the people of that area, probably because Dad had lived up the road in Margrove Park for many years.

Not until I was 19 did I buy my first motor vehicle and that only after suffering the embarrassment of sharing the bus home with supporters after breaking into the Boro first team. That in itself was fine as long as the result had been a good one. However, after a less than impressive performance, the comments reverberating around the bus were not too pleasing on the ear. I would probably have bought a motor earlier had I not witnessed the immediate aftermath of a bad car crash on the old A19 while travelling back on the club coach from an away match with the reserves one night. Seeing a blanket-covered body carried from behind a smashed vehicle sent a shiver down my spine and I promised myself I would delay purchasing my first car for as long as possible. On breaking into the first team, I would usually get a lift home in Dad's car but when his night shifts forced me back on to that daunting bus journey I knew buying my own motor was an absolute necessity. I consequently paid £360 for my first car, a three-year-old green VW Beetle, considered by the players 'in the know' to be the in-car at the time.

But in the summer of 1969 first team football and even VW Beetles were still

Extra Time – The Final Chapter

beyond me. I was thrilled to have been taken on as a professional footballer but was fully aware that I was just one of several talented young players at the club and I would have to work hard to outshine the likes of Alan Murray, Alan Moody, Brian Myton, David Mills and, most of all, Joe Laidlaw.

And yet if I had expected to receive words of encouragement from the club's senior staff I was in for a shock. First team coach Jimmy Greenhalgh, a man for whom I always had tremendous respect, ensured my feet remained firmly on the ground when he asked in a rather serious tone: "How the hell does someone like you get signed on professional forms?"

The switch to professional terms also meant I would now use the first team or Home dressing room rather than Ayresome Park's Away team dressing room traditionally used by the club's apprentices. I was happy as Larry after my first day's training until I accidentally picked up the towel of first teamer Mike Kear believing it to be my own. Seeing me using his towel to dry myself, Kear - who was a good eight years older than me - snatched the towel off me and aggressively warned: "You're on the wrong side of me right from the f***ing start." I don't know whether he saw me as a potential threat to his first team place but from that moment on he was always hostile towards me. He would go out of his way to bully me and criticize my performances for the reserves, telling me I couldn't play. I had little regard for Kear as a person but, inevitably, my confidence nose-dived. His barracking continued for several months until the day I dumped him on his backside with a deliberately physical challenge during a five-a-side training match at the club's gym in Whinney Banks. As he climbed to his feet, I could see he was ready to square up to me but pumping with adrenaline I pushed him back to the floor and left him in no doubt that I'd had quite enough of his antics. I did wonder what the other older players would make of it all and was thankful when Arthur Horsfield reassured me that I had done the right thing. "He's had it coming," he insisted. Any worries I had that my actions might have simply added fuel to the fire soon vanished and Kear never bothered me again. The episode had served as a good lesson in sticking up for myself and ensuring no-one got away with pushing me around.

On the pitch, I did not have to wait long for my reserve team debut, going on as a substitute central defender for the experienced Bill Gates against Halifax Town at Ayresome Park. A kick in the testicles from the former Manchester United player Mark Pearson - quite probably retribution for one of Bill's aggressive tackles - saw Gates stretchered off in agony. But Bill's pain was my joy as I passed another milestone in my progression towards first team football, acquitting myself well during the final 40 minutes of the game. I was quietly pleased with myself until I received a tongue-lashing from Don Masson, a player who had regularly featured in the first team in the past but had been relegated to the reserves that night. Having played through what could only be described as a perfect pass no more than a foot off the ground for Don to volley narrowly wide, I was stunned when he angrily yelled at me: "Maddren - I want the ball on the ground next time!" The truth was I was in awe of Don, having witnessed him yelling at Stan Webb during an earlier reserve team game when he had shouted to Jimmy Headridge: "He can't play, get him off!" But I was to learn that only when you had proven you could play would a youngster like myself or Stan be accepted by senior pro's. In fact, never again did I have a problem with Don who was, of course, to go on to become a Scotland international as a star of the QPR and Derby teams of the late 1970s.

The following months brought more reserve team action alongside my friends and the club's manager Stan Anderson soon recognised the fact that he had an outstanding crop of young players bursting with potential. So impressive were our performances for the second team that Stan publicly stated that 'The M-Squad' of Moody, Myton, Mills and Maddren would save him hundreds of thousands of pounds in the transfer market. A reflection of just how good we were came when the reserves took on Doncaster's normal first team line-up - forced to turn out for the reserves as punishment for a disappointing display the previous Saturday - and duly hammered them 7-2 on their own patch. With just 10 minutes left, snow began to fall and I was amazed when Alick Jeffrey, one of Doncaster's most experienced players, pleaded with the referee to abandon the match. His defence was that the players could no longer see the markings on the pitch but the simple truth was he was trying to save his team from further embarrassment. Unfortunately, the gloss was taken off the night when the team coach broke down at Wetherby on the way home and we were forced to sit for three hours while we waited for a relief coach to arrive from Hartlepool. My head didn't hit the pillow of my bed until after 3am but I doubtless enjoyed pleasant dreams about my blossoming career that night.

Even so, all of the young pro's were on steep learning curves and, despite their encouragement, the club's coaches always ensured our feet remained firmly on the ground. I was reminded just how much I still had to learn whilst playing at left-half during a reserve team match at York City. As we sat down in the dressing room at half-time, Jimmy Greenhalgh shot a glance in my direction that told me he was not best pleased with my performance. "Why is it, Maddren, you think you have a divine right to win every ball in the air?" he demanded. Embarrassed to be the focus of his anger, I gave him a blank look. I had no idea what he meant but Jimmy explained himself: "When a centre-forward receives a quality pass at a good height, don't be climbing all over his back trying to get the ball and giving away free-kicks like you have done for the last 45 minutes. No-one can win every ball. Sometimes you have to be patient and wait for your chance, wait for the player to make a mistake."

Throughout my career one of my best traits was the ability to listen and learn. I needed telling only once and the penny would drop. Jimmy was right and I knew it and from that moment on I determined to put those words of advice into action on the playing pitch to the benefit of my game. But not all players have the ability or desire to put into practice what they are taught. Many years later during a coaching spell at Hartlepool, I remember watching John Bird, a former Newcastle United defender I had rated highly at his peak, still crashing into the back of players and needlessly conceding free-kicks. Even in his mid-30's, John was still making the same basic errors I had cut out of my game from an early age.

Another memory of my reserve team days remains strong in the memory. It was the night, under Ayresome Park's floodlights, I realised I would hardly be missed if ever I disappeared. During this particular second team game, I chased after a ball to the outside left position towards the corner flag at the ground's deserted Holgate End. Running hell for leather, I just managed to reach the ball before it went out of play and swept over a cross into the penalty area. With the momentum I had built up, however, I was unable to stop myself and twisted 180 degrees before the back of my knees hit the small wall which divided the pitch from the terraces. Falling fully five feet, my back hit the concrete terrace below with a thud. With the wind knocked right out of me, I lay there out of sight of the rest of the ground for fully two minutes. Only then did I realise that no-one was coming for me! Eventually, I staggered to my feet and was dismayed to look over the wall to see the game continuing without me. I felt like shouting: "For Christ's sake, here I am." Had the fall rendered me unconscious it is quite possible I'd have remained there until the groundsman discovered me the following morning! Shaking my head, I gingerly resumed the game untreated. I guess everyone was so engrossed in the game that they had forgotten about me - either that or the physio couldn't be bothered running over to the ground's furthest corner on such a cold night.

Even so, after an indifferent start with the reserves, I was playing with a degree of confidence though I knew I was not the finished article in terms of either technique or the physical development of my upper body. I seemed to do equally well in either defence or attack but it was as a right half-back that I was called up for one of the Football Association's occasional youth training and selection weekends at Lilleshall early in the 1968-69 season. I was naturally delighted to be named by coach Wilf McGuinness among the cream of the country's best young talent and travelled to Shropshire with a real sense of pride. Among the players included in that squad who would go on to make their names in the game were Bob Latchford of Birmingham City, Tottenham duo Steve Perryman and Jimmy Neighbour, Alan Hudson of Chelsea and Orient's Tommy Taylor. I thought I did reasonably well and was disappointed when I was not named in the following England under-19 squad.

However, my more regular position for the reserves was up front, either at centre-forward or inside-left. With Joe Laidlaw frequently featuring in the first team, the responsibility for scoring second team goals fell between Stan Webb and me, though David Mills was also beginning to feature regularly. I believed I was edging into the manager's thoughts in terms of a first team call-up and was determined to take every opportunity I could to press my claims. One such opportunity arose during a morning training session at Hutton Road. Concerned that the first team defence had been conceding goals from set pieces, Stan Anderson set out to work on the problem with the reserve team acting as the opposition against the club's regular defenders. That put me, as the opposing centre-forward, in direct opposition to the vastly experienced Dicky Rooks and Bill Gates. As only the second corner of the session was swung into the box, I got a yard or two on Bill and planted a firm header into the corner of the net. Given the nature of the exercise, Stan understandably went berserk that the defence had allowed me a free header. Tiring of Stan's ranting, Dicky set out to ensure that the mistake was not repeated. "Leave Maddren to me, Bill. I'll pick him up," he told his central defensive partner. Just two corners later, however, with Rooks on my shoulder, I moved in one direction, checked back and headed the ball past goalkeeper Willie Whigham. I had left my marker for dead and the manager's mood turned black. He gathered the players around him and began his own version of the Spanish Inquisition.

Eventually we were ready to resume with the session. Before we did so, however, I was approached by Dicky Rooks who had a troubled look on his face. "For Christ's sake, Willie, leave it out. I've got the kids to pick up at 1.30. He'll have us all here till four o'clock if we carry on like this." It was a significant moment for

Extra Time – The Final Chapter

me. Until then I had been known to senior players like Dicky only as "Maddren". Now he had used my Christian name as he implored me to take training a little less seriously. I knew I had gained respect among the more experienced players that day. However, I had plans of my own that afternoon and granted Dicky's request. The session ended 20 minutes later at one o'clock with manager and players all happy - the manager believed the problem was solved, the players got to go home on time and I had made a good impression on all concerned.

Stan Anderson must have made a mental note of my contribution that day because just two weeks after, in late October 1968, I was included in a first team squad for the first time. It came as a huge surprise. Indeed, I left Ayresome Park after Thursday's training session without even checking the squad of players listed on a team sheet to travel by train to London the following day in preparation for Saturday's Second Division clash at Oxford United. There had been no hint that I would be included and it was only that evening when Dad pointed out my name among the squad of players listed on the back page of the local newspaper, the Evening Gazette, that I realised I would not be spending the weekend on Teesside. Despite seeing my name in black and white, I doubted my inclusion and wondered if there had been some sort of mistake. If I was included I would have to be at Ayresome Park at nine o'clock the following morning - rather than my usual 9.30 - in time to catch the team coach that would take the players to Darlington Railway Station. I was in a dilemma so decided I should hear it straight from the horse's mouth. I ran the mile-and-a-half to the manager's house on Billingham's Sandy Lane to ask Mr Anderson if I had got the story right. I was quite breathless as he opened the door to his house and I asked him if I was to travel to Oxford. "Did Jimmy Greenhalgh not tell you?" he enquired. "No, boss, he didn't," I answered nervously. "Of course you're f***ing travelling." With that, the door was slammed shut and I raced home to tell my parents the exciting news.

Travelling to London by train as a wide-eyed teenager proved to be quite an experience but it was only on arrival at our accommodation for the night that I was left with eyes agog and mouth gaping in wonderment. My humble upbringing in Haverton Hill and Billingham was a far cry from the magnificent Waldorf Hotel in the heart of a bustling capital city. That evening, I shared a dining table with Willie Whigham and a couple of other experienced players. The food was exquisite though I was unsure of exactly what some of it was. A glance down the menu was of little help. Upon finishing my main course, I asked Willie what pineapple flambé was all about. At 17 shillings and six pence, it was the most expensive dessert on the menu but Willie was insistent that I should give it a try. "Have it! You're not paying!" Eventually, he ordered the flambé on my behalf. Oh, how I was to wish he had not done so. All heads turned my way as this flaming dessert was wheeled in to the restaurant and served on to my plate. The last thing I wanted to do as the rather shy newcomer was draw attention to myself. Instead, my nervous glance towards the directors' table was met with glares from the faces of club chairman Eric Thomas and director George Wood. At that moment, I felt sure I could read their minds - "That big time Charlie, he's only a kid and he's already trying to be flashy..." I was mortified but my embarrassment gave Willie and the rest of the lads a good laugh at my expense.

That evening, after we had eaten, I experienced another eye-opener. Two more first team regulars, Derrick Downing and Ray Lugg, took me under their wings and invited me to see the latest movie at a West End cinema. I readily agreed to pay the taxi fare and pay my own way into the cinema. Only later did I discover that the senior pro's had been given expenses for the whole squad and I had needlessly spent part of my own weekly wage. Arriving back at the Waldorf after our evening out, we were greeted with huge plates of sandwiches and I thought to myself: "Wow, what a lifestyle this is." It was the sort of life most people could only dream about and yet here was I, just 17, living it up. I wasn't even a substitute for the following day's match - a 4-2 win - but I was thrilled with the experience and desperate for more of the same.

If my inclusion on that trip to Oxford was designed to make me even keener for a first team breakthrough, then it had the desired effect. Although I spent the next six months back in the reserves, there was a new edge to my game as I now had the belief that I was in the manager's thoughts. Consequently, when I was told I was substitute for an away match against Bolton Wanderers in early February, I was confident I was not the victim of a wind-up. The game at Burnden Park, soon after my 18th birthday, was played on a cold winter's night and after 80 minutes sat on the sub's bench my feet were like ice when Stan Anderson told me to start warming up. I thought my chance had finally come and I would make my first team debut but after a couple of minutes of nervous jogging and stretching along the touchline, I was told to sit down again. And there I remained until the referee blew his whistle to signal the end of a rather dull goalless draw.

Coming within a hair's breadth of my first team debut only served to make me hungrier for a taste of the big time. And I was soon to be handed a chance to show what I could do...

4

Joy...and Pain

MY HEAD was full of self-doubt the night before I made my first team debut. It was April 1969 and a disastrous run of results and below par performances had seen Middlesbrough slip from the thick of the promotion chase to no more than mathematical possibilities for promotion. The fans' dreams had been shattered for another season and manager Stan Anderson had clearly decided to give youth its chance when we faced Bury in our final home match of the season.

The day before the game, Stan called me upstairs to his Ayresome Park office and asked me to sit down. "How do you feel about playing for the first team against Bury tomorrow?" he asked. I thought it was an unusual question and gave him the only possible answer: "I'd be over the moon, boss." With that, he stood up and told me: "Fine, you'll be starting the game then."

I felt a rush of adrenaline course through my veins but before I left, Stan reassured me: "Willie, whatever you do tomorrow will please me." Those words helped to put me at ease.

I was filled with a combination of excitement and apprehension but could hardly wait to get home to tell my parents the good news. I wasn't the only young player who had been told he would get his chance the following day - Brian Myton, Alan Moody and Joe Laidlaw were all included too - but while they oozed with confidence, deep down I wondered if I was even good enough to play at such a level. Typically, I spent the night worrying about what Saturday would bring and wishing I was of the same temperament as my fellow young professionals. I have always been a worrier about what might happen instead of simply having the attitude that I would cross a bridge when I came to it. I always found transition hard and yet I would always comfortably leap every hurdle I came to throughout my career.

After a sleepless night, I reported to Ayresome Park to begin the countdown to my league debut. On arrival in the dressing room, I glanced up at the team sheet pinned on the wall. There, in black and white, was the team to play relegation-haunted Bury that afternoon:

1. Willie Whigham
2. Alan Moody
3. Brian Myton
4. George Smith
5. Bill Gates
6. Frank Spraggon
7. Ray Lugg
8. Eric McMordie
9. Joe Laidlaw
10. Willie Maddren
11. Johnny Crossan

With no less than four teenagers in the starting line-up it seemed to the fans that the manager had thrown in the towel as far as the promotion challenge was concerned. Indeed, the manager came in for a good deal of criticism for resting John Hickton, the club's only regular goalscorer, when promotion was still a mathematical possibility. The fans' frustration was reflected in a disappointing attendance of just over 10,000. That was way beyond any crowd I had previously played in front of but Ayresome must have seemed like a morgue to the first team regulars who had come to expect gates of over 25,000 during the previous months. Despite their perilous position towards the foot of the table, Bury were up for the game from the very start as they fought for every loose ball in a desperate bid for two points which might provide an escape from the relegation trapdoor. With the former Leeds United midfielder Bobby Collins marshalling their midfield, Bury ensured the first 10 minutes of the game were played at an electric pace and I quickly began to realise the gaping divide between reserve and first team football.

One or two early first time passes helped me to find my feet on the heavy pitch and my confidence built with every touch. But even if I say so myself, my debut was bloody brilliant. Or rather bloody *and* brilliant. With 15 minutes on the clock, Boro won a left wing corner and I quickly took my position on the edge of the six yard box. Full of raw energy and enthusiasm, I saw only the ball and no danger as I rose at the far post to meet the corner. A second later I was prostrate on the Ayresome Park turf with a bloodied and broken nose. In a bid to intimidate a young player like myself into tactical submission, a Bury defender had butted the back of his head into my face as I rose to meet the ball. With blood pouring from my nostrils, physio Jimmy Headridge had no option but to lead me from the pitch as he sought to stem the flow. There he packed my nose full of cotton wool, waited for evidence that the bleeding had ceased and told me to get back on.

Within five minutes a left wing cross was floated into the Bury box and from an almost identical position to the one in which I had been head-butted, I this time rose above the same centre-half and powered a header into the Bury net off the far post. It was a marvellous moment. I had achieved every football-mad boy's dream of scoring on my first team debut. As I looked back at the goal, I noticed a mark the ball had left three-quarters of the way up the left-hand post before it had bounced into the net. That mark would remain there to remind me of my magic moment for the next two months while the pitch was being re-seeded during the close season.

The goal gave me huge confidence and I went on to enjoy a good game, though I really should have scored again from another cross in the second half. I put everything into the game and was completely shattered during the final minutes, so much so that I turned my ankle and hobbled from the field at the final whistle. The supporters were far from happy with Boro's 3-2 defeat to a team facing relegation and there were looks of depression on the faces of the players back in the dressing room. Selfishly perhaps, I cared nothing for the result. I simply felt immense pride that I had not only done well but scored on my first team debut.

That night as I lay in bed suffering from a migraine attack, a broken nose and a chipped ankle bone, I was the happiest boy on Teesside.

Such was the severity of the migraine that I was unable to enjoy the plaudits of my family when I arrived home that evening. The whole family had witnessed my performance and were clearly delighted for me but I wanted only a dark room as relief from my nauseous headache. As I walked into the living room of my parents' home, as always I asked my brother Dave: "How do you think I did?" His answer, delivered with a proud smile, was predictable: "I thought you should have scored that header in the second half."

Joy...and Pain

I returned to Ayresome Park the following Monday morning having thankfully recovered from my migraine. Unfortunately, the chipped ankle bone I had suffered on my debut would take longer to heal and I was forced to sit out the final game at Birmingham City as David Mills got his chance as a second half substitute. Although friends, there was always a measure of rivalry between David and I as we were not only the same age but were frequently competing for the same positions right through from the intermediates to the first team. The season ended in disappointment for Boro, who signed off with a 3-1 defeat at St Andrew's, but I was already looking forward to the new campaign with great anticipation.

I began pre-season training with a real sense of optimism that this would be my year but the months that followed were the most frustrating of my career as I spent week after week in the reserves without even a sight of first team action. I could not understand why much of the time I was not even named among the larger squad to travel to away games and this began to pray on my mind. One day I revealed my feelings of frustration to Eric McMordie, Boro's vastly experienced Northern Ireland international, and he advised me to express my feelings to the manager. "Unless you knock on his door and tell him you want first team football, he'll think you're not bothered and give others the chance instead," he insisted.

After a few encouraging displays for the reserves, I eventually plucked up the courage to confront Stan in his office.

"I feel I'm wasting my time in the reserves, boss," I told him. "I can't understand why you haven't picked me for the first team."

He didn't hold back in his response. "It's because you're not f***ing good enough, son. That's why you're not in the first team."

That was the one reply I had not expected and I had no answer to it. I was gobsmacked and nervous silence followed.

Embarrassed and belittled, I stepped towards the door before announcing in a determined manner: "I'll prove you wrong."

I was desperate to do so but wondered if my chance would come. I needn't have worried. Within weeks I was named in the starting line-up to face First Division West Ham United's star-studded team in a FA Cup third round tie at Ayresome Park. When Stan told me I was selected, I couldn't help but think how less than four years earlier as a schoolboy I had watched - along with millions of other worldwide television viewers - as Bobby Moore, Martin Peters and Geoff Hurst had helped to win the World Cup for England. Now I was about to perform

Extra Time – The Final Chapter

on the same stage. I was given a midfield man-marking job on Peters, a role with which I was unaccustomed. That didn't bother me - I was just delighted to be in the team and if the manager thought I had the versatility to carry out such a job then I would give it my best shot. My brief was to mark Peters whilst getting forward whenever I could to support the forwards but that was to prove easier said than done. Peters had a tremendous reputation as a player who scored goals by arriving late in the box and I knew I would have my work cut out trying to keep him quiet.

Wearing the number 11 shirt, the atmosphere created by over 32,000 supporters raised the hairs on the back of my neck. This truly was the big time. Like all the players, I spent the first 15 minutes trying to find my feet on a treacherous pitch that was like glass after several nights of frost. The Hammers stars were far from happy that the game had gone ahead and it showed in those opening minutes. But not once did I actually even touch the ball in the opening 10 minutes and I knew I needed a few good touches to settle my nerves. I was totally in awe of the crowd, the opposition and the occasion and was in danger of letting the game pass me by. Then after about 15 minutes I rose above England captain Bobby Moore to flick the ball on for a colleague and I realised he was only human after all. From that moment I began to get to grips with my task.

However, Boro left-back Gordon Jones was getting a hell of a chasing off Ronnie Boyce. Mid-way through the first half Jones, my team skipper, ordered me to leave my man-marking job on Peters and play in front of him to stop Boyce from gathering momentum along the wing. I was reluctant to leave a job the manager had designated to me but neither did I want to upset my captain. What I ended up trying to achieve was do the best of both jobs for the rest of the half and hope that

In action in my second first team game, against West Ham United.

Joy...and Pain

Stan would back Gordon's judgement. With my support for Jones, Boyce's threat diminished during the remainder of the half and I headed for the dressing room at the interval feeling pleased to have both kept Peters quiet and my club captain happy. Indeed we went in at half-time a goal up thanks to striker Hughie McIlmoyle who seemed to be the only player on either side who was comfortable on the icy pitch. On one occasion he left Moore on his backside with a superb piece of skill. Given his supremacy, it was no surprise to see him rise above the Hammers defence to nod Boro into the lead with a typical header from a left wing corner. The crowd erupted into a crescendo of noise that sent a shiver down my spine as players and fans alike realised we had within our grasp a tremendous victory. At the time, Boro's most vocal supporters, who would traditionally stand in the Holgate End, were affectionately known as the Ayresome Angels, and they were in fine voice that afternoon. We knew, however, that we were somewhat fortunate to have that slim advantage as West Ham had actually had the ball in the net three times during those first 45 minutes, only to see each strike ruled out for offside.

Having matched our more illustrious opponents in the first half, we took the game to them in the second 45 minutes, resulting in a big cup upset. The game was over when late in the game Derrick Downing met a right wing cross from John Hickton with a brave diving header to put Boro two up. Though West Ham rallied after pulling a goal back, we were not to be denied and held out for a memorable win. My feelings at the end of the game were the complete reverse to those I'd had after my debut against Bury. This time the result was everything and yet I didn't feel I had contributed as much to the game as I would have liked. Stan, however, would have disagreed. After all, my mission was accomplished and Peters had not scored.

Further victories followed as Middlesbrough progressed to their first FA Cup quarter-final in almost a quarter of a century. There we faced the might of Manchester United - including three of the game's legends, Bobby Charlton, George Best and Denis Law - though we did have the advantage of a home draw. To help us prepare for the big game away from the glare of the media, Stan took the first team squad to train in Scarborough in the days before the tie. There we stayed at the magnificent five-star Grand Hotel where we enjoyed first class treatment amid a relaxing atmosphere, enjoying a game of snooker or table tennis when we weren't in training. Having been an unused substitute in the previous round against Carlisle a fortnight earlier, I was not surprised when I was named on the bench again against United's all-stars. The game ended in a 1-1 draw and

Extra Time – The Final Chapter

although I didn't play a part I immediately began to look forward to the Old Trafford replay.

I had no reason to believe I would not be substitute once again but I was in for a shock. I was horrified when two days before the game I read the team-sheet to find my closest rival David Mills, who had missed a fortnight's training due to a knee injury, named as 12th man in my place. I couldn't understand the manager's thinking. To rub salt into the wound I wasn't even named in the squad to travel to Old Trafford. On the night Boro went down fighting before bowing out to a 2-1 defeat watched by over 63,000 excited fans, I was 20 miles down the road playing for the reserves at Halifax in front of no more than 50 people. I was utterly dejected and didn't play at all well that night. Needless to say, my mind was elsewhere.

Little did I know that events taking place at Old Trafford that night were to change the direction of my career...

5

The Case for the Defence

GOALS bring glory. Glory makes heroes of footballers. Those facts alone ensure that most young footballers want to be the team's goalscorer. Centre-forward or striker, call it what you will, but that is the glory position. At least it is if you get the goals. If you don't, of course, then you can just as easily become the fans' public enemy number one. Even so, up front is the glamour position that many young boys across the world dream of playing for their local team.

As a teenager growing up on Teesside and playing in local football, I was no different from most other boys though my natural ability enabled me to score more than my fair share of goals from midfield. And yet in my early years as a professional with my boyhood heroes I was to have many a heated debate with Stan Anderson about why I did *not* want to play up front for Middlesbrough. I was fully aware that for many such an opportunity would have been a dream come true. And, for a while at least, it was for me too. Then came the realisation that I had the potential to go much further as a centre-half than I could ever hope to do as a forward. From that moment on, a long-running psychological battle raged between Stan and I about what was my best position.

And yet it was Stan who initially gave me a regular first team place at the centre of Boro's defence and an idea of just how good I could become if I really put my mind to it. Almost from the word go, I had an overriding feeling of confidence at centre-half that I had never experienced either up front or for that matter whilst playing in any other position.

Like many other young players, I played in several different positions during my formative years as an apprentice and young professional with Middlesbrough

Extra Time – The Final Chapter

as the club's coaches tried to decide which was my best position. But not until my third start did I pull on the first team's number five shirt for the first time.

As I trekked disinterestedly around the Shay's pitch against Halifax Town's reserves on that late February night in 1970, I could not imagine that events taking place in Middlesbrough's first team match at Old Trafford were contriving to shape my future career path. Bill Gates had played the match in the only way he knew how - hard and uncompromising. It led to retribution from Manchester United striker Brian Kidd that left Bill with a broken jaw which would keep him sidelined for the next six weeks. In an off-the-ball incident midway through the second half and with play at the other end of the pitch, Kidd threw a wild punch at his marker and tormentor which almost severed Bill's jaw altogether. Such was the damage that his jaw was completely severed on one side and left hanging only by the smallest thread on the other.

It was immediately obvious that Gates would not be fit to play for some time to come. That created a dilemma for Stan Anderson. Dicky Rooks had departed for Bristol City the previous summer and, as neither Gates nor his central defensive partner, Frank Spraggon, had missed a game in the entire season, there was no recognised cover for that position. On the fringe of the promotion chase, Boro had a vital league fixture against struggling Preston North End at Ayresome Park that Saturday and Stan knew he had to find a replacement for Gates.

Alan Moody, the reserves' regular centre-half, was favourite to get the nod though I had played a number of second team games at left-half as part of a three-man half-back line in the old W formation involving two full-backs, three half-backs and five forwards. On the

A typical Monday morning training session, running across the moor tops. I still wonder just how much significance those arduous sessions were in bringing my career to a premature end.

The Case for the Defence

Friday, Stan arranged a first team against reserves practice match at Hutton Road to help him decide who should be given the role as Bill's stand-in. For the first half, Frank Spraggon was partnered in the centre of defence by Alan Moody. For the second half, Alan was replaced by a forward, Stan Webb. I played the entire practice game for the reserves. It seemed Stan had decided to make a straight choice between Alan and Stan. When the training session ended at 11.30, I had no reason to believe I would be involved in the following day's match against Preston.

As I waited for the team-sheet to be pinned on the notice board back at Ayresome, however, I was summoned to the manager's office. "How do you feel about playing centre-half tomorrow?" he asked. Somewhat taken aback, I gave the same answer I had given him last time I had been called to his office. "I'd be delighted," I replied. But I was curious as to how he had come to ask me when it seemed only Alan and Stan had been considered for the role. The manager explained that he had not been happy with the performance of either player during the practice session. However, two of his senior players, Willie Whigham and George Smith, had been impressed with my previous reserve team displays at left-half and felt I would do a better job than either Alan or Stan. I certainly wasn't going to argue with that assessment and left the manager's office with a spring in my feet and determined to make the most of this somewhat unexpected opportunity.

I can't actually remember too much about the game itself though I still have the newspaper cuttings from the following day which tell me that I must have impressed. 'Local boy Maddren makes good as Cup heroes slump' is a headline which tells its own story. While Boro dropped a vital point in a 1-1 draw with relegation threatened Preston, I surprised even myself with the level of my performance. I felt immediately comfortable at centre-half though I was thankful for the support I received from Frank Spraggon. Ironically, he was criticised by some elements of the media who felt he over compensated for my lack of experience to the detriment of his own game. But I was delighted to read in one of the Sunday morning newspaper reports: "Saturday's performance at least provided one consolation in the shape of a lanky 19-year-old boy called Willie Maddren. Maddren, playing only his second senior game of the season, stepped into the boots of injured Bill Gates with barely a ruffle of his curly hair. Granted that the heavy footed Preston attack posed few problems. But the local boy's cool handling of every situation at the back must have booked him the centre-half spot for the rest of the season." The same report did, however, add: "The more the pity

Extra Time – The Final Chapter

that his one piece of slack marking, midway through the first half, should lead to an out-of-the-blue equaliser by Preston."

I fully agreed with coach Jimmy Headridge's guarded thoughts when he commented: "We"ll be happier when Maddren gets a couple of away games under his belt. But we were very pleased with his performance. He did the simple things well and looked very composed." I was fully aware that my limited first team experience had all been gained at Ayresome Park and that playing in front of a partisan away crowd would be a more daunting task. The real test would come three days later at Charlton when the Middlesbrough defence would undoubtedly come under great pressure.

By half past nine the following Tuesday night I was convinced that I had arrived as a first team player. From that game forward, any lingering doubts I had that I might not make the grade were banished from my mind. When things go as well for a player as they did for me that night, there is no need to be told that you have played a blinder. You just know it. That evening I knew I had played out of my skin in helping my team to an impressive 2-0 success. I still vividly remember among the complimentary articles in the following morning's London newspapers a photograph of me towering above Charlton's centre-forward to head the ball out of the defence. As we travelled home that day there were clear signs that I was now completely accepted by the club's senior players. I was a proud young man. And I had also made up my mind that my best position would be as a centre-half and not in my regular role as an attacker.

But if I knew then what I know now, I would have known better than to think that those who had seen me play would agree with that assessment. Only injury ended my run as the first team's centre-half during the final stages of the 1969-70 campaign but by the opening day of the following season I was back on more familiar territory up front. This time I was called upon as stand-in centre forward for the injured Hugh McIlmoyle with the manager stating publicly: "Maddren has played at centre-half but he is primarily a forward. I want to see how he looks up front." So it was there that I played as Boro opened the season with a 2-1 home win over Carlisle United. It was a short-lived spell as the side's main attacker for I collided heads with an opponent during the first period of the game and had to come off suffering from impaired vision.

The truth is, I was disappointed that Stan did not consider me to be one of his first choice centre-backs as I believed I had proved that I was at least as good as

The Case for the Defence

Gates and Spraggon at the latter end of the previous season. But I felt my chance would come if I remained patient and I did not have to wait long. Stan rang the changes when a lack-lustre home performance saw Boro slump to a 2-0 home defeat to Oxford United in only our third match and Gates was dropped to make way for yours truly alongside Spraggon. That day a youthful Boro side gained an impressive 1-0 victory at Birmingham.

I had barely settled into the role, playing just three times, when injuries to Alec Smith and Michael Allen left us without a recognised right-back. Would I play at right-back, asked the manager, for the sake of the team? Of course, I agreed. I was fast earning a tag as Boro's Mr Versatile but it was a label that did not bother me. Indeed, at that stage I positively encouraged it as I felt my versatility would increase my chances of being selected over players who were less flexible. With Gordon Jones as my partner at left full-back, I felt I did reasonably well over the following five weeks though I couldn't help but wish I was back in my favoured central defensive role.

I was still on a steep learning curve, of course, and I still remember the embarrassment of being on the wrong side of the pitch as the man I was supposed to be marking scored an early goal for Swindon in October 1970. In the dressing room before the game, Stan had given me specific orders to mark Swindon winger Don Rodgers, a player with exceptional pace and dribbling ability. Forget about the rest of their players," he had told me. "Go wherever Rodgers goes and stick to him like glue." Having checked the team-sheet I noted he was wearing the number 11 shirt and so simply assumed he would be playing on the left flank. But as I awaited kick-off, there was no sign of Rodgers and I wondered where the hell he was. Eventually, as the game kicked off, I spotted him on the opposite wing. Determined not to panic, I decided to simply pick him up as the game got going. It was a fatal mistake. Within two minutes of the start Swindon were in front - and Rodgers had scored the goal. I didn't need to ask Stan what he thought of the goal. "You f***ing w****r!" he yelled at me from the touchline. No prizes either for guessing that he went through me like a dose of salts back in the dressing room at half-time. It was to no avail, however, as former Boro player Arthur Horsfield scored twice to give Swindon a comfortable 3-0 win.

Eventually, when Smith returned to fitness, my wishes were granted and I was switched back to centre-half. Injury denied me a chance to establish myself and I had to wait my chance before being handed a new role as a sweeper when Frank Spraggon was sidelined. But this was to be a season when my ability to be used as

Extra Time – The Final Chapter

the team's utility man was to be tested to the full. During those nine months, I appeared in no less than seven different positions - right-back, centre-half, left-half, sweeper, midfield, left wing and centre-forward. In one astonishing game against Orient, I was instructed at half-time to move from central defence to midfield, then to the wing and finally into a central attacking role. Sadly, it was all to no avail as we lost the match 1-0 but I felt I adapted quite well to each job.

Award winner: receiving the Evening Gazette Player of the Year trophy after my first full season of first team football.

I certainly must have been doing something right over the course of the campaign, for I was voted the club's Player of the Season by the supporters. Naturally, I was flattered to receive such an accolade, especially at the tender age of 20 years old and in my first full season in the first team. I was beginning to feel part of the furniture at the club and felt accepted by the more experienced pro's, several of whom I had once idolised as a supporter from the Boys' End. I was proud of the fact that wherever I had played I had won rave notices in the media, whilst I was clearly catching the eye of players and supporters alike.

Indeed, I was proud as punch the day Hughie McIlmoyle stated on the record in an interview with The Weekly News: "Willie isn't just going to make the grade, he is going to become a great England player. He has everything - great in the air, with the ball coming from both sides, an outstanding temperament, fine ball control, a wonderful striker of the ball. Of course, players with loads of talent are open to the temptations of life. Well, Willie just isn't a nightclub type. He is quietly dedicated and a terrific trainer."

It was heady stuff to win such praise from a player I admired so much. Hughie did, however, urge a few words of caution. "If there is any weakness, it's in his ability to read the game. But that will come with confidence and experience. At 20, he is one of the finest prospects in the country."

Years later, in choosing me as one of his top five best Boro players of all-time in the book Boro's Best, Hughie added: "Willie was only a young lad while I was at the club but even then he looked like he would go all the way to the top. He was good in the air, strong, determined and enthusiastic. He was also a sensible lad and listened to advice which a lot of youngsters tended to brush aside. He had the potential to play for England but I think the fact that he was seen as a utility player may have counted against him."

Even the characteristically conservative Jimmy Greenhalgh went out of his way to sing my praises at the end of that memorable season, this time in the News of the World. "I'll stake my reputation on Willie becoming a star," he said. "Already I think he is the best defensive prospect in the League and in my opinion will eventually settle in a back four role."

With those words from the club's first team coach ringing in my ears and having ended the season wearing my favourite number six shirt, I felt things were finally pointing towards a long run in the centre of defence. Until I read another newspaper article which quoted Stan Anderson.

In it, the manager insisted: "I don't think Willie quite realises that he could become a very fine front-line player. He has scored some truly great goals. For a young player he has the balance and accuracy of shot needed up front. Some players, however, settle for the 'easy' position. Willie has found that he can do well as a defender. I am sure his reaction is to say to himself 'I know I can keep my place and do well here'. But I feel Willie would not fulfil his potential by staying as a defender. He must raise his sights."

It was clear we had a difference of opinions. I knew, however, that Stan was the manager and his decision would be the one that mattered. And yet the following season was to bring no respite in my role as Boro's flexible friend, able to fill in for injured players throughout the side. I began to fear that I would become a jack of all trades and a master of none.

I began the 1971-72 campaign at right-back, having once again agreed to sacrifice my own ambitions for those of the team. Stan was most persuasive in talking me into the tactical switch but I was far from happy. We lost the opening match at Portsmouth and over the next couple of weeks I began to feel disillusioned. I could not get it out of my head that I was not being played in what

Extra Time – The Final Chapter

I saw as my rightful position and was highly bemused that Stan had seen fit to pair Spraggon and the club's new £50,000 signing Stuart Boam in my coveted defensive positions. When a new player came to the club I always wanted to show them that I was a good player but I didn't feel I was doing myself justice at right-back. That hurt when a player of the calibre of Nobby Stiles - a former Manchester United star and World Cup winner - was among those seeing me in action for the first time.

I wasn't the only one mystified by the manager's team selection. Writing in his column in the Evening Gazette, the former Middlesbrough and England captain George Hardwick said: "To play a youngster with Maddren's skill, stature, speed and flair for the game as a defender is nothing short of a tragedy and a disgraceful waste of a lot of talent."

Whilst George and I agreed that the number two shirt was not for me, we were some way apart in terms of my best position. He further wrote: "For the sake of the team (and Willie Maddren) he must be moved forward either as a striker with John Hickton or at least into midfield where his many talents can both materialise and mature into international recognition. As a midfield player Maddren could be worth £150,000 to the Boro, as a number two maybe £25,000 at the most, for I am sure Willie has neither interest nor enthusiasm for the position, and it showed in his play last Saturday."

Then came another twist in the tale. Or rather two twists. The first came with Boro trailing 2-0 at Bristol City in our third league match. We were temporarily reduced to 10 men when I was carried from the field suffering from a nasty gash to my forehead, the result of a collision with City striker Chris Garland. After treatment - three stitches applied without anaesthetic - I returned to the pitch wearing a white bandage around my head and in a forward position with orders from Stan to get us a goal. And within 15 minutes I had done just chat, outstripping the home defence before hitting a crisp left foot shot past Pat Cashley in the opposition goal. Sadly, that was my only goal that afternoon and Boro fell to a second defeat in three outings - but I had once again impressed Stan as an attacking force.

The second twist came two days later when Boro announced the club record £60,000 signing of Newcastle United's reserve team right-back John Craggs. It was obvious that Stan had not paid such a fee to play Craggs in the reserves so I knew I would not continue at right-back in Tuesday night's match against Sheffield Wednesday at Ayresome Park. And it came as no great surprise when I was given the number nine shirt and asked to partner John Hickton in attack against the Owls. With McIlmoyle having departed for pastures new, Boro were lacking firepower and had even tried little Eric McMordie as centre-forward against Bristol.

Midway through the first half, I got my bandaged forehead on to the end of a cross to head Boro in front. Hickton added a second as we ran out 2-1 winners watched by an excellent crowd of just under 24,000. With two goals in two games, I had every right to feel pleased with myself - and I wasn't the only one happy about my display. In his post-match interview, I was embarrassed to learn that Stan had told the press that I would soon make people forget about fans' favourite McIlmoyle. "If Maddren fulfills his promise people will forget the past," he said. "McIlmoyle had more experience but Willie has time on his side. It was necessary to play him at full-back earlier this season but I think he will prove a success at centre-forward. He is brave and holds the ball well. In fact, he's a natural."

Of course, I was flattered my manager thought so highly of me. I fully appreciated that the chance to make a name as a centre-forward would be tempting to most young players and, of course, I had enjoyed scoring the goals. Who wouldn't? But one-and-a-half decent games wasn't going to change my opinion that my best role was in central defence. In the meantime, however, I knew I should simply be pleased to be in the team.

Even when I followed up with another goal in a 2-0 home win over Fulham, I remained sceptical that this was my natural position. I was so unhappy, in fact, that I went in to see Stan on the Monday morning following the Fulham game to tell him that I would rather be playing in defence. Stan was disappointed with my view and told me so. He felt I was being unreasonable. I had scored in three successive games and in his opinion had the makings of a very good centre-forward. He ended our conversation by asking me to persevere up front. "I want you to stay at centre-forward and I'm confident you'll make the position your own," he said. "With a few games under your belt to reach an understanding with John Hickton, the two of you could be an even better partnership than when Hughie McIlmoyle was here."

Once again, I had to back down. No doubt it would have shocked the fans if they had known that I was so unhappy as their new goalscoring hope. Naturally modest, I was flabbergasted to see a newspaper headline that week which read: "Maddren can be a £200,000 star". The article beneath it was written by the great Jackie Milburn of Newcastle and England fame, who wrote: "Even though

Extra Time – The Final Chapter

Maddren is just learning the trade, it's my guess it won't be long before he will be worth £200,000. Maddren is every bit as good as Colin Todd was at this age. Defence, midfield or up front striking all comes naturally. He has the head and footwork to make defenders miserable. But he also shows that all important change of pace that separates the average players from the greats." It was nice of him to pay me such compliments but I knew I still had a lot to learn. But when two goals at Charlton took my tally to five in just four league games, my switch from defender to forward was beginning to look an inspired move. Imagine Stan's dismay, therefore, when on the Monday morning I walked into his office to tell him I didn't want to play up front any longer.

"Boss, I consider myself to be the best number six at the club," I told him.

Stan went berserk. With my goalscoring record, he probably had good reason "How the hell can you say that?" he demanded. "I've just recommended you to Alf Ramsey who is monitoring your progress very closely. You're not a million miles away from being picked for the England under-23 team at centre-forward - and yet you tell me you don't want to play there!"

I hadn't imagined that I was being considered for such an honour but I had no reason to disbelieve Stan. Even so, I insisted: "My heart isn't in it, boss. I want to play at the back where I feel the most comfortable."

We were a million miles from one another on the subject but Stan eventually persuaded me once again that I should continue to give it a go. I have no reason to doubt that Stan truly believed I was a better forward than defender. Many years later he was quoted as saying: "Willie settled for a sweeping role at the back, but I believe he might have turned out to be one of the best strikers around. If he had grabbed his chance, those England caps would have been there for the taking."

When, two games later, I was on target again at Luton Town, my six-goal tally was twice that of Hickton's. To put that into perspective, Big John had finished three of the previous four seasons as the Second Division's top scorer. But my goals didn't kid me. I knew I had certain skills and physical attributes which I simply made the best of. It wasn't in my nature to do anything but my best and, of course, I was still trying to improve as a player. For instance, I had always considered myself to be quite fast but had discovered that I had to speed up over short distances of five to 10 yards. That was vital if I was to nip on to half-chances in the box. At the same time I was working on sharpening up my ball control to enable me to hold up the ball until I received support from team-mates. The striker I tried hard to emulate in style was the one I considered to be the best in the business at the time, Martin Chivers of Tottenham.

My experience as a defender was also paying dividends in my role as a centre-forward as I went out of my way to do all the things that annoyed me in opposition strikers when I played in the back four. For instance, I would make every effort to wander around the field, always keeping on the move. As a defender I had always hated forwards who backed right up to me to ensure I couldn't make a running jump for a high ball. That meant a standing jump, thus losing that little bit extra height. So, of course, I would now back into defenders at every opportunity!

But then - as I had known they would - the goals began to dry up. Boro went into a league match at Swindon in late October on the back of an outstanding run of results which had made us promotion favourites and yet I had not scored for six games and had become a target for the Ayresome Park boo-boys. For the first time in my young career I had received criticism from the supporters and I couldn't conceal my hurt. I had gone from being the club's Player of the Year to the butt of criticism within a matter of months and I went into the Swindon game with my confidence at an all-time low. I actually scored the only goal of the match that day - and a good one too - but it did little to boost my confidence.

Deep down, I just knew I wasn't a forward. I had simply got away with it for a while. I could volley and head the ball as well as most prolific goalscorers but I had one crucial weakness that left me begging. Whenever I found myself in a one-on-one situation, running from the half-way line with only the goalkeeper to beat and with time to think, I would invariably miss. I simply wasn't a natural goalscorer. With experience, perhaps I might have improved. Indeed, years later at Hartlepool it was to dawn on me that I had all the necessary skills to have made a top class forward. At the time, however, I was convinced that it wasn't for me.

Consequently I went into a home game against Preston North End a week after the Swindon victory feeling frustrated and miserable. And things were about to get much worse.

In the first five minutes of the match I collided with Preston defender John Bird, leaving me with blurred vision and suffering from a severe migraine attack. Nowadays a player who suffers such a head collision would be taken off as a precaution but at the time teams were inclined to give it 20 minutes to see if the vision cleared. Consequently, I played the remainder of the half with blurred vision - and lived to regret it.

Extra Time – The Final Chapter

I missed a couple of half chances and the crowd quickly got on my back, heckling my every touch. Little did they know I could hardly see the *ball*, let alone the *goal*. And yet, by a cruel injustice, I ended the game believing my previous reputation and credibility as a young player of great potential was in tatters.

Within a fortnight I had been dropped. I had known it was coming, of course. I knew I wasn't doing well. And I knew the reason. I was annoyed with Stan for putting me through such a confidence-draining experience. I had always thought it right to give priority to the team's needs and was still ready to do that despite the fact my own game was suffering. But I was desperate for a break and, in an interview which appeared in the national press, pleaded for Stan to give me a chance. "I want to settle down where I know I'm at my best," I said. "I'm a left-half and that's it. I'm not a centre-forward and I don't want to be a jack-of-all-trades. I should be playing at the back where I know the qualities I have would be used most effectively. There's talk now about me playing in midfield. I will go there if I'm wanted, of course, but that's not where I'd be happy."

But the manager hit back publicly, telling the press: "Willie has hardly been a great failure, his goals testify to that. He is going through a bad patch that all players get. We all know that Willie's a great player at the back but you have to use your resources according to your needs. I think that outside influences have partly convinced him that he is not suited to playing up front and when things have gone a little bit wrong he started to think this way." Once again, we were at loggerheads. Even so, I decided to suffer a few games on the subs bench and see how things turned out.

I was to be glad of my patience. Press reports suggested that I might be on the verge of a transfer request and I must admit I did consider that option. But I was delighted when I was recalled to the starting line-up to play at Hull in early December, even though it was now as a midfielder. However, within a few games I was switched to my favourite central defensive role where I was to remain for the rest of the season.

My new partner in the centre of Boro's defence was big Stuart Boam and we hit up an instant understanding on the pitch. Like all good strikers, centre-backs do best when they are a pair and we were to form a formidable partnership. Our understanding was uncanny in that we didn't have to speak to each other to know what the other was doing. It had been my opinion that Stuart and Bill Gates - his centre-back partner until then - were too similar in style in that they were both contact players who would invariably go for the same ball. But I was a different kind of player to Stuart. He was the hard man who you could always rely on to win the ball while I was perhaps a little more cultured though not as brave as he was. But the whole defence quickly hit up an excellent understanding. When the opposition attacked down the right flank, without even looking I would leave the middle of the field to support left-back Gordon Jones, knowing that Stuart would automatically move into my position and right-back John Craggs into his, with the right-sided midfielder dropping into John's place. The same thing instinctively happened in reverse when we were attacked down the left wing.

But it was the team-work Stuart and I had that was special from the very start. We played with such confidence in each other's ability and yet we never truly trusted each other completely. For instance, even if Boamy appeared to have a free header under no pressure I would still be there to cover him in case of a rare mistake. Likewise, he would do the same for me. Boamy was to get even better over the years but it was clear even then that he was an outstanding defender. We rarely played an offside trap because Stuart and I preferred to mark forwards tightly. In fact, Stuart was the best one-on-one defender in the game. When I say that I mean this: the ball might go past him or the player might go past him - but very rarely would the two go past him together. If it looked like they would, then he would quite crudely take the player out. Believe me, it was an effective policy!

I was different in that I would pitt my wits technically against opponents. And our very difference was the main reason why Stuart and I gelled so well. Our styles complemented one another and we soon became known as the best defensive partnership outside the First Division. That reputation was cemented with an excellent display, by ourselves and the team as a whole, in two FA Cup ties with top flight Manchester City that were to result in Boro creating a big upset in dumping them out of the country's top knock-out tournament.

I was thrilled when Nobby Stiles sang my praises in his next Evening Gazette column. I doubted Nobby had been overly impressed with me in my roles as a right-back, centre-forward or midfielder but he wrote: "There was no-one more outstanding in these games than Willie Maddren. Mind, his form was no surprise to me. In fact, I'm prepared to state here and now that young Willie will one day play for England. He's already played at full-back and striker for us this season, but there can be no doubt that sweeper is his best position. He reads the game so well, he displays such authority in his tackling, such maturity in his general play. Maddren's coolness has done a lot for the man who plays alongside him at the

Extra Time – The Final Chapter

heart of our defence, Stuart Boam."

Stuart and I were at the beginning of a wonderful partnership which would thrive for the next six seasons, four of them in the top flight against the best forwards in the country. From that moment I rarely looked back and I doubt very much that Stan Anderson ever again considered playing me at centre-forward. He must surely have known even then that I was far happier when facing the game from the back.

Given his input, however, perhaps I should leave the final words on the saga over my best position to Stan. Speaking to Doug Weatherall in the Daily Mail in December 1972, less than a year after finally handing me my defensive chance, he said: "Hardly anyone skins Willie twice because he stores knowledge quickly and keeps it in mind. His basic asset is that he reads the game sharply. He also has a great positional sense - just like Bobby Moore."

What better compliment could I have from the manager who thought I was a centre-forward than for him to compare me with perhaps the greatest central defender in England's history?

6

When Stan was the Man

DESPITE my battle of wills with Stan Anderson, I always had the utmost respect for him as a manager. He always in turn had enormous faith in me and did much to encourage me during my formative years as a professional. He was to put together an excellent squad of players that should really have taken Middlesbrough into the First Division. Instead, time after time they faltered at just the wrong time and it was left for his successor Jack Charlton to take Boro into the promised land.

I felt sorry for Stan as he had provided the nucleus of the team that Jack shaped and organised so professionally in our promotion year. Among those around throughout my early years with the club, from first team breakthrough and on to the verge of international honours, were the likes of Gordon Jones, Derrick Downing, Willie Whigham, John Hickton and Eric McMordie.

Whigham and George Smith were particularly supportive to me during my first months as a first team regular and both displayed tremendous faith in my ability. During those early games, I would be constantly aware of the watchful eye of Willie in goal behind me, shouting out in his broad Scottish accent a constant stream of advice and praise - "Well done, Willie!"; "Magnificent!"; "Great header!" Everything I did was met with a positive comment, doing my confidence a power of good at a time when I needed to know I was doing well. As a young boy, it was fantastic to get such words of encouragement from a senior pro and a special bond built up between us. Willie - or 'The Whig', as he was affectionately known - was quite a character and a good goalkeeper who was popular among players and fans alike.

I became firm friends with George Smith almost from the moment he joined

Extra Time – The Final Chapter

Boro in a club record £50,000 transfer from Portsmouth and we often roomed together. I was only a youngster but George took me under his wing and gave me tremendous confidence. In fact, I think he often had more confidence than I did in my ability. I was gutted when he later left Teesside for Birmingham as I had not only lost a good friend but I felt the club had made a mistake in selling one of their best players. With his terrific stamina and top class passing ability, he was our engine room. I did, however, stay in touch with George and he was best man at my first wedding.

Another with a likeable personality was Eric McMordie, a Northern Ireland international who was particularly adept at holding the ball under pressure, helping his team-mates to get a breather and to push out of defence. As skillful as he was, Eric could also be a nasty piece of work in the way he would often leave his foot in, as no doubt a number of opposition players would bare testimony to. Beneath what was a pleasant exterior, Eric had a fierce will to win at all costs, perhaps a result of his tough upbringing on the streets of Belfast. But Eric's boyish humour did much to help me settle into the first team dressing room. A good friend of George Best's, he would often entertain the dressing room with tales of watching Besty in action *off* the pitch from the benefit of a hotel room wardrobe. In those early days he would often flash a cheeky grin before asking me: "So Willie, are you getting plenty?" Indeed, it sometimes seemed that all conversations between Eric and his best mate Gordon Jones had a sexual connotation.

Club skipper Gordon possessed an exceptional left foot and from left full-back he was the perfect provider for Hugh McIlmoyle during the striker's two years with the club. Gordon's positional play was second to none and, but for his lack of pace, I am sure he would have followed his former Boro team-mate Mick McNeil into the England team. Initially, I felt in awe of Gordon but I soon came to recognise him as an astute captain to whom Stan gladly gave permission to change things around on the pitch as he saw fit.

It has to be said, however, that both Gordon and Willie Whigham occasionally struggled with some of Stan's tougher fitness sessions. Every Monday morning, come hail, rain or shine, we would work the hills. We would often run up the steep side of Roseberry Topping, down the left side, along the moor top, down a set of steep steps and finally up to Captain Cook's Monument. From there, it was all the way back again along the same route, about seven miles across rugged terrain. One cold winter's morning, many of the early finishers were already sat on the bus, the windows wet with condensation from our hot bodies, when I wiped the glass clear to notice two tiny figures still on the summit of Roseberry Topping. It was Jonesy and Willie, who were known not to favour that type of running, struggling some way behind us!

Up front in that team was big John Hickton, a player who I'm sure would have won England caps had he played for a more fashionable club in the First Division. As it was, he was just past his peak by the time Boro achieved top flight status but did well to adapt his game from that of an out-and-out goalscorer to hard working target man and battering ram under the management of Jack Charlton. Under Stan, there were times when if John didn't score he would contribute little to the game. But his goals output, powerful finishing and strong running down the left flank made him one of the best strikers outside the First Division during the late 1960's and early 1970's.

In those days Middlesbrough were not a team of stars. But there were those who will live long in the memory of supporters who saw them play. Derrick Downing provided the pace on the wings; David Chadwick was a terrific dribbler on the opposite flank; full-back Alex Smith was as honest as the day is long and a great defensive organiser; Bill Gates was a commanding centre-half, a good tackler and positional player, who was always helpful in talking me through games; and Frank Spraggon was to emerge as one of the most consistent centre-halfs in the country. Frank's lack of height held him back in terms of his aerial ability but he was a superb reader of the game who did well to overcome blurred vision in one eye following a cartilage operation.

In charge of us were Stan Anderson and Jimmy Greenhalgh, two real task masters who contrived to make our training sessions something an army general would have been proud of. No player who had the misfortune to tackle it will ever forget the assault course Stan and Jimmy devised at our Hutton Road training ground. The course started with a line 20 yards from a purpose-built five foot wall. As you cleared the wall, you had to crawl under a bench which was no more than 18 inches high and then over another wall. The next challenge was to crawl some 20 feet under a net. As you got up, you would run maybe 10 yards, duck under a three feet high pole, jump a dozen hurdles, go under another net and then run a further 30 yards before vaulting two six foot fences about 10 feet apart. A few yards later you had to pick up a medicine ball and hold it whilst jumping over a bench and back. Then you had to go back the way you came! And we had to negotiate that damn assault course three times at each training session, leaving us with scrabs on our knees and hips from crawling under the netting. One frosty morning

Extra Time - The Final Chapter

I arrived sure we wouldn't be subjected to the course when the ground was so hard. My heart dropped as I saw Jimmy shovelling sand on to the area under the net.

If there were no "stars" in the Boro side, there's little doubt I came up against some wonderful opposition players as I learned the first team ropes. Two outstanding players were Huddersfield's Frank Worthington and Rodney Marsh of Queen's Park Rangers, both of whom would go on to win England caps. I came up against Worthington during my first run in Boro's defence in March 1970 and he impressed me not only with his excellent touch but as an extremely physical player who could give it as well as take it. Despite being in absolute agony with a torn groin, I played through the pain barrier and felt I did well in a good team performance as Boro grabbed a 1-1 draw against a side which went up as champions that season.

Early in the following season, Marsh - brimming with flashy skills - came to town though we were to give him and his QPR team-mates something of a football lesson that day. Marsh and co. started the game like a house on fire and were 2-0 up within five minutes of the kick-off. I remember thinking to myself that I had never been part of a team beaten 5-0 but at that time there seemed every likelihood that that would be the outcome come the end of the 90 minutes. Marsh was really turning it on and scored one of the two goals and yet I couldn't help but wish I was playing centre-back instead of right-back. I would have loved to have pitted my wits against his and, despite my inexperience, had the confidence to believe I could have stubbed out Marsh's menace.

Despite that early dominance by Marsh and QPR, the game was to be named in honour of a Middlesbrough player for his part in an astonishing comeback which transformed a 2-0 deficit into a terrific 6-2 victory. This was the McIlmoyle Match. The majority of the supply to Hughie came from Gordon Jones and myself, but mainly Gordon. With that special left foot of his, he was angling balls from the halfway line to the opposite corner of the penalty box with unerring accuracy. But I have never seen such complete aerial dominance as McIlmoyle displayed that day. He won everything that came to him, heading ball after ball across the front of QPR's goal from which Hickton reaped the benefits. We were 4-2 up by half-time and left the field to a standing ovation. In the second half, Hughie started where he had left off in the first 45 minutes and continued to torture their back four to the point where further goals were inevitable. As it turned out, he scored two himself whilst setting up a hat-trick for John and another goal for Downing.

When Stan was the Man

Undoubtedly the most impressive team I faced during my early days as a first team player was Chelsea. The record books show that Boro lost that League Cup tie in October 1970 by just a single goal in five but the gap between the two sides was enormous. Having been caught in the London traffic on the way to Stamford Bridge, we hardly had time to collect our thoughts before leaving the dressing room for kick-off. Within 12 minutes, we were 3-0 down, having fallen behind within the first five seconds. Receiving the ball from the kick-off, Gordon Jones caught his studs in the ground in attempting to pass the ball back to Whigham. The ball fell invitingly into the path of Keith Weller - 1-0. I had never before played in a game where the pace was so frantic and Chelsea's ball playing was quite breathtaking at times. Players like John Hollins, Charlie Cooke, Peter Osgood and the wonderful Ian Hutchinson were so impressive that, in that opening quarter of an hour, I wondered if we would lose the game by 10 or 11 clear goals. Instead, Boro rallied, though the 3-2 scoreline was rather flattering to us.

As good as individuals like Worthington and Marsh were, they were not the players I would consider to have been my most impressive opponents as my game developed. Indeed, many will not have heard of the man to whom I would give that accolade. His name was Chris Chilton, a prolific goalscorer for Hull City who taught me a football lesson during one of my first games at centre-back. Despite my youth, I was quite well developed physically but Chilton knocked me from pillar to post, employing every trick in the book to leave me feeling beleaguered and disheartened. On one occasion, he grabbed me by the scruff of the neck, daring me to kick him in retribution and give away a needless free-kick. The truth is he talked me out of the game. As I sat in the Boothferry Park dressing room after a 3-2 defeat, I made my mind up that I would learn from the lesson I had been given.

I was learning the game and sometimes I did it the hard way. I was filling my favoured centre-back berth at home to Millwall in November 1970 when I suffered an injury that should have seen me leave the pitch. Naively, I played on for the remainder of the half. There were less than five minutes on the clock when Millwall's Gordon Bolland deliberately went over the top on me, his boot scything into my shin bone about an inch above my ankle. As I lay on the ground, I felt a numbing sensation in my shin. I put my hand down my sock and pressed a finger what seemed at least an inch into the bone. With adrenaline rushing through my body, I didn't even stop to check the wound and carried on with the game, convincing myself that what I had felt was simply fluid that often appeared on my shin as a result of my ongoing problems with my knee. It was only at half-time that

Extra Time – The Final Chapter

the full extent of the injury was to be revealed. On inspecting my shin, physio Jimmy Headridge announced: "If it's a clean wound, I think you cay play on." But his assessment was some way from that of the club doctor's. Dr Phillips took one look at the injury and immediately packed me off to Middlesbrough General Hospital where a hole measuring three inches long by an inch wide was treated with 12 internal and three external stitches, not to mention a series of anti-tetanus injections.

When Stan realised the extent of the injury, he was not pleased. And yet the target of his anger was not my aggressor but yours truly. Stan threatened to fine me if ever again I played a competitive match without wearing shinpads. Until that time I had never worn shinpads as I found them uncomfortable but that incident - and the manager's words of warning - convinced me it was time to put up with the discomfort.

The injury forced me on to the sidelines for two weeks but I was to suffer a further setback just as it seemed I was ready for a return to action. Tackling that infamous army assault course at our training ground, I reached the final wall feeling completely knackered. As I dropped down on the other side of that final obstacle, I failed to notice half a brick at the foot of the wall. It was Sod's Law that I landed awkwardly on the brick, spraining my ankle and ruling me out for a further three weeks. I was completely brassed off but to make matters worse my spell on the injury list coincided with Boro's momentous FA Cup success over Manchester United in January 1971. I was also absent for a defeat to Everton in the following round and I cursed my luck that I had missed a chance to play against Joe Royle, a player I rated as one of the best centre-forwards in the country.

I eventually returned to the side and began to win some rave notices in the press. One outstanding moment came in a home win over Swindon Town as Boro sought to keep up with the promotion pace-setters. There are certain instances that most players look back on and believe that was the moment that launched their careers. Mine came that day in March 1971 at Ayresome Park. Picking up a square pass from a team-mate, I advanced about five yards before letting fly with a left-foot shot which saw the ball rocket into the net from fully 40 yards out. For a split second, the ball hung in the left-hand corner of the net as I launched into ecstatic celebration. It was the best goal I ever scored and the Tyne-Tees Television cameras - on a rare visit to Ayresome - were there to catch it in all its glory. Indeed, I was to be reminded of my magic moment every Sunday for many months to follow as they included the goal in the opening title sequences of their football show. It's ironic to think that had I been more experienced I would never have even contemplated such an outlandish shot. But I was young and enthusiastic - and, when the ball hit the back of that net, quickly gaining in popularity among the Middlesbrough supporters!

Sadly, the 1970-71 campaign was to end in disappointment as Boro once again flattered to deceive. A 1-1 draw at QPR on the final day completed an amazing sequence of no less than eight consecutive draws to leave us some way short of a promotion spot. The game at Loftus Road did, however, provide me with a belated opportunity to come face to face with Rodney Marsh in the centre of Boro's defence. I was only 20 but such was my confidence that I had a good game against a striker who was undoubtedly already among the best in the country.

The following season was to be a time of change as Stan looked to replace the old brigade with new, younger players to give the club fresh impetus. Johnny Vincent, who had been signed late in the previous season, was joined at the club by Nobby Stiles, Stuart Boam, Jim Platt and John Craggs. It was to prove the end of the road, however, for Hughie McIlmoyle, Alex Smith and Willie Whigham, all of whom would move on to pastures new. Stiles, Jones, Hickton, Downing and McMordie were the backbone of a young team, while less experienced players like Boam, Craggs, Platt, David Mills, Joe Laidlaw, Alan Moody and myself were maturing as footballers. With such a wonderful blend of young talent and experience, there was a belief that Stan had the recipe for success. The signing from Manchester United of Stiles, a player who needed no introduction, was an exciting prospect for players and fans alike and it seemed the club was showing some signs of real ambition. When the season kicked off at Portsmouth, hopes were high that this could be the team to take Middlesbrough into the First Division.

With so many new faces it was perhaps no surprise that we struggled to live up to our promise that season though we did make a good start, winning five of the opening seven league games. However, two early season goalkeeping errors were to cost Willie Whigham his first team place. A good positional 'keeper, Willie had always had a habit of leaving long distance shots to whizz past the post, with 30-yard efforts often missing the target by no more than an inch or two while he looked on without so much as a flash of concern. "Good judgement!" he would shout as he saw the looks on our disbelieving faces. But apparent over-confidence in his own judgement was to prove his downfall.

During our third match of the 1971-72 campaign, at Bristol City, their centre-

Extra Time – The Final Chapter

back Ken Wimshurst hit a long, hopeful free-kick forward from deep within their half. The ball cleared our back four, bounced once, twice...and into the net just inside the right-hand post, while Willie swung around the post in the belief that the ball had bounced wide. A red-faced Willie, having made no attempt to stop the ball, finished outside the post with the ball nestling in the back of the net and City on their way to maximum points. That match was the beginning of the end for Willie. Just a few games later his fate was sealed when he let a tame looking shot from Sunderland's Bobby Kerr slip through his legs in an embarrassing 4-1 defeat at Roker Park. That was The Whig's last game for the club. For the following match against Blackpool, Stan handed a league debut to Jim Platt who remained the club's first choice 'keeper for more than a decade.

After spells at right-back, centre-forward and midfield, I cherished the opportunity that season to pitt my wits from the centre of defence against a top flight Manchester City side rated second favourites to lift the the FA Cup. We went into the match at Maine Road rated by many pundits as no-hopers but emerged with our heads held high after securing a fully deserved 1-1 draw. Indeed we held a 1-0 lead courtesy of Millsy until the dying seconds when City's Franny Lee took his usual dive inside the box. Known as Lee One Pen for his accuracy from the spot, Lee scored 15 penalties in that one season alone and he made no mistake as City grabbed an unmerited replay. But we were fuming to lose a late goal in such circumstances having played so well against supposedly superior opponents. Stuart Boam was the closest player to Lee as he raced into the box but he made no contact with him whatsoever. Lee simply threw himself to the ground and the referee was fooled. The first of football's "professional" divers, Lee was looked upon as nothing more than a cheat by opposing defenders who fell foul of his antics.

Thankfully, justice was done when a strike from Hickton clinched a 1-0 win in the replay three days later, though the game should never really have gone ahead. The Ayresome Park pitch was covered in two inches of snow, making it hard for players to retain their balance while the ball was always likely to do the unexpected on the uneven surface. But we found the pitch a great leveller and I enjoyed a good game in marking Lee. Despite his unfair gamesmanship, Lee was an England international and a highly skillful player who had given us plenty to think about in the first game. Like Stuart Pearson with Manchester United a few years later, Lee liked to keep in actual contact with his marker and would constantly back into you as he waited for passes from his defence. Using his bodyweight to great effect, he

When Stan was the Man

An unorthodox last-ditch challenge to deny George Best a goal during our FA Cup tie with Manchester United in January 1971. Jones and Gates look on.

would attempt to unbalance you before racing past as you tried to regain your balance. But I prided myself in doing my homework on opponents and had weighed Lee up by the time the replay came around.

Lee wasn't the only player who didn't stick to the rules of the game that day. Mike Summerbee began by standing on my toes. Then, as we waited for a City free-kick to be floated in from the edge of the Middlesbrough penalty area, he punched me in the Adam's Apple before racing to the opposite corner of the box to meet the cross. I'm sure I don't need to explain I suffered some pain from the blow but I made up my mind: don't get mad, get even. About 20 minutes later, I saw my chance to take divine retribution as Summerbee overran the ball in attempting to go past Gordon Jones - and I had no hesitation in taking it. As he raced after the ball, I crashed into him, sending him hurtling to the floor. I prided myself in not being a dirty player, no matter what the intimidation, but I felt Summerbee had gone too far. As he picked himself up from the cinder track by the pitch, he shot me a glance that seemed to say: "Well, I probably deserved that."

Having disposed of Millwall in the following round, we were once again drawn to play Manchester United, who it seemed we were destined to meet in the cup every season. It was a home-coming for Nobby Stiles and the team did not let

Extra Time – The Final Chapter

him down. In front of almost 54,000 fans, we fought out a goalless draw and felt we were unlucky not to have won. We were convinced Hickton had clinched the match with a late header that looked to be at least six inches over the line before United 'keeper Alex Stepney plucked the ball away but the effort was not given. The reputation Stuart and I had as the game's most up and coming defensive partnership was being built on performances against legends like Law, Best and Charlton.

Power cuts resulted in the replay being played at Ayresome Park on the afternoon of the following Tuesday, causing a 10-fold increase in truancy among the town's schoolchildren that day. After our fine showing at Old Trafford, we fancied our chances of completing another cup upset on our own turf and in front of almost 40,000 passionate fans. Sadly, we made a bad start from which we were unable to recover, Gates conceding a penalty in the opening 15 minutes, with Willie Morgan converting from the spot. Mills couldn't make the most of a chance to equalise late in the first half and United went on to win the game by three clear goals, Best and Charlton both scoring in the second half. Despite the result, I enjoyed playing against George Best and felt I did well over the two games.

Nobby Stiles always made sure I kept my feet on the ground and that I knew I still had much to learn. On one occasion, I almost caused the team to concede a late goal when I played a cross-field pass instead of opting for an easier ball to a defensive colleague. The ball was cut out and could easily have resulted in a needless equaliser in the game's closing minutes. No sooner had the ball gone thankfully wide of the post than Nobby - bloodshot eyes glaring and steam coming out of his ears - raced over to me and proceeded to give me an almighty bollocking. In no uncertain terms, he let me know that with the match won I should have been killing the game rather than looking for flashy passes. He was right of course and I simply accepted his lecture and made a note to learn from it. With Nobby's fiery temperament and experience at the highest levels, players with a far bigger reputations than mine would sit up and take notice of him when he was in a mood like that. What made Nobby look even fiercer was the fact that his eyes were always bloodshot, a result of enormous contact lenses he would wear during games, placed into his eyes on the end of long suction pads.

Sadly, a season that had promised so much fizzled out long before the final game and a crowd of less than 10,000 attended Ayresome for our final match against Hull City. And yet our home form had been quite wonderful throughout the season, winning 16 and losing only one of our 21 league fixtures on Teesside.

When Stan was the Man

Our promotion push had faltered on our travels where we took maximum points only three times. But it was my belief that we would have faired far better had Stan shown faith in Stuart and I as a defensive partnership right from the start. However, it was always likely that it would take time for the new-look team to blend together and I felt we would be far better equipped for promotion the following season.

Our attitude as we approached the start of the 1972-73 campaign was that this time we would have no excuses. Promotion had to be our aim and we honestly believed we would do it. Instead, it was to end in tears. Or, more accurately, in the resignation of Stan Anderson.

It was an action-packed and memorable season for me as I began to grab a few headlines away from Teesside for the first time in my career. My partnership with Stuart Boam and my own development put me firmly in the public glare - so much so that England honours and interest from a First Division club followed. And yet it was to be a season of unfulfilled promise for the team as a whole.

The season began brightly enough with a 2-0 opening day win over our north-east rivals Sunderland at Ayresome Park. The goals both came courtesy of the boot of an 18-year-old local lad called Malcolm Smith who, in the absence of the injured John Hickton, enjoyed the sort of league debut Roy of the Rovers would have found hard to believe. Sadly, that sensational start raised the fans' expectations of Malcolm to a level which he struggled ever again to attain. Everything he did after that was compared to his debut and what seemed the perfect start to his career quickly became a weight around his neck.

Hickton aside, the responsibility for scoring goals rested on the shoulders of Smith and the still developing David Mills. Still learning his trade as a goalscorer, Millsy was given a tough time by the hyper-critical Boro fans. That's not to say he wasn't getting the chances to score goals, it was simply that he wasn't converting enough of them. To his credit, he was always brave enough to keep getting into goalscoring positions when a lesser man may have ducked out.

But Boro's lack of goals was a major problem and placed extra pressure on a young defence to keep the ball out of the net at the other end of the pitch. Fortunately, we were able to do that regularly, while Stuart and I both scored early season winners, mine a 90th minute header to clinch a 1-0 home win over Millwall. But results were hit and miss. Indeed, a run of just one win in seven league games

Extra Time – The Final Chapter

followed the success over Sunderland, leaving the prospect of First Division football a distant dream.

Then, out of the blue, came news that I might be playing in the top flight sooner than I had anticipated. As I prepared to leave Ayresome Park after a morning training session, Bill Gates pulled me aside. "Has Stan had a word with you about Ipswich Town?" he asked quietly, careful not to let anyone overhear our conversation. I had no idea what he was referring to but Bill quickly brought me up to speed with the facts. It turned out that Ipswich manager Bobby Robson had bid £90,000 for me. Bill's young brother, Eric, was a player at Portman Road and had passed on the information.

I was amazed. Certainly I was flattered too - £90,000 was a huge a fee at the time. And I would be lying to say I wasn't interested. Ipswich were flying high in third place in the First Division and I knew I would be mad to turn down a chance to join a club battling for the leagues top honours. But my ambitions were tempered by apprehension. I was always a home-boy and at the age of 21 the prospect of moving to the other end of the country was not particularly appealing.

Within days the story was in the newspapers and the figure being quoted had increased to £100,000. Though I was never told the truth behind the rumours, the Evening Gazette's chief sports reporter Cliff Mitchell reported that Ipswich had offered their midfielder Peter Morris plus cash in exchange for my signature but that Stan had given Bobby Robson a prompt and uncompromising refusal. Stan was quoted as saying: "Our estimation of Maddren's worth is higher than Ipswich's estimation. There aren't many better back-four players in the First Division, let alone the Second, than Willie Maddren. If he goes it would certainly be for more than £100,000." Mitchell went further, suggesting Boro would only be tempted if the offer was increased to £150,000. I found that staggering considering the British record transfer at the time was little more than £200,000.

It was amid such speculation that Boro took on another First Division side, Tottenham, in the League Cup at Ayresome Park. We proved a worthy match for our more illustrious opponents though we were forced into a White Hart Lane replay by the likes of Martin Chivers, Alan Gilzean, Pat Jennings, Cyril Knowles and Mike England. An impressive team display took the tie to a second replay when neither side found the net during 120 minutes at White Hart Lane but my mind was on other matters when I was told after the game that Bobby Robson had watched my performance from the stand. I knew I had done my chances no harm with a confident display against Chivers. According to Gates, Ipswich had now upped their bid to a straight £100,000 in cash.

Over the following couple of weeks, the speculation was intense - Manchester City boss Malcolm Allison was also said to be watching me - and there was little doubt it contributed towards a dip in my form. Quite simply, I didn't know whether I was coming or going. However, I did ask Bill to enquire with his brother about property prices in the Ipswich area as I felt there was every likelihood that I would be on the move.

More press speculation suggested that Ipswich had increased their bid still further, to £120,000. Then came news, through the Gates grapevine, that Middlesbrough's board of directors had accepted in principle Ipswich's offer and that the transfer should be completed that Thursday. So it seemed my destiny would lay away from Teesside and I prepared myself mentally for a move to East Anglia.

Then came the surprise intervention of Stan Anderson. The manager quashed the deal, insisting that if Middlesbrough were serious about their ambitions to win promotion then the club must keep its top players. "Obviously, if a club offered £300,000 for Maddren it would have to be considered," he told the media. "But Maddren is not for sale." Stan was also concerned that Stuart Boam's form would suffer if I was to move on, such was the excellent understanding we had developed. I later discovered that privately he had gone to great extremes to ensure the deal did not go through, threatening to resign if the board insisted on my transfer. In the event, Robson converted his reserve team left-back to central defence and Kevin Beattie went on to become one of the game's top centre-backs of the era.

Years later, writing in my testimonial programme, Robson recalled his attempts at signing me: "At the time Willie was not widely known. But I regarded him as the most promising number six in the country. Willie had everything going for him - power, pace, skill, heading ability, confidence and composure. I realised his outstanding potential. So did Stan Anderson. He would not sell him. I was disappointed but I understood. No-one recommended Willie to me. I saw his ability myself and so did the chief scout. Cyril Lea, my coach, made two checks and was impressed. In one game, at Spurs, he said two players were magnificent...Stuart Boam and Willie Maddren."

I was disappointed, of course, that the deal did not go through. And yet I was

Extra Time – The Final Chapter

also relieved because a major decision had been taken out of my hands. I was a home-bird at heart and was about to be married. My fiance Diane was hardly thrilled at the prospect of moving so far from home and was happy when the status quo remained. What was more, I still hadn't given up hope of playing top flight football with my hometown club.

I made up my mind to concentrate on the job in hand - doing my best for Middlesbrough Football Club and comments made by my friend and former teammate George Smith in the Northern Echo confirmed that I was back to my best. George, who was on Birmingham's injury list, took time out to watch Boro's 1-1 draw at Aston Villa. Afterwards, he commented: "Willie Maddren played with such great authority. He was very cool in difficult situations and his confidence must be a wonderful help to those around him. His positional play was so perfect that I thought he was Middlesbrough's top player by a mile. I am not surprised Middlesbrough turned down an Ipswich bid of £120,000 for him. That is peanuts when you consider today's sky-high prices. Maddren has an old head on young shoulders and must have a great future. It would be a crime if he does not get a chance to prove himself in the First Division."

Sadly, our form deteriorated almost from that moment on. It was clear that in Jim Platt, John Craggs, Stuart Boam and myself, Middlesbrough had the basis of a young defence which would form a foundation for years to follow. Unfortunately, our forwards could not capitalise on our fine defensive record, a run of just six goals in nine league games leaving us well adrift of the promotion hopefuls at the turn of the year. Even so, with so many young players blossoming, it seemed there was every reason for optimism about the future.

It was out of the blue, therefore, when after a disappointing FA Cup defeat at Third Division Plymouth, Stan Anderson announced his resignation as manager. I was stunned and could not understand his decision. Looking back, however, I think he felt he had taken the club as far as he could after almost seven years in charge. Perhaps his batteries had worn down and he no longer had the energy to see the job through. On the day Stan resigned, he called me into his office and advised me to seek a wage rise from the club. "Your wages should be twice what they are," he told me. It was good of him to offer such forthright advice but I couldn't help but ponder his hypocrisy. After all, if Stan knew I was worth more than I was earning, why hadn't he increased my salary while he had been in charge?

When Stan was the Man

Although almost half of the season still remained, the club decided not to rush into appointing an immediate successor to Stan, preferring instead to give first team coach Harold Shepherdson a role as caretaker manager. After losing his first match in charge, Boro hit a fine run of form that saw us lose just three more games. Indeed, four wins from our final four fixtures left Boro in a final position of fourth, just three points off a promotion slot.

A former England trainer, I rated Harold highly and felt he had so much to offer. At the time, I therefore found it surprising that he chose not to put his name into the hat when the club's directors considered their options for the next manager during the summer of 1973. With hindsight, I now understand that he just didn't want or need the pressure that went with the job. He was happy as a trainer, to remain in the background and get on with doing his job to the best of his ability. He was to spend almost 50 years at the club in all capacities so his devotion to Middlesbrough could not be questioned but this was one job he would not consider.

It was clear, however, that Stan had left for his successor the foundations of a very good team indeed. There were real signs that the defence was beginning to gel as a unit, David Mills and 18-year-old David Armstrong were both earning their stripes as regular first teamers while, before his departure, Stan had added to the squad two more names which would be synonymous with the club's success in the following years - Alan Foggon and Graeme Souness.

But I could not have imagined the great days we would enjoy over the next 12 months...

7

Up the Boro!

THERE was a presence about Jack Charlton that made people look up to him. Here was a man who commanded respect, whose knowledge of the game was second to none and who knew what he wanted to achieve. You couldn't help but be impressed.

I learned of Jack's appointment as manager of Middlesbrough in a newspaper article and felt intrigued rather than excited. His reputation as an honest, wholehearted player who was quite outspoken went before him and I hoped some of the success he had enjoyed under Don Revie at Leeds United would have rubbed off on him. Certainly, I knew his appointment would be good for the club's profile.

When Jack gathered the players together at Marton Country Club for our first meeting soon after his appointment, I was immediately impressed with the way he came across. There, he issued a statement that set us all thinking. "I've watched you all play and I can see that there are some good players, some bad and some indifferent." I couldn't help but wonder which category I fell into in his estimation. It was clear, however, from that first meeting that Jack knew what he was talking about and he let us know in no uncertain terms that he would not suffer fools gladly. It was the start of a memorable spell in the history of Middlesbrough Football Club.

Few teams have ever been good enough to dominate a division in the way Middlesbrough did in the 1973-74 season. It was a campaign that was to go down in football folklore on Teesside, a wonderful season that would stay fresh in the memory for many, many years to follow. Indeed, even now as I write this book almost a quarter of a century later, those who witnessed that team still talk about it with great affection. Names like Souness, Armstrong, Foggon, Boam, Hickton and Mills established their place in the hearts of the supporters forever. And yet no-one, least of all I, could have predicted what was to come as we prepared to kick off the campaign with a long trip to Portsmouth in August 1973.

Our pre-season friendlies certainly gave no indication of the fairy tale season we were about to enjoy. We had done reasonably well, though a shock defeat at lowly York City had served to keep our feet firmly entrenched on the ground. And, though I felt we had the makings of a good team, I was concerned that once again we had not spent a penny on incoming players. Indeed, our squad had been weakened by the £30,000 departure of Nobby Stiles to join Jack's brother Bobby at Preston North End. Without Nobby's experience, I was apprehensive about our ability to handle the pressures of a long, hard season. I needn't have worried.

What perturbed me more, however, was that I was once again being asked to play out of position. During the pre-season build-up, Jack had told me that he felt I was "too good" to be playing at the back and that he wanted to give me a try in central midfield in place of the departed Stiles. Yet again, the Mr Versatile tag which I had fought so hard to shake off had returned to haunt me. I was far from happy about the idea as I knew I was the best number six in the club but decided to give it a go, if only to keep the new manager happy. To my amazement, Jack handed my cherished central defensive role to a teenage rookie, Brian Taylor.

But I was to receive another blow during Jack's Saturday morning team talk before our opening game at Portsmouth. There, without forewarning me, he announced to the squad that Stuart Boam would be club captain for the season. I was gutted. I had captained the team throughout our pre-season friendlies and felt I had done a good job. Now, just a few hours before our opening league match, Jack had dropped this bombshell. Inside, I was both hurt and angry but I knew this was no time for confrontation and decided to concentrate my efforts on the game ahead and speak to Jack on Monday morning. I later discovered from Stuart that Jack had offered him the captaincy as an incentive to sign an extension to his contract which made me feel no better whatsoever. Surely your captain should be the best man for the job - it was not a responsibility to be dangled as a carrot.

In stark contrast to Boro, our opening day opponents Portsmouth were the Second Division's big spenders, having brought in almost £400,000 worth of new players in Ron Davies, Peter Marinello and Phil Roberts. They were rightly the pundits' pre-season promotion favourites. Welsh international Davies, signed from Southampton, had been a tremendous top flight goalscorer for many years; winger

Extra Time – The Final Chapter

Marinello, a club record £100,000 signing from Arsenal, had once been labelled "the new George Best"; and promising full-back Roberts had been considered well worth his £52,000 fee from Bristol Rovers.

As kick-off approached, I turned my thoughts away from the injustice of losing my captaincy to the tactics that we would employ during the game. In the brief time we had been together during pre-season, Jack's game plan had been quite simple. When the ball was at the back, we would need movement towards the left channel from the front men and Alan Foggon would make runs into the opposite right channel or vice versa. When the ball was in wide areas, David Mills was to go to the near post and get in front of the opposition goalkeeper, while John Hickton was to go to the back post. Meanwhile, Foggon would arrive late at the centre spot for any balls cut back. It was a tactic that was to work a treat.

Before the game, I was a little bit apprehensive about the lack of ball winners we had in the middle of the park. I thought there might be too much onus on me. Although David Armstrong was a wonderful ball player and Foggon had been told to get back behind the ball whenever we lost possession, there was really only Eric McMordie who we could expect to help me dispute possession with Portsmouth's midfield. As the game started in scorching temperatures touching the upper 80's, little Eric surprised me with his tenacity and we quickly began to win the midfield battle. And, although it peeved me to acknowledge it at the time, young Brian Taylor was doing a super job at the back alongside Stuart Boam in containing Ron Davies and his fellow forwards.

Then, just before half-time, one of the moves on which we had worked so hard in pre-season came to fruition. The ball was delivered wide to John Craggs who cut it back for the on-rushing Foggon who arrived behind the front two to steer the ball wide of the goalkeeper and into the net. The goal was no more than we deserved and from then on there was really only one winner. We handled everything Portsmouth threw at us, an ability which was to become our hallmark as the season progressed. Even from that opening fixture, it was clear that the strength of the side was going to be based on a firm defence.

One specific incident from that game, when Portsmouth's experienced midfielder Bobby Kellard attempted a one-two on the edge of our box, stands out in my memory. Call it a mini premonition or whatever you like, but as Kellard approached our box I made the instant decision to leave the man I was marking, recognising the danger if he attempted a one-two and went through on goal. Sure enough, he played the ball in to Ron Davies who flicked it on to give him a free run at goal. But as the ball was played in, I went beyond our back four and made a last-ditch sliding tackle to knock the ball out for a corner just as Kellard was about to pull the trigger. If I was ever to sum up my major strength as a player it was my ability to see things in advance of them actually happening, albeit often a split-second before. It is that aptitude to anticipate, rather than react only when things happen, that distinguishes great defenders and great attackers apart from the rest. That last-gasp tackle earned my team a 1-0 win but the following day's newspaper headlines were not about the good job I felt Eric and I had done but about how well Boro's back four had played in handling the likes of Davies and Marinello. The honest truth is I felt quite jealous of Brian Taylor as I read the press plaudits over Sunday morning breakfast back home in Billingham. I wanted to be the one pitting his wits against top stars but instead I was consigned to a midfield role to which I felt neither suited nor enjoyed.

As I had promised myself, I went in to see Jack in his office at Ayresome Park on the Monday morning following that opening game. Despite the result, I could not come to terms with the fact that Jack had not only taken from me the captaincy but had not had the decency to tell me personally before announcing it to the rest of the players. But I was to receive no joy.

In typically blunt fashion, Jack told me he wanted his captain to be a back four player who could see the whole picture in front of him.

"But that's even more reason why I should be playing in defence," I reasoned with him, adding that I was particularly disappointed that he had not told me personally of his decision.

But Jack had no intention of backing down. "That's the way it is - you can like it or lump it," he insisted. It was impossible to argue with him. But I couldn't escape the feeling that my versatility had not only now cost me my favoured position but the team captaincy too. Whilst I did not agree with the decision, I knew I had to accept it and was glad I had got it off my chest. In the meantime, I decided to get on with my job and try to enjoy the season ahead.

The visitors for our first home game were Fulham. After our success at Portsmouth, we were regarded as home bankers but it was not to be and for some reason the wheels came right off. I can't remember too much about the game but I will never forget Jack's flaming temper as we returned to the dressing room after the referee's whistle had brought to a close a 2-0 defeat.

Extra Time – The Final Chapter

"Everything we worked on in pre-season we tossed out the window," he yelled furiously. "You just played off the bloody cuff and did it how you liked. That's the last time you'll do that. From now on, you'll play it my way."

We were in no doubt that he was angry with every last one of us and he told us in no uncertain terms how he wanted us to play from then on. But, as I recall, he directed the worst of his anger at poor Alan Foggon. He had preached to Foggy that he should never drop back to receive the ball off the back four but instead to make runs in behind the opposing defence and into the channels as the opposition pushed out to play offside. In Jack's view, Foggy had shown a lack of discipline in not following his orders to the letter.

He pointed his finger at Alan: "If I ever see you drop back like that again to take the ball off the back four, I'll fine you."

But he wasn't finished yet. Eyeing each of the lads, he added: "What's more, if any member of the back four gives him the ball on the edge of the box, they'll be fined as well. From now on, the only pass you give Foggon is over the top."

Jack's uncompromising words of warning, coupled with many hours of tactical training, were to have the desired effect. The defeat to Fulham was to be our last in the league for five months and we would lose only once more before clinching the Second Division championship the following March. The week after the Fulham game we spent hour after hour on the training ground as Jack drummed into us the team pattern that was to carry us through the season. Our confidence, which had been dented with the home defeat, was restored with a 3-2 win at Malcolm Allison's Crystal Palace - another team among the promotion favourites - with the scoreline flattering the home side.

A new battling spirit among the team was epitomised by a fight during that game between Boro team-mates John Craggs and Stuart Boam. Amazed supporters saw the pair push and jostle each other and raise their fists after Palace nearly scored. I told them both to shut up, calm down and settle their differences after the game. And they did - the row went on long and loud in the dressing room after the final whistle. It all started because Stuart thought John shouted "leave it" when in fact he shouted "keeper". They both got a bit angry and upset in the heat of the moment. I was actually pleased to see the fight. It summed up the new attitude of the players - that they cared enough about what happened to fight over it if necessary.

Despite feeling elated with the result, I personally was still not happy with my midfield role and a return to the defence looked further away than ever as a result of another excellent display from young Taylor, whose winning goal capped a fine performance. I was becoming increasingly depressed with the situation and it got to the stage where I seriously considered handing in a written transfer request.

The next game against Carlisle, however, was to prove a watershed not only for the team but for myself and two young men whose careers would shoot off in starkly contrasting directions from that moment on. Whilst a string of impressive performances had made Brian Taylor the talk of the terraces, a young lad almost a year older than Brian and already out of his teens had become the forgotten man of Ayresome Park. But the Carlisle game was to prove to be the launchpad to a great career for a lad called Graeme Souness and the death knell for poor Brian who would not play again all season.

Plucked from Tottenham's reserves by Stan Anderson the previous season, Souness had flattered to deceive on the few occasions he had been given a first team opportunity and was hardly flavour of the month with Big Jack. More often than not, he had not even featured in the squad for our opening games as the manager had felt his attitude had been some way off the mark. It was hard to argue against such an assessment. I had hit it off with Souey right from the start but his brash, even arrogant personality had put the majority of the lads off him and he had not been welcomed into the fold as well as a new player might have hoped. I counted Graeme as a pal of mine but even I had to admit that he wasn't doing himself any favours, particularly as he was mixing in less than desirable circles away from the club.

More importantly, his early performances simply weren't good enough. He was quite unrecognisable from the player that was to become one of the best all-round midfielders of the modern game. I will never forget the look of horror on his face as he walked from the field at half-time during his Middlesbrough debut at Fulham the previous season. "I didn't realise how fast the pace would be," he admitted to me. Having been plucked straight from the Combination League with Spurs' reserves, it was obvious that he was not prepared for the harsh realities of Second Division football. At reserve team level, he had been allowed the luxury of putting his foot on the ball and spraying it about almost at leisure. There was no chance of such niceties at this level. I told him straight: "Heh, in this league, if a bouncing ball comes your way, don't try to get it down and control it, just hook the f***ing thing over the top and out of danger - otherwise you'll get halved in two." Even so, his subsequent appearances were quite unimpressive. There was little

Extra Time – The Final Chapter

doubt he was a passer of the highest order, as we witnessed on many occasions in training, but there was no evidence to suggest that he would become one of the game's most aggressive players. In fact, there were many occasions when he seemed reluctant to head the damn ball as if it would spoil his hair!

On the team bus to Cleethorpes for a pre-season friendly with Grimsby, I felt the time had come to give him a few home truths. "I don't think Jack fancies me as a player," he confided. I told Graeme that he hadn't exactly done himself proud and that he needed to show a better attitude and knuckle down to business. I mentioned the sort of people he was knocking about with, that they were bad company. He had to prove to Jack that he cared and wanted to be a success. To do that he would have to turn in a series of a good performances for the reserves. Then, perhaps, the boss might give him a chance. Thankfully, Graeme took my advice on board and several years later, the night before he joined Liverpool, he thanked me for it.

Several much improved displays for the reserves earned Graeme a place on the bench for the visit of Carlisle to Ayresome Park. He never looked back. Unfortunately, for every winner there is a loser and on this occasion the "victim" was Brian Taylor. Amid a derby-like atmosphere, the game was both frenetic and physical. Subsequently, within the first 20 minutes my former Boro team-mate and holiday companion Joe Laidlaw elbowed Brian in the face - I'll give him the benefit of the doubt and say it was probably an accident - resulting in Taylor being carried from the pitch suffering from a depressed cheekbone. The sight of Souness preparing to join the fray would not have sent even a ripple of anticipation through the crowd and yet it was to prove a major turning point on three fronts. The most immediate effect of Graeme's arrival was that I returned to my true position in central defence alongside Stuart Boam with Souey slotting into the central midfield role I had previously occupied. The second turning point was for Souness. It was a fierce match but at long last Graeme began to show a side to his game that we had not even known he possessed. From the first seconds, he began to dispute possession and win the ball with determined harrying and tackling of the opposition. We all knew he was a good passer but this was something new. I sensed that he knew he had to make an immediate impact and he did just that, turning in a terrific performance that would prove just the first in a long run of games which would make him hugely popular in the dressing room and on the terraces. More importantly, his introduction to the team was, in my opinion, the most significant point in the entire promotion season.

Up the Boro!

A third turning point was for young Brian. Although naturally disappointed for Brian, I knew his absence through injury over the following weeks would present the perfect opportunity for me to re-establish myself in my favourite position. But you have to feel sorry for Brian. The repercussions of that day were such that, while the game proved a springboard for Graeme and I, he made only a handful more appearances for the club over the next two-and-a-half years before leaving Boro for Doncaster Rovers.

That momentous game against Carlisle sticks in my mind for one further reason. Boro were defending a 1-0 lead, courtesy of John Craggs, in the final 10 minutes when an opponent chipped the ball in behind our back line. As the ball spun dangerously in the air between Frank Spraggon and myself, I made the instinctive decision to launch myself at it in the hope of putting off any onrushing opponent. As I did so, I felt the back of my head crunch into someone's face. As I turned around, thankful that the ball had trickled past the post instead of over the line, I was faced with the sight of Carlisle's Brian Tiler, his nose splattered horrifically across his face. There was no intention on my part to break Brian's nose. It was just an instinctive thing that, as a defender, you have to do, if only to see how brave an opponent is, to discover how determined they are to get their head on the ball. On this occasion, my attempts to simply put him off had resulted in him needing medical attention but I knew that this was a fact of life in football. Without wishing to sound uncaring, my job was done. I had saved my team a goal and, when the final whistle sounded, I knew I had won a vital point for Middlesbrough.

The addition to the team of Graeme Souness gave us a new impetus. But Graeme was not the final piece in the jigsaw. That came with the arrival two weeks later of a beer-drinking, cigar-smoking, overweight Scot. If that doesn't sound the ideal description of a player to inspire a promotion success, then I cannot disagree. But then Bobby Murdoch was no average beer-drinking, cigar-smoking, overweight Scot. For this was a man whose range of passing was simply out of this world. For all his apparent physical failings, this was a player who simply oozed class. When rumours first abounded that Murdoch was about to join the club, I was immediately excited. I had seen Bobby's performance for Celtic in a European Cup semi-final against Leeds United some years earlier and had been left in no doubt that here was one of the finest midfielders in British football. When he subsequently joined Middlesbrough on a free transfer, it soon became apparent that Jack had made one of the bargain buys of the century.

Although his debut at Blackpool ended in a third successive goalless draw,

Extra Time – The Final Chapter

Bobby did enough to suggest he was going to form a tremendous understanding with the improving Souness and ever-enthusiastic David Armstrong. With the wonderful long range passing of that talented trio, things quickly began to click into place. But it was becoming apparent that Souey was blossoming into the real star of the team. Not only was he able to win the ball but his passing was now on a par with Murdoch's - a finer tribute I could not give anyone. We could see that what had been pure optimism at the beginning of the season was now something far more tangible. We may not have been setting the world alight in terms of scoring goals, but we had built a sound platform in defence and our confidence was blossoming. But Murdoch's arrival signalled the end of the road at Middlesbrough for Eric McMordie. A wonderfully gifted player, Eric obviously wasn't Jack's kind of midfielder. His range of passing was typically 30 yards but Jack wanted the ball shifted over longer distances and the new-look midfield was ideally suited to this.

With five successive clean sheets and just that solitary defeat, there was now a belief among the players and supporters alike that this could be our season to return to the top flight. A few days after Bobby celebrated his home debut with the opening goal in a 2-0 win over Bristol City - a result which took us to the top of the table - we met our fellow promotion challengers Orient in front of an Ayresome Park crowd of over 22,000. In a tight game, it took a John Hickton penalty to clinch a 3-2 win and take us to the top of the table. Despite the two goals conceded, our belief that we were now pretty much unbeatable at home had been strengthened with that success. The new-found professionalism Jack had instilled in the team meant we were also going to be hard to beat on our travels.

Everyone was on a high and full of confidence as we prepared for the following Saturday's visit to Swindon Town. But I was left with a mountain to climb simply to make the starting line-up when I turned my ankle during a Thursday morning training session. The ankle immediately became swollen and by the Friday was black and blue with bruising. With my ankle heavily strapped and supported by a U-pad, I undertook a late fitness test outside our Swindon hotel on the Saturday morning, under the watchful eye of Jimmy Headridge. It was immediately obvious that the injury was still extremely tender and my warm-up was a case of step one, limp one. I felt I had no chance of being ready for the game. But Jimmy wasn't prepared to listen to such negative thoughts and, being his usual persuasive self, insisted we continue with the fitness test. Half an hour later, I was very gingerly breaking into a jog, still unable to confidently plant my foot firmly on to the floor.

Up the Boro!

More time passed before Jimmy threw me a football which I found almost impossible to kick with any power, such was the pain in my ankle. Even so, Jimmy felt my experience would carry me through the game and eventually talked me into playing.

With the injury praying on my mind, I was far from my usual confident self. After about 20 minutes of the game, I went shoulder-to-shoulder with Swindon's centre-forward to chase a long ball through the middle. Without the injury, I would normally have made a fairly elementary tackle, but this time I made my challenge in three stages with the result that my opponent skipped easily past and on for a free shot at goal. Thankfully, Jim Platt made a terrific save to keep the scoreline goalless but I knew it was a lucky escape. At half-time I approached Jack and told him I felt he ought to take me off because I felt I could cost the team the game. Instead, he told me he was quite happy for me to continue. I was surprised at his decision because in substitute Bill Gates he had an ideal replacement for me. As it turned out, we pinched the sort of 1-0 win that was to become our hallmark and I got through the game without further embarrassment.

Old Trafford was our next destination for what was becoming an annual cup clash with Manchester United. Incredibly, it was the fourth time in five years we had been drawn to play them in one of the two major knock-out competitions. On a proud night, we won 1-0 through a goal from Malcolm Smith and I was immensely pleased with my own performance. After the game Jack's assistant manager, Ian McFarlane, told me that United manager Tommy Docherty had asked if there was any point in pursuing the idea of an exchange deal involving Martin Buchan and myself. He asked Ian what he thought Jack's reaction to the idea would be, to which Ian had left him in no doubt that the club would not even consider letting me leave. In Ian's opinion I was one of the most integral parts of the team and he would often call me his "diamond". Even so, I was hugely flattered about Docherty's approach as Buchan was a regular Scotland international who would go on to captain his country.

I liked and respected Ian McFarlane, who was known to all at the club as "The Big Man". A great motivator, he left Boro under a cloud at the end of that season, citing Jack's lack of appreciation for his efforts as his reason for leaving. Such was Jack's single-minded approach at the time, he was oblivious to Ian's frustration and was shocked to read of his former assistant's public rebuke in a newspaper article shortly after he had taken up a role at Manchester City.

Extra Time – The Final Chapter

Despite another three games without defeat, taking our unbeaten run to 11, we weren't winning ourselves many friends in the media with our controlled football. There seemed a reluctance to pay credit where credit was due and I wondered if this was a result of the fact that Jack had been such an integral part of the successful but unpopular Leeds team under Don Revie. I do admit that sometimes we might have gone over the top in ensuring we killed games off during the latter stages when we had the points in the bag. One tactic was to hold the ball in the corner whenever possible during the final five minutes or so to ensure the opposition created no further goalscoring opportunities. There were occasions, too, when I was guilty of this type of professionalism myself, especially in games when the home team, urged on by loud support, might rally in the closing minutes. It was then that I would occasionally slump to the floor as if injured. As the physio ran on to the pitch I would give him a knowing wink to let him know I was OK. He would get the message that I was simply attempting to take the steam out of the match, take a look at my imaginary knock and leave the pitch. It was all part of Boro's game-plan which was already proving so frustrating for opposing teams. Such tactics were to earn us the label of 'boring, boring Boro' but that hardly mattered to us when we were doing so well. In any case, the truth was that we were simply far superior to any other Second Division team.

Players like Murdoch, Souness and Armstrong were head and shoulders above your average Second Division players, while it was hard to find a defensive partnership anywhere near as good as the one forged between Stuart and I. In addition, Alan Foggon was beginning to play the sort of crucial role that few of us could have imagined on seeing him in his first days with the club during the previous season.

I will never forget witnessing Alan's first training session with Middlesbrough after joining us in a £10,000 deal from Cardiff. He was not only completely out of shape, appearing to be at least a stone-and-a-half overweight, but was bordering on the totally inept in all he attempted to do. During that first training session, he was given the apparently simple challenge of collecting a football from the halfway line before running with it to the edge of the penalty box and shooting into an empty net. I and the rest of the lads watched in disbelief as our new signing proceeded to stub his toe into the ground with two of his attempted shots. On the two occasions he did manage to make contact with the ball, he toe-ended it high over the cross bar. As I stared incredulous at what I had just witnessed, I made the judgement there and then that Stan Anderson had bought a complete duck egg of a player. And yet he was to prove to me the old adage that you should never judge a book by its cover.

A regular scorer from the word go, Foggon played a crucial role in our promotion challenge. By the time Jack Charlton arrived at Ayresome Park, Foggy was looking a far slimmer version of the tubby figure he had owned on his arrival. His electric pace and ability to arrive late in the box was now paying dividends and the fans had a new goalscoring hero now that the ageing Hickton's output was decreasing.

And yet neither Foggy nor his good friend Murdoch would have found it easy to combine their lifestyles with careers as professional footballers in the modern game where fitness and speed are everything. Indeed, it is fair to say that the pre-match preparation favoured by Alan and Bobby was hardly what could be described as conventional, as Souey and I often discovered on joining them in their hotel room for away trips.

Before Boro's game against Millwall at The Den in the late October of 1973, the team enjoyed our usual stay in the Waldorf Hotel. When in the capital, Graeme and I would usually take the opportunity to visit the West End to watch one of the latest film releases which might not arrive in Middlesbrough until several weeks later. One evening, on our arrival back at the Waldorf at about 10.30 on the night before the game, we went to the room shared by Foggon and Murdoch. I knocked on the door. "Who is it?" came a voice from the other side. "It's me, Willie," I replied. As the door creaked open, the over-powering but unmistakable smell of gin, tonic and King Edward cigars bellowed out into the corridor. Entering the room, there stood two profiles that Alfred Hitchcock would have been proud of, each silhouetted against thick, choking smoke. They were both naked but for their Y-fronts, huge guts camouflaging their waistlines. They toasted us with a small gin, their usual pre-match tipple despite the fact that, as with all football clubs, alcohol was strictly prohibited for 48 hours before a game. Perhaps Jack knew what they were up to but when results were going so well he probably never felt a need to question them. They never drank to excess but clearly found a wee tipple a good way to relax before a big game and it was clear that this rather off-beat pre-match preparation suited them down to the ground as their performances rarely fell below excellent.

The following day's game against Millwall was a perfect case in point as we once again went into the game feeling invincible. At the time, Millwall were almost unbeatable in front of their own hostile fans and before the match were full of

Extra Time – The Final Chapter

confidence that they could upset the league leaders. In his autobiography some years later, Eamonn Dunphy recalled marking Murdoch and how he couldn't believe the size of him. What amazed him far more, however, was that he simply couldn't get anywhere near this portly guy who he had been given specific orders to mark. That day Bobby played the sort of one-touch football that Dunphy and his team-mates simply could not contend with and, as Dunphy admitted, Middlesbrough murdered them 1-0. Though the actual scoreline may sound close, the result was never in question and our usual rearguard shut-out was followed by a goal from Malcolm Smith on a rare appearance.

Jack had used only 14 different players in his starting line-up by this stage and had already settled on the team that would almost pick itself throughout the next two seasons. The line-up which, barring injuries, appeared on the team-sheet without fail was:

1. Jim Platt
2. John Craggs
3. Frank Spraggon
4. Graeme Souness
5. Stuart Boam
6. Willie Maddren
7. Bobby Murdoch
8. David Mills
9. John Hickton
10. Alan Foggon
11. David Armstrong

The understanding between those 11 players was so instinctive to be almost radar-like and it was little surprise that Jack stuck to that same line-up whenever possible.

But those 11 individuals didn't just happen to knit together. They were made into a team thanks to the outstanding coaching of Jack Charlton. Training was always very enjoyable and no doubt Jack took great satisfaction in seeing many of his set plays, practiced on the training ground, come to fruition on the playing pitch the following Saturday. Although many of our games were tight, often with only a goal in it, we created massive problems for opposition defences with our free-kicks and corners. When we weren't training at Hutton Road, we would spend hour after hour on the pitch at Ayresome Park. One tactical observation Jack made was that we wouldn't get the same sense of dimension at Hutton Road and that we needed to practice set plays at Ayresome. Consequently, our free kicks were to be aimed in the direction of particular advertising hoardings around the ground, obviously depending on where the free-kick was taken. When the ball was delivered into the box, we would know it would be delivered in the direction of a particular hoarding.

Jack drummed into us the importance of ensuring the opposition goalkeeper was not allowed to catch the first cross of the game. "If he catches the first one, he'll catch them all day," he would tell us. Basically, his philosophy was all about ensuring the 'keeper was not given the chance to build up his confidence. If he dropped or missed the ball from the first cross of the game, then there was every chance that he would go on to have a bad match. If we had to clatter the 'keeper to make sure he didn't collect that first cross, then so be it.

Another move we worked on until we had perfected it was what could be best described as a cross-over throw-in. Whenever we won a throw-in parallel to the 18-yard line, Armstrong would make a run infield from the corner flag while Foggon would run towards David from the corner of the penalty area. Craggs would throw the ball down Armstrong's left side so he could make the cross while Alan's job was simply to obstruct David's marker. We probably had a 90 per cent success rate of David either hooking the ball into the penalty area or getting in a shot on goal.

Another thing Jack drummed into us was that whenever a player broke through in a one-on-one with the opposition goalkeeper, a team-mate had to get up to support him. He preached that rather than shoot himself, it was the player's job to then pass the ball across the face of the goal for a simple tap-in for his team-mate. That very tactic worked to perfection during a 2-0 win at Oxford United that season. The second goal was a carbon copy of the one we had practiced over and over again at Hutton Road. Late in the game, John Hickton broke clear on the left and, of all people, the less than pacy Murdoch got alongside him to slide home the easiest of chances from Hickton's square ball. Despite the result, however, we again came in for criticism for the way we had killed the game in the final minutes.

But even the most hard-bitten critic could not have doubted Boro's superiority over the rest of the Second Division. Teams would push on to us at their peril. We were wonderful at absorbing immense pressure before hitting teams on the break.

Extra Time – The Final Chapter

Just as importantly, every last man - from the front two right through the team - would work hard in closing down opponents whenever we lost the ball. The defence tended to win the praise for our outstanding goals against record but it was by defending as a unit that we were so successful.

Personally, I looked forward to our away games far more than our home fixtures as we tended to dominate visitors to Ayresome Park so much that games tended to be something of a doddle for me. I simply played one-touch football, feeding the ball to Souness, Armstrong or Murdoch in midfield. With their delightful skills and passing ability, they would spread the ball to all angles of the pitch. I took more enjoyment from our away games as we naturally had more to do defensively.

That season, another of Jack's regular ploys was the use of an incentive scheme we dubbed The Golden Carrot. At the time, he had connections with a Leeds-based clothing company and early in the season promised to get us all a blazer if we won eight points out of the next 10. Mission accomplished, we asked him what the next carrot was. Win six points out of the next six, we were told, and we would get the trousers to go with the blazer. Although it wasn't a tremendously valuable incentive, all the lads were up for it and that season we went on to earn ourselves blazer, trousers, shirt and tie!

Our unbeaten run continued into December with a 2-2 draw at Notts County that sticks in the memory, if only for the gale force winds which made good football all but impossible. In truth, the game should never have been played. We were 2-0 down at half time, having played against the wind throughout the first 45 minutes. Such was the strength of the gale, one particular Jim Platt goal-kick got no further than the penalty area before catching in a gust of wind and bending back over on itself and going out for a corner. We struggled even to get the ball out of our own half and probably did so no more than four times during the entire half. Naturally, we were looking forward to turning round for the second half when the elements would be on our side. As it turned out, we dominated the following 45 minutes and were disappointed not to win the game.

Whilst our defensive record had been impressive from the very start, we had initially struggled to score goals regularly but had overcome that problem well before Christmas. No less than 14 goals were scored in a run of just six games, though no doubt Jack took particular satisfaction from a 3-0 home win over Preston North End, as the opposition manager was his famous brother, Bobby, whilst their former World Cup colleague and ex-Boro star Nobby Stiles appeared in the North End line-up. As the goals began to flow, I was pleased to see David Mills start to get on the score-sheet regularly as he began to reap the rewards for his unselfish running. We would drop ball after ball behind opposition defences and David would chase many seemingly lost causes, turning some of them into goals. For all his early criticism from the supporters, Millsy was now recognised as an important component in the Boro machine.

Indeed, by Christmas there was clearly an enormous gulf between Boro and the rest and it seemed only a disaster would deny us promotion. We were now six points clear of the chasing pack which was quite a gap at a time when it was still two points for a win. On the back of a wonderful 20-game unbeaten run, we went into a Boxing Day derby clash with Sunderland bubbling with confidence. Amid an electric atmosphere created by a 37,000-strong crowd - Ayresome Park's biggest league gate for over six years - Sunderland, as usual, grabbed the first goal. But whereas in previous seasons we might have gone hell for leather in search of an equaliser, at the risk of falling further behind, we stuck to the patient pattern of play that Jack had drummed into us over the previous five months. After sustained pressure on the Sunderland goal, Foggon put us on level terms. Then, as the game reached an exhilarating climax, Boamy popped up to grab a late winner to spark off emotional scenes of celebration from players and fans alike.

Despite all the pre-season optimism, no-one connected with the club could have anticipated such a magnificent first half to the season. The sheer pride and determination to be the best that now ran right through the club was exemplified perfectly after a 1-1 draw at Aston Villa in mid-January. Having gained a goalless draw at Ayresome earlier in the season, we knew Villa were no mugs and expected a hard game from them. However, we appeared to be coasting to victory during the dying minutes thanks to a deflected John Craggs free-kick. But we made the mistake of defending too deep and Bruce Rioch's speculative shot through a crowded goalmouth resulted in the ball creeping agonisingly over the line. Normally, a point from a visit to Villa Park would have been viewed as highly creditable but such was the professionalism among that Boro team that a sombre atmosphere pervaded the dressing room after the final whistle.

There was more joy, however, as an easy 3-0 home win over Portsmouth saw the unbeaten run extended to 24 games. It seemed we truly were invincible. But we were about to receive one hell of a shock from a most unexpected source.

Extra Time – The Final Chapter

It seemed the FA Cup fourth round would provide a nice distraction and, though they were flying high at the top of the Third Division, we felt we had little to fear from little Wrexham. At the time, Wrexham were managed by John Neal, a future Boro manager who had one or two surprises up his sleeve that day. More gale-force winds ensured the game kicked off amid horizontal driving rain and we had to weather an aggressive start from our hosts. Things took a turn for the worst on 20 minutes when I was forced to leave the field after a head collision left blood pouring from my forehead. On entering the dressing room, Doctor Phillips had antiseptic wipe, needle and cat gut at the ready. He quickly wiped the mud and blood from the wound before inserting three stitches. Within five minutes I was back on the pitch but was unable to stop Wrexham from scoring what proved to be the only goal of the match soon afterwards. We bombarded their goal during the second half but to no avail. On the final whistle, the disbelief that our wonderful run had come to an end against a team from a division below us was clear to see on the faces of the Boro players. We made our way to the dressing room, anticipating a bollocking from Jack who was never the most mild-mannered of people. I was amazed therefore that he was quite philosophical about the defeat, reminding us that all good things had to come to an end.

Despite Jack's words of comfort, this was one occasion when that football cliche of being sick as parrots rang very true. We were embarrassed by the defeat but, after a few days of physical training, put thoughts of the cup out of our minds and turned our attentions to taking out our disappointment on Nottingham Forest the following Saturday. But, once again, it didn't quite turn out like that.

Jack kept faith with the side which had lost at Wrexham. After all, these were the very players who had swept all before them over the previous months and Forest were no great shakes. But the match at the City Ground was one of the most unusual I ever played in. When I say that, I mean that what appeared to be an evenly fought game saw Boro crash to a humiliating 5-1 defeat. Everything Forest hit seemed to end up in the back of our net and we were left totally bemused long before the final whistle. One player who had a particularly outstanding game for Forest, in direct competition to Stuart Boam and myself, was striker Duncan McKenzie. Whilst I had always prided myself on my ability to weigh up a player's strengths and weaknesses, McKenzie was one of those unpredictable characters who always had a new trick up his sleeve. You simply never knew what he was going to do next. What made his clever little flicks, twists and turns all the more confusing for defenders like myself was that I have serious doubts that even

Duncan knew what he was going to do next! Although not a tall guy, he had this wonderful knack - like Hugh McIlmoyle before him - of appearing to hang in the air for that extra split second, just enough to gain an aerial advantage.

For the second time in a week there were looks of bewilderment on the players' faces as we made our way back to the privacy of the dressing room after the final whistle. Despite Jack's cool response to our cup exit, this time we did anticipate a fierce rollicking. We had been on the wrong end of some stinging remarks from Jack when we had won games so it was natural to expect a real ear-bashing after such a mauling. But, once again, Jack amazed us all with his reaction. The blunt and cutting remarks we had expected were replaced by a calm, quiet exterior. Jack seemed determined to keep things in perspective, insisting that it was just one of those days.

And yet there was a real fear among the players that the bubble might have burst. We were still five points clear of second placed Orient at the top of the table but the manner of the Forest defeat had shocked us all. Despite Jack's assurances that this was only a blip, our confidence had been dented and we wondered if we had been "found out". Sure, this was only one league defeat in five months but to lose our unbeaten run like that raised real questions about our ability to stay the course.

Those concerns were hardly tempered by an inept performance at home to Blackpool the following Saturday when we were completely devoid of our usual swagger and style. Had Micky Burns converted a goalscoring opportunity in the dying seconds of the game we would have been left contemplating our third successive defeat - a situation that only a fortnight earlier had seemed unthinkable.

We need not have worried. We were about to embark on a nine-game winning sequence which would put even the performances of the previous five months into the shade. For the first time, the goals began to flow and we were no longer reliant on the defence to keep a clean sheet to enable us to clinch maximum points. Having said that, only three goals were conceded during that winning sequence, the first of those in a 3-1 success at Hull City that put our promotion drive firmly back on track.

One of those enjoyable wins came at Sunderland's Roker Park, a 2-0 success over our north-east rivals helping to wipe clear the painful memories of all too many drubbings suffered there over the previous years. At the time, Sunderland were the FA Cup holders, having shocked mighty Leeds United in the previous

Extra Time – The Final Chapter

year's final, but we played them off the park on their own patch to move nine points clear at the top of the table - and with just 11 league games remaining. Such was their frustration that both Dennis Tueart and Bobby Kerr earned themselves red cards for remonstrating with the referee.

That win left the top of the league looking like this:

	P	W	D	L	F	A	Pts
Boro	31	19	10	2	46	22	48
Luton	30	15	9	6	43	34	39
Orient	31	13	12	6	46	31	38
Blackpool	32	13	11	8	43	30	37
WBA	31	13	11	7	40	30	37

Frank Spraggon was among the scorers in the following week's 2-1 victory against Millwall, leaving yours truly as the only regular outfield player yet to have found the net. I was getting quite paranoid about it, especially as Boamy was taking great pleasure in reminding me that he already had two goals to his name. We always had a friendly rivalry about who would score the most goals from the centre-back position and I cursed the manager over his tactics for set pieces. He insisted that I should always position myself in front of the near post for flick-ons when I preferred to attack the ball from central areas.

Even so, I was delighted to hear that week that I had been chosen by my fellow professionals in the Second Division's team of the season. I was only surprised that John Craggs was my only Boro colleague in that select team which read: King (Millwall), Craggs (Boro), Watson (Sunderland), Maddren (Boro), Gorman (Carlisle), Rioch (Aston Villa), Masson (Notts County), Hartford (WBA), Tueart (Sunderland), McKenzie (Forest), Rogers (Crystal Palace).

The following two fixtures, away at WBA and Fulham, were for me the highlights of that fairy tale season. West Brom were second in the league and, if their pre-match press quotes were to be believed, they were confident of turning us over at the Hawthorns. Instead, Boro blitzed them of the park, winning 4-0. With the likes of Jeff Astle, Tony Brown and the promising Asa Hartford in their line-up, West Brom were a good side on their day but that afternoon it was just one-way traffic from start to finish.

Three days later, on the Tuesday night, we visited Craven Cottage for the much-hyped Fulham debut of former England skipper Bobby Moore, an occasion which helped to double the ground's usual attendance. The game couldn't have started better for me as, from a free-kick, I managed to wriggle free of my marker to plant a firm header beyond their 'keeper to register my long-awaited first goal of the season. I'm not ashamed to admit that I felt huge relief at finding the net after so long. My blank had started to pray on my mind, especially as local sports writer Cliff Mitchell, in his weekend reports, had reminded me and the rest of his readers that I hadn't scored. An absolute belter from Souness made it 2-0 with about 15 minutes left. And just like buses, having waited so long for one to come along, I was soon celebrating a second goal, when left completely unmarked at a corner to head home again. As I ran back to take my place in our defence, I nodded to Boamy and signalled to him 2-2, to remind him of the fact that we were now all-square in our little goalscoring competition.

I was given the chance to complete my one and only first team hat-trick before the end of the game. With just minutes remaining, I found myself completely unmarked in the Fulham box, with the ball dropping nicely my way. As I drew back my head and prepared to nod home a back post header from no more than five yards out, a long streak of misery called Boam threw himself in front of me and powered the ball into the net. Cheated of my hat-trick, I didn't know whether to laugh or cry. But Boamy took great pleasure in reminding me that he was now one goal ahead again in our race to be Boro's number one goalscoring centre-back. The entire second half must have been 45 highly embarrassing minutes for man-of-the-moment Moore. Fulham, Moore included, really didn't know what had hit them as we dropped ball after ball in behind their defence and generally pulled them all over the park. It was a terrific result and, with the goals beginning to flow, we began to receive some long overdue recognition from the national press.

The league table now looked like this:

	P	W	D	L	F	A	Pts
Boro	34	22	10	2	56	23	54
Luton	33	17	9	7	50	38	43
Orient	33	13	13	7	48	35	39
Carlisle	33	15	8	10	48	37	38

With only a statistical improbability now between us and promotion to the

Extra Time – The Final Chapter

First Division, training during the days following those two 4-0 away wins was more relaxed than usual. Indeed, such was Jack's relaxed state of mind, that we were joined in one session at Hutton Road by comedian Freddie Starr, who was appearing in cabaret at the local Club Fiesta. After filming Freddie clowning around in goal, the Tyne-Tees Television cameras turned their attentions to a light kick-about to end the session. As he occasionally did, Jack played in one of the teams and, possibly for the only time in his life, achieved a nutmeg by pushing the ball through the legs of John Craggs. Jack laughed as he raced around Craggsy to continue his run - until John stuck out his right foot, tripping Jack in full stride. Jack hit the deck with an almighty slap which could be heard right around the training ground. I'm sure steam was coming out of his ears as he lifted himself from the floor, his face blushed red with anger, and proceeded to chase after Craggsy around the perimeter of the ground. In a scene more reminiscent of a Tom and Jerry cartoon and all witnessed by the TV cameras, Jack's big strides would occasionally enable him to catch up with Craggsy and lash out at him - John avoiding a kick up the backside by hurdling every attempt. After numerous unsuccessful attempts to connect, Jack gave up the chase and yelled after him: "Nobody does that to *me*!" This was met by howls of laughter from the players.

Though we mocked Jack that day, it should be said that it really was quite some achievement to have put the ball between the legs of John Craggs. Craggsy had legs like a snooker table - solid and short. In fact, Jimmy Headridge once described him as the sole survivor of a lift crash, telling us that Craggsy was seven feet tall before he got in the lift. Although John won't thank me for bringing this to the fans' attention, I feel that this is the right time to reveal that he was affectionately known by his team-mates as Mr Cube, such was his rather odd physique!

The whole day was quite hilarious, though I was less amused by an incident back in the Ayresome Park plunge bath once the session was over. As I happily scrubbed myself down with club issue carbolic soap, I was horrified to see Freddie Starr urinating down the back of our young reserve team player Tommy Paterson. Tommy, who had a stammer, told Freddie: "Eeeeee, d-d-d-don't d-d-do that t-t-t-to m-m-m-me." Freddie thought it was hilarious but I couldn't help think I'd have punched him there and then if he'd done the same to me.

It was soon time to turn our minds back to the important business of winning promotion. The statisticians had worked out that, if results went in our favour, a win against Oxford United the following weekend would clinch our return to the

Up the Boro!

top flight. I don't actually remember too much about the game itself, apart from the fact that it was a tight affair with David Armstrong netting the all important goal. We returned to the Ayresome Park dressing room still not knowing if we were promoted but, as we listened to the radio, we soon realised that each and every result had gone our way. We were up! We were 13 points clear of our nearest rivals Luton and fully 17 ahead of fourth placed Orient. With only 16 points still available for Orient, it was impossible for them to catch us.

Knowing that we might soon be out to celebrate, the supporters had stayed behind and there were joyous scenes as we jogged a memorable lap of honour around the perimeter of the pitch, shaking hands with as many of our jubilant fans as was possible and chairing Jack on our shoulders. Words can't describe the feelings of joy I had as I listened to the fans saluting our promotion. I was overjoyed to have realised my ambition of securing top flight football with my home town club, a dream I had often believed I would have to realise at a more ambitious club. To have secured promotion as early as March 23rd was really quite something. Indeed, seven league games remained but we knew we still had the important work of ensuring the Second Division championship was Teesside-bound.

We did not have to wait long for an opportunity to clinch the title in style, with our visit the following Saturday to Kenilworth Road, to take on our nearest rivals Luton Town. After the euphoria of the previous week, we made the trip south in high spirits, taking with us tremendous support. I was completely taken aback by the deafening roar which greeted us as we ran on to the pitch before kick-off. Jack had suggested that a draw might be the best result to allow us to clinch the championship in front of our own fans back at Ayresome Park the following week. But we had got into a wonderful habit of winning every game and, knowing the competitive spirit of that team as I did, I would have been surprised if the result had been anything other than a Boro win. In a display typical of our performances that season, we thrashed Luton 1-0. David Mills scored the winner, his mis-hit shot bobbling in off a post. It was hardly the goal with which you would hope to clinch the championship but, nevertheless, the resulting eruption of noise from the Middlesbrough end lifted the roof off the ground. The feeling of absolute ecstasy that I felt with the sound of the final whistle that day remains vivid in my memory. With champagne awaiting us in the dressing room, we celebrated in style with our fantastic supporters who had made the long journey south.

Along with four or five team-mates, I travelled back to Teesside accompanied

Extra Time – The Final Chapter

Going up! Celebration time in the dressing room after a 1-0 win at Luton, had clinched promotion. I'm pictured back row, far right.

by hundreds of joyous fans, having readily agreed to join them on the League Liner train, one of the football specials which were so popular at the time. I will never forget the scenes at Luton Station as what must have been a couple of thousand Middlesbrough fans packed the platform. The Supporters Club chairman Peter Hodgson, who was a good friend of mine, had organised crates of champagne and beer to be distributed throughout each of the 10 carriages. I took it upon myself to accompany the delivery and I think I personally handed a bottle of beer to at least half the people on the train.

There was a magical atmosphere among the supporters as we made the journey home that evening. With the beer to keep us company, it is fair to say that I wasn't the only one feeling extremely merry by the time the train pulled into Middlesbrough train station some hours later. My own feelings of jubilation that promotion had been achieved were magnified by the fact that I had achieved that ultimate goal for the people that I had grown up with on Teesside. I was bursting with pride that at long last we had given them something to cheer about after so many years of under-achievement. Here was a team that could produce on the big occasion.

Going in for training was a joy in the days which followed our success at Luton as we eagerly awaited our first opportunity to parade the Second Division championship trophy to our supporters. Before Saturday's home game with Notts County, we celebrated by kicking footballs into the crowd as a token of our appreciation to our wonderful fans. We were actually a little bit worried that such goings on would distract us from the job in hand but there was never much chance of an upset from the moment John Hickton put us ahead. We ran out 4-0 winners, the perfect preparation for scenes of absolute joy and celebration after the final whistle. Parading the championship trophy around Ayresome Park that day is a memory that will live with me forever. It was one of those wonderful occasions that make the hairs on the back of your neck stand on end and sends shivers down your spine.

The following three games, however, were something of an anti-climax. With the title won, Jack decided to experiment and give some of the club's younger players an opportunity to shine at first team level. A drab goalless home draw with Bolton Wanderers was followed by an even more disappointing 3-2 defeat at relegation-threatened Cardiff. The only consolation in the latter result was that I scored my third goal of the season to draw level with Mr Boam. Two days later we lost 2-1 at Bolton, our goal coming from the head of Stuart to win our personal scoring duel - something which would result in unprecedented Micky-taking in my direction.

For our final home fixture, against Sheffield Wednesday, I was pleased that Jack returned to the starting line-up which had swept all before them. I couldn't help but feel disappointed with the attendance of just over 25,000, some 3,000 fewer than had attended the match against Bolton a couple of weeks earlier. Having clinched promotion and the title so early, it seemed that the run-in was something of an anti-climax for the fans but we were determined to sign off in style. In a game of exhibition football, we completed dominated the match from start to finish and eventually ran out 8-0 winners. It was Middlesbrough's biggest win for 15 years - and yet I can honestly say I really didn't enjoy it. That may sound hard to believe but the fact is that I hardly got a touch, such was our dominance. I don't think poor Jim Platt touched the ball once.

There was a real carnival atmosphere around the ground. And yet the one thing which always sticks in my mind about that night was that between the seventh and eighth goals some of our so-called supporters actually had the audacity to give us a slow hand clap to show their disapproval that we hadn't scored for 15 minutes or so! The criticism, as usual, came from a notorious part of the Ayresome Park terracing known as the Chicken Run. Graeme Souness scored a

Extra Time – The Final Chapter

hat-trick that day but was so infuriated with that section of our supporters that, at one stage, he put his foot on the ball and pointed a V-sign in their direction. Such was the fickleness of those who occupied the Chicken Run, their jeers were turned to cheers when Souey completed the rout with his third of the day.

Celebrating promotion to the first division.

The last game of the season brought together the two famous Charlton brothers, Jack and Bobby, in opposition as managers. The gulf between Jack's Boro and Bobby's Preston could not have been wider, however. While we sat 15 points clear at the top of the table, Preston were already relegated. We beat Preston 4-2 at Deepdale to make it 29 goals in our final 10 league games of the season - burying the "boring, boring Boro" tag which had dogged us during the early part of the season.

I was actually relieved that we won that final game as I'm sure Jack would have blamed me had we not done so. In our hotel on the morning of the match, Jack had proceeded to go through his opposition dossier with his usual attention to detail, highlighting every potential strength and weakness about Preston. To have to sit and listen to detailed dossiers when we were hammering all before us had become quite tedious and I'd had just about enough. It was as if Jack wanted us to know when the goalkeeper would make his last visit to the toilet before going on to the pitch, such was the meticulous nature of those dossiers.

Some 20 minutes into his talk, Jack got to Preston's centre-half John Bird, presenting me with an opportunity for some childish humour. Turning to Millsy beside me, I quipped: "I thought Bird played on the wing and was a bit of a flier." Unable to contain himself, David laughed out loud, cutting Jack dead in mid-sentence.

Jack was furious and demanded to know what Millsy found so funny. Millsy pointed the finger of blame my way. "It's him, Jack."

I was given a lecture about how much work had gone into this dossier, the time that had been spent watching the opposition, often three or four times. I wasn't to take such matters lightly and should bloody well pay attention.

The rebuke over, Jack returned to his opposition run-down - and back to explaining the attributes and weaknesses of Bird. Once again, I couldn't resist the temptation for a quick gag. "I can't *swallow* that," I whispered. Millsy burst into laughter, a reaction which was met with a look of fury on the manager's face.

In a fit of temper, Jack made a few strides my way, ripped up the dossier, threw the remains into my lap and stormed out of the room. The lads were gob-smacked and I knew there would be hell to pay if the incident was followed by a lacklustre performance on the pitch. Thankfully, my team-mates dug me out of what could have been quite a hole with a thoroughly professional performance in ending the season with another impressive win.

This was the Second Division's top three in the final league table of that season:

	P	W	D	L	F	A	Pts
Boro	42	27	11	4	77	30	65
Luton	42	19	12	11	64	51	50
Carlisle	42	20	9	13	61	48	49

What a season that was. The celebratory open top bus ride through the centre of the town saw scenes I will never forget. The whole town seemed to be on the streets to catch a glimpse of their Boro heroes and I still have vivid memories of cheering supporters hanging out of the windows of offices and shops right the way along Linthorpe Road as the bus made its way towards a civic reception at the Town Hall.

The words to the popular club anthem of the era were: "Up the Boro, the Boro's going up, the Boro's going up to stay!" Well, we were certainly going up. Whether it would be to stay would be down to the response of the players who had got us there. First Division, here we come...

Celebrating promotion with Frank Spraggon (centre) and Stuart Boan

8

The Team that Jack Built

IF THERE was one season I look back on and wonder what might have been, it was the 1974-75 campaign. Not only did I suffer heartbreak with my international aspirations but that was the season Middlesbrough could, and perhaps even should, have been crowned champions of England. That may sound like an exaggeration given the fact that we actually finished a highly disappointing seventh. But I firmly believe it to be the truth. We were that good.

All that was missing from that Boro side was a proven goalscorer and Jack Charlton's unwillingness to plunge into the transfer market almost certainly cost us the title. That may sound harsh on Jack but he himself admits he could have taken the club further had he added players to the excellent squad we already had. That is to take nothing away from Jack, who was to prove himself to be perhaps the best tactician in English football. So much of our success was down to him - and yet some of the blame for our failure to fulfil our potential must also lie at his feet.

Nevertheless, it was to be a great season for the club and one of great joy for the success-starved Teesside public. Still bubbling from the previous season's promotion success, we made further huge strides, despite Jack's surprising decision not to add new signings to the side which had clinched the Second Division championship in such style. The same 11 regulars who had dominated game after game in Division Two simply continued where they had left off and there is little doubt in my mind that this was the best team in Middlesbrough's long history. The balance of the team was near perfection in all areas but for the lack of a prolific goalscorer. That is no criticism of our centre-forward John Hickton. Big John had been a great goalscorer in his younger days but he was now on the wrong side of 30 and could no longer provide the constant flow of goals that is so vital to any title-chasing team.

The Team that Jack Built

Our rock solid defence was the envy of the First Division and formed the platform from which the likes of Souness, Murdoch and Armstrong could weave their midfield magic. Graeme Souness was quickly establishing himself as a major force and the range of passing he possessed was in my view unparalleled. On Graeme's left, David Armstrong was still a very young man who many would argue matured into an even greater player by the end of the 1970's and into the 1980's whilst with Southampton. But in those first two seasons following Boro's promotion, 'Spike' played with an arrogance in his game that often made him breathtaking to watch. And out on the right hand side of our midfield was that man Bobby Murdoch who, like Souness, possessed a range of passing that was out of this world. Receiving the ball, he would frequently let it run before making pin-point passes over distances of 50 and 60 yards, hit with such perfection that the likes of David Mills and Alan Foggon would rarely have to break stride to control the ball. Foggy, perhaps the most vital cog in our promotion machine, continued to wreak havoc in the First Division and few defences could cope with his devastating runs from deep which brought a high proportion of our goals.

We were among a group of seven or eight teams chasing the title for the vast majority of the season, though it did initially appear Jack's gamble not to strengthen the squad was going to prove a bad mistake. Such was the belief that ran right through the team, we were always confident that we could do well in the top flight but a series of early setbacks left one or two doubts in our minds. Personally, I was always surprised with Jack's decision to keep his faith in the lads who had won promotion. Although we had romped away with the title, we had been lucky with injuries and had been able to pick the same 11 players in 90 per cent of the games. But it was hard to imagine we could go through another season with so few injuries and I wasn't the only one concerned that our squad would lack quality in depth if we picked up a few knocks. But Jack's confidence in the players he had was based on the fact that not only had the first team won the Second Division title, but the club's reserves and juniors had won their respective championships too. He believed there was enough young talent coming through the ranks to hold us in good stead should we need to call on a bigger squad.

Such worries were far from my mind on August 17th 1974 when we became the first Middlesbrough team since 1954 and the days of the great Wilf Mannion to play a First Division fixture. And that opening game against Birmingham City at St Andrew's could not have given us a better start. Playing the very same game that proved so successful in the Second Division, we dropped ball after ball behind their

Extra Time – The Final Chapter

defence, pulling their back four all over the park with our non-stop movement and hard work. The final scoreline of Birmingham 0 Middlesbrough 3 was flattering - to Birmingham!

I played a big part in our opening goal midway through the first half. I think even I was surprised to beat no less than three Birmingham players before cutting the ball back towards the penalty spot from the left dead ball line. To my great joy, there was John Hickton arriving late to meet the ball with his head and I knew immediately that we would score our first goal of the season. John never passed up opportunities like that and duly bulleted a header past Brummie 'keeper Peter Latchford. With Stuart Boam and I containing the home strikeforce of Trevor Francis and Kenny Burns with remarkable ease, we completely outclassed Birmingham and they could not have complained if we had won by five or six goals given the opportunities we created as they chased the game during the final minutes.

Heading home in an early season win over Chelsea in 1974. Alan Foggon (no.10) can only stand and admire the quality of my finish!

And yet the harsh lessons of the previous season were repeated in our second game as we tarnished a great opening day away win with an inept home performance. We were ecstatic after our success at St Andrew's and enjoyed the plaudits as the media began to talk about us as a team that might make a real impact rather than simply making up the numbers. We were brought back down to earth with a bump as we fell to a humiliating 2-0 home defeat to Carlisle United, a team which had finished fully 17 points behind us in clinching one of promotion spots the previous season. We disappointed a crowd of almost 29,000 as former Boro star Hughie McIlmoyle gave us a torrid time in the air. I knew all about Hughie's aerial ability from his days at Ayresome Park and believed I had the know-how to handle him. How wrong I was. Quite simply, I couldn't even get near him in the air as he won header after header, much to my embarrassment.

Despite gaining revenge with a 1-0 win over Carlisle on their own patch seven days later, we flattered to deceive in the early weeks of the season. England manager Don Revie was in the Ayresome Park stands for the visit of Chelsea and I was delighted to score my first goal of the season with a header from Murdoch's corner. Again replacing the injured Souness in midfield, I felt we were on our way to our first home win of the season but the wheels fell off in the second half and we ended the game relieved to have taken a point.

It seemed we had finally turned the corner four days later when we visited Tottenham for a League Cup tie and ran out comfortable 4-0 winners. I marked Steve Perryman out of the game to play my part in a highly professional team display. But if we had expected plaudits in the newspapers the following morning, we hadn't banked on the blatant bias of the London-based press. I could hardly believe the reports which again labelled us as "boring, boring Boro". For heaven's sake, we had won the game by four clear goals. The only conclusion I could make was that it was not considered "the done thing" for an unfashionable northern club to come to the big city and turn over one of the so-called glamour teams. It all left a decidedly bitter taste in the mouth.

With three wins on our travels already, our away form had been impressive. And yet our trip to play Sheffield United in mid-September was a disaster. We actually lost the game by just a single goal but the alarm bells were ringing as United were the first team to work out our tactics of playing those long balls over the defence. To nullify our threat, they defended deep, almost on the edge of their own penalty area, and made it all but impossible for our midfield to drop balls behind their back four for Millsy and Foggon. For perhaps the first time, Jack's tactics had been sussed and we found it hard to adjust our style of play in an effort to break them down.

With only two wins from our opening seven league fixtures, there seemed good need for concern. And yet we were about to embark on a run that would restore our self-belief and take our confidence to a new high. The run began with an outstanding 3-0 win over what was a very good Manchester City side, boasting the likes of Mike Summerbee, Rodney Marsh and Colin Bell. With Souey still injured, I continued in midfield where I felt I did well in carrying out Jack's orders to nullify the threat of Bell's frequent forward forays. But this was Bobby Murdoch's match. That day I simply won the ball and gave it to Bobby. He did the rest. His demonstration of first-time passing over 40, 50, even 60 yards, simply took the breath away. Those defence-splitting passes were like manna from heaven for Alan Foggon who galloped on to them time after time without having to break stride. The game finished in a 3-0 win but it is not an exaggeration to say we murdered City that Saturday afternoon.

The marvellous team spirit which had played so strong a role in our promotion success would now help us make a quick rise up the table. But an all-consuming will to win occasionally bubbled over into slanging matches between us that would have dismayed our supporters. Arguments would flair up between us in the dressing room or even on the pitch, irrespective of whether we had won the game or not. Just such an occurrence took place during the closing stages of a 2-1 league win at White Hart Lane. Jack had always preached to us never to try to play killer square balls in the last third of the pitch. Rather, in the final stages of a match, we should kill the game by keeping the ball in the corners of the pitch or by making small triangular passing movements.

Inside the final five minutes, we were 2-1 in front and had two valuable points within our sights when Millsy attempted a crossfield pass to Armstrong. The ball spun off the outside of Millsy's left foot and bounced into the path of Spurs' right winger who launched an attack which ended with Boro nearly conceding an equaliser. The whole team were furious that Millsy had almost cost us the match and both Stuart Boam and I raced over to David to give him a piece of our minds. Stuart got there first and had grabbed David by the throat by the time I got there. The referee appeared to be perplexed by two team-mates jostling one another and was clearly considering whether to send off one or both players. I decided to pull them both apart but the row continued back in the dressing room after the final whistle. Eventually Jack separated the three of us and demanded to know what the hell was going on. When Stuart and I reminded him of Millsy's crossfield pass, Jack's tone changed and he began to bollock David too! That was typical of the whole team's desire to continually improve. Even when we had won, we were never satisfied and there would always be much after-match analysis.

A third successive league win, this time at home to Wolves, took us to the heady heights of joint-top of the First Division. However, it is not our performance that sticks out in my memory about that game but my clash with the evergreen Derek Dougan. White haired but brimming with experience, The Doog came on as a substitute with Boro 1-0 up. Some time later he challenged me for a high ball from which I - quite by accident, I must add - smashed my forehead into the back of his skull. As he picked himself up off the floor, he looked at me, rubbed his bruised head and frowned: "I'm getting too f***ing old for this game." And yet it was he who would have the last laugh at my expense that day. In Jack's pre-match dossier, delivered with the usual enthusiasm and detail, he had told me: "Willie, if Derek Dougan comes on, deny him the space and push him on to his right foot - he's absolutely useless with it." I took Jack at his word. So when The Doog latched on to the ball about 35 yards out from goal in the inside right position, I egged him on to have a crack as I gave chase. I was thinking "Go on, hit it! Hit it!" When, still 25 yards from goal, he drew back his right foot, I prepared myself for a shot that might hit the corner flag. Instead, the ball rocketed into the back of the net for one of the most spectacular goals of the season. It was egg-on-your-face time for Jack and yours truly. As Jim Platt picked the ball out of the back of the net, I turned to the dug-out to see the manager shrugging his shoulders in bemusement. Thankfully, a late goal from our young striker Alan Willey saved our blushes and we were able to go into the following match against Liverpool with confidence sky high.

Anfield was a fortress at the time and few teams took even a point, let alone won there. But all the Boro lads looked forward to their first visit to Anfield and their famous Kop. The atmosphere that day was electric and I was amazed to see what must have been 25,000 fans already in the ground when we took a walk on the pitch about an hour before kick-off. We were all experienced players but it was only human to feel a few pre-match nerves in such circumstances. Our coach Jimmy Greenhalgh must have spotted that one or two of us were looking a bit anxious because back in the dressing room he broke the ice with a couple of one-liners about Liverpool's Tommy Smith, a player infamous for his no-nonsense defending. As the lads made their final preparations, Jimmy quipped: "I don't want you boys to think that Tommy Smith is a bit of a nutter but I've just seen him shaving with a blow lamp!" With the lads warming to his humour, he added: "Did you know he carries a Norwich Union insurance policy under his left arm and hands them out after every tackle!"

Jimmy's wisecracks helped to relax the lads and relieve the big match tension and we did very well in the first 45 minutes in front of a crowd in excess of 52,000. It's football legend that the Kop could "suck" the ball into the net when Liverpool

Extra Time – The Final Chapter

attacked that end and I couldn't help but wonder if it was true during a second half which saw them lay siege to the Boro goal. In fact, we rarely got the ball out of our half and they were full value for their 2-0 win.

I did, however, get a closer look at the Kop than I had bargained for. Late in the game, as I shepherded a ball out of play for a goal-kick, Kevin Keegan pushed me in the back in a half-cocked, attempted challenge. The force of the push took me over the small barrier and into the crowded Kop. Thankfully, their supporters were all good natured as they celebrated a comfortable win and I was pushed back on to the pitch with no more than a bruised ego.

Late October saw us come face-to-face with Derby County at the Baseball Ground, a terrific team who - though we didn't know it then - would go on to be crowned First Division champions that season. Though their England defenders Roy McFarland and Colin Todd were missing that day, Derby's Archie Gemmill, Francis Lee and Kevin Hector were all household names and their supporters must have felt it fair to assume their team would retain an unbeaten home run which stretched back nearly a year. I guess we just didn't read the script. We hammered them that day, going 3-1 up before Hinton grabbed a late consolation. There was now a genuine belief among the Boro players that we could mount a sustained title challenge. Coming only a week after a 4-4 home draw with Coventry, there was certainly no reason to believe that a lack of goals would prove our downfall.

A goalless home derby with Newcastle in gale-force winds a couple of weeks later was dour and instantly forgettable but for the fact that I came within a whisker of scoring what would have been the only own goal in over 350 first team games for Middlesbrough. I still vividly remember the incident. We were into the last five minutes and I was marking Supermac himself, Malcolm MacDonald, when United's Terry Hibbitt took a corner on the left. As the ball floated into the penalty box, it caught in the wind and swerved towards the six-yard area just as I was about to rise for a header. In a desperate bid to deny Supermac, I dived backwards and connected with the back of my head. As I looked around, I was relieved to see the ball shave our crossbar and bounce to safety. It was the nearest I ever came to an own goal for the club. Indeed, only once in first class football did I ever put the ball into my own net and that was, in my opinion, to cost me an international chance. But more of that later.

Meanwhile, we reached the quarter-final of the League Cup with a famous victory over mighty Liverpool at Anfield just a month after they had beaten us so convincingly in that same arena. Everything went like clockwork in the first half and we reached the interval all square. I had moved into a midfield role in place of the injured Murdoch when, early in the second half, I conceded a penalty - or rather Steve Heighway took a theatrical dive over my right foot. Jack Taylor, who had refereed the previous summer's World Cup final, proved that even he was susceptible to the intimidation of the Kop End, pointing to the spot when no contact had even been made. I was furious but, thankfully, Jim Platt saved Alec Lindsay's resulting penalty.

The stage was set for perhaps the sweetest goal of my career. The tie was into its second minute of injury time and a replay was beckoning when Hickton dragged the ball square across the edge of the Liverpool penalty area. From the right hand edge of the box, I raced on to the ball, ordered John to leave it and, without breaking stride, curled a right foot shot into the far corner of the net past a disbelieving Ray Clemence. There was not even enough time for Liverpool to mount another attack before the final whistle blew to signal a Boro win that committed Liverpool to what I believe was their first home defeat in well over 18 months.

Having dispensed with Liverpool, we now faced a quarter-final home tie with Manchester United, who led the Second Divison promotion chase after suffering an embarrassing relegation the previous season. That night United 'keeper Alex Stepney performed the sort of heroics that we all felt he could never repeat. Countless Stepney saves helped United grab a goalless draw and took us to an Old Trafford replay. Some how, he simply carried on where he had left off at Ayresome Park, making stupendous saves from Murdoch and Craggs to set up an eventual 3-0 win for his side. So dreams of Wembley glory, in that competition at least, were forgotten for another season.

Back in the league, we played one memorable game with Leeds, the reigning champions, at Elland Road which initially looked certain to see us hammered but ended with Hickton letting United off the hook. With the great Johnny Giles and Billy Bremner dictating the play at their classy, arrogant best, Leeds took the game to us from the start and raced into a two-goal lead inside the first 15 minutes, both goals courtesy of the ever-dangerous Duncan McKenzie. Then, mid-way through the first half, Bremner had the chance to wrap it up with a third. Needing only to simply stoop to head the ball over the line, he inexplicably attempted a spectacular bicycle kick which resulted in the ball spinning off the outside of his boot, crashing against the underside of the crossbar and bouncing at least a foot over the line

Extra Time – The Final Chapter

before being cleared by a desperate defender. That should have been curtains for Boro. Instead, the referee waved play on and slowly but surely we began to stamp some authority on the match. Just before half-time, I got in a header that Leeds 'keeper David Harvey saved at full stretch, only for Boam to follow up with a close range tap-in that put us right back in it. We grabbed what had earlier seemed an unlikely point when Malcolm Smith volleyed home a terrific goal in the second half but we really should have won it. Late in the game, Hickton made a burst down the left wing and found himself completely free with just the 'keeper to beat. In his wisdom, John decided to go for glory and ignore the manager's tactical rule of laying the ball off to an onrushing team-mate. He tried - and failed - to beat Harvey at his near post. At the final whistle, we were all ecstatic with a 2-2 draw. All, that is, but for Jack, who had a few harsh words to say to Mr Hickton.

Our league form through to the end of the year remained quite outstanding and we were about to embark on an impressive run in the FA Cup. Confidence was high - and rightly so. And yet we weren't the closest of teams off the pitch. In fact, I often considered us to be quite cliquey in the way that certain players had particular friends but would never socialise with other members of the team. During a trip with England's under-23 squad, Burnley goalkeeper Alan Stevenson told me how his team would, without fail, socialise at least once a week. In stark contrast, the Boro squad never went out together for a night on the town. But once we went over the white line on a Saturday afternoon, we had a team spirit which was the envy of every side. We would fight tooth and nail for one another - and often against one another, as the incident between Millsy, Boam and myself at Spurs suggested.

Whatever our feelings about each other, there is no question that the team Jack built was special. We oozed class in every department and the majority of that side formed the backbone of the Middlesbrough team for at least three years. Our strength was based on that rock solid defence but quality ran right through the team. We were often criticised by the media for being defensive and yet we created as many chances as any other side - we just couldn't put them away. On one occasion, after a good result at Stoke, their manager Tony Waddington told reporters to give the Man of the Match award to "Boro's 10 defenders". I thought that was unfair as we had given as good as we got. Indeed, I still look back and wonder just what that side might have been capable of had Jack taken a few risks in the transfer market and added a quality striker to finish off the good work of the rest of the team. Just look at the players we had...

Jim Platt

A vital cog in the promotion team and a great reaction goalkeeper. Jim wasn't the sort of 'keeper to dominate his penalty area but then, with Stuart and I in the centre of defence, he really didn't need to. Such was the strength of the defence in front of him, Jim was often redundant for long spells but his concentration levels were such that he had the knack of producing saves when called upon. In my opinion, Jim became a far better 'keeper a few years later under John Neal when Boro's new attacking style meant he was called upon more often.

John Craggs

The best attacking right full-back in the First Division, Craggsy should have been an England international. John had all the attributes required of an international full-back in that he was a good tackler, a great dribbler, was an exceptional crosser of the ball on the run and could pass it accurately, often low and hard over 40 or 50 yards to our front men. Unfortunately, like myself, John's international aspirations suffered due to the fact that he played for an "unfashionable" club which rarely featured on Match of the Day. Even so, he maintained a great consistency over many years, right into the early 1980's. Like Jim, John was a quiet lad off the pitch but had a very dry sense of humour.

Frank Spraggon

Although not blessed with great pace, Frank had great positional sense and his reading of the game was second to none. He was our left-back by the time we were in the top flight, having been converted from wing-half. His lack of height might have held him back in the First Division had he remained a central defender but he did particularly well at left-back, such was his ability to produce the right tackle at the right time. If Frank had a weakness, it was in his distribution but he remained a great servant to the club for over a decade.

Stuart Boam

The press dubbed Stuart and I "the telepathic twins" and it was easy to see why, such was our understanding at the heart of the Boro defence. I don't think it is any exaggeration to class us in the company of the era's great defensive partnerships like Derby's Todd and McFarland, Hughes and Smith at Liverpool, or earlier Jack Charlton and Norman Hunter at Elland Road. A great tackler and as hard as nails, Boamy was the best one-on-one defender I have ever seen. Very few opponents beat him on skill - and if he couldn't stop them fairly, he wouldn't think twice about taking a player out. Having said that, Stuart had reasonable pace for his build and there weren't many strikers who did him for speed. He did, however, fancy himself as an attacker and, in moments of madness, would occasionally set off on these mazy runs down the right wing, leaving yours truly to cover for him. For me, his only weakness was that he occasionally didn't show for the ball as he was uncomfortable about passing the ball out of defence. Stuart and I had a great relationship on and off the pitch and had many great times together. My nickname for him was Youth. In a broad Yorkshire accent, I would take the Micky out of his strong accent with a daily greeting of: "Ay up, Youth. I want to talk to thee."

David Armstrong
David could drop a ball on a sixpence with that super left peg of his. His fantastic vision gave him the ability to change the play, whilst he had great composure in front of goal and was deceptively good at winning headers. Without doubt he was one of the best, if not the best, left-footed player to have pulled on a Middlesbrough shirt. My only criticism of David was that, at times, I felt he didn't go in where it hurt. Anyone who can play over 350 consecutive games cannot be of the physical type, in my opinion. Indeed, Souey and I did occasionally have a go at David about his tendency to avoid getting "stuck in". David picked up the nickname of Spike as he had only thin, whispy hair when he first broke into the first team. By the time he was 21 he was almost totally bald and I think many people quite understandably believed him to be much older than he was throughout his career. In those early days, David was quite a shy lad and you would rarely get much out of him. On the coach home after away games, however, he would always shout to the driver: "Whip them snails, driver!" and "Get that boil in your foot lanced!"

Graeme Souness
The best player I have ever seen in a Middlesbrough shirt. And I make no exceptions to that - not Murdoch, not Juninho, not Merson, no-one was as good for Boro as Graeme Souness. It saddens me that many people remember Souey for the rather cynical side of his game and overlook the fact that he was one of the best

passers of a ball the British game has ever seen. The range of Graeme's distribution, long or short, was unparalleled. A turning point in his playing style came when Leeds United's Terry Yorath and Johnny Giles went over the top on him in one of our typically tough derbies, resulting in Graeme spending several weeks on the sidelines with ligament damage. He decided there and then that no-one would ever do that to him again and he became very much the aggressor from then on. But Graeme was our play-maker throughout his time with the club, receiving the ball off the back four and spreading the play to either wing with that pin-point passing of his. Graeme and I became instant friends on his arrival at Ayresome Park from Tottenham. Most of the other lads were put off by his arrogant nature but I thought he might need help in settling in and made a point of getting to know him better. Having made the breakthrough, he was always ambitious and it was no surprise to me when he became Boro's record sale in a £350,000 move to Liverpool in 1978. The night after his Liverpool debut against WBA, he complained to me that he had hardly got a kick. I had to remind him that he was now playing alongside 10 fellow internationals who would all want a piece of the action. To his credit, he became a great play-maker in that outstanding Liverpool team. What surprised me was that Bob Paisley made him club captain. At Middlesbrough, he was always a Jack the lad type, a rebel who enjoyed the social scene. At Liverpool, however, he seemed to thrive on the sort of responsibility he had never seemed to want during his Ayresome Park days.

Bobby Murdoch

Graeme Souness always said that he learned a great deal from playing alongside Bobby Murdoch. There certainly couldn't have been a finer player to teach you your trade. Bobby had won everything the Scottish game had to offer, including a European Cup medal, during a glittering career with Celtic. Quite why Jock Stein agreed to let him leave Parkhead is beyond me because he was a very special player whose range of passing was quite stunning. He was the pulse of our team, able to quicken the tempo or reduce the speed of the game at will. Although his extra bulk meant he wasn't the quickest of players, he was still an extremely good competitor and was never frightened to go in where it hurt.

David Mills

Millsy was a manager's dream in that he would run all day, chasing lost causes and

Extra Time – The Final Chapter

making bad passes look like decent ones through his own workrate. Although not a prolific goalscorer, David always had the bottle to get into the right positions in the box, even when he faced the wrath of the fans during lean spells. Only someone with great strength of character can do that. Eventually David won over the fans and went on to win England under-23 caps and was included in full squads on occasions. Apart from his unselfish running, which would create space for the likes of Hickton and Foggon, he was also surprisingly good in the air for his size. Having known Millsy since we were kids playing for the town's boys team, I have always classed him as a great friend. Like me, he has a weird sense of humour. Given that I'm a friend of his, I know he'll forgive me for saying that big Ron Atkinson must still wake up screaming in the middle of the night when he recalls how he thought he could convert Millsy to midfield at WBA. David was always a front man, who is remembered by Boro fans as honest and brave.

Alan Foggon

First and foremost, Foggy was a great runner - a strength Jack Charlton utitilised to exploit the weaknesses of opposition teams who would push up in an attempt to play us offside. Alan's well-timed runs from deep caused havoc in defences across the country and, once in a one-on-one position, he had the cool head of a great striker and could put the ball away with contemptive ease. At times, he looked ungainly as he always carried excess weight and yet he had that ability to leave defenders in his wake. A jovial lad, Alan was a popular guy in the dressing room.

John Hickton

Until the arrival of Juninho, Big John was the most popular player in Middlesbrough's history. The best volleyer of a ball I've ever seen and, at his best, a clinical finisher. In training, John was the one to model yourself on if you wanted to improve your finishing because he hit the target nine times out of 10. In the promotion year, he had to adapt his game from that of an out and out goalscorer to more of a target man and he made the change with ease. He became our battering ram who would knock the opposing centre-half from pillar to post, allowing Millsy, Foggon and others to pick up the pieces. Boro fans will also remember John for his penalties, which involved extraordinarily long runs followed by blasted shots, hit with unerring accuracy. Suffice to say, he didn't miss many.

The Team that Jack Built

What a team that was. Though Souness was perhaps the only household name beyond Teesside, we had so many excellent players and it was no surprise at all that we did so well. Behind it all, of course, was our uncompromising manager Jack Charlton. But as good a coach as he was, there were times when I didn't like Jack during my days as a player. In those early days of his managerial career, he could be arrogant, rude and self opinionated. More than once he interrupted private conversations to express his own views.

I also felt he was rather mean, especially with the club's finances, too often treating them as though they were his own. No doubt he was a dream for the club's directors. One such occasion occurred that season when I asked him for a pay rise. Having been involved in several England under-23 squads, I had discovered the sort of salaries being paid to most good players in the First Division and approached Jack for an increase in my own wage. On his arrival at the club, he had proudly announced that he was a players' manager and that if we did it for him he would look after us. With that in mind, I told him what I was looking for, only to be told: "I can't afford those kind of salaries. If the team goes down, it would financially cripple the club if you lot were on top salaries." I told Jack: "You know this team will not go down." I was never motivated by money but left Jack's office feeling hugely disappointed as I felt I was being far from greedy with my request. About a fortnight later, after further discussions, a compromise was reached though I still felt Jack was being mean considering the success of the team in the First Division.

But he was to remain the same uncompromising man throughout his time in charge of the club. A couple of years later, David Mills and I were looking to negotiate new pay rises as we were at the end of our contracts. David had read reports that Liverpool were ready to pay £100,000 for his services and therefore felt he should be on the sort of wages a player of that value would expect to be on. Whilst I sat in Ayresome Park's reception, David went upstairs to Jack's office to discuss his new contract. After about 10 minutes, I heard the door to Jack's office open. I would not like to repeat the sort of language being exchanged between Jack and David. Millsy was giving as good as he got but it was clear Jack was in no mood for compromise. Eventually David slammed the office door and marched angrily down the stairs and out through reception without stopping. The office door opened again and the angered sound of Jack's voice boomed down the stairs: "Next!" Realising this was not a good day to discuss wages, I did an immediate about turn and left the ground. Several days later I returned but still did not get

Extra Time – The Final Chapter

Jack Charlton labelled me Boro's scruffiest dresser and I think it's fair to say I rarely looked as smart as I do in this early modelling photograph!

what I wanted. Over the years Jack has mellowed to become a much warmer person who I have the utmost respect for but, in those early days, I think he was keen to ensure no players got too close to him to enable him to motivate them and keep their respect.

Our final game of 1974 saw us maintain our position just off the top of the league, thanks to a 1-1 draw at fellow title-chasers Everton. It was a game of contrasting emotions for me as I had a hand in both goals. Just before half-time, their left winger John Connolly got to the touchline and hit a swerving cross which deceived me in a strong wind. I missed the ball completely and I turned back in horror to see big Bob Latchford creeping in behind to bullet a header past Platt. I was hugely disappointed as I blamed myself for the goal and was determined to do something about it. I kept pushing into attack and, with time ticking away, was rewarded when a left wing cross evaded Hickton but arrived in my path for me to strike home a fierce shot with my gammy right leg.

Our first league game of 1975 was a pivotal point in our season. For the next two months we completely lost our way, a run of six games without a win leaving us with a mountain to climb in our quest for the championship. Away to another of our fellow title challengers, Ipswich Town, we were trailing by a single goal until late in the game, having failed to capitalise on a steady stream of chances to equalise. Ipswich clinched a flattering 2-0 win with a second goal in the final minute and we were left to rue those missed chances. We were desperate for a proven goalscorer and by March 1st had scored just one league goal since the turn of the year.

But this was a team of great character and from our most heart-breaking moment we were to re-launch our title bid in dramatic fashion. The heart-ache came at Birmingham City's St Andrew's ground in the quarter-final of the FA Cup. We had quietly put together an impressive cup run and confidence was high that this could be Boro's year for a first ever Wembley appearance. Ironically, we almost fell at the first hurdle, coming all too close to an embarrassing cup exit at the hands of non-league Wycombe Wanderers on their infamous sloping pitch. We never looked like scoring and only clinched a replay when a diving header flashed inches wide in the final minute. But the minnows had had their chance and an Armstrong penalty back at Ayresome Park saw us through to face the old enemy, Sunderland, in the fourth round. Nearly 40,000 fans packed into Ayresome Park to witness Sunderland take an early lead when Souey's careless back-pass was intercepted by Pop Robson. Our patient build-up play brought an equaliser before half-time, Murdoch the man on target, and we wrapped up a 3-1 win in the second half. Twice Millsy was brought down inside the box. Twice Hickton smashed home the resulting penalty. Goodnight, Sunderland!

In the last 16, we faced a tricky away tie at Third Division Peterborough United, who pulled in a full house of almost 26,000. In the days before the game, a young boy called David Gregory made a few outlandish predictions about what he was going to do to "big-time Boro" and I saw his boasting as a challenge, as I would be the man to mark him. To be fair, Gregory was a good player but I kept him quiet for most of the game and we eventually got a 1-1 draw, before winning a replay back on Teesside.

Now it was Birmingham City for a first ever place in the FA Cup semi-final. We had every reason to feel confident. After all, we had already twice beaten Birmingham by 3-0 scorelines that season, including that opening day win at St Andrew's. We had nothing to fear - but it all went disastrously wrong. We lost 1-0 and, as I left the ground after the match, I couldn't help but wonder if I could have denied them the goal. City centre-back Joe Gallagher rose unchallenged for a far post cross and directed a great header right across our goal, from where Bob Hatton pulled away from me and knocked home a simple header.

Over the years, much has been said about that disappointing day as we saw our cup dreams left in tatters once again. I have heard it said many times that the reason we lost the tie was because Jack had set his stall out for a draw to bring them back to Ayresome Park. In Jack's defence, I can honestly say that it was never mentioned that we should play for a draw. The fact that we lost the game was simply a result of the occasion being too big for several Middlesbrough players who just didn't perform on the day. Personally, I look back on that defeat as one of

Extra Time – The Final Chapter

the most disappointing games of my career. There was great expectancy from the Middlesbrough fans before the game but, once again, we let them down on the big occasion.

And yet from the despair of that cup exit, we lifted ourselves to build a run of victories which resurrected our title aspirations. A major boost was the arrival during that period of left-back Terry Cooper from Leeds United. An England international, Terry had recovered from serious injury and was still the best left-back in the country. His dribbling ability was second to none and there was no question in my mind that, with John Craggs on the opposite flank, we now boasted the two finest attacking full-backs in the country. With Cooper replacing the unfortunate Spraggon in the starting line-up, March saw wins over Stoke City, Tottenham, Everton, Chelsea and Burnley follow in quick succession and, while the championship looked to be a long shot, we had every chance of being the first Middlesbrough team to qualify for Europe.

A 2-0 home win over Burnley on March 29th left the top of the league looking like this:

	P	W	D	L	F	A	Pts
Liverpool	37	17	11	9	53	35	45
Everton	36	14	16	6	49	35	44
Ipswich Town	36	20	3	13	55	37	43
Boro	37	16	11	10	50	36	43
Stoke City	37	15	13	9	59	46	43
Derby	35	17	8	10	57	45	42
Burnley	37	16	9	11	60	53	41
Sheffield Utd	35	15	10	10	47	46	40

It was the tightest championship race in years and never can so many teams have still been in with a shout of the title with just five or six games to play. The visit to Ayresome Park of Derby County in our next game in early April offered us a great opportunity to strengthen our challenge and hammer what would be a nail in the coffin of their title hopes. We were really up for it that afternoon and played Derby off the park. It was a mystery how we had only a solitary David Mills goal to show for our complete dominance. Even so, we were coasting towards two crucial points when, in the last minute, disaster struck. At a time when he should have been taking no chances and simply hoofing the ball up the pitch, Stuart Boam uncharacteristically attempted to play a square pass across our defence midway inside our half. Derby striker Kevin Hector intercepted the pass and strode forward before planting the ball past Platt. The silence in all but the small corner of Ayresome Park which housed the away supporters was quite deafening. Players and fans were in complete disbelief. The ball hadn't travelled two yards after the re-start before the referee blew the final whistle.

As the players trooped dejectedly into the dressing room and the equally sombre fans out of the ground and home, the full horror of the situation began to sink in. Without doubt any lingering hope of winning the championship had now disappeared. Of course, there was no way Stuart's rare mistake could be blamed for us failing to win the league. He had enjoyed a great season and it was unfortunate that his one mistake came in such a big game. The goal was his fault, however, and back in the dressing room he felt the full brunt of Jack's fury. Jack went ballistic, launching a scathing verbal attack on Stuart. In his fit of temper, Jack threw a milk crate across the room, the plastic crate smashing against the wall inches from Stuart. I don't think I need to explain that Stuart wasn't best pleased with Jack's antics and I know he seriously considered asking for a transfer in the aftermath of that game and resulting showdown.

The top of the table now looked like this:

	P	W	D	L	F	A	Pts
Liverpool	39	18	11	10	55	37	47
Everton	38	15	17	6	51	36	47
Stoke City	39	17	13	9	64	46	47
Derby	38	19	9	10	65	49	47
Ipswich	38	21	4	13	58	39	46
Boro	38	16	12	10	51	37	44

We found the disappointment of that game hard to overcome and lost the following away games at relegation strugglers Leicester and Wolves. Those were to prove crucial defeats. A 1-0 home win over Liverpool all but handed the championship to Derby County. A final day 2-0 win at Coventry would normally have been a pleasing result but we were left with a sour taste when Stoke City's goalless draw at Burnley ensured their qualification in the following season's

Extra Time – The Final Chapter

UEFA Cup instead of us.

The final table was:

	P	W	D	L	F	A	Pts
Derby	42	21	11	10	67	49	53
Liverpool	42	20	11	11	60	39	51
Ipswich	42	23	5	14	66	44	51
Everton	42	16	18	8	56	42	50
Stoke City	42	17	15	10	64	48	49
Sheffield Utd	42	18	13	11	58	51	49
Boro	42	18	12	12	54	40	48

Coming so near and yet so far was a bitter pill to swallow after so much hard work. But it had been a wonderful return to the top division. To finish seventh in our first season at that level was a great achievement, especially given that Luton and Carlisle, the two teams promoted with us the previous summer, were both relegated. But when I look back on that 1974-75 season, I can't get away from an overriding feeling of disappointment. We were so close to a team that could have brought a first ever league championship to Teesside. All that was needed was a prolific goalscorer. All too often we had a heavy reliance on our defence to keep a clean sheet in the hope that we might pinch a single goal win. We were so difficult to beat but we simply didn't score enough goals. Only Liverpool conceded fewer goals but we scored fewer than any other team in the top half of the table. That was our downfall and, frustratingly, it was to remain the case for several years to follow. The truth of the matter is that we peaked as a team that season.

9

Tales from Down Under

THE RAIN was hard, the pitch resembled a muddy bog and the sun was nowhere to be seen. Not quite what I'd expected of my first visit to Australia. But much, much worse than the uncharacteristically inclement weather was my own rather sensitive condition. There are few ways to say this without drawing too vivid a picture so I think it's best if I just tell you straight - I was suffering from the worst bout of diarrhoea imaginable and I have never yet seen a public convenience on a football pitch. Yes, I was in a pretty bad way.

Welcome to Perth, Western Australia in the May of 1975. This was our end-of-season tour Down Under, taking in Norway, Denmark and Russia along the way before reaching the normally warmer climes of Thailand, Australia, New Zealand and Tahiti. If that sounds exciting and exotic, well who am I to argue? Certainly, it was great fun and a fantastic experience. But that awful day in Perth stands out in my mind for all the wrong reasons.

We had arrived in the city at 10 o'clock two nights earlier feeling extremely jet-lagged after a series of exhausting flights. From Norway, we had first flown to Denmark for an overnight stay in Copenhagen before embarking on a horrendous 11-hour flight to Tashkent in Russia. After a thankfully brief stop-off, we were back on the 'plane for a 10-hour journey to Bangkok. Another stop-off, this time for five hours, was followed by a four-and-a-half hour flight to Singapore, a four-hour wait for a connecting flight and finally a five-hour trip to Perth.

I was frustrated by the fact, that while most of the lads had enjoyed several hours' sleep during the journey, I had not slept a wink. I have to be horizontal before I can sleep so long flights have always simply been a case of grinning and bearing it. I'd had plenty to drink and taken two sleeping tablets and yet

Extra Time – The Final Chapter

throughout the flight remained seated bolt upright with eyes like Marty Feldman that just would not close. Suffering from severe fatigue, I was naturally relieved to reach the sanctity of our hotel where my head hit the pillow within minutes of our arrival.

I awoke the following morning to the sound of children playing outside. Further investigation revealed that opposite our hotel were five rugby pitches on which local youngsters were competing. It thrilled me to think that, although the noise I was hearing sounded just like any kids I'd ever heard enjoying recreation, this was the other side of the world. It was 75 degrees outside so, after a light training session, I and the other lads spent the majority of our day sunbathing next to the hotel pool - much to the amusement of the Aussies, who were in fits of laughter at the sight of the white bodies on the Poms.

That evening, I was still feeling dizzy from all the travelling but hunger got the better of me and, along with most of the lads, ordered a take-away pizza which turned out to be the biggest I've eaten in my entire life. As it happens, it was also the first pizza I'd eaten as I had never previously seen one back in England. Having satisfied both my hunger and my curiosity by consuming the entire pizza, I retired to bed. But what I had hoped would be a peaceful night's rest before the first of our friendly games against a local side the following day was soon transformed into long hours sat on the toilet. Following violent stomach pains, I began to pass the pizza through the eye of a needle. Let's just say I had never before nor since suffered such chronic diarrhoea.

Knowing the team had a three o'clock kick-off against Western Australia the following afternoon, I made my predicament known to coach Jimmy Headridge soon after rising, fully expecting to be relieved of the burden of a game of football. No such luck. Jimmy informed me that I would have to play as Stuart Boam was still suffering from jet-lag and had apparently developed a rather nasty rash and lumps all over his body. I was far from thrilled about the prospect of playing in such a state.

I spent most of what remained of the morning on the loo and even missed Jack's pre-match team talk as I was occupying the toilet at the time. Given my condition, I thought it wise to wear two slips under my shorts. They were to be fully utilised. Playing alongside Brian Taylor in central defence, my first jump for a high ball was accompanied by the excretion of a certain amount of the previous night's pizza. The secretions gathered momentum with every lunge, tackle or leap until I could feel it trickling down the inside of my leg. Long before half-time, I was horrified to notice that the brown liquid was beginning to gather at the top of my sock, behind one of my knees. At that moment I was grateful for the hard rain that had greeted our arrival on the pitch before the game, the muddy conditions helping to camouflage my embarrassment.

I was grateful to hear the sound of the half-time whistle and headed for the dressing room expecting to receive much sympathy and be replaced. Instead, I was informed that travel sickness among many of the players meant we were down to the bare bones and I would have to play on. Having spent the majority of the interval back on the toilet, I left the dressing room for the pitch wearing two clean white slips as replacements for the rather brown-coloured pairs I had worn in the first 45 minutes. Back on the pitch, I looked around for the guy I had marked during the first half, only to discover he had withdrawn to a midfield role. Whether this was a tactical move by their coach or this guy's own decision, I will never know, but I rather suspect he would not have enjoyed being too close to me during those first 45 minutes!

Returning to the hotel after the game, I was again desperate for the loo and headed quickly for the room I shared with Stuart Boam. As I turned the key and opened the door of the room, there was a rather chirpy Stuart horizontal on his bed. "Ay up, Willie. How did you get on, lad?" he asked in a broad Yorkshire accent.

"Never mind that," I responded. "I suppose the rash and the lumps have disappeared now, have they?"

I could have guessed his reply. "Yep," he smiled. "I'm feeling a million dollars now, thanks very much!" I could have killed him - but for the fact I was back on that damn toilet.

I'm pleased to be able to say the rest of the tour was far more enjoyable. After hearing of the club's plans to treat us to the trip, none of the married lads had looked forward to telling our wives that we were about to disappear for five weeks of the summer holidays. Needless to say, the news went down like a lead balloon with my wife Diane. But I was excited about the trip from the word go and it was to live up to my expectations.

We began the tour somewhat closer to home, playing Norwegian sides SK Brann and Viking Stavanger. Before those fixtures, however, there was drama at the airport when Harold Shepherdson got into an almightly argument with Customs. Hidden at the bottom of the players' boot skip were two dozen bottles of

Extra Time – The Final Chapter

whisky which the eagle-eyed Customs officers had discovered. The price of whisky in Norway was probably quadruple its price in England at the time and I have a sneaking suspicion this little perk was one of the main reasons why Jack was so keen on our annual trip to Scandinavia - especially considering he was such good pals with Brann's coach Billy Elliott. Jack had travelled on ahead of us and there was a look of horror on Shep's face when the Customs officers told him they would have to confiscate the booze, but he knew he was fighting a losing battle and eventually left the airport empty-handed.

From Norway, we flew to Copenhagen before the long journey to Tashkent. Jack told us that we could relax and enjoy a drink or two during the flight but once we were Down Under we were to get down to the serious business of winning games and making new friends in the hope that the club might be invited again in years to follow. Not being the best of flyers, I quickly devoured several lagers in an attempt to relax. It was then that I spotted Graeme Souness drinking Moet Chandon. No wonder he was later dubbed a Champagne Charlie! Being a working class northern lad, my sophistication levels hadn't stretched far beyond lager and bitter but I decided to join him for a bottle of bubbly. At Graeme's suggestion, we soon added orange juice and arrived in Tashkent, high in the Russian mountains, in a rather happy state of mind thanks to an over-indulgence in Buck's Fizz.

As we disembarked the plane, I was disturbed to spot our escort to the airport building. There at the bottom of the steps were 20 Russian soldiers, each carrying a machine gun. I consoled myself with the thought of spending the next hour in duty free whilst our plane was refuelled. But my naivety was driven home when we were handed an "information sheet" which was nothing but a blank page. Amid the most primitive of surroundings, there was nothing but tea and coffee for sale and the prospect of another 10-hour flight suddenly began to seem strangely appealing. Certainly, our stay in Tashkent was the longest hour of my life and I was relieved to get back on the plane.

Next stop Bangkok. This was to be only a brief stop-over in a hotel as we were to fly on to Singapore five hours later but we had a change of plans when a Ronnie Corbett look-a-like jumped on to our bus just as we prepared to leave the airport. For one English pound each, "Ronnie" offered to give us a guided tour of the city and we all readily agreed that it was too good an opportunity to miss. So we travelled into Bangkok instead of taking the opportunity to rest and I was soon wishing we were staying in that magical city for much longer. The atmosphere of Bangkok was absolutely wonderful but we were soon back at the airport and on our way to Singapore and finally my date with destiny in Perth.

The hectic schedule of our tour continued unabated following our 1-1 draw with Western Australia. We had to leave our Perth hotel at the ridiculous time of 5am to catch an early morning internal flight to Adelaide. After touching down at about one o'clock, we were horrified to discover that a tour of the local naval base had been organised for later that afternoon. The courier who told us of the many beauty spots along the way that afternoon spent much of the coach journey talking only to the driver and Mr Insomniac himself, Willie Maddren. As I looked around the bus, I noticed one head after another bouncing off the windows as the lads took the chance to get in some much-needed rest.

The fun really got going the following day. In preparation for our next friendly against South Australia, Jack had organised an evening training session under floodlights on the Adelaide pitch. In their wisdom, Jack and Jimmy Greenhalgh went off on their own for an afternoon's fishing, instructing me and Boamy to organise taxis to take the players to the ground if they weren't back by six o'clock. That afternoon, seasoned drinkers Bobby Murdoch and Alan Foggon took John Craggs to the pool bar and proceeded to get him completely and utterly pissed on Bacardi and Coke. By the time six o'clock came around Craggsy was blotted with a training session about to take place in front of a thousand curious locals and the Australian TV cameras.

By 10 to seven, there was still no sign of manager or coach and Stuart and I were busy making plans for the training session. Five minutes later, Jack and Jimmy arrived back from their fishing trip, looking more than pleased with their afternoon's work and no doubt having enjoyed a few beers along the way. Arriving at Adelaide's ground, we quickly got on with training. Jack started with a session of shadow football. For those not in the know about such things, this involves the ball being played out from the goalkeeper, to the back four, through the midfield and up to the front men to finish with a shot at goal. All this is done without opposition.

For the first five minutes, Craggsy would go on overlapping runs without ever receiving the ball. Given the audience and the watchful glare of Jack, we attempted to protect John by refusing to pass to him. This only inflamed the situation as, in his alcohol-induced state, he began to yell: "Give us that f***ing thing!" Unfortunately, a square pass from Armstrong accidentally bypassed Murdoch and arrived at Craggsy's feet. As he attempted to take the ball in full stride, he trod on it and fell full length on to the pitch. Realising that something was amiss, Jack turned to Boamy and demanded to know: "Where the hell has Craggsy been this afternoon?" Stuart shrugged his shoulders.

Somewhat embarrassed with one of his player's antics in front of the media, Jack changed the session to shooting practice in which each individual would play a one-two with him before shooting. I distinctly remember that Jim Platt did not have a save to make from the first five shots on goal as all missed the target. As I prepared to shoot, Jack turned to me, a look of exasperation etched on to his face: "For f***'s sake, Willie, hit the target," he pleaded. Whack - my shot was hit true and hard, straight over the bar! Next in line was young Peter Brine, all too often Jack's whipping boy. As Peter played the ball up to Jack and got the return, the ball hit a divot with the consequence that the resulting shot not only went over the bar but over the stand and out of the stadium. Mortified and angry, Jack drew a line under our shooting practice there and then and moved on to something a little more basic before we embarrassed him further.

But that was not the end of the drinking. Having fought out another 1-1 draw with South Australia, we decided to celebrate Souey's birthday that evening in our Adelaide hotel. Of course, Graeme, in his own inimitable style, ordered the usual Moet Chandon and invited Boamy and I to join him for a few drinks in his room. After about an hour, there was a knock at the door. One of the boys had pulled a young lady and was about to engage in sexual activity in one of the rooms at the far end of the first floor. Wearing only briefs and Y-fronts, the three of us decided to investigate.

We hadn't gone 50 yards when up went the panic-stricken shout: "Here comes Jack - quick, get back to the room!" With a quick about-turn, we raced back towards Souey's room. Graeme and Stuart got there seconds before me and slammed the door behind them. I was still beating the door and shouting to be let in when Jack ascended the staircase to my right. His glare told me he was not best pleased. "What the hell is going on?" he yelled, staring at my attire and banging on the bedroom door. Graeme opened the door, rubbing his eyes as if he had been awoken from a deep sleep. Inside the room, Stuart was under the sheets imitating a deep snore. But Jack wasn't buying any of it. He was furious with all three of us and fumed: "That's it - no more drink on the tour. If you can't behave like adults, that's the last of the booze."

Realising it was futile to continue pretending, Souey admitted that we had perhaps been a little vociferous but this was only due to the fact that it was his birthday. Suddenly Jack appeared more sympathetic, to the point that he accepted our offer of a glass of Moet and even began to see the funny side of the story.

Even so, Jack wasn't to be messed with and was very much his own man - as I had witnessed in the hotel restaurant the previous evening. The club's vice-chairman George Kitching let it slip that chairman Charlie Amer was about to knock down The Shaw's Club outside Ayresome Park to make way for a new sports hall. As we quietly ate our meal, our attentions were suddenly drawn to the raised tones of Jack's voice, demanding that George got on the phone to England immediately to tell Charlie that he was not to start any building work without his permission.

George began to stutter his protest: "B-b-but J-J-Jack..."

He was cut dead before he got out more than two words. "Get on the phone NOW!" yelled Jack.

As the club's vice-chairman left the room to make that phone call at the manager's insistence, an embarrassed silence fell on the room. But poor old George had no chance as Jack had the sort of personality to dominate most people.

Boamy and myself had several heated debates with Jack during the tour and every time it was about money. The club had granted us only £2 a day in expenses and none of the lads felt it was anywhere near enough for five weeks away from home. In fact, on refreshments and incidentals alone I spent over £400 of my own money during the tour, quite a sum in those days. But Jack refused to buckle. His blunt reply remained: "That's all you're getting. End of story."

From Adelaide, we travelled to Brisbane to play Queensland in what turned out to be a comfortable 4-0 win. The morning after, we moved on to Surfers' Paradise on the Australian Gold Coast, about 90 minutes from Brisbane. Before an overnight stay, we took up an invite to visit a local marine park where Flipper, the dolphin of TV fame, performed tricks. An enjoyable morning with Flipper was followed by a visit to a private beach where we all had a go at surfing for the first time in our lives. It really was paradise. In fact, I was enjoying myself so much in the surf that I accidentally strayed outside the protection of the shark nets which surrounded the beach. I was blissfully unaware of this until a lifeguard pointed out to me that unless I wanted to be eaten alive, I had better get back behind the marker buoys. Naturally, I acted on his advice and the idea of a shark attack began to prey on my mind. Indeed, five minutes later, whilst back within the safety of the net, a piece of seaweed touched my foot and my paradise found suddenly seemed far less attractive. My arms never stopped beating until I had reached the safety of the shore and I did not venture back into the water again that day.

With my heartbeat back to its normal rate, we spent that evening at an orange garden with outdoor pool tables. As Souey and I enjoyed a few free lagers, courtesy of our hosts, I turned to him and reflected: "What a magnificent life we live, Souey. To think that we're getting paid for this." I couldn't help but think back to the early winter games some months earlier when my outlook was at a low ebb. Now, here I was enjoying all the benefits of a truly luxurious lifestyle.

Having said that, not all the lads were as happy as I was about the tour. Several spent much of the time whinging about our accommodation and all the travelling. Admittedly, the travelling was hard. We had a tight schedule and were constantly on the move but I loved every minute of it. Witnessing such a different culture on the opposite side of the world was a truly wonderful experience for a working class boy from Haverton Hill.

The adventure continued when we made our way to Wollongong, an industrial area close to Sydney. There, a crowd of almost 5,000 saw us beat a team called Balgownie. But I remember Wollongong far more for the late night phone call I received in my room at the Cabbage Street Hotel - a hostelry the lads inevitably nicknamed the Cabbage Patch. Boamy and I, sharing a room as always, were fast asleep when the phone rang at about three in the morning. I answered it to be greeted by the deafening voice of my now ex-wife Diane, demanding to know why I had sent only one postcard in the two weeks I had been away. She went on to tell me that Pat Cuff, our reserve team goalkeeper, had sent a postcard to his wife Christine for every day of the tour. It was just my luck that Diane had invited Christine to stay at our house during my absence. As I sat in pitch darkness listening to Diane's furious rantings, I was embarrassed to think that Stuart might be listening to me receiving such a verbal blast from my wife. Trying to keep the conversation to an absolute minimum, I was saying things like "Yes", "Right", "Fine", "I will". Eventually Diane rang off and I quietly replaced the receiver, hoping Stuart had slept through it all.

Just as I settled back to sleep, Stuart sat up in bed, flicked on the bedroom light and grinned: "You've just had the biggest bollocking of your life, haven't you?" I could only answer "Yes."

The following morning I gave Cuffy - who was obviously still in love - the most almighty verbal stick in front of the rest of the lads, informing all and sundry how he had got me into hot water. "And what the hell do you find to write about every day?" I asked.

That day I kept an appointment to visit an old ICI colleague of my sister's, Pauline Kearton, her husband Colin and her brother Dave. On hearing my tale of woe, Pauline had the wonderful idea that I should make a taped message for Diane, to send back to the UK. With a recorder and 90-minute tape at my fingertips, I sat in the Kearton's garage for an hour - by which time I had found enough words to fill only about two minutes of the tape. Every few minutes I would record a message, rewind it, listen to it and think it was far too soppy. Then I would start the process again.

But Pauline and Colin's hospitality was fantastic as I shared a mouthwatering afternoon meal with them. We enjoyed huge king prawns which I said must have cost a fortune. But that was far from the case. They explained that all they needed to do was go to a little inlet nearby after dark, shine a torch into the water and these giant prawns would swim to the surface. The prawns could then be fished out with a big net. "Mind you," said Pauline. "You have to be aware of the sharks when you're at the water's edge." I recalled my time back on the Gold Coast and thought to myself that I wouldn't have ventured near the water's edge for the tastiest prawns in the world.

Our short stay in Balgownie over, the team moved on again, this time to Newcastle and a friendly with Northern New South Wales. There, Jack picked himself as a substitute after informing us that he had a bet with the chairman, who with director Mike McCullagh had now joined us from England. Jack's bet meant he stood to win £50 for every goal he scored. If we helped him score, he promised, then he would share his winnings with us after the game. No sooner said than done. Just before half-time Terry Cooper went on a typical mazy dribble, beating four players and rounding the 'keeper, before leaving the ball on the line for Jack to toe-poke it into the net. As we ran riot to the tune of 8-0, Jack was given a second goal on a plate. But much to our irritation, he never so much as mentioned our financial arrangement after the game.

One good thing did, however, come out of our comfortable win. Watching from the stands that day was a teenager who had a talent for soccer but was growing frustrated with the lack of opportunity for his skills to flourish in his homeland. Watching Boro gave him the impetus to pay his own airfare to England

Extra Time – The Final Chapter

some months later for a trial with the club. His name was Craig Johnston, later to star for both Middlesbrough and Liverpool.

We left Australia for New Zealand with Christchurch our first stop. There, I met a former Whitby Town player called Kevin Mulgrew who I had known well before he had emigrated Down Under. On hearing of my forthcoming visit, Kevin had written to ask me to bring him some Adidas boots as they were about twice the price in New Zealand. In his letter, he had also revealed that Christchurch was one of the most beautiful cities in the world and I considered it something of a tragedy that I would see nothing of the place due to our tight time schedule. I rang Kevin on the morning before our game with Christchurch and arranged to meet him in town. Needless to say, our meeting point was a bar and I took Souey along as extra company. After enjoying a swift half of lager, we agreed to join Kevin on a grand tour of Christchurch, despite Jack's orders that we should spend the afternoon in bed for our usual pre-match kip.

As we followed Kevin around the city's streets, yours truly capturing the sights on my movie camera, little did we know that we had been spotted by Jimmy Greenhalgh and Jimmy Headridge. As a consequence, we were summoned to Jack's room on our return to the hotel later that afternoon. He was far from happy that we had disregarded his orders and told us we were both lucky that we weren't being sent back to England on the next available flight for breaking club rules. Actually, I can't help thinking that we may well have been on our way home but for the fact that we were two of his better players. Even so, I was happy to receive Jack's rebuke as Graeme and I were the only two players to see Christchurch in all its glory.

That evening Kevin, who had represented his adopted country on many occasions, played centre-forward for Christchurch as we ran out comfortable 2-0 winners. The game was memorable only for the fact that late in the game Jack gave in to sub Malcolm Smith, who had pestered him throughout the match to be given a run-out. With about 15 minutes to go, Jack told Malcolm to take off his tracksuit and prepare to go on. Moments later, Mally missed the simplest of chances and, out of sheer devilment, Jack pulled him off. It was the first time I had ever seen the substitute substituted. Poor old Mally left the field in disgust and I don't think he has ever forgiven Jack to this day.

On we went to Auckland where we ran up an easy 5-1 win despite playing our third game in three days. Afterwards, Jack relaxed his no drinking rule to allow us to enjoy ourselves prior to flying out for the final leg of our tour, in Tahiti. Our

Tales from Down Under

Who said I was a donkey?

'plane touched down in the capital, Papite, at the usual unearthly hour of 3am and we eventually arrived at our hotel an hour later. We were informed that there would be three to a room so Souey, Frank Spraggon and myself lugged our cases to our room on the far side of the hotel complex. As we entered the door, we were greeted by a huge cockroach that came scuttling towards us. Frank took off his shoe and hit the roach several times without success before finally splattering it across the floor. I was last into the room and noticed that Frank and Graeme had already claimed the two single beds. All that was left was a small camp bed in the far corner of the room. After undressing, I climbed in only to find the bed's short legs would collapse every time I put my weight on them. After several unsuccessful attempts to remedy the situation, I gave up and spent the night flat on the floor with the discomforting thought that the friends of the creature zapped by Frank's shoe would soon be crawling all over me. I had no option but to simply pull the blanket over my head and try to drift off to sleep.

We were woken at 10 o'clock the next morning by Jimmy Headridge, with orders to pick up our cases and meet in the reception. We were moving accommodation. There had been several complaints about the quality of the rooms, not to mention the creatures inhabiting them. Graeme and Frank quickly disappeared out of the door but I was delayed. Finally, as I picked up my case and headed for the exit, I was stopped in my tracks by the sight of a huge rat with nine-inch tail scurrying by the door. "What kind of place is this they've brought us to?" I wondered to myself. Moments later, my question was answered. As I carried my case along the pathway and turned a corner, I was awestruck with the sight before me. From my lofty viewpoint, I could see the thatched cottage roofs belonging to another part of the hotel complex and the full splendour of the Great Barrier Reef.

Extra Time – The Final Chapter

This time we had truly arrived in paradise. It was a magnificent place, boasting a jetty on the end of which was an area from which we could dive into the warm waters of the Pacific. It was like diving into a warm bath while the colours of fish swimming beneath us were quite breathtaking.

I well remember the day during lunch when Millsy raced in to tell the lads that a Tahitian girl was nude and diving into the sea off the end of the jetty. It takes a lot for footballers to down tools and leave a scrumptious meal but every last member of the squad made their way out to the jetty that day. We sat watching the grace of the girl's performance and I was amazed that her male companion took our attention in such good humour. Indeed, when club director Jack Hatfield arrived, this guy was quite happy for his girlfriend to pose topless with us for an impromptu team photograph!

After such excitement, the following day's friendly against a Tahitian Select XI was something of an anti-climax, though we won at a canter, 6-0, with Big Jack getting his name on the scoresheet once again. Yet again, there was no mention of Jack's winnings from Charlie Amer being shared out among us but we were to have our revenge. The following evening, we played what was supposed to be another team from the island, but, as we lined up before the match, we recognised all the same faces from the previous day's game. Before the match, Charlie had a quiet word with me and Boamy to suggest that, as the Tahitian president's son was playing centre-forward for the opposition, it might be a nice gesture to let him score. We didn't give Charlie an answer. One glance at one another was enough to confirm that the idea was a non-starter. It was totally foreign to either of us to let anyone have an easy time. In fact, such was our effect that night, I don't think the poor lad got a kick. Late in the game, he took his frustration out on young Spike, as a result of which he was shown the red card. It was a brave decision by the referee as I had visions of him being deported to the Tahitian version of Siberia!

We completed our visit to Tahiti and the tour itself with a trip around the island. As we boarded the mini-bus for the tour, I couldn't help but notice the five grass-skirted Tahitian girls sat smiling on the back seats. Someone had kindly arranged for them to play their guitars for our amusement throughout our journey. In all the letters the lads sent home to their partners, there were stories full of cockroaches and rats - but nobody to my knowledge ever mentioned those beautiful girls!

Tahiti truly was a wonderful experience, though I'm not sure I would choose to return again with 16 uncouth footballers. After all, staring into Stuart Boam's eyes isn't quite the same as enjoying a romantic experience with the woman of your dreams...

10

Boring Boro?

THE FARCICAL events of January 21st 1976 haunt me to this day. What could and should have been the finest hour not only for that Middlesbrough team but any in the club's previous 100-year history was transformed into abject humiliation and humble surrender. Such was my desperation that I decided that my future lay away from Middlesbrough Football Club. I had suffered disappointment before but this was something new.

It was an evening which began with players and fans alike full of hope. Boro were just 90 minutes away from a first ever Wembley final. By the end of the night, the hope in our hearts had been replaced by a boiling, gut-wrenching concoction of negative feelings. I personally felt a combination of anger, despair and embarrassment that our dreams of reaching the League Cup final had been shattered, not because we weren't good enough but because the club as a whole simply hadn't prepared properly for such a big occasion.

As a Middlesbrough lad, I was absolutely gutted for the fans. I was embarrassed to look them in the eyes when the team bus stopped off at a motorway service station on our journey home, after a humbling semi-final second leg defeat at Manchester City. Even as I walked away from the services to climb back on board the team bus, it crossed my mind that perhaps I would have to leave my beloved Boro if I was to fulfil my ambitions of winning major honours and representing my country. That in itself was a heart-breaking prospect but it was one I knew I would have to seriously consider, such was my frustration at that time.

And yet such negative thoughts were far from my mind in the days leading up to that semi-final clash at Maine Road. Just eight days earlier, back at Ayresome

Boring Boro?

Park, we had hosted City in the first leg in front of 35,000 excited and expectant fans. That night you could have cut the pre-match dressing room atmosphere with a knife, such was the tension and sense of occasion. And yet we were all confident of beating City, especially on our own patch. It was City's second visit to Ayresome Park in just three days, a David Armstrong goal having clinched both points in a league encounter the previous Saturday.

As it turned out, another 1-0 win - courtesy of John Hickton - gave us a slim one-goal margin to take across the Pennines for the second leg but there was a strong belief that it would be enough. I was delighted with my own performance in that first game as I did a good job in marking City's dangerous attacking partnership of Joe Royle and Dennis Tueart, the latter in particular being a man in form and a regular member of the England squad. Watched from the stand by Les Cocker, England's assistant trainer, I was determined to prove not only to him but to myself that I was a big game player and was pleased to end the match feeling that I had performed at the top of my game.

The one-goal advantage wasn't as comfortable as we might have hoped but I was confident that we could keep it tight for the first 20 minutes at Maine Road and score a vital away goal on the break as City pushed forward. We thought we could beat anyone at the time. My only slight apprehension was that we hadn't been scoring too many goals - just 14 in the previous 16 league games - but, such was the capability of our defence, that we felt one goal could be enough to see us through.

We had reached that semi-final second leg stage having conceded just one goal in the whole competition - and that in an early round 2-1 win at lower division Bury. A lone Alan Foggon goal had seen us through in a tight home encounter against Derby in the following round before a comfortable 3-0 Ayresome victory over Peterborough had given us a quarter-final clash at Burnley's Turf Moor. In a league match earlier in the season, a Burnley side featuring the likes of Ray Hankin, Leighton James and Peter Noble had thrashed us to the tune of 4-1 but this game was a different story. Going into the match, I was consumed with a feeling that no-one was going to get past me. The game meant so much to local lads like me and David Mills who had dreamed of getting to the final stages of a major competition with our hometown team. But in the dressing room that night I could sense the mood among all the players that this was a game we weren't going to lose. And that's exactly how it turned out. Millsy put us in front in the first half and I scored a far post header midway through the second to clinch Boro's first semi-final in a major competition.

Extra Time – The Final Chapter

With our local rivals Newcastle United drawn to play Tottenham in the other semi-final, there was a confidence around the club that this would be our year for cup glory. Oh, what a shock we were in for during a night of disaster that would turn Teesside into Tearside.

I felt uncomfortable with our preparation for that second leg against Manchester City, right from the morning of the match. I couldn't believe the club's decision to travel to Maine Road on the same day as such an important match. Surely, this was one game where we should have travelled the previous day and made our preparations within the relaxed confines of a local hotel, away from the glare of the media and public. Instead, we boarded the team coach for our trip across the Pennines only on the morning of the match itself, stopping off at the Saxon Hotel, just off the M62 near Huddersfield shortly after midday. After the usual lunch, the boys retired to their bedrooms for a traditional afternoon rest or sleep, rising again for tea and toast around four o'clock in the afternoon.

We set off on the journey of 30 miles or so to Maine Road at around five o'clock. But things were about to go very, very wrong for that happy, relaxed band of players. It had been raining for three days solid and we quickly hit the sort of weather conditions that those who pass Saddleworth Moor on a regular basis have come to expect over the years - unrelenting, driving rain. Approaching the outskirts of Manchester, we hit the most horrendous congestion and found ourselves stuck in a traffic jam to end all traffic jams. We had no police escort to the ground and what should have been an hour-long journey eventually took us over two hours.

There were only 40 minutes to kick-off when we finally arrived in our Maine Road dressing room and I was not best pleased. As with the majority of my team-mates, I always liked to be in the dressing room at least an hour before kick-off, not just to sort

Flicking on a near post header against Ipswich Town's Paul Cooper, Paul Mariner and Trevor Whymark (no.10). Boamy is ready to reap the rewards on the back post.

out my footwear and get dressed at a controlled and leisurely pace, but also to prepare myself mentally for the challenge ahead. But our late arrival meant that the normal relaxed build-up was replaced by scenes of near chaos. Just 20 minutes before the most important match in the club's history, players were rushing around trying to sort out tickets for family and friends. Worst of all, it was clear that the pitch was quite waterlogged and we would need the longer style leather studs for our boots, to keep our footing. Farcically, there was just one pair of pliers to change the studs on our footwear and there was clear concern on the faces of some players as they waited their turn to prepare their boots. It was a complete nonsense.

By the time we left the madness of our dressing room and walked on to the pitch to the deafening roar of over 44,000 supporters, my frustration with our poor preparation had evaporated. I felt confident that we would not be beaten and would clinch our place in the League Cup final. We were just 90 minutes away from creating club history and there was every reason to believe we could do it.

That confidence was shattered within a little over 10 minutes of the game starting. By then, we were 2-0 down and all our pre-match tactics to contain and frustrate City had been thrown out of the window. It had been my experience that whenever a team arrived late at the ground it would inevitably concede an early goal. This match was to be no exception. The game was less than five minutes old when Peter Barnes chased what looked like a lost cause down their left flank and whipped in a near post cross that little Ged Keegan met with an acrobatic diving header, leaving our defence as embarrassed onlookers.

Five minutes into the game and the tie was all-square. But it was about to get much, much worse. There were only 11 minutes on the clock when a speculative 25-yard shot from Alan Oakes skidded across the wet turf and past Jim Platt into the back of our net. I could not believe that our hard-won 1-0 home advantage had been wiped out in the space of just 11 mad minutes. So much for keeping things tight early on.

As I looked around at my team-mates, devastation and disbelief was etched on to their faces. Believing that all was not yet lost, I shook my fists at one or two of them and ordered them to pull themselves together. It was imperative that we did not concede another goal before half-time and now was the time to dig in, to stand up and be counted.

With a crescendo of noise from the home fans, City launched countless attacking waves. They had their tails up and were going for the kill but we battled on against all the odds. Experience tells you that eventually you will get into the game and that the tempo will subside. I kept telling myself and encouraging others to hang on in there and, whatever happened, not to concede another goal. By the midway point of the first half, we hadn't featured as an attacking force whatsoever but the remainder of the half saw us slowly settle down and take a foothold on the match. A golden opportunity to get back in the tie came our way seconds before the interval, the ball falling at the feet of David Armstrong with only City 'keeper Joe Corrigan to beat. It would have been the perfect time to score but David miscued the ball off the outside of his foot and on to a post. The chance was gone.

Big Jack had an awful lot to do back in the dressing room at half-time in an effort to try and bring some semblence of order to the team and install some much needed confidence. We didn't need telling that coming back now was going to be a tall order but we returned to the pitch shaking our fists at one another and generally trying to gee each other up. I still believed we could pull it out of the bag but I was not prepared for what happened soon after the re-start. Bobby Murdoch, one of the world's greatest passers, played a square ball deep inside our half. The pass was weak and inaccurate and was easily intercepted for Barnes to run clear and beat Platt for City's third goal of the night. It left us with a mountain to climb and, with our goalscoring record, a comeback like that simply wasn't on.

In a desperate bid to get something from the tie, Jack pushed me up front during the final 10 minutes or so. But my switch to the attack left us short at the back and Joe Royle scored a fourth goal for City late in the game. That was that - it was a sickening feeling to be out of the cup, having been so full of hope. But I was to gain retribution for the arrogant manner of an opponent as City celebrated that fourth goal. "How about that then!" Mike Doyle yelled into my face. Humiliated and angry, I threw a punch that would have done Joe Bugner proud, smacking Doyle hard in the mouth and knocking him to the floor. Thankfully, the incident wasn't spotted by any of the officials or a night of disaster for the team would have ended in a red card for me, to rub more salt into the wound.

Back in the dressing room, the atmosphere was one of quiet despair and despondency. In a fit of temper, I remember hurling my boots against the wall. I wondered how many of the lads felt as gutted as I did. Once again, we had let down the fans on the big occasion and I felt for them.

Whenever I recall that night I am quickly consumed with frustration. I have so many questions that will never be answered. Why didn't the club book a hotel in

Boring Boro?

Manchester the night before instead of having us travel there on the same day? Why did no-one organise a police escort to the ground? Why was there only one pair of pliers between 11 players in the dressing room? It's easy to say now, of course, but I firmly believe that, had we prepared correctly for that game, instead of the slipshod manner in which we did, we would have won our way through to Wembley. Having said that, I also believe that three or four Middlesbrough players bottled it on the night, just as they had done in our FA Cup quarter-final defeat at Birmingham a year earlier.

Time is a great healer but the pain of that defeat did not subside in the days and weeks which followed. Inside, I was hurting and angry. Eventually, I felt I had no other option but to leave the club and handed in a written transfer at the end of the season. By then I had become completely disillusioned with the club as I believed we would never win a major honour and I felt myself slipping away from the England scene. I wondered why, when it was so obvious that we were crying out for one, we had not bought a new striker, a player who could guarantee us at least 20 goals a season. David Mills was our top league scorer that season with just 10 goals.

Even Alan Foggon, our top scorer for the previous two campaigns, had moved on to pastures new but he had not been replaced. Alan's success at getting in behind opposition defences had gradually waned as the penny dropped with teams that, by defending deep, they could prevent us from dropping balls over their back four for Foggy to run on to. As soon as that happened, Alan's days were numbered and Jack knew we had to start to play a more controlled system. After a spell on the wing, Alan found himself out of the side but it was not for want of trying by Jack. Unfortunately, Alan was beginning to look on the heavy side once again and, in an effort to remedy the situation, Jack sent him for a week's stay at his mum Cissie's house in the Yorkshire Dales. The idea, for Alan to eat the right food and lose a bit of excess weight, was a good one. Where it fell down was that his hosts spent too much time feeding Alan up while he also became rather popular at the local pubs where he accepted one too many lock-ins after closing time. All this had the result of providing the opposite effect to the one Jack had hoped the break would have. By the time he returned to Ayresome Park, Alan had actually put on a few pounds, much to Jack's dismay and anger.

Jack's next attempt at improving Foggy's diet was to give him a meal allowance at Newbould's, the local butcher. For three or four months, Alan got the best money could buy - sirloins, fillet steaks, you name it. And all on the club. At

Extra Time – The Final Chapter

the time, Alan had lost his driving licence so I was his chauffeur to and from the ground each day - and getting the occasional fillet steak into the bargain. But, typical of Alan, the novelty soon wore off and the healthy meat diet was replaced by a dozen mince and pork pies. Eventually, Jack discovered that the meat allowance wasn't being used as he had intended and Foggy's little perk was hit on the head.

By now, Alan was affectionately known among the supporters as the Flying Pig, such was the excess weight he was carrying. One game, a dour goalless home draw, in which Alan was sub, stands out in my memory. Frustrated with the complete lack of goals, the crowd began to chant for Foggon to be brought on. Typically stubborn, Jack initially refused to bow to the pressure - the more they chanted, the more determined he became not to send Alan on. With about 10 minutes remaining, he relented and sent on our overweight super sub. Moments later, Alan ran on to a perfect ball over the top of the defence, took it in full stride and promptly trod on the ball and fell flat on his face. As a perfect demonstration of just how fickle the Boro supporters, especially those in the infamous Chicken Run, could be, those very same fans who had chanted his name minutes earlier now demanded to "Get the fat bastard off!" Eventually, Alan was dropped and moved on to Sunderland via a short spell with Manchester United. But he was the sort of character I was sorry to see leave.

Young lads like Alan Willey and Billy Woof were given the chance to shine in the attack but Boro's only outlay was on Phil Boersma from Liverpool. Phil was a super lad and a man I had much time for but he was never going to be the answer to our goalscoring problem. As Kevin Keegan's deputy, he had done well for Liverpool and scored his fair share of goals over the previous couple of years. On the strength of that, Jack paid Liverpool a club record fee of £72,000 but Phil simply never produced the goods for Middlesbrough.

It was the same old story for three full seasons. As our need for a first class goalscorer became ever more desperate, Jack continued to rely on a series of teenage rookies and bargain basement style signings. We scored only 17 goals in the opening 17 games of the 1975-76 season and yet we weren't far off the title pace. Jack made a move for Coventry City's centre-forward David Cross, a player both Stuart Boam and I had recommended to him on several occasions. Cross, who we had always found to be a real handful, was a great target man who scored his fair share of goals. He would have been a great addition to the Boro team. Unfortunately, we heard that Jack refused to meet Coventry's £90,000 valuation of him. Jack valued him at £10,000 less and refused to go any higher. End of story. Jack pulled out of the deal rather than settle on a compromise figure. I heard that similar bids for both Paul Mariner, then with Plymouth, and Burnley's Ray Hankin came to nothing for similar reasons as Jack stubbornly refused to pay more than what he considered to be the going rate for first class forwards.

Things got worse the following season when we scored just 10 goals in the opening 17 league games, by which time young Alan Willey was our top scorer with three. The over-reliance on our fabulous defence was becoming unbearable as we knew we had little chance of winning if we conceded even one goal. We were constantly relying on nicking 1-0 wins - a feat we achieved six times during that opening spell. Another four goalless draws underlined just how much our defensive capabilities were our only hope. The situation did nothing to convince either me or any of my team-mates that the season ahead would be anything but a battle and that mid-table survival was the best we could hope to achieve. I say that despite the fact that we were top of the league after nine games and there was much talk of us being title challengers if we could start scoring more goals.

If Jack and the directors of the club had been serious about finding Middlesbrough a top quality goalscorer, there was one player who fitted the bill perfectly. It's true that they would have had to shell out far more than the fee they paid for Boersma but I am talking about a player who would have been a revelation for Middlesbrough. That man was Malcolm MacDonald. Perhaps if Boro had shown the sort of ambition they have done in more recent years we may well have brought him to Teesside.

Supermac was tailor-made for Middlesbrough's style of play. As teams pushed forward in an effort to break down our stubborn defence, Malcolm would have been devastating alongside Millsy as their electric pace took them on to the passes of Souness, Murdoch and Armstrong. Malcolm scored 25 goals in a bad season in a Newcastle side that wasn't a patch on the Boro team of the era. In fact, I have no hesitation in saying that, had Boro signed Supermac at the start of 1974-75, we would have won the championship. Even at £333,000, the figure Arsenal paid Newcastle for his services in 1976, he would not have been a risk. After all, the club had huge assets in the likes of Souness, Armstrong and Mills and were like the Bank of England in terms of financial stability.

Perhaps the reason why Jack never considered signing a player of Supermac's quality was because he did not want to upset the club's pay structure. To attract a

Extra Time – The Final Chapter

player like MacDonald, that structure would have had to have been broken. But so what? I would have been quite happy for Supermac to have been paid twice my salary because his arrival would have boosted my ambitions with club and country. As long as I was happy with what I was getting, I wasn't bothered what other people were on, and I would hope my team - mates would have felt the same.

One thing I hadn't considered was that the club might only buy a new striker if they sold me! But that was exactly what legendary Boro skipper George Hardwick, writing in his regular column in the Evening Gazette, suggested Boro should do. Hardwick was deeply critical of the lack of fire power and wrote: "It looks as though Jack is going to play another of his trump cards in the shape of young Alan Willey. If Alan fails to score goals, then Billy Woof will have his chance to provide the answer, and if he doesn't then Malcolm Smith is liable to be thrown into the deep end yet again. It seems that if and when Smith has failed to make his mark, the Boro boss will play his final trump card, he will sign a striker, and the new man will make his debut at Ayresome Park to an almost empty stadium." It was heavy stuff and Hardwick went on: "If the cash is so tight, then I wouldn't hesitate to sell our current top star Willie Maddren and I know that that is going to disturb a lot of fans to a cry of No! But if it would get a great goalscorer to replace a great defender, it would be a good deal, for it is goals which attract the public, and not the players who stop them."

Eventually, in October 1976, Jack relented and signed a centre-forward. But the arrival from Hull City of 31-year-old Alf Wood, an experienced lower division player, was hardly the big transfer plunge we had hoped for. Alf, who had been converted from centre-back to centre-forward, was a whole-hearted player but he

Another near post header, this time against Manchester United at Old Trafford.

was not the prolific scorer we needed. Indeed, he found the net only twice in 23 league games for the club before moving on to Walsall the following summer.

Jack's reluctance to buy a truly first class striker left a big question mark against his ability in the transfer market. Jack's strengths lay on the training pitch. Within eight weeks of that traumatic defeat to Manchester City, he had given me reason to strengthen my belief that he was the best tactical coach in the country.

In February 1976, we went into a First Division clash against Leeds United at Elland Road on the back of just one win in seven league games and confidence understandably at a low ebb. That week as we prepared for what on paper was an extremely tough fixture, Jack worked on a new system of play that was not to catch on in this country for another two decades. It involved a system of three centre-backs and two full-backs - what we now, of course, call wing-backs - pushing forward into advanced positions. With young Tony McAndrew drafted in to play alongside me and Stuart Boam, it would be my job to "sweep" behind and in front of Tony and Stuart. To mislead United, I would also wear the number 10 shirt rather than my usual number six jersey. We worked on the system morning and afternoon, Monday to Thursday until everyone was absolutely sure what was expected of them. Personally, I loved my role as sweeper because it gave me licence to join in with attacks when we won the ball.

By the Thursday, however, I had grave doubts about the whole idea. Jack had taken the system to an extreme by congesting the midfield with no less than six players, leaving Millsy on his own up front. Eventually, I had to question Jack about his plans. "Yes, boss, I can see how this could work defensively but how the hell are we going to score any bloody goals?" I asked him. Supremely confident, Jack explained that if we kept it tight for the first 20 minutes, United's centre-backs, Paul Madeley and Norman Hunter, would start to push into midfield. We should simply let them play shadow football across their back four. Eventually, the home crowd would begin to give them so much stick that their full-back, Paul Reaney, would become frustrated and would start to push forward too. "By then," said Jack, "the midfield will be so congested that there'll be no hope of the likes of Bremner and Giles in the centre and Lorimer and Gray on the flanks dictating the play."

He had obviously thought long and hard about the tactics and I listened intently. But I was still not satisfied with his answer. "Yeah, but how are we going to score goals?" I repeated. With a reassuring smile, he answered: "Simply by winning the ball at the back and knocking it into the channels for Millsy. With Madeley, Hunter and Reaney all pushing up, David will find himself in one-against-one situations. From the moment David gets the ball, we must push up quickly from midfield and the back in support of him. The key is keeping it tight and not conceding a goal for the first half hour."

As we prepared for the game that day, I and many of the lads still had reservations about this pioneering tactical approach but Jack was brimming with confidence. Maybe he had played under a similar tactic at Leeds under Don Revie but I had never seen any other First Division team operate this system. I had seen glimpses of players like West Germany's Franz Beckenbauer playing the system in the World Cup but, in 1976, the traditional flat back four was used across the board in the English First Division.

Our new system worked to perfection. Everything Jack said would happen took place just as he had predicted. Every last word of his tactical advice proved prophetic. After half an hour of watching the Leeds back four stroking the ball from one side of the pitch to the other without even a glimpse of a breakthrough, the Yorkshire crowd began to give their heroes some almighty stick. Just as Jack had predicted they would, Hunter, Madeley and Reaney began to push forward and added to the congestion in the middle of the field. As we won the ball, we pushed forward from the back and quickly knocked the ball up to Millsy. The resulting 2-0 Boro win was no surprise but I couldn't help but wonder if we would have kept our own discipline had we gone a goal behind.

Two weeks later the exact same system worked again, this time helping us to inflict a truly rare home defeat on Liverpool, who were to go on to lift the league championship six weeks later. Liverpool's central defenders, Tommy Smith and Emlyn Hughes, made the same mistakes that Hunter and co. had made for Leeds a fortnight earlier and we ran out worthy 2-0 winners to further enhance our reputation as Liverpool's bogey team. That system was effective but no-one would argue that it was pretty to watch. In fact, Kevin Keegan was to famously say that he would rather go shopping with his wife on a Saturday afternoon than play against Middlesbrough. It was meant to be an insult but I took it as a tribute to our effective play.

To be fair, Keegan later qualified his criticism whilst making flattering remarks about me. "I don't withdraw that criticism," he said. "But I exempt Willie from it. He is calm, a good reader, quick and strong. He is a fair player too. He plays it hard but will do nothing untoward. He will not kick anyone - and that is rare these days."

Jack's tactical master-stroke worked wonderfully well away from home but it was not so successful at Ayresome Park when the onus was on us, as the home side, to attack. Arsenal were the first team to suss this out the week before the Liverpool win. They simply sat back and waited for us to attack them. The result was a midfield stalemate and they actually sneaked a goal to win the game. In hindsight, Jack could perhaps of changed the system to a flat back four for home games as I felt we had the versatility at the back to adapt to different tactics for home and away fixtures.

For all the disappointment of that League Cup semi-final defeat against Manchester City, we did not end the 1975-76 season empty-handed. However, the trophy we lifted came in the less-than-glamourous Anglo-Scottish Cup. It was, however, the first competition Middlesbrough had won in 100 years since the club's formation so fans and players alike took pride in the achievement.

Cheers! Jack pours me more champagne into the Anglo - Scottish Cup - a trophy I believed would be just the start of our success.

Extra Time – The Final Chapter

Regarded as something of a Mickey Mouse competition by bigger clubs like Liverpool and Manchester United, the Anglo-Scottish Cup still attracted a good standard of teams and right from the start we set our stall out to win it. Having topped a north-eastern qualifying group ahead of Newcastle, Sunderland and Carlisle, we achieved a notable 7-2 aggregate victory over Aberdeen before comfortably seeing off Mansfield Town in the semi-final. Our opponents in a two-legged final were Second Division Fulham so we had every reason to feel confident of success.

Keen to live down our reputation as a defensive, boring team, we hoped to win the trophy with a hatful of goals. It was with some embarrassment, therefore, that all that separated the two sides over 180 minutes was an own goal from Fulham defender Les Strong. The sound of the referee's whistle that brought to an end a second leg goalless draw at Craven Cottage gave me an overwhelming feeling of disappointment as we had failed to either score goals or entertain in winning that historic first trophy. We were left in no doubt about just what the Fulham fans thought of us as boos rang out around the ground as we were presented with our winners' medals and tankards on the pitch. Nevertheless, we were determined to enjoy the moment and our celebrations went on long into the night with the result that I was suffering from an almighty hangover on our return to Teesside the following day. A reflection of just how little the competition meant to all concerned was the complete lack of any sort of civic reception or official event to commemorate our success. But what the players and everyone else believed was that this would only be the appetiser and many more honours would follow in the years to come. How wrong we were.

Jack's reluctance to strengthen the squad with quality signings meant it was downhill all the way. Don't get me wrong, we were still a match for anyone on our day but as we progressed through the 1976-77 campaign it was clear that key players simply weren't being replaced. From our promotion team of three years earlier, Bobby Murdoch had hung up his boots to become the club's youth team coach, the ageing John Hickton was fading out of the first team picture and both Alan Foggon and Frank Spraggon had moved on to pastures new. Spraggon's replacement at left-back was Terry Cooper, a star of many a game and hugely popular with the Middlesbrough fans. He had the ability to drift past three or four opponents with consummate ease and, in all fairness to Spraggon, it was clear he had helped the attacking side of our game. Having said that, he would at times infuriate me as he would not cover me like Frank did. If he thought I was favourite to win a header against an opposition forward, he would simply let the winger he was meant to be marking run on. "Terry - get yourself on cover!" I would cry out. He would smile back at me and flippantly dismiss my concerns, saying: "You always win the thing anyway." If the truth be known, I think Terry had more trust in my ability than I did. It also appeared to him a good technical arrangement as it would set him up on the counter attack.

Tony McAndrew, a determined Scottish lad, who had come through the club's ranks, had replaced Murdoch in the team. Tony, however, was naturally defensive-minded and did not have the craft and cutting edge of Murdoch. We had adopted a more controlled four-four-two system but were no longer good enough to challenge for the title as the likes of Liverpool, Ipswich and Manchesters United and City added more and more quality players to their squads.

With the majority of the promotion side still at the heart of the team, however, we were still good enough to mount an impressive FA Cup run in 1977. In the third round, we were drawn against Wimbledon - though it seems incredible now, they were at that time still a non-league club - at their aptly named ground, Plough Lane. Despite protests from Jack, Wimbledon's groundsman - no doubt acting on orders - had not replaced divots on the mud-strewn pitch following a mid-week fixture and the playing surface was to prove a great leveller. Ironically, that day Boro gave Wimbledon a taste of what was to become their own trademark medicine during their rise through the the Football League. In his pre-match team talk, Jack emphasised the need for the ball to be played quickly to the front men as any attempt to play a short-passing game through the midfield would prove impossible on such a poor playing surface. In the event, neither side looked like scoring and the game ended in a goalless stalemate. The Ayresome Park replay was settled with a penalty and we marched on with an easy 4-0 success over Hereford United in the following round.

That win presented us with an exciting home draw against an Arsenal side whose new hero was that man Malcolm MacDonald. Having thrashed Arsenal 3-0 at Ayresome 11 days earlier, we were confident of progressing. This time we did not let our supporters down and tore the Gunners apart to run out 4-1 winners, courtesy of a David Mills hat-trick and a lone strike from David Armstrong. Once again, there was a belief that this could be Boro's year for cup glory but our hopes were dealt a blow with a draw which took us to Anfield to face league champions Liverpool. Even so, with two wins and a draw from our three previous visits, we went into the game believing we could win.

Extra Time – The Final Chapter

I faced a personal fitness battle even to be ready for the tie, having spent the best part of a week in bed suffering from a bad bout of bronchitis. Only on the Wednesday, three days before the quarter-final, did I rise from

Jogging around the Ayresome Park pitch in a race against time to be fit for the FA Cup quarter final with Liverpool.

my sick bed to take my baby daughter Lucy for a walk in her pram around our Hartburn home. I reported into Ayresome Park the following afternoon, still feeling breathless and very much under the weather. In his wisdom, Jack decided to send me to Blackpool for the night "to get some fresh air", where I would be accompanied by coach Jimmy Greenhalgh and Stuart Boam. Stuart had a bit of a cold himself but I think he was only really sent along to keep me company. From Blackpool, it was Jack's plan that we would rendezvous with the rest of the squad in Liverpool on the Saturday morning. "I could get the fresh air at Seaton Carew, boss," I pleaded but Jack was insistent. "Willie, you're going to Blackpool."

Having arrived on the west coast on the Thursday evening, Jimmy arranged a Friday morning training session at Blackpool's training ground alongside Pontin's holiday camp. I had been jogging in the chilly air for no more than 10 minutes when Jimmy called a halt to the proceedings and told me he would have another look at me the following morning. I think he had drawn the conclusion that I had no chance of being ready for the big game little more than 24 hours later, especially as I had failed to train in well over a week. I anticipated another training session on the Saturday morning but instead Jimmy simply told me to take a stroll down the promenade for 15 minutes and report back to him. Back at the hotel, I told him I didn't feel too bad after my brisk walk. The truth was I felt like death but the prospect of missing out on a quarter-final tie affected my judgement. On meeting

Boring Boro?

up with the rest of the lads in Liverpool later that day, our club practitioner Doctor Phillips asked me how I was feeling. Again, my answer was in the positive and I was told the final decision on whether to play would be left to me. In my mind, there was nothing to consider - I was playing.

Looking back, I was foolish to subject myself to the rigours of a crucial cup clash when I felt so sick but I simply couldn't bring myself to admit I was in no fit state for the game. There had been much media speculation that I would miss the tie so, when I walked on to the pitch a good hour before kick-off, I was greeted by a huge roar from several thousand Boro fans who had already packed into the ground in anticipation of the game ahead. Their wonderful reception sent shivers down my spine.

Though I was completely breathless, I was at the top of my form during a goalless first half and, with the Kop behind us, the team as a whole defended comfortably. In fact, I felt we were desperately unlucky not to go in at half-time with a 1-0 lead. Late in the half, Alf Wood had a header scooped from behind the line by Liverpool 'keeper Ray Clemence. There was no doubt it was a goal but, to our horror, the referee waved played on. Had the goal been given, I'm sure we would have gone on to win the game but if only Alf had made sure the ball hit the back of the net. Without any disrespect to Alf, I can't help but think that a player of Malcolm MacDonald's calibre would not have left the referee in any doubt about the validity of the goal.

Having appeared to weather the storm during those first 45 minutes, we fell behind in the second period to a 30-yard effort from David Fairclough. I was particularly disappointed with the goal because our midfield backed off and allowed Fairclough a free shot. Liverpool added a second, killer goal as we chased the game and I finished the match almost on my knees and feeling extremely ill.

Such was my fierce pride in playing whenever possible, I insisted on retaining my place in the starting line-up three days later against Birmingham despite the fact I was still very much suffering from the affects of bronchitis. In all honesty, I wasn't fit to play for several weeks after but continued to do so out of stubborn pride. It was a decision that was to hit my pocket. I didn't usually take much notice of the merit marks carried by the national newspapers but I was well clear as the country's top defender in the Sunday People until my illness. With a £500 cash prize to the winner - a considerable sum in those days - I don't have to explain that I was keen to win. But my form was less than impressive during my illness and I fell away in the ratings. Leeds United's England player Paul Madeley eventually won the award, beating me by a tenth of a point. But the deciding factor was that Paul, who had played just 32 league games, had obviously had the sense not to play when he wasn't fit while I had taken part in all but three league games.

In the eyes of the Sunday People reporters, the top players in the country that season were: 1. Gordon Hill (Manchester United), 2. Paul Madeley (Leeds), 3. Tommy Hutchison (Coventry), 4. Alan Hudson (Stoke), 5. Willie Maddren (Boro), 6. Archie Gemmill (Derby), 7. Lou Macari (Manchester United), 8. Howard Kendall (Birmingham), 9. Tommy Craig (Newcastle), 10. Liam Brady (Arsenal) and Colin Todd (Derby).

I was proud to be classed among such company. I always had the confidence to know I was among the best defenders in the country, though I know some pundits have suggested that I could have been even better if I had been a bit "tougher". I was well aware of my "Mr Nice Guy" image, which was probably a result of the fact that I refused to resort to physical or even verbal retribution when a player got the better of me. But never did I allow opponents to physically intimidate me and if revenge had to be exacted then so be it.

One player who could be particulary nasty was Kenny Burns, especially during his days at Birmingham City, and I still remember a challenge he made on me during Boro's FA Cup quarter-final tie at St Andrew's in 1975. With Birmingham ahead from what proved to be the only goal of the match, Burns went over the top of the ball in a 50-50 challenge with me, his studs leaving a painful gash in my thigh. I was incensed and made up my mind there and then to get even with him - but decided to bide my time to gain retribution. In fact I had to wait until the following season when City paid a visit to Ayresome Park for a league game. The match was only minutes old when I hit him from behind with a tackle that left him clutching his ankle. And two minutes later I deliberately cracked the back of my head into his face as I recalled how easily he could have broken my leg with that horrendous tackle. Kenny didn't need to ask what it was for and, to his credit, made no attempt to retaliate. He was always a tough competitor and, of course, became a world class defender under Brian Clough at Nottingham Forest.

Being naturally cool-tempered, it was rare for me to retaliate to a bad challenge. But I made an exception the day QPR's Stan Bowles made an over-the-top challenge on me and then had the nerve to suggest I had deliberately caused him to be sent off. I admired Bowles as a talented player and we had actually shared a few jokes during the game. But then he just snapped. I had possession of the ball in the last minute when I spotted Bowles coming in. I played the ball and attempted to jump out of the way of his challenge. But he made no attempt to win the ball and caught me on the knee. The foul brought me down but my evasive action meant he didn't actually hurt me. But it was the sort of tackle that could have resulted in a bad injury. Infuriated, I jumped to my feet and grabbed him by the scruff of his shirt. Fortunately, I didn't punch him. I thought better of it and walked away. Justice was done when the referee sent him off for serious foul play.

The 1975-76 season was a huge anti-climax after all the promise of the previous couple of years. As we all knew, we couldn't go on winning games only when we kept a clean sheet at the back and from February onwards our form nosedived as we entered a disastrous run of 12 league games without a win, all but three of them ending in defeat. It was by far our worst run since Jack's arrival at the club but it soon became evident that his time on Teesside was coming to a close.

On our way to a training session at Hutton Road one morning, I was shocked to hear Jack tell me that he would be calling it a day and leaving the club at the end of the season. I was dumbstruck as I still felt we could achieve so much if only he replaced the quality players we had lost. But Jack felt the run of defeats was ample proof that he no longer had the ability to motivate the players. I tried to reason with him, telling him that by changing the personnel he *would* motivate the team and bring about a change in the club's fortunes. But he insisted that four years as manager of one club was long enough for anyone and it would be time to move on in the summer.

Over the following weeks, Jack spent less and less time at the training ground and devoted far more of his time to his other loves of fishing and shooting, whilst he was also in big demand with the media. I found that hugely disappointing because whenever he was on the training pitch, the level of performance throughout the squad would be lifted immediately. That is meant as no disrespect to the coaches but Jack's training methods were always interesting and innovative. Sadly, Jack appeared to have become disenchanted with the game.

Sure enough, he followed through his promise and resigned at the end of April. It was a huge blow to see the big fella go. It marked the end of an era. I'm not even sure why he chose to stay those final few months once he had made up his mind he was going because it was obvious he was no longer taking the club forward. I think he was just seeing out the four years but he had completely lost his appetite for management. Like myself, I'm sure all the lads regarded Jack as a brilliant tactician, arguably the best in the game at the time. Of course, we know now that he simply needed to recharge his batteries and he subsequently went on to achieve huge success in charge of the Irish national team. His achievements with the Irish came as no surprise to me because he always had an ability to make the best out of what he had and to adopt the best playing system for the players available to him.

His departure, however, left a huge void at the club. Over the following weeks, rumours abounded about who Boro would bring in as his replacement and it was widely felt it would have to be a larger than life character with a big game background. We were in for a surprise on that front but I had far more serious matters on my mind. Within months, my career as a professional footballer was to come under threat as the knee injury which I had carried throughout my playing days finally caught up with me...

11

Game Over

TEARS rolled down my cheeks as I wept uncontrollably in the living room of my parents' house. The soft, comforting words of my concerned mother and father could do nothing to stem the flow. There was nothing they could say to make the painful truth any easier to accept. The crumpled letter which I held in the fist of my right hand was the cause of my agony. There, the type-written words of my specialist David Muckle confirmed the facts. My career as a professional footballer was over.

Deep down, I had known for some time that I would not play again. It had been 16 long and often painful months since I had last kicked a ball for Middlesbrough's first team and the excruciating agony I suffered in my right knee was the clearest possible signal that I was no longer capable of continuing a career as a professional sportsman. But to see the bitter truth, the heart-breaking reality, written down before me in black and white was a catastrophic blow. As I passed Dr Muckle's letter to my parents, the cold reality that it was all over became too much to bear and I broke down in tears.

It was the end not only of a 16-month battle to save my playing career but of a dream that I might go on to play for my country, to win major honours, to break the appearance record for my hometown club, to achieve the numerous ambitions I still had inside me. It was so hard to accept that only a month after my 28th birthday my playing days were over. To have been robbed of the best years of my career was a bitter pill to swallow and I wondered what the future held for me. A life without football, my life for as long as I could remember, was a truly frightening prospect. Since playing my last first team game for the club I had put my all into regaining fitness and concentrating my mind on the positive thought that I would one day be back in Boro's colours playing my heart out in front of thousands of passionate supporters. The idea that it might all be over was a prospect I had tried to keep out of my mind. It had been too painful to consider. Now I had to face it as fact and the reality threw up far more questions than I or anyone else had answers.

And yet it had always seemed likely that sooner or later the injury to my right knee would deprive me of the career I loved. Even from my days as a 16-year-old pro, I was carrying the knee problem that was to finish my career a decade later. During games the cartilage in my right knee would often jump out but immediately spring back into place. Despite the pain this caused, it did not give me too many problems. The cartilage would simply jump out and lock my knee for a second or two. On straightening my leg, however, the cartilage would quite violently jump back into place.

At the time, no-one but me was aware of the problem and I did my utmost to keep it that way. I didn't want to give the club's coaching staff any reason for leaving me out of the side. Little did I know that it might have cost me a career in the game had things not come to a head. Years later, Stan Anderson recalled the day Harold Shepherdson went to see him after watching me in a junior match. He was worried by what he had seen, telling Stan that Willie Maddren had been afraid to tackle.

The game was truly up, however, the day Boro's intermediate team entertained Darlington in a Youth Cup tie at Ayresome Park. That day, the cartilage jumped out and refused to go back in. As I lay prostrate trying to straighten my leg, our trainer Alec Brown raced over to me and proceeded to try and force the cartilage back into my knee, causing me considerable pain. Eventually, I could bear no more and, through gritted teeth, pleaded with him: "Christ, Alec, it's not going to go back in - just leave it." In agony, I was carried from the field.

The following day, at Middlesbrough General Hospital, the need for a full cartilage operation was diagnosed. I was informed that the tear in my cartilage was the worst of its kind, known as a bucket handle tear due to the shape it cut across the knee. The cartilage, normally a tough elastic tissue, was virtually in tatters. To this day I do not know how exactly the tear first happened. From the early age of 14, I had an ongoing problem. Nowadays, with advanced medical knowledge, the cartilage would simply be stitched back in to retain the bone's cushioning. Sadly, my right cartilage was removed, leaving the knee with no cushioning, and I was to suffer the consequences many times over.

In those days, normal recovery time - for those lucky enough to recover at all - was about six weeks. As we approach the 21st Century, cartilage injuries are no longer career-threatening but that was not the case in the late Sixties, particularly for a 16-year-old. Eager to get back to playing, I made a swift recovery until the fourth week after the operation when I was allowed to take part in a five-a-side match in an Ayresome Park gymnasium - later to become the 100 Club - in which there was barely room to swing a cat. Needless to say, the tight nature of the gym resulted in a particularly physical game. After just five minutes, an opposing player smashed a full-blooded drive into my right knee. Within seconds, the knee began to visibly swell. From that day on it would often swell after a game.

I eventually took twice the expected time to return to fitness. On the 13th week, I was picked to make my comeback for the intermediates against Bradford Park Avenue. The match coincided with my brother Dave's wedding for which, some six months earlier, I had accepted his invitation to be best man. For me, there was no option. Middlesbrough had to come first. Fortunately, Dave was understanding about my predicament.

Psychologically, however, I believe that the realisation that my dreams of becoming a professional footballer had come so close to being snatched from my grasp was the turning point of my career as I began to play with a new enthusiasm and confidence that was to make me a regular first team player whilst still a teenager.

The knee dogged me throughout my playing days. After games, it would often swell to quite shocking proportions and I frequently left the ground with heavy strapping around my knee. Although I was very rarely sidelined when it came to a Saturday afternoon, even training was a risk and, as my career progressed, I often had to sit out the rigorous mid-week fitness work my team-mates were put through. That I was ever-present during our promotion season of 1973-74 was quite amazing given the problems the knee was giving me.

I was just 22 years of age when the rigorous hill - running I had endured, mainly under Stan Anderson, finally began to take its toll. Monday morning training usually comprised running up and down the steep slopes of one of the two local landmarks, Roseberry Topping or Carlton Bank. Though going up the hill was obviously far more physically demanding, it was coming back down that gave me all the problems, particularly at Carlton Bank. We made the mile-and-a-half descent of the bank from the top of the moor down into Carlton village at full sprint, a task which subjected my knee to pounding pressure which it was ill-equipped to bear. Without the cartilage to cushion the joint, each stamp-like step down the bank would send shudders into the knee, resulting in dramatic swelling. Eventually, I knew the knee could stand it no more and was given permission to give the hill-running a complete miss.

My subsequent training was limited to flat, softer surfaces. Avoiding the tougher elements of training did, however, result in a good deal of Micky-taking from my team-mates, who took great delight in ribbing me about being a soft touch. While they all realised I had a serious knee injury, there was no way they would allow me to get away with an "easy life" without relentlessly pulling my leg. But the simple truth was that, had I trained as rigorously as they did, I would not have been able to turn out on a Saturday.

On several occasions, I had to pay visits to Middlesbrough General Hospital to have the knee manipulated, a process which involved a syringe being inserted into the joint to withdraw a build-up of fluid around it. This process was necessary as often as twice a season, though I, and those who knew about my knee problem, ensured it remained a closely guarded secret from the press and supporters.

The knee was always syringed while I was under general anaesthetic. On one occasion, however, after laying down in the operating theatre and receiving the anaesthetic, I noticed that it was exactly 10am on the clock on the opposite wall. I drowsily awoke some time later as a nurse wearing a face mask walked into the theatre. A glance at the clock told me it was now four minutes past 10 and I was horrified to think I had awoken before the operation. I closed my eyes in an attempt to get back off to sleep but to no avail. Two minutes later, I nervously pointed out to the nurse that I was awake and it seemed the anaesthetic had not worked. You can imagine my relief when she smiled: "That's alright, Mr Maddren, the knee has already been manipulated - you can wake up now." Until then I simply hadn't realised that it took such a short space of time to syringe the knee.

During a time when I was on the brink of the England squad and performing in a top First Division team, my typical training week was quite different to that of either my team-mates or any other professional player. While my fellow professionals were out pounding the hills on a Monday morning, I would be constrained to the Ayresome Park gym where I would work on weights to improve my strength and abdominal fitness. That day of relative rest from hard physical

Game Over

work would allow the swelling in the knee to subside in time for me to play in any mid-week fixtures. If there was no mid-week game, I would perhaps undertake some light training on Tuesday while Wednesday would be a day of rest for the whole squad. On Thursdays I would take part in any tactical work Jack might want to work on, particularly set pieces

I am proud to say that, despite my injury problems, I am a member of an elite club to have played over 300 games for Middlesbrough.

like free-kicks and corners. Naturally, it was important for me to be involved with practice sessions for such an important part of our play, though teenager Tony McAndrew would occasionally stand in for me while I watched from the sidelines if it was felt an extra day was needed for my knee to recover from the previous game. Fortunately, Friday was traditionally a day of light training which didn't pose any problems for me but it was always a case of getting through the week from Saturday to Saturday.

The lack of physically demanding exercise resulted in the leg losing much muscle bulk and it was clear that no amount of weights was a substitute for lots of running. It eventually reached the point where I was forced to play everything with my left foot. Until then, my right had always been my best foot though I had prided myself on being two-footed in terms of being able to use either foot in football. Nevertheless, I had to adapt to using my left foot more in order to compensate for the weakness in my right leg. It was particularly worrying that my central defensive partner, Stuart Boam, had to take all free-kicks from deep positions as I had lost so much power in my right leg and could no longer achieve the desired distance with either foot. At the same time, my turning circle began to get bigger and I was increasingly forced to rely on my own experience to get me through games. Despite this severe handicap, I was proud to receive rave notices in the media, who remained in the dark about my knee problem.

Of course, such was the seriousness of the problem, that it was occasionally

Extra Time – The Final Chapter

touch and go as to whether I would be fit to take my place in the team. One such occasion came in November 1974, shortly after Boro's return to the First Division. During a goalless home draw with our arch rivals Newcastle United, I remember chasing a long ball over the top of our defence with Malcolm MacDonald on my heels. As Supermac closed in, I stretched to toe the ball back to Jim Platt in the Boro goal. In doing so, however, I caught the studs of my boot in the heavy pitch, causing my knee to bend more than 20 degrees further than it was capable of doing. A sharp pain told me all I needed to know and the joint began to swell by the second. I was more than thankful to hear the sound of the referee's whistle a couple of minutes later and limped off the pitch wondering what damage had been done.

I eventually left Ayresome Park with the usual cotton wool bandage strapping around the knee in an attempt to reduce the swelling. As was to become the norm, that day I wore a club blazer, shirt, tie and tracksuit bottoms as I limped gingerly out of the ground. Goodness knows what those who saw me must have thought of my dress sense but this was a medical necessity rather than a fashion statement. Quite simply, it would not have been possible to get a normal pair of trousers over such heavy strapping.

Three days later, on the Tuesday night, we were due to play Liverpool in a League Cup fifth round tie at Anfield and it was obvious that I would be struggling to be ready for such a crucial match. On the Monday morning, Jimmy Headridge removed from my knee two layers of cotton wool, two layers of elastic strapping and a sticky elastic bandage to reveal an enormous amount of swelling. Further inspection revealed the knee to be very warm which meant there was still plenty of activity going on inside the joint. Erring on the side of caution, Jimmy strapped me back up and I limped into Anfield the following evening knowing a final decision on whether I should play was still to be made. In the away dressing room, the strapping was removed once again. It was clear for all to see that although it had settled slightly, the knee was far from well, but the final decision on whether to play was left to me. I wasn't about to miss such an important game if I had the choice so the name of Maddren was duly added to the team-sheet that evening.

In a game that will live with me forever, I scored the last minute goal which sealed a shock 1-0 win and a place in the League Cup quarter-final. But I didn't get through the game without a scare. Mid-way through the second half, I was involved in a thumping 50-50 challenge with Liverpool's Alex Lindsay, a player who was built like the proverbial s***house door. Neither of us were the sort to shirk a challenge and the ball flew into the air between us as we crashed into one another. My right knee took the brunt of the force behind's Lindsay's tackle and I limped away from the challenge wondering what damage I had done. That night, however, I limped out of Anfield wearing a collar, tie, tracksuit bottoms, the heaviest strapping you have seen in your life and a grin as wide as the River Mersey itself, having scored the winning goal with my gammy right leg.

I continued my week to week existence for the next two seasons, each week ending five days of painstaking training by playing what I believed was the best football of my career. All the time, I was on the brink of international honours but became increasingly frustrated by the club's lack of success. Eventually, at the end of the 1975-76 campaign, I had had enough. Although I knew it would break my heart, I decided it would be in the interests of my career to move on to pastures new. I would have asked for a transfer anyway but my hand was forced when I received an anonymous call at my auntie's house tipping me off that Coventry City had offered £220,000 for me. However, if I wanted to get away I was told I would have to act as Middlesbrough had turned down the bid and were determined to keep Coventry's offer out of the papers. Coventry may not have been the most glamourous of clubs but I might have considered going there at the time. Although they were a decent team going forward, they tended to leak goals at the back and I might have been able to stem the tide.

Having heard of Coventry's interest, I made my move. With a written transfer request to the club's directors in my hand, I went to see Jack in his office at Ayresome Park where I told him I wasn't happy and wanted a move. There wasn't a long discussion. In fact, the only words I remember him saying were: "I don't think it will be considered." That didn't surprise me. I knew I was one of the club's best players and they would not be keen to sell me. But all clubs know it is folly to force an unhappy player to stay when his heart is no longer in it. I also knew that every player had his price and felt that if Boro received the right offer for me they would let me go. Instead, within 24 hours my whole world was turned upside down.

The call came from club chairman Charles Amer at my home in Billingham. Hearing Amer's voice on the other end of the line wasn't a complete surprise. I had half expected him to call, either to accept my transfer request or inform me they wouldn't consider letting me leave. But I was not prepared for his words of advice. "I've received your transfer request," he told me. "But before you take it any further, Willie, I think you should have a word with Dr Phillips about your knee."

Extra Time – The Final Chapter

Dr Neil Phillips was the club doctor who I had spoken to on numerous occasions about my knee. On Amer's instructions, I contacted Dr Phillips immediately and was stunned by what he had to say. In his opinion, due to the severe arthritic condition of my right knee, no other club would consider buying me as they would not be prepared to take a risk with my fitness. Given the day-to-day problems I was suffering, I had no reason to doubt his words but told him I would seek a second opinion on the matter. After all, I had missed just three games in the previous four years.

With my mind in a whirl, I quickly arranged an appointment with an orthopaedic surgeon in Newcastle, an acquaintance of my old pal George Smith. Sadly, after examining X-rays of my knee, the second opinion was the same as the first. He confirmed that if he was employed as a consultant by a football club, he would have to advise them that the severity of my knee problem would make me too big a risk in the transfer market. I was hugely disappointed with the diagnosis. Not only had it confirmed just how bad the condition of my knee was but it left me in a very uncompromising position. Not only would I never now have the chance to sign for another club but I would be disadvantaged in negotiating a new contract. After all, what other option did I have if I wasn't happy with any new contract offered to me by Middlesbrough?

Despite that desperately disappointing news, I decided to knuckle down and get on with giving my all to Middlesbrough Football Club. Now I knew where my future lay, it was easy to focus on doing my best and I continued to perform well throughout the following season. Indeed, many media pundits resumed their calls to award me full England honours at a time when I knew my injury was not getting any better. Throughout this time, barring the medical practitioners I had consulted, no-one outside the club suspected I had any problem with my fitness. I found that amazing, given the number of times I left Ayresome Park in my odd-looking get-up. I spent many an uncomfortable and sleepless night with the knee throbbing like toothache. But such was my in-built desire to play the sport I loved I never once considered the consequences that playing on would have on my life in later years.

By the end of the 1976-77 season, I believed the knee needed a long rest from the rigours of professional football. It had become progressively worse over the previous months and, with Jack Charlton having departed the club, I expressed my concern to the club physiotherapist Jimmy Headridge. The first team squad was about to embark on an end-of-season tour of Australia, taking in Norway and Hong Kong along the way, and I felt it would be prudent for the club to give me a

Game Over

rest whilst giving some of the younger players a chance. The problem was that our new manager John Neal would be meeting us during the tour and, like the rest of the lads, I was keen to impress the man who would be selecting the team in future. I consequently played in the vast majority of games during our sortie Down Under.

But the tale of the aching knee was about to take another surprising twist that would leave my career hanging in the balance. After returning home from the club's tour, I decided to give the knee a complete rest instead of my normal pre-season schedule of a couple of hours' training every Tuesday and Thursday morning. That was a mistake I would regret.

By the time I reported back to Ayresome Park for pre-season training, the knee appeared to have seized up like an old working part without vital lubricants. For the new campaign, John Neal took the team to Aberystwyth where he had taken his former club Wrexham in seasons gone by. Just two weeks before the season's big kick-off at home to European Champions Liverpool, we took on John's old club in a friendly. After 45 minutes of excruciating pain, I limped from the pitch at half-time knowing that I could not play on. It was clear the rest I had given the knee had done it more harm than good and time was ticking by in my bid to be ready for our big opening day fixture. To add to the pressure-cooker feeling, I suffered a bout of bronchitis shortly after returning home from Aberystwyth.

I consequently went into that massive game against the English and European champions having played just 45 minutes against Wrexham and a further 45 against the might of Whitby Town three days before the opening day to the season. By this time, though there was plenty of movement in the joint, it was clicking and grating like an old hinge. I was naturally concerned but was eager not to disappoint the new manager in his first competitive match in charge.

The truth was that I had done nowhere near enough preparation for such a big match and I should never have played. The decision on whether I was fit to play should have been taken out of my hands but instead it was left to me and, letting my heart rule my head, I took the decision to play. Nowadays, with all the medical advice available to top players, there is no way I would even have been allowed to consider playing in such a state but, in the mid-1970's, it was left to the player to the choose.

Of all the players I might have been marking after such minimal preparation, one of the last I would have chosen was Kenny Dalglish. But that's exactly who I was forced to mark. Dalgish, full of twists and turns to test the turning circle of

Extra Time – The Final Chapter

even the fittest defender, was making his Liverpool debut after being signed from Celtic as a replacement for Kevin Keegan. Watched by a crowd of almost 31,000, the game kicked off at a white hot pace and it was immediately apparent Liverpool were in irresistible form. Within five minutes, I was absolutely knackered but kept telling myself that the pace would slow as the game settled down and I would have a chance to get my second wind. But I was horrified when Liverpool took the lead in those opening minutes. As I tracked an opponent out to the left flank, they played the ball from midfield into the heart of our defence and I could only look in dismay as Dalglish raced through unmarked to beat Jim Platt with contemptible ease.

At that moment there was fear on my face. It crossed my mind there could be an avalanche of goals and, with the condition of my knee and general fitness, that I would be the main cause of it. Fortunately, the game did settle down and after the opening 20 minutes we began to impose ourselves on Liverpool. So much so that David Armstrong scored a second half equaliser to give us a share of the spoils. I, however, did no more than get through the game. How the hell I did so - either mentally or physically - I really have no idea. Dalglish frequently left me in his wake and by the end of the game the sole of my left foot was a sea of blisters - the result of having to put so much weight on to my left leg in an effort to protect my bad knee.

That day, as always, I left Ayresome Park with my knee bandaged and strapped. But the pain was something new. I had always suffered a nagging pain after games but this was something I had never previously experienced. This was a shooting pain from my knee right up to my hip and I began to worry if I was doing myself serious damage.

I managed to get through a full 90 minutes in the following game at Norwich and a 2-0 home derby win over Newcastle United a week later but my turning circles were becoming bigger and bigger as I was unable to put any pressure on my right knee. What's more, the shooting pain meant sleeping on the night after a game was almost impossible. I was in agony throughout Boro's 2-2 League Cup draw at Sunderland but once again got through the game through sheer stubborn determination.

Our next match, against West Bromwich Albion at the Hawthorns, was to be the last of my career. I was just 26. I didn't know then, of course, that this would be the end. In fact, I naively believed I could go on and on and the knee would simply improve in time. The game was significant also for the debuts of two centre-forwards - Billy Ashcroft for Boro and Cyrille Regis for Albion - but it is a match that still haunts me to this day. Regis would go on to prove he was a handful for anyone on his day but I was far from happy that he marked his debut with a goal. He scored what looked like a terrific goal, waltzing past me, Terry Cooper and Stuart Boam to score. I was hugely disappointed with myself at being beaten with apparent ease and I knew that even a 90 per cent fit Willie Maddren would have cut out his run at the first attempt.

At half-time, I told Jimmy Headridge that I needed to come off as I wasn't performing at anywhere near my full potential due to the pain in my knee. But Jimmy persuaded me to persevere a little longer. "Give it another 10 minutes," he said. "If it doesn't get any better by then, we'll bring you off." No surprises for guessing that the knee didn't get any better and I was preparing to signal to the bench to make a substitution when Terry Cooper told me he was going to have go off as he had tweaked a cartilage and his knee had locked. By this time I was suffering real trauma and told Terry in no uncertain terms: "You can't f***ing well go off - it's me that needs to be substituted!" But we were both in for a surprise. No sooner had we finished our brief conversation than Peter Brine limped from the pitch and our sub, young Graeme Hedley, was on in his place. I couldn't believe it. After all I'd said at half-time, neither manager nor physio had even signalled to me to see if I could make it through the match. Now I had no choice. With Terry and I facing a rampant Laurie Cunningham down one side of the Boro defence, it was like Custer's Last Stand down our left flank in that second half and we did well to lose the game narrowly, 2-1.

But by the end of those traumatic 90 minutes, I knew the writing was on the wall for me. Back in the dressing room, I was in horrendous pain from a knee which now resembled a balloon. If that wasn't enough to tell me that I had gone as far as I could, then my own pride was. I had played at no more than 25 per cent of my ability that day and that was something I could not accept. It was time for meaningful action. Either I would have to rest the knee for a significant amount of time or I would have to undergo an operation to rectify the problem.

The full extent of the way arthritis was gripping my knee was revealed by an X-ray taken by a specialist the following week. Not only did the condyles - the edge of my femur and tibia - resemble craters on the surface of the moon but a loose piece of bone had flaked off and was moving around inside the joint. With the knee in such an obviously bad way, I was naturally concerned about my future in the

Extra Time – The Final Chapter

game. Watching the following Saturday's game against Birmingham City from the Ayresome Park stands was an experience which was completely foreign to me and I didn't enjoy it one bit. One of the club's talented teenagers, Alan Ramage, stood in for me and was to go on to make my position his own that season as I struggled along the long, long road which I believed would lead to recovery.

A couple of days after our defeat to Birmingham, John Neal took me to Manchester to see an orthopaedic surgeon called Mr Glass, who had looked after his former players at Wrexham. After viewing the recently taken X-rays and examining my knee, it took Mr Glass only five minutes to tell me that unless I had corrective surgery I would never play competitive football again. That news in itself, though it hurt to hear it, was no surprise to me. However, I was concerned about the success rate of such an operation and asked him what he felt the chances were of me making a full recovery. I was relieved when he told me I had every chance of getting back in the game as he had performed a similar operation on the great Denis Law some years earlier and he had made a full recovery.

I had no hesitation in agreeing to undergo the operation and was duly booked into Manchester Royal Infirmary for the following week. I asked myself what other choice did I have. I desperately wanted to continue in the career which had been all I had known since leaving school and this seemed to be my only chance. I later discovered that there was a second option that was never put to me. John Neal's decision to seek the opinion of Mr Glass ended a long-standing relationship between Middlesbrough F.C. and a local consultant orthopaedic surgeon called Mr Leach. He resented Neal taking me to another specialist and, as I later discovered, strongly disagreed with the decision to open up my knee. Mr Leach believed it would have been far better to give the knee complete rest before hyper-developing my quads to help support the knee. But that option was never given to me.

The operation itself involved smoothing off the rough edges of the joint line on the femur and tibia whilst removing the loose body that was floating around in the knee. For two days after the operation, I was in agony despite taking the strongest of pain-killers. After four days, with the pain thankfully subsiding slightly, I was allowed home to Hartburn to begin my recuperation. But if I believed the recovery process would be straight forward, I was to be sadly disappointed.

After such an operation, a patient was normally expected to be able to achieve a 90 degrees bend in the joint after two to three weeks. But fully 12 weeks later, I had achieved only a 20 degrees bend. It seemed almost as if the knee had stuck in that position as, no matter how much I tried to bend it, it simply would not budge.

Eventually, the club's new orthopaedic consultant, Mr Muckle, decided that the best policy would be to manipulate the knee. This involved bending it by up to 90 degrees whilst under general anaesthetic. But I will never forget how Mr Muckle and his medical staff turned me on to my stomach and continued to bend my knee, by up to 120 degrees, as the anaesthetic wore off and I awoke in excruciating pain. I always felt I had a high pain tolerance and yet I found myself begging them to stop as I hung on to the edge of the operating table, yelling out in agony. But rather than stop, Mr Muckle insisted that they had to keep going with the movements now that they had broken through the adhesions - basically congealed blood which had solidified within the joint. I don't know what sound was the worst - my screams of pain or the violent cracking noise which emanated from my knee as it was bent. Indeed, such was the whip-like crack, a young physiotherapist who assisted Dr Muckle that day later revealed to me that she thought he had broken my leg!

Much intense physiotherapy followed but 18 long weeks after the operation I had only achieved enough bend in the knee to enable me to walk normally. The pain and the long recovery period told me that all was not well and that the operation had not been the success Mr Glass had hoped it would be. Deep down I still hoped beyond hope that I might be able to make a full recovery and play football once again. I clung on to the notion that I could develop my quad muscles to such an extent that they could provide the knee with the required support. In all honesty, I was clutching at straws. But I had little else to keep me going. Doing what daily exercise I could, I began the long haul back

By a twist of fate, that season was also my testimonial year at Middlesbrough and I was thankful for a busy social calendar to keep my mind off more depressing thoughts. Thanks to the hard work of testimonial year chairman Ray Robertson, a local reporter, secretary Mike Holmes, and in particular my treasurer and old friend Peter Hodgson, the year was turning into a great success. Most of my evenings were taken up with sportsmen's dinners and visits to working men's clubs who had kindly agreed to support my testimonial year. At the same time, I took every opportunity I could to travel away with the Boro first team, not only to keep me sane but so that I could approach Scotland internationals to ask them to take part in my testimonial match at the end of the season. The Scots were close to qualification for the 1978 World Cup finals in Argentina and their manager Ally McLeod had given me his blessing to approach his players and ask them to represent their country against a Middlesbrough side at Ayresome Park the following May.

Without the distraction of my testimonial year, I'm not sure how I would have got through that season. It truly was an annus horribilis. Not only was I having to cope with the mental torture of dealing with the possibility that my career might be over but my wife Diane and I were growing increasingly incompatible. Finally, midway through that horrible year we reached the point of no return. Following one of our regular barnstorming arguments, I decided enough was enough, packed my cases and headed for my parents' house. I told Mam I'd been unhappy for some time and hoped that she might be able to put me up for a month or so until I found alternative accommodation. I was somewhat surprised when she revealed that she had known I had been unhappy. I guess you can never disguise your true feelings from your mother.

Moving in was the easy bit. Living there was a little harder, despite the welcoming attitude of my parents. I wasn't the only one living back at home at the time as my elder brother, Dave, had only recently separated from his wife. The two of us ended up sharing a bed which resembled a hammock in the way we would both roll into the middle together. I was relieved that, with Dave set to leave for a job in Libya, we would only have to suffer this rather uncomfortable and embarrassing arrangement for one week. It was a rough time for me and I remember feeling particularly lonely. Having made the break from Diane, I missed my young children, Lucy and Steven, terribly.

Over the following weeks my parents killed me with kindness but I knew I had to find my own space. With Mam having had a major operation some years earlier, Dad took on the household duties and would iron for all three of us. I felt I couldn't burden him like that and eventually found myself a semi-detached on the Wynyard estate. I needed my own space so was relaxed about living on my own, though I wasn't what you could call a happy bachelor. Never having been a nightclubber, I became quite lonely in the evenings. I found the idea of increasing my social activities quite foreign but began joining my friends, John Johnson and Peter Binks, for a drink in the Station Tavern in Norton. Initially, I would go maybe once a week but this soon became two and three nights a week.

Meanwhile, my rehabilitation wasn't going as well as I might have hoped. My progress was painstakingly slow and I missed Boro's old physio Jimmy Headridge, who John Neal had replaced with Lew Clayton. Jimmy had been a tough task master and, under him, injured players were expected to spend mornings and afternoons in the gym working on abdominal and leg strengthening exercises. Lew was a nice guy but he was too soft with me. I needed someone who would work me night and day but too often he would leave me to my own devices. As a result, I became a little indisciplined over the course of the season and would occasionally arrive late for training without ever being challenged about my time-keeping. I became increasingly frustrated as I could not see a light at the end of the tunnel.

At a time when I was already lonely, I lost the daily friendship of a good mate in Graeme Souness. In December of 1977, there was much speculation linking Graeme with a dream move to Liverpool, making him increasingly unsettled on Teesside. When Liverpool's £350,000 offer was confirmed, he sought my confidence and asked me what I would do in his shoes. I admitted that if I was purely selfish I would want him to stay with Middlesbrough because I would be losing a friend and a team-mate who was vital to the Boro cause. But I told him he couldn't turn down an opportunity to join the best club in Europe. In all honesty, I don't think he needed me to convince him what was the right thing to do as Souey was an ambitious lad who had always known just where he wanted to go in life. When the move finally went through, however, I was delighted when he took the time to thank me for the straight-talking advice I had given him four years earlier.

Seeing him leave was a sad moment. With Souey gone and with severe doubts over my future, I could see the promotion team of four years earlier was beginning to be broken up as John Neal introduced his own ideas and his own players into the side. Centre-forward Billy Ashcroft was doing a reasonable job as the team's target man while the experienced Wales international John Mahoney, signed from Stoke City, was proving a good asset in midfield with his neat passing and competitive edge.

But the real find of the season was a pocket dynamo of a striker with an explosive left foot. His name was Stan Cummins. Still just 19, he had been hailed by Jack Charlton as the man to become the first £1 million footballer at a time when the record transfer was still less than half that figure. He looked a great little prospect but perhaps Jack's prediction of such a star-spangled future was just too much of a burden on the little lad's young shoulders, for he never quite fulfilled that early promise. He eventually left the club for a third of the figure Jack had predicted it would take to prise him away - and that came long after Trevor Francis had become the first £1 million footballer.

Extra Time – The Final Chapter

During my long fitness struggle, I always kept a watchful eye on the talented youngsters at the club. There were several promising apprentices but one stood out. Every afternoon after training, I would see him kicking a ball against the ground's car park wall. Left foot, right foot, left foot, right foot... with monotonous regularity. Long after his fellow apprentices had gone home, this young lad was still practising his skills. His future success was living proof of what you can achieve with dedication. For the young man was later to leave Middlesbrough to make his name in an all-star Liverpool team. Asked who I thought was the club's best young prospect, Daily Express writer Tony Hardisty put forward three names - Stan Cummins, David Hodgson and Mark Proctor. "No, there's one kid better than all three of them," I replied. "He'll be a big star - his name is Craig Johnston."

With Alan Ramage proving a capable deputy for me alongside Stuart Boam, the team were doing quite well in the league while they put together an impressive FA Cup run. I hoped the climax to my benefit year would see Middlesbrough playing in their first ever FA Cup semi-final and, when Boro drew Second Division Orient at home in the quarter-final, it seemed my hopes would be realised. With Boro going into the tie on the back of seven consecutive wins, there was huge expectation throughout the town that this would be our year for cup glory and yet my own joy was tinged with a feeling of regret that I would miss out on such a special occasion if we did reach the final. As it turned out, I needn't have got so excited. Once again, Boro disappointed in being held to a goalless draw at Ayresome Park. I travelled down to London to watch the replay and, like every other Teessider, was heart-broken to see us beaten 2-1. Once again, the poor old Middlesbrough fans were left in despair.

As the season drew to a close, I began to concentrate my mind on my testimonial match between Middlesbrough and Scotland's 1978 World Cup squad, Ally McLeod's team having qualified for the finals in Argentina in some style. The game was scheduled for May 9th, the day before the Scottish players were due to report to McLeod for their final get-together before departing for South America. Though it might seem surprising now, at the time I could not have picked more glamourous opposition for the game. The whole of Scotland had been whipped up into a state of near hysteria, such was the belief in some quarters that they could actually win the World Cup itself. Of course, it would all end in tears with an embarrassing first round knock-out after a disastrous 3-1 defeat to Peru in their opening match but at that time few people believed that such a catastrophe was possible.

Game Over

In all, I had approached 35 Scotland international players to ask them to play in my match and every last one of them had said they would be delighted to turn out for me. Experience, however, has taught me that it would have been far easier to have chosen a club team as my opposition rather than a group of individuals. Two days before the match was due to take place, just six of those players were now prepared to make themselves available for my big day. I was in a panic and shuddered at the embarrassing prospect of a so-called Scotland World Cup team lining up with several stand-in Middlesbrough players within it. The match programme had already been printed, complete with the names and faces of the Scotland stars who were supposed to be appearing on the night. Apart from my testimonial committee, I felt completely alone in facing this potentially disastrous problem as not one director of Middlesbrough Football Club ever offered words of advice. It would have been so comforting if they had told me not to worry and that, if it didn't work out, the club would make up any lost revenue.

It was the players who had let me down, however. One player who particularly angered me during this stressful period was Aston Villa's Andy Gray, now a well-known football pundit for Sky TV. On several occasions, I rang the telephone number Gray had given me earlier in the season in order to confirm his availability for my big night. On the first occasion, I believe it was his Villa team-mate and house-mate Colin Gibson who answered the phone. Gibson told me Gray was in the bath and asked me to call back in 20 minutes. This I did, ringing back on the dot, only to be told: "Oh, he's gone out." The following day, I rang again and got an identical answer. "He's in the bath - can you ring back in half an hour?" 30 minutes later, I called again, only to be told he had, once again, gone out. I was fobbed off in a similar fashion twice more until, in complete frustration, I gave up on Gray.

On Sunday May 7th, two days before the game, Ray Robertson and I sat in the offices of the Northern Echo where he worked, two very concerned men. Ray made one last attempt to contact Andy Gray, only to be told - you've guessed it - he was "in the bath". He must have been the cleanest footballer on the go - or simply a man who didn't have the common good manners to say he didn't want to take part in my game after all. Ray told Colin Gibson that he was disgusted with Gray's lack of courtesy. "If he doesn't want to play in Willie's game, all he needs to do is say so," he said. "To leave him in the lurch like this is totally unacceptable". Later, I told Graeme Souness to tell Gray that if ever I did get fit again I would look forward to the next occasion I would play against him. Souness himself was a key member of

Extra Time – The Final Chapter

the Scotland squad but, like Kenny Dalglish, was unavailable for my game due to Liverpool's involvement in the European Cup final the following night.

In sheer desperation, Ray called Brian Clough to ask him to reconsider his decision to insist none of Nottingham Forest's Scottish players took part in the game. Having inspired Forest to the league championship in their first season back in the top flight, Clough felt they had already played too many games and had informed us some weeks earlier of his decision. But if he would release Archie Gemmill, John Robertson and Player of the Year Kenny Burns, then we would be close to a full Scottish team. Ray rang Brian at home and gave him the sob story about how so many players had let us down and could he possibly reconsider his decision and let his players take part. "Give me 15 minutes," came Cloughie's reply and the phone clicked. I think they were the longest 15 minutes of my life. But exactly a quarter of an hour later, the phone rang. As I sat tensely waiting to hear his decision from the other side of a table, Ray listened intently to Cloughie, nodded and finally, to my huge relief, gave the thumbs up sign. "You don't need to ring my chairman, all three lads will be there," Clough assured Ray. "I will guarantee that. And don't give them any gifts or money for turning out - they've earned enough this year as it is." It was a marvellous gesture by a man often painted in a less than positive light.

There was more good news from Manchester United's Martin Buchan who rang my mother to say he would, after all, be able to play in the game for at least 45 minutes. A couple of weeks earlier, Buchan had been in touch to say he would not be available after pulling his groin. Another player I contacted to confirm his appearance was Sandy Jardine at Glasgow Rangers. "No problem, Willie," he confirmed. As we chatted, I revealed to him the struggle I was having in putting a

Back in training at Ayresome Park - but I was never to play professional football again.

189

Game Over

team together, to which Sandy suggested his Rangers team-mate John Greig might be willing to play. Although he was no longer a current Scotland international, Greig had won many caps and was still a mainstay in the Rangers team. "Give me 10 minutes and I'll ring you back," Jardine told me. Sure enough, he called back and I was delighted with his message: "Yes, John will come down - but only if he plays the full game." I was more than happy to confirm he could play the full 90 minutes. After my experiences with Andy Gray and others who had let me down, Sandy Jardine and John Greig had helped to restore my faith in my fellow professionals. Now I would have 11 full Scotland internationals on show and I would not face the embarrassment of appearing to deceive the Teesside public about Middlesbrough's opposition on the night.

In terms of numbers through the turnstiles, the game was a huge success, attracting 18,000 fans. Given the fact I had been out of the first team for almost a full season, that was a great turn-out and I will always be grateful to those fans who supported that important night for me. Newcastle United's Micky Burns turned out as a guest for Boro while Sunderland's Bobby Kerr helped to swell the Scottish ranks alongside internationals like Gordon McQueen, Derek Johnstone, Ian Wallace, Jim Blyth, Tommy Hutchison plus, of course, Burns, Gemmill, Robertson, Jardine, Greig and Buchan. The result itself, a 5-5 draw, was almost irrelevant.

I celebrated the success of the game in the Dragonara Hotel where I presented gifts to my committee and the Scotland players as tokens of my appreciation. We moved on to the Madison nightclub where well over 1,200 people danced and drank the night away. I left there at about 3.30 in the morning, feeling very happy. After just three or four hours' sleep, I rose to set off for London to see Graeme Souness play for Liverpool against Bruges in the European Cup final at Wembley. Joe Harrington, a member of my testimonial committee, accompanied me to the national stadium where we were thrilled to see Graeme give a great performance as Liverpool retained the trophy thanks to a single strike from Dalglish.

I found my testimonial year physically and emotionally draining and was relieved it had come to an end on such a high. After so many frustrations with my knee, I particularly looked forward to an end-of-season break in Portugal which John Neal had arranged for the first team squad. Each morning at nine o'clock, John accompanied me to the beach where he got me jogging, though it was very much a case of jog one, limp one as I was still in quite obvious pain. After training, we would go to one of the local bars and I found we got on very well with one another. Very easy going, John was a quite different character to the single -

minded guy Jack Charlton was in his early days. It was clear we shared similar opinions on how the game should be played.

Back on Teesside in the build-up to the new season, John called me into his office where he gave me a surprising offer. "How would you like to become Boro's first team coach?" he asked me. I was quite taken aback and asked him why he was making such an offer. He revealed to me that he was not seeing eye to eye with Jimmy Greenhalgh, who was the first team coach at the time. I was flattered by John's approach but told him that I still thought I could regain my fitness and get back into the first team. As tempting as it was, I felt being the first team coach would have been too much of a distraction from my main priority of getting fit again. John was disappointed but ended our conversation by saying: "Never mind, there will always be a job for you at this club as long as I am manager." It was a promise he would not keep.

At the start of the following 1978-79 season, having kept fit as best I could throughout the summer, I joined John and the rest of the first team squad for pre-season training in Aberystwyth. The first week back in training after a long summer was always tough but much of our work involved running on the sand dunes, something I found almost impossible. I was still a long way from being fit and consequently took part in no more than 50 per cent of the training.

Nevertheless, I continued to work as hard as I possibly could on the knee. But the harder I worked, the more fluid I seemed to get on the knee. Finally, about six weeks into the season, I was pushed into a reserve team game at Hull City. It was my first competitive action in well over 12 months and, if I'm honest, I think it was a case of make or break. The club's coaching staff knew they had to put me under a bit of pressure and see if I could last through 90 minutes.

Before the match, I remember Hull player Alan Worboys was shocked to see me in Middlesbrough's reserve team. I had to explain to him that this was my first return after a long-term injury. Later in the game, I was on my last legs as Alan and I chased a long ball through the middle. As we both gave chase, he tried to give me encouragement by shouting "C'mon, Willie, you can do it." I eventually got through 80 minutes but I was operating at no more than 40 per cent of my full fitness. Quite honestly, I was embarrassed and was only glad the match was away from home. Worst of all, it took me two weeks to recover. It took that long for the swelling and pain to subside. I realised there and then that I was nowhere near ready for a return.

Game Over

When the pain had subsided, I was again picked for the reserves, this time at Rotherham on a frosty October evening. The ground was frozen hard - the last thing I needed in my condition. Once again, I struggled even to get through the game. In the crowd that night was my old boss Jack Charlton, by now manager of Sheffield Wednesday. One glance from Jack after the match was enough to tell me he knew I was struggling badly.

But I wasn't the only one who was struggling. Boro were at the wrong end of the First Division table, having taken only four points from their opening nine league games whilst being dumped out of the League Cup by little Peterborough United. Everyone in the club was feeling the pressure and though winger Terry Cochrane was signed in a record deal, it was clear money needed to be spent on more players if we were to pull out of the slump. As a consequence, I think the club wanted the insurance money that they would only receive with the official announcement that I had hung up my boots and retired.

In action for Boro for the last time, against Sunderland reserves at Ayresome Park.

Whatever their reasons, the club began to hype it up that it was make or break time for me. If I didn't play in the first team game at home to Norwich on October 14th - a game which would see Cochrane make his Boro debut - they claimed my career may be at an end. It was announced that a reserve team outing against Sunderland three days before the match would be my final warm-up game before making my first team return. I knew I had no chance of being ready. It was taking me at least 10 days to recover in between each reserve match and I couldn't even train afterwards. It was plain to see I was being set up for a fall.

The Sunderland game itself could not have started any worse. With Billy Woof sent off in the opening five minutes, the back four - including me - was forced to work overtime for the next 85 minutes. With a larger than average crowd at

192

Extra Time – The Final Chapter

Ayresome to see Boro take on our north-east rivals, I was embarrassed for myself. Many of the young lads in the reserves that night sensed my embarrassment too. I played the entire match on one leg and as I sat in the bath after the game I could see my knee visibly swelling. I hadn't a cat in hell's chance of being ready for the Norwich match.

The inevitable duly happened. I accepted that I wasn't fit to play against Norwich. Even I was now beginning to concede that my playing career was over. The attempted salvage job on my knee had simply accentuated the problem.

Even so, I was disturbed and angry by what the club did next. As I watched 'On the Ball' on my TV at home on Saturday lunchtime, I was shocked to hear it announced that it looked as though my career was over. If I was dismayed at that, I was sent into a rage when I picked up the morning paper the following Monday to read a statement from the club confirming my career was over. I couldn't believe it. I was honest enough to realise that it was probably the truth but there was surely protocol to follow in such situations. At no time had I been told by a specialist or anyone of note that my career was officially over.

Now they were trying to take the decision out of my hands. That day I received a telegram from Graeme Souness, who had obviously heard news of the club's announcement. Graeme's message read simply: "Sorry to hear about the news. Will ring you soon - Graeme." It seemed it was commonly believed that Willie Maddren had retired - and yet I was completely in the dark. I was so angry with the way the club had gone about the situation, I immediately called a press conference to announce that, in my opinion, my career was not over at all. I did it out of sheer awkwardness.

After reading my comments in the press the following morning, Charles Amer summoned me to John Neal's office where they both sat waiting for me. "What the hell do you think you are doing, Willie?" Amer demanded. I left him in no doubt about the way I felt over the club's handling of the situation, telling him: "I think it's absolutely atrocious that the club could make a statement about me like that without my knowledge or approval." Amer asked me what alternative I felt I had. Determined not to back down, I insisted I would continue trying to get fit until I was personally convinced there was no way back. Throughout our heated conversation, I was embarrassed by Neal's silence. He never offered a single opinion. This, the man who only months earlier had promised me there would always be a job at the club as long as he was manager. Whether Amer had told John

Game Over

not to offer me a job, I don't know, but it was clear that the offer was no longer on the table.

I was just 27 but I wasn't going to allow anyone to bully me into retirement. It was my belief that the club wanted me to retire so it could claim the insurance money on me. If I remember rightly, I asked Amer for £2,000 in return for which I would formally announce my retirement and walk away. I didn't want the money. But I wanted to prove in my own mind that this was all about money. His only response was to say I had already made money through my testimonial match the previous year. I was furious that the club was prepared to offload me in such an off-hand manner. I had given them 10 years of my life and left myself a virtual cripple in the process. I had always believed that in return for my loyalty the club would look after me and keep me on in a coaching capacity once my playing days were over. But here they were showing me the door in no uncertain terms. I was desperately disappointed that my long association with Middlesbrough should end in such bitter acrimony.

To be fair, I had no real gripes with Amer. Although he was never a popular man among the supporters, until that moment I had not had much to do with him. But I bitterly resented the way he handled my final days with a club to whom I had devoted my entire career. Had he approached me in a sensible manner and said: "Look, Willie, I think we need to make an announcement that your career is now over", I would have found it far easier to accept.

Instead, I simply refused to go and eventually left Amer and Neal, promising to stay on at the club. For another four months I battled on against all the odds, training as best I could and desperately working on the knee. In truth, I was probably fooling no-one but myself. Though I still held on to even the slightest hope that I might play professional football again, I knew it was useless. The knee was not getting any better. I was finished.

Finally, I had to concede defeat and get on with my life. It would be a new life away from Middlesbrough Football Club - a frightening prospect in itself - but one I knew I had to face. Finally, in early February 1979 - 17 months after playing my last game - I officially hung up my boots. I did so after being examined by the club's orthopaedic consultant David Muckle who confirmed what I already knew - that my right knee would never again be able to cope with the demands of the professional game.

Two days later, I received a copy of Mr Muckle's letter to Charles Amer and

Extra Time – The Final Chapter

John Neal confirming his diagnosis. It was dated the previous day, February 4th, and read:

Dear Mr Amer and Mr Neal,
re: W. Maddren Middlesbrough F.C.

I examined this player on 2.2.79. Reluctantly I had to advise him to give up his occupation as a professional footballer with Middlesbrough F.C. or any other club.

I explained that the injuries and problems with his right knee had led to impaired mobility and power in this knee and that he would risk further, and perhaps more serious, trauma if he continued to play football. The player understood the nature of the problems involved and the future risks and agreed with this advice.

I would like to add that no player could have worked more diligently in an attempt to overcome the knee problems and he is to be complimented on achieving the muscle power and tone in the right lower limb he has accomplished.

Yours sincerely,

David S Muckle.

Clutching the letter in my hand, I left Ayresome Park for the last time as a Middlesbrough player for that tearful visit to my parents' home. After 354 first team games and 21 goals, my career was over and it hurt like hell.

A couple of days later, the club got in touch to offer me the chance to do a lap of honour at the following game at Ayresome Park. I rejected the idea out of hand, a decision I regret to this day. Although such an event would have been extremely emotional, I wish I had shown my appreciation to the Middlesbrough fans and equally let them show theirs. But I could not escape the feeling that injury had robbed me of greater honours and I would be forever left to wonder "What if..."

In his programme notes for the following home game, John Neal wrote: "Recently the sad medical verdict was announced on Willie Maddren. This has

Game Over

been one of the bitterest blows I have had in my management career. I recognised when I was a manager of another club the value of this great player and it has been my misfortune not to have seen Willie playing in my time here when 100 per cent fit. You can judge by the inflated prices paid for top class players, the shortage of players like Willie. I feel sure that had he been 100 per cent fit, my job here would have been just that little less difficult. You proved what you thought of this popular local lad last year when you gave him a magnificent testimonial and I am sure you would want me to wish him on your behalf the very best for the future. To finish playing when in one's prime must be a bitter blow, but at least Willie must have known in his own mind that it was inevitable."

12
In Retrospect

I HAVE often wondered just what I might have achieved in the game but for that knee injury which dogged me throughout my playing days and eventually brought a premature and painful close to my career. I might have been tempted to move on to a more ambitious club than Middlesbrough, perhaps following a similar line to Graeme Souness at Liverpool. I feel I was good enough to have played for Liverpool, Manchester United or any of the top clubs of the era. Many fans remember me as a great player and that is comforting. But I know in my heart that given an injury-free run to the age of 30 I would have been twice the player I was. I also believe I would have been a regular England international. That is not an idle boast as I believe the facts speak for themselves.

I was on the brink of the England team for several years but was never capped due to a number of reasons. Playing for an "unglamorous" club who were rarely featured on TV or challenging for honours didn't help. And, of course, but for the injury I might have moved on to pastures new. Equally, but for the knee, I honestly believe I could have played until I was 40 as I wasn't a big drinker, looked after myself and found playing at the back an absolute doddle. The majority of players do not peak until their late 20's and early 30's and I would still have had all that to come. Even at Middlesbrough, I feel I could have forced my way into the England team as I reached the peak of my form. My main attributes were an ability to read the game and see things early.

Fellow professionals, fans and members of the media have often stated over the years that I was the best uncapped centre-back in the country during the mid-1970s. Of course, their words are meant as praise but I have never liked that "uncapped" label. I would much rather have been simply *one* of the best capped centre-backs of the era or one of the best internationals in Middlesbrough's history. Instead, I ended my career with five England under-23 caps but none at full international level.

In my testimonial programme, Malcolm MacDonald presented his theory as to why I had not been capped by England, commenting: "The ironic thing about Willie Maddren's testimonial is that he should not really be having it. In my opinion, loyalty to Middlesbrough has cost him his rightful place in the international spotlight and a chance to move around the Football League circuit. For me, Willie was the natural progression from Bobby Moore. His reading of the game and on-the-field command ranked him alongside England's World Cup winning skipper."

Even so, I took immense pride when I was voted by fellow former Boro professionals as the club's fifth best player of all-time in a book called *Boro's Best*, published two decades after my last game for the club. Only Graeme Souness, Juninho, Gary Pallister and Wilf Mannion received more votes. When you consider that I had only half a career - albeit over 340 games - that is the highest accolade.

Of course, I was tipped for an international future from a young age when both Stan Anderson and then Nobby Stiles stated publicly that I would go on to win England caps. And yet when the first of my under-23 appearances came along it was completely out of the blue. That first chance at international level came in March 1973 when Ipswich Town's Kevin Beattie was a late withdrawal from the squad prior to a game against Czechoslovakia at Villa Park. Boro trainer Harold Shepherdson, who was also trainer for the England team, recommended me to the national coach, Sir Alf Ramsey, as an able replacement.

With Boro lagging behind the Second Division pacesetters at the time, an international call-up couldn't have been further from my mind and it actually took some time for my wife Diane to persuade me that she was not joking when she informed me that the club had rang to say I was to travel to the West Midlands the following day.

With Harold Shepherdson giving me such support, I was delighted to read the comments of Boro coach Ian MacFarlane who said: "Willie has performed heroics for this club. He is one of the best - and certainly one of the most consistent - sweepers in England at the moment."

Having travelled down to the England hotel in Sutton Coldfield with Harold on a Sunday evening, I teamed up with the rest of the squad and had a rather

Willie Maddren   Extra Time - The Final Chapter

Above: The Farraday Hall school team. That's me holding the ball (front centre).

Left: Getting into the party spirit on my 21st birthday

Below: On an Anglo-Italian Cup trip to Italy with George Smith (centre) and Alan Moody.

Willie Maddren

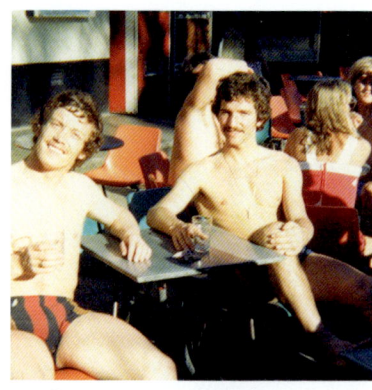

Extra Time - The Final Chapter

Left: Me and Graeme Souness step out in style. Now that's what you call fashion victims!

Above: Enjoying a drink during a summer holiday with Souey during our Boro playing days.

Below: Well, it has taken me more than 20 years, Jack, but I finally got you with this picture. This is Jack Charlton doing his traditional collection of the players' tracksuits before kick-off – with slight addition to his jacket.

Willie Maddren   Extra Time - The Final Chapter

Above: Marking Franny Lee during the 1974-75 season which saw Boro and Derby vying for the First Division title. Franny was known by many defenders for his ability to dive in the box.

Right: In action for Middlesbrough. I pride myself at having played over 350 games for the club before injury brought a premature end to my playing career.

A look of concentration hides the stress as I watch my struggling Middlesbrough team during my managerial days. Flanking me are physio Steve Smelt and club doctor, Lawrie Dunne. In the dug-out behind us is young Stephen Bell, whose whinging almost resulted in my resignation.

Trying to keep my emotions in control as I walk on to the pitch at the Cellnet Riverside Stadium with my youngest children, Laura and David, before my benefit match in 1996.

Willie Maddren **Extra Time - The Final Chapter**

I have never appreciated the time I have spent with my family more than I have done over these last three difficult years. Here, I am pictured after my benefit match with my children, Steven, Laura, David and Lucy. Oh, and some guy called Juninho!

With Hilary and Jack Charlton at a MND fund-raising event. The effect the drugs I take to combat the MND can be clearly seen on my face.

The love I share with Hilary and my children keeps me going when I am at my lowest ebb.

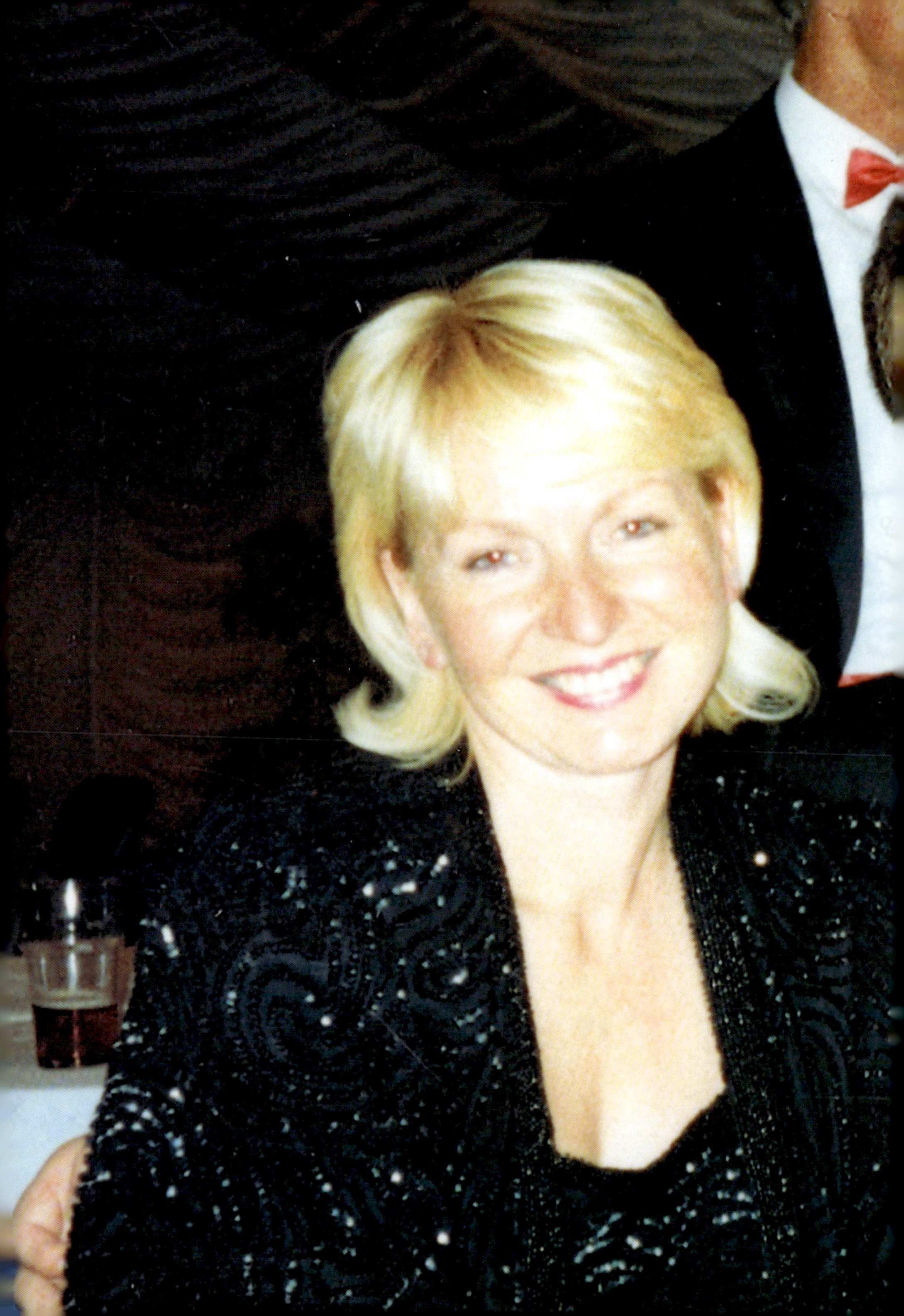

Hilary has been a pillar of strength for me since the day I was told I was suffering from Motor Neurone Disease.

Match of the Day: With my wonderful wife Hilary on our wedding day.

embarrassing first meeting with Sir Alf. That evening, Alf took it upon himself to greet each of the players individually and I can still recall him going around a table shaking hands with each player and greeting them by name. "Hello, Charlie." "Hello, Tony." "Hello, Tommy." When, however, he arrived at yours truly there was a deafening silence as he gave me a blank look. "Hello, err..." It was obvious he did not have a clue who I was. Fortunately, Harold tactfully brought an end to the silence and introduced me to a man I was hoping would pick me to represent my country three days later! To be honest, it reminded me of home as Big Jack had insisted on calling me Tony McAndrew for his first three months with Boro.

Despite that rather unpromising introduction, I started to feel very much part of things during training over the next few days and was greatly impressed with Ramsey, who insisted on players calling him by his Christian name. There was no standing on ceremony. I found him to be a shrewd tactician who could motivate players in a quiet, persuasive way. I was delighted when I was picked in the starting line-up to take on Czechoslovakia, who were the reigning European under-23 champions. My mother, who was in the Villa Park stands along with several members of my family, still remembers the deep intake of breath I took whilst standing for the national anthem prior to the kick-off. I'm not ashamed to admit I was extremely nervous about the challenge ahead as the only times I had previously been among such distinguished company had been when Middlesbrough were drawn against First Division teams in the FA Cup. Before the game, Alf told us that the Czech side included nine full internationals and it crossed my mind that I may well be out of my depth.

But I did not disappoint either myself nor anyone else that night. Following a nervous opening 10 minutes, I managed a goal-saving tackle which gave me the confidence to settle down and go on to enjoy a fine debut. The pace of the game was quite frantic and it took me time to become accustomed to the ball being passed at such speed and accuracy. I was particulary amazed to see one of our midfielders, Tony Currie of Sheffield United, constantly dropping back towards me when I had the ball in defence. Currie wanted the ball whether he was marked or not. I found this quite strange as in the Second Division we were taught to bypass the midfield and knock the ball directly to our forwards. But Currie was so good that he could receive the ball despite such intense marking. In truth, the quality of the players around me helped make my debut relatively easy and we eventually won the match 1-0, courtesy of Charlie George's goal. In fact, I was unfortunate not to score in the second half but my glanced near-post header from

In Retrospect

a corner hit the upright and rebounded to safety.

As I walked from the pitch at the sound of the final whistle, I was proud as punch to have played at the top of my game for my country and against such quality opposition. As I entered the dressing room, Harold Shepherdson gave me a nod of approval. Naturally, he was proud and no doubt relieved I had played so well, having recommending me to Sir Alf in the first place. He had risked allegations of being biased towards a Middlesbrough player if I had been overawed by the occasion. Later, Sir Alf thanked me for a fine performance - and even remembered my name! "Thanks for coming, Willie - and well done." I thought this quite unusual, the England manager thanking me for playing for my country. I would have thought anyone would have given their right arm for such an opportunity. I couldn't help but think that the thanks were all mine. I would have walked to the Midlands in by bare feet for the chance to represent my country. The next morning I was pleased to read the media agreed with my own thoughts that I had given a good account of myself. I was well aware that national newspaper reporters could be quite scathing when covering England games at any level. That first international experience, albeit at under-23 level, gave me a new found confidence which spilt over into my Second Division performances with Middlesbrough.

When Beattie withdrew from the under-23 squad for a close-season tour of Denmark, Holland and Czechoslovakia, I was again called upon as his replacement. Having enjoyed such a good debut, I was disappointed not to be in the original party but when Harold called me to give me the good news, I was over the moon. Sadly, I was suffering with my knee injury at the time and was never fit enough to play. But Ipswich Town's commitments in Europe meant Beattie was again not available when the under-23's took on Denmark at Portsmouth in November 1973 and I duly won my second cap in a 1-1 draw. From then on, I was a regular in the under-23 squad alongside players who would go on to make big names for themselves - players like Trevor Francis, Bob Latchford, Terry McDermott, Charlie George and Gerry Francis.

I was grateful to both Graeme Souness and Jack Charlton at this time for publicly backing my international claims. Souey gave me a glowing tribute when he stated in the press: "If Willie shouldn't be in the England side, I know nothing about the game. He is without doubt the best professional at our club and he has helped me a great deal. I can't but admire his tremendous talent for the game and appetite for training. I can't remember the last time he made a mistake on the field.

Extra Time – The Final Chapter

That is a measure of just how much he means to Middlesbrough. What better example could a bloke like me, with no real ties and no responsibilities, have? I reckon that he has played a major part in making me the player I am today. A couple of years ago I was down in the dumps, convinced I had made a bad mistake in leaving Spurs for Boro. I let myself go, put on weight and I suppose I didn't really care. Then one day, over comes Willie and gives me a right going over. He asked me did I really want to play the game and if I did, there was only me who could do anything about it. It made me stop and think alright. Since then I have never looked back." It was good of Souey to acknowledge my contribution to his rise within the game.

Receiving the Boro Player of the Year award from the Old Codgers Association as Stuart Boam, John Hickton and David Armstrong look on.

Meanwhile, big Jack stated: "There is no better back four player in the league than Willie." That was some accolade considering I was still playing in a Second Division team at the time, albeit one gunning for promotion. Personally, I felt the best central defender in the country was Leeds United's Norman Hunter.

Further England recognition followed in March 1974 - and this time I was joined in the under-23 squad by my Boro team-mate and old friend, David Mills. It was a special moment for the two of us, having come through the ranks together, right from our pre-Boro days in the Stockton Boys team. We both played well in a 2-0 win over Scotland at St James' Park, Millsy scoring the first goal, though Souey was not so chuffed with my progress on this occasion - he was on the losing Scotland side!

Shortly after celebrating Boro's wonderful promotion that summer, Millsy and I joined up with the England party once again for a series of games against Turkey, Yugoslavia and France. I wasn't involved in the opening match of the tour against Turkey in Ankara, a game which was abandoned at half-time due to heavy rain, but I went on as a sub in Yugoslavia and then won my fifth and final under-23 cap

In Retrospect

four days later against France in Valence.

When the former Leeds United boss Don Revie succeeded Sir Alf Ramsey as England coach during the summer of 1974, it initially seemed my international fortunes would take a marked upturn. Sadly, this was not to last long. However, I was pleased to be included among the 80-man squad of prospective England players Revie named for his first get-together. Those players, he said, were in the running to help England qualify for the 1976 European Championships. Both David Mills and David Armstrong were also named in the party which met in Manchester as way of an introduction to what Revie expected over the forthcoming months.

Of course, Revie would have to leave the majority of those players out of the full squad when the first competitive game came around but I was delighted to be named in the party to take on Czechoslovakia in a European Championship qualifier in October 1974. I was now being ranked alongside players of the highest calibre and yet it is heart-breaking to look back and consider that I was the only member of that 23-man squad who did not go on to play a full international. Don Revie's first ever England squad was: Shilton (Leicester), Clemence (Liverpool), Madeley (Leeds), Nish (Derby), Hughes, Lindsay (both Liverpool), Watson (Sunderland), Beattie (Ipswich), Hunter (Leeds), Maddren (Middlesbrough), Todd (Derby), Dobson (Everton), Bell (Manchester City), G. Francis (QPR), Currie (Sheffield United), Brooking (West Ham United), Hudson (Stoke City), T. Francis (Birmingham), Clarke (Leeds), Worthington (Leicester), Thomas (QPR), Channon (Southampton), Keegan (Liverpool).

Coming just a couple of weeks after Revie selected me for a 16-man "All-Star" squad to take on Sheffield Wednesday in a benefit match for the late Eric Taylor, I was full of confidence that I was very much in his mind with regards to the European Championship qualifying campaign. At the time, Boro were flying high in the First Division, having just beaten Derby County at the Baseball Ground, but I was struggling to keep down the swelling in my knee. I was at a stage when quite substantial strapping was required after every game to reduce the swelling. It was difficult enough knowing I had to impress the new England manager without having to disguise the fact that I was carrying what had become an irritating injury. However, I took the precaution of taking off the strapping back in the hotel before a training session which involved a full scale practice match.

On a wet Sunday morning, I took my place in the defence of a Possibles line-up against a Probables team. From the bench, England's assistant coach Les Cocker shouted a series of orders, telling me to drop off, get hold of the ball and spread it about. This I did with great effect and with the utmost confidence and I could see Les was delighted with my performance. Only half an hour into the game, however, my whole world was turned upside down in a freak incident. A harmless long ball came over our midfield towards me, about 25 yards out from goal. I was under no real pressure but, at the last second, decided to back-head the ball to our goalkeeper Peter Shilton. Little did I know that, without calling, Peter had raced off his line to take the ball. As I turned around, I was horrified to see the ball bouncing over the goal line with Shilton stranded just yards behind me. I wanted the ground to open up and swallow me there and then. What if this had been a full international in front of 100,000 fans instead of a Sunday morning training session with no spectators to witness my error? And yet in over 340 career games, I scored not a single own goal. Indeed, Jack Charlton once complimented me by saying that I made fewer mistakes than any other player in the First Division. And yet I look back on that occasion and wonder whether that one error convinced Don Revie that I would not be reliable in a full England shirt. I would be extremely disappointed if that was true, of course, but I do believe it could have been a deciding factor in my future non-selection.

In fact, Jack went out of his way to point out that I was the sort of player who only tended to get a mention when I made an uncharacteristic mistake. "Take it from me, he is as good a defender as there is anywhere," he told Tony Hardisty of the Daily Express. Such praise from my club manager was a great boost but it was clear that on the international front I still had to convince Revie of my worth. I retained my squad place for a second Euro Championship qualifier against Portugal at Wembley in November '74 but again failed to make the starting line-up.

Derby's defender Colin Todd was very much the man in the driving seat in terms of England selection in the central defensive position and Jack admitted that it was possible I could remain in his shadow for some time. In another press interview, he said: "For years Norman Hunter lived in the international shadow of Bobby Moore. All the pro's knew how good Hunter was and how effective he would have been in an England shirt, but with Moore so firmly established for his country, Norman had to wait years before getting the chance to prove himself at that level. Maddren could have the same misfortune. It is now assumed that Colin Todd is in Don Revie's team to stay. It is difficult to argue otherwise. He is a tremendous player - although Maddren is much better in the air. Kevin Beattie would get a lot of votes if Todd was not available - both are great competitors - but neither is better equipped than Maddren."

He is also quoted as saying I was "too good to be noticed". That might seem a strange comment to make but I think I know what he meant by it. Jack's words were: "Willie was a good all-round player but, if anything, he lacked a gimmick to attract attention. He was not brilliantly outstanding. On the other hand, he was never bad. I established a reputation through the fact that I scored goals standing on the goal-line. This brought me more attention. There was very little about Willie's game I had to work on. There were problems with everyone else but not him. I would say he made fewer mistakes than anyone else in the Football League."

And yet that cherished England chance never came my way and I couldn't help but wish Todd would just disappear. By the summer of 1975, having been named Boro's Player of the Year, I was dismayed to be out of the squad altogether. When Boro's two David's, Mills and Armstrong, were selected in a 35-man squad for a get-together in May of that year, I stayed at home and I was left to wonder why. From that moment on, I was completely overlooked. Calls for my selection continued right through to my last full season before my injury but confirmation that I was no longer in Revie's plans came in a newspaper article early in the 1975-76 season. In the article, Revie defended Boro's playing style and named four players he obviously rated. I wasn't one of them. At that moment, I knew he simply didn't fancy me as a player.

Of course, I wasn't stupid enough to say I wasn't interested in playing for my country. I would have been deeply honoured had the opportunity arisen but I had privately accepted that I was unlikely to win a recall to the full squad. Then, in March 1977, I knew it was time to write off all hope of being selected as long as Don Revie was in charge of England. When Mick Doyle, Brian Greenhoff, Roy McFarland and Kevin Beattie were all ruled out of a World Cup qualifier against Luxembourg at Wembley, I thought my chance would come and I would be called up as a replacement. Instead, Revie chose to bring in Bolton's Paul Jones. If he was ever going to select me, that was the time.

Over those years, I had to come to the conclusion that Revie had some sort of bias towards players from Middlesbrough. And I say that knowing that he was born in the town. For while Mills and Armstrong were included in full England squads, like me, they were overlooked when it came down to selecting the team.

Extra Time – The Final Chapter

Mills was never capped at full level, while Armstrong had to wait until a tour to Australia, under Ron Greenwood, in 1980. In addition, John Craggs, Stuart Boam and Terry Cooper were all overlooked despite having strong claims for recognition by their country.

Without doubt, the media influenced the selection of England players - and none more so than BBC Television's Match of the Day, presented by Jimmy Hill. Basically, it boiled down to one thing - if you were a friend of Jimmy Hill's, you had a great chance of getting in the England team. He would often go into raptures about Manchester United defender Brian Greenhoff. Without wanting to blow my own trumpet, I know full well that I was quicker, read the game better, possessed more aerial ability and passed the ball as well as Greenhoff. And yet he won 18 England caps whilst I won none. Where Greenhoff had an advantage over me was that Manchester United - "a glamour team" - were featured on Match of the Day every other week while Boro were lucky to make it on there even once a season. The sheer lack of profile given to Middlesbrough contrived to disadvantage the international prospects of anyone who played for the club. On the few occasions Match of the Day did make the effort to make the long trip up to the north-east, they seemed to pick goalless draws. That would give them all the excuse they needed not to return for another year!

Like Greenhoff, Emlyn Hughes of Liverpool undoubtedly stood out more as he had the benefit of playing for a high profile club. I will concede that perhaps Middlesbrough's system of play might have had a detrimental effect on the international hopes of individuals. We used to hit the ball to our front men early and were never encouraged to play it out from the back in the way that Liverpool or Manchester United tended to do. In doing so, their defenders would certainly have stood out more and perhaps looked more cultured in their play.

In my opinion, however, Revie should have considered the entire Boro back four for England selection. Instead, he capped none of us. No-one can tell me that not one player from that fabulous defence, with one of the best goals against records in the country for several years, was worth a single cap. John Craggs, Terry Cooper, Stuart Boam and myself must surely have done enough to justify at least one of us being capped over the years. The likes of Liverpool's Phil Neal deprived Craggsy of England caps while Leicester right-back Steve Whitworth played for his country several times under Revie - and yet he was not fit to lace John's boots.

John's partner at left full-back was Terry Cooper. Terry had suffered with injuries during his final couple of years with Leeds United but when he joined Boro he was still the best left-sided full-back in the country. Revie, who had of course been Cooper's manager at Elland Road, had even called him up on his return to fitness with Leeds. But his move to Boro brought an end to all international recognition. I found that extremely puzzling.

Alongside me in central defence, I had Stuart Boam. Again, Stuart was one of the best centre-backs in the country during the mid-70's and our defensive partnership was the equal of Todd and McFarland at Derby or Hughes and Thompson at Liverpool, four players who won a combined total of 160 England caps. But Stuart's profile had one fatal flaw. He played for unfashionable Middlesbrough. End of story.

When I look back and compare myself to the players selected ahead of me by Don Revie, I can only wonder why I never got a chance. But don't just take my word for it. Tony Hardisty of the Daily Express wrote: "I think of Emlyn Hughes and Phil Thompson (Liverpool), and Mike Doyle (Manchester City) getting cap after cap. None of those players has been more skillful or consistent than Willie Maddren. Had Willie played for a more successful club I am certain he would have played time and again for his country." Players like Phil Thompson, Roy McFarland and Dave Watson all played regularly for England. Kevin Beattie was far better in the air than I was. Indeed, I would go as far as to say he was the best header of the ball I ever saw - and that includes Hugh McIlmoyle. During crossing sessions in training for England's under-23's, Beattie would bury nine out of 10 headers on goal, such was the power and accuracy he achieved. However, I think I had the edge over Kevin in terms of reading the game. I also made fewer mistakes than he did - and that is ultimately how a good defender should be judged. Colin Todd, meanwhile, was not as good as I was in the air, mainly down to his lack of height, though he was maybe a tiny bit quicker and had the edge over me in terms of his tremendous passing range and ability on the ball.

Whether I would have won England caps had my career not been cut short at such an early stage, we will never know. I do know, however, that I enjoyed the sort of career and lifestyle that the vast majority of people can only dream about. Despite the bitter disappointment of being robbed of half my playing days, I take great comfort from my many wonderful memories of playing for my hometown club in a golden age of football. I know I can hold my head up and say I played my part in one of Middlesbrough's best ever teams and gave the Teesside public many happy memories. I know too that I was highly respected among the football press and was delighted when the Daily Mirror's Charlie Summerbell wrote this tribute to me in my testimonial programme: "It's trite to say that Willie has given Middlesbrough consistently brilliant service. He's an education in soccer, a veritable throw-back to the days when flair and native skill counted as against the modern pre-cast types."

Cliff Mitchell, the Evening Gazette's chief sports writer, added: "Willie could and would play a blinder in any position on the park. He is that rare bird, a natural footballer, of whom there will never be enough."

I pride myself that I gave many exceptional forwards a good run for their money on numerous occasions. Indeed, I am often asked who the best forwards I encountered were and it is a tough question to answer. There were so many. But I have tried to outline below those who particularly stood out and just what made them the special players they undoubtedly were.

Malcolm MacDonald
The man who could have won Boro the title. He never actually did play for a championship-winning team though he was a prolific goalscorer wherever he played. Along with Allan Clarke, the best finisher I came up against, Supermac had explosive pace and a lethal shot. In my games against Malcolm, I adopted a special tactic to counter that pace. Whenever Newcastle played the ball back for their playmaker Terry Hibbitt, I knew the ball would be played first time over the top for Malcolm to run on to. Before Hibbitt even received the ball, I would automatically take 10 paces back towards my own goal to allow for Malcolm's speed out of the blocks. A terrific header of the ball, he would instinctively shoot on sight and was particularly dangerous in and around the six-yard box. I pride myself in the fact that I believe he scored only three goals against Boro in all the games I came face-to-face with him throughout his time with Newcastle and Arsenal. One of the secrets to my success was the way I would push him on to his right-foot whenever I confronted him bearing down on goal, knowing that Malcolm would try to work the ball on to his favoured left foot. One occasion when he did get the better of me was the day he scored a very cheeky goal following a quickly taken throw-in at St James' Park. Both Stuart Boam and I were guilty of turning our backs to the play and Malcolm was on the end of the resulting quick throw and had toe-ended the ball past Jim Platt before we could even blink. That was Supermac for you - like every great striker, he was at his most dangerous when

you thought you had him in your pocket.

Duncan McKenzie

Another player who was exceptional in the air, McKenzie always seemed to do well against us. Stuart and I still have nightmares about the day, as a Leeds United player, he turned us inside out during the opening 20 minutes, scoring twice. I always prided myself on being able to learn from my first encounter with a player and few forwards got the better of me more than a couple of times. But Duncan got the better of me technically on at least three occasions. With great balance and close control, he had that rare ability to do the unorthodox and I remember his Leeds strike partner Allan Clarke admitting that even he rarely knew what Duncan would do next.

Trevor Francis

My most difficult opponent. Tricky Trevor was perhaps the only other player who edged the majority of his battles against me. Certainly, it is fair to say he had more good games against me than I had against him. Trevor had electric pace and, similar to McKenzie, always had another trick up his sleeve. From the age of 16, he was the golden boy at Birmingham and matured into arguably the most exciting front runner in the country. Though not brilliant in the air, he was so deceptive when the ball was at his feet and was always comfortable in front of goal. It always frustrated me, however, that Francis never reproduced his fantastic club form at international level. He had so much composure on the ball and yet he seemed to treat it as though it was red hot whenever he pulled on an England shirt. Even so, an exceptional player.

Kevin Keegan

Although not as naturally gifted as Francis, Kevin Keegan worked at his game and perfected his skills through hours of dedication on the training ground. I did well against Keegan on most occasions and there was a mutual respect between us. Of course, Kevin became a household name but he didn't have the tricks possessed by the likes of McKenzie and Francis. Considering his lack of height, however, Keegan was dangerous in the air, had great awareness of the players around him and was always on the move, demanding a defender's full concentration for 90 minutes.

Extra Time – The Final Chapter

Paul Mariner

Oh, what a difference Paul Mariner would have made to Middlesbrough's progress had Jack Charlton followed through his interest in him while he was at Plymouth Argyle. Instead, Mariner moved on to Ipswich Town for £220,000 where he scored goals for fun and won England caps. Boasting a good shot with either foot and lethal in the air, Mariner was one of the best target men of the era. An easy mover, he had a big, athletic physique and wasn't afraid to put himself about and go in where it hurt.

Allan Clarke

Sniffer, as he was affectionately known, was an exceptional goalscorer. One particular goal Clarke scored against Boro stands out in my memory. It came at Ayresome Park during our first year back in the First Division. As he chased a long through-ball about three feet from the ground, I felt sure Clarkey would need a touch to control the ball before having a crack at goal. That, I thought, would be my chance and I would make the tackle. He didn't take the touch and I never got the tackle in. Instead, he volleyed the ball from what seemed an impossible height and nearly broke the back of the net, such was the force behind his shot. That was that - Leeds won the game 1-0. Like many of the best players, he also had a nasty streak. Occasionally, when I was clearing my lines near the touchline, he would come across me and leave his studs up in case I followed through. I always knew that, with Clarke coming at you, it was best to simply stab the ball up the line without any follow through whatsoever.

Stuart Pearson

The sort of player who invited physical contact, Stuart Pearson always gave defenders a hard game. I first came across him at Hull City and found him to be a livewire and quite a handful, but Stuart went on to play for Manchester United where he was their key player on their return to the First Division in 1975. He liked defenders to get in tight against him and would constantly back into you. If you dangled a leg in to try and poke the ball away, he would use his weight to turn you and go bounding away. It took me a couple of games to realise that, when playing against Pearson, I had to drop off an extra yard or two and not allow him to keep in contact with me. He became less effective after that. One occasion he did get the better of me, however, was at Old Trafford when he scored a good goal after making a monkey out of me. As I closed in to challenge for a header, Pearson made a back for me and I went flying over the top, missing the ball completely and allowing him to go on to score. It was a hard lesson learned.

Martin Chivers

A regular England international centre-forward and a collosus of a man, Chivers had such broad shoulders it looked like he hadn't taken the coathanger out of his shirt. I came up against him during my younger days when Boro took on Tottenham in three successive cup games. For a big man, he had the deftest of touches, was an excellent dribbler of the ball, possessed a fair amount of pace and was naturally exceptional in the air. Of course, above all he was a prolific goalscorer, one of the best of his era.

Andy Gray

Andy was exceptionally good in the air and it didn't surprise me how many goals he scored. I always knew it would be a physical battle against him. I played against him on his debut for Aston Villa, who had signed him from Dundee United, and I made a mental note to remember he wasn't bad for a Scotsman, who tended to be a yard off the pace when they first moved into English football. He was one of the first players I'd seen raise his elbow when attacking an aerial ball. In one game, I remember back-peddling after a high up-and-under whilst marking Gray. The ball was dropping under our crossbar and I was expecting a shout from Jim Platt which wasn't forthcoming. At that moment Gray elbowed me, splitting my nose, as I headed the ball against my own bar. Little did I know, Jim had come for the ball and kneed me in the crease of my backside a split second after Gray had made contact with my face. I didn't know which part of my body to hold first. Fortunately, the ball bounced to safety off the top of our bar. Along with Old Trafford and Anfield, Villa Park was always my favourite ground. At the other end of the scale, I hated playing at Norwich City. Carrow Road may be a modern stadium nowadays but in the 1970's it was dull and depressing. The playing surface was only moderate and the dressing rooms were dismal - a total contrast to the town itself which has always been a beautiful part of the country.

Of course, there are many more forwards I could mention. Occasionally, I came up against a little known player who would give me a hard time, only to disappear back into reserve team football, never to be heard of again. I guess it was a case of

Extra Time – The Final Chapter

horses for courses and some players were ideally suited for my game and others were never going to give me a problem.

Whatever the case, I cherish the memories of my playing days. I may never have won a major honour nor a full international cap but I achieved an awful lot and take huge satisfaction from my position on Teesside as a local hero. With my playing days over, however, it was time to move on to pastures new.

13

It's a Funny Old Game

WHEN I look back on my playing career, the many humourous moments I enjoyed with the game's characters often come to mind. Here's just a few of them...

The Lying, the Pitch and the Wardrobe

I felt I had good reason to suspect the sexual leanings of Graeme Souness when I first roomed with him during a pre-season tour of Scotland. It was in a Scottish hotel that he invited a friend of his, a Hibs player called Eric Carruthers, back to our room to share our night's accommodation. I already had my suspicions about Eric, with his albino white hair, but my mind went into overdrive the minute Graeme revealed a hairdryer and began blowing his hair. After all, this was 1974 and I can assure you that blow-drying your hair was not the done thing among males in the north-east of England at the time. Such was my concern, that night I went to sleep with one eye closed - and the other on Graeme and Eric! Let's just say I was relieved to see daylight arrive with my 'virginity' still intact.

My concerns were laid to rest the moment I saw at first hand Graeme's ability to pull attractive members of the opposite sex. He was the best. On one occasion, the Boro team was staying in a hotel when he chatted up a young lady in the bar. Such was his confidence that night, he offered to demonstrate to David Mills and I his love-making ability! Handing us his room key, Graeme told us to go up to his room and hide in the wardrobe. Try to picture the scene with David and I squashed together in a small wardrobe, peeking through the gap and giggling like two silly schoolboys as we awaited the arrival of Souey and his girl. Every couple of minutes, my dodgy knee would make a cracking sound, sending us into another fit of the giggles. After almost 20 minutes, however, there was still no sign of the pair.

Eventually, we decided they were not coming but, just as we stepped out of the wardrobe, we heard the unmistakable sound of the lift doors opening outside the bedroom door and promptly dived back inside. Five minutes later, however, there was still no sign of Graeme and the lady in question. We waited there, in the most uncomfortable wardrobe I've ever been in (!), for fully 45 minutes in all before finally giving up on them. Quite whether Graeme ever got his wicked way with her, I have never found out, but he certainly ensured David and I enjoyed one of the most laughter-filled hours of our lives.

Jack's Jacket Jape

Millsy and I were always like two big kids when we got together, laughing and joking constantly. We also loved playing practical jokes and could not resist the chance to carry one out on Jack Charlton the day we saw his favourite jacket hanging up in the Ayresome Park treatment room. This was a rare opportunity. The jacket - Jack called it his "lucky jacket" - was rarely off his back. Despite its shabbiness, with at least two of its buttons hanging on a couple of inches of thread, the lads would often joke that it would take anaesthetic to get it off him. But this was our chance.

Having spotted the jacket, Millsy and I proceeded with our plans. With the risk that Jack might return to catch us in the act at any second, we were both in hysterics as we cut up strips of inch tape, which was normally used to support our shinpads. We stopped only when we had enough small pieces to spell out the words "Hell's Angels" which were quickly transferred on to the back of Jack's cherished jacket. With the job completed, I folded the jacket in a way which ensured only its lining was visible and hung it back on the same peg we had found it.

At the time, Jack's usual pre-match routine included walking on to the pitch to personally collect the tracksuits of each player. David and I could bearly contain ourselves at the prospect that this matchday tradition would not only mean our little wind-up being witnessed by over 30,000 fans but by the nation's television cameras too as we were about to face Manchester United in a League Cup tie. Commentator Barry Davies let out a little chuckle as Jack turned away from him after a pre-match interview while each of the lads cottoned on to our prank as they walked past Jack as he sat on a remedial bike in the club's treatment room during the build-up. In fact, such was the apparent happy mood around the dressing room, Jack even commented on the players' "good spirits".

But just as our anticipation of what was to follow reached its peak, physio Jimmy Headridge spotted the addition to the manager's jacket and thoughtfully pointed it out to him. Jack had been saved from the ultimate embarrassment but he was furious and vowed to find out who had set him up. He never did discover who his tormentors were. Until now - of course, but I'm sure Jack wouldn't hit anyone in a wheelchair!

I'm Alright Jack Jack!

Jack was always good for a laugh - though he didn't always appreciate my sense of humour. Going through one of his infamously detailed dossiers on the opposition before a game against Aston Villa one day, he warned me: "Willie, I want you to keep a careful eye on that little Little." Smiling, I replied: "Alright, Jack Jack." His response to my quip was one of his customary glares.

During another team talk, he became tongue-tied and announced: "Let's be *realastic* about this." I couldn't resist the temptation to cut in with the quip: "I think that's stretching it a bit far!" I'm pleased to say that, on that occasion, he did see the funny side.

Then, there was the time he held a pre-match talk at the Medhurst Hotel while little Peter, his son, sat twanging the springs of the lounge chairs. Jack enquired if any of us knew anything about the opposition's reserve goalkeeper who had been drafted in at the last minute. "Anyone know anything about this 'keeper?" he asked. Deftly silence. "No-one heard of him before, then?" Again, we looked nonplussed. At that moment, Peter stood up from behind one of the chairs and yelled: "I have, dad!" As the lads roared with laughter, Jack twisted round and shouted: "Get out, you little sod!"

What a Card

Graeme Souness didn't share with Millsy and me that childish - some would say immature - sense of humour. He was, however, a glutton for being cajoled into taking part in our infantile pranks. On one memorable occasion, I spotted three training balls as I sat at the back of the club coach with Graeme, on the way back from an away game.

Further up the bus, Jack Charlton and Jimmy Greenhalgh were enjoying a quiet

Extra Time – The Final Chapter

game of cards but I was keen to ease the boredom of a long journey. I began winding Graeme up by saying: "I bet you daren't throw one of those balls down the bus." His initial answer was the usual: "Don't be so immature." But I goaded him relentlessly for the next half an hour. "C'mon Souey, don't be such a chicken," I mocked. "You're a right woman, aren't you?"

Finally, as I had known he would, Souey had heard enough of my childish teasing. Cursing me under his breath, he picked up one of the balls, stood up and hurled it half the length of the bus. His aim was near perfection. The ball whacked an unsuspecting

John Hickton (left), Terry Cooper and me taking some time out for some serious training

Jimmy on the back of the head, sending his pack of cards into the air. The whole bus was in uproar but Jimmy was in no mood to see the funny side. In a fit of temper, he grabbed Souey's case, marched to the front of the coach and ordered the driver to open the doors. It was his plan to hurl Graeme's case out on to the busy road as we motored along at 60mph. Responding to Jimmy's threat, Graeme went tearing after him and yelled: "If you throw my case out, Greenhalgh, I'll hold it against you for the rest of my life." Jimmy's response was: "Get back to reading your Dandy." The lads were in hysterics - most of all me, the incident's instigator. Eventually, the pair were separated by Jack who insisted that Graeme's case be handed back to him in the name of team spirit!

A 30-Second Wonder

I still vividly remember the day Millsy and I spotted a rather seedy massage parlour on our way back to the Waldorf from London's West End before an away game whilst we were still teenagers. Being inquisitive, we popped our heads around the door like two giggly schoolboys and slowly made our way into the foyer.

On the wall was a "menu" of choices on offer, from standard massage to masturbation. The prices quoted were for half an hour or an hour but Millsy jangled the change in his pocket and enquired to the receptionist: "How much for 30 seconds, love? That's all it will take me!" The bemused receptionist frowned: "Get out, you silly boy." We laughed all the way back to the Strand as we considered Millsy's staying power.

Pillow Talk is a Pain in the Neck

Another player with whom I enjoyed a good relationship, especially in our younger days together, was my central defensive partner Stuart Boam. In the first couple of years after Stuart joined Middlesbrough, we invariably roomed together on away trips and I still remember the somewhat unorthodox wake-up call he devised for me. It solely comprised a pillow being whacked over my head.

Retaliating only made things worse. In one of the pillow fights which inevitably ensued, I put my neck out and was forced to play that afternoon's game against QPR in much discomfort. Not only could I not attack aerial crosses with my usual determination but I had the added problem of marking Stan Bowles, who had the annoying habit of running behind me before suddenly switching directions. With my cricked neck, it's fair to say I struggled to tie Bowles down that day. Afterwards, when Jimmy Headridge enquired why my neck seemed to be a bit stiff, only briefly did I contemplate explaining that it was the result of an early morning pillow fight!

Eric's Crustacean Cracker

Perhaps the biggest dressing room prankster I encountered throughout my career was Eric McMordie. When he wasn't exchanging sexual innuendo with one of his team-mates, Eric loved a joke and would go to almost any lengths to carry them off.

One day we sat together in Ayresome Park's big plunge bath after a particularly muddy training session and heard Eric ask: "How long do you think it would take me to get you lot out of this bath?"

Our questioning glances brought a cheeky grin to Eric's face. "What do you mean by that?" we asked.

"How quickly do you think I could empty this bath?" he persevered. Again, blank looks all around. Until a couple of small live crabs popped to the surface of the scum-filled water. The bath was empty in seconds as each of us dived for safety.

Only a laughing Eric remained in the water. "Yeah, I thought it would take about that long," he smiled.

I Take Cliff's Hat off to you, Eric

Another humorous memory I have of Eric was the day the team travelled to an away match on an old fashioned rail carriage with private compartments. Gordon Jones had stolen the Trilby hat of Evening Gazette sports writer Cliff Mitchell who was accompanying us on the journey.

Pointing up to a tiny open window, Gordon dared Eric: "I bet you couldn't throw that out of the window from here."

There was no need to ask him twice. In a flash, Eric took the hat and spun it out of the window at the first attempt. The window was so small, if he had tried it another hundred times, I doubt he would have achieved the feat again. But that was the end of Cliff's Trilby.

Moments later, the doors to the carriage slid open and Cliff's face peered in. "Anyone seen my hat?" he enquired. "No, Cliff!" we all answered in unison - but the smiles on our faces must have given the game away.

Eye, Eye Frank!

I will always remember how the less than perfect eyesight of Frank Spraggon gave us all a laugh during what proved to be the first of several tours to Norway in May 1974. Frank was left almost blind in one eye due to a problem with general anaesthetic administered to him during a cartilage operation early in his career. However, he always seemed to do well enough with his one good eye so we were amazed by what he did during our opening game in Norway, against Viking Stavanger.

Rolled back from the field was a plastic pitch cover which was a quite unmissable feature to anyone but Frank. As he placed the ball and took a few strides backwards in preparation for a corner, the back of Frank's knees hit the rolled plastic and he theatrically fell backwards over the roll. As he lay prostrate on the ground, the lads were in fits of laughter, as just a couple of weeks earlier he had given us a similar idea of just how bad his eyesight was. During a friendly at Tunbridge Wells, Frank had again placed the ball for a corner kick. But instead of connecting with the ball, he sent the corner flag itself flying a good 10 yards through the air!

Norway was a place I loved during our regular close season tours there under Jack and all of our games would be played amid a relaxed though professional atmosphere. One side we took on was SK Brann, a team we nicknamed the All Bran XI, while I remember during one of his pre-match team talks Jack jokingly warned us that the Norwegians had strong legs as a result of all the skiing they did.

Against SK Brann, we were entertained at half-time by a pop group, who were set up behind one of the goals. We were surprised to hear they sounded quite good as the only half-decent band to come out of Scandinavia at the time was Abba! However, they had well and truly outstayed their welcome when fully 10 minutes into the second half they were still bashing out tune after tune - despite numerous attempts by the referee to silence them.

Don't Fall for that One

It was during our stay in Tunbridge Wells that one of the lads agreed to give us all a performance of his love-making technique - with rather painful consequences for one of us.

In the knowledge that one of our team-mates had gone back to his room with a young lady, several players made their way on to the hotel roof from where they had a bird's eye view of the action through the bedroom window. Adjacent to the window - or so I'm told! - was a large skylight and, such was the excitement of the performance, one of the lads took a couple of paces backwards and fell straight through it on to the floor 15 feet below. Not surprisingly, the player in question suffered considerable lacerations though, thankfully, most were superficial.

The next day, as we prepared to leave the hotel on the team coach, Jack rather angrily addressed the squad. "I've had a complaint from the hotel manager," he said. "One of you guys has smashed through a skylight. I'm not letting this bus leave until that person owns up and pays for the damage."

No-one dared own up to the mischief so we eventually had a whip-round to enable us to leave. Jack never did find out who the culprit was. Don't worry, I wouldn't tell on you, Cuffy! (Sorry, Pat, but I know Christine will be understanding!)

Extra Time – The Final Chapter

A Question of Priorities

Of course, the fans are often even more passionate about the game than the players and can sometimes get things a little out of perspective - as was the case on the day my first wife Diane gave birth to our daughter, Lucy.

At the hospital, I went to collect a white gown to wear during the birth and walked past a room in which I could see through the window a lady in obvious discomfort with her contractions, whilst her husband administered the gas and air. With his wife screaming in pain, the husband noticed me walking by. As only a die-hard football fan could, he completely forgot about his wife's distress and walked over to the window.

"Willie!" he shouted. "Are you OK for the weekend - are you fit?" Astonished with his actions, I gave the thumbs up sign and told him to get back to his wife.

In my mind, everything I achieved and experienced in football does not even compare to witnessing the birth of my children. It is the greatest gift that we can have. The sound of the first cry of a new-born child is better than the roar of any crowd.

The Day Nobby was Out for the Count

Perhaps Frank Spraggon's only rival in terms of poor eyesight was Nobby Stiles. There is a famous story about Nobby during his Manchester United days when he used to pretend his eyesight was better than it really was just to avoid being forced to wear glasses whilst off the pitch. The game was up, however, the day his team-mates spotted him attempting to read a newspaper upside down!

However, his reading ability was not actually much better even when he could see the words in front of him - as we discovered when Nobby led several Boro players "back to school" one summer. Four or five of us, Nobby and myself included, decided to further our education at the nearby Kirby College, taking English and Maths O-levels. But Nobby's mathematical ability was found wanting right from the start.

In our first lesson, our tutor set us a short test to discover our capabilities. As I got stuck into the paper, I couldn't help but notice that five minutes on Nobby was still to start writing. On asking him what the problem was, I was amused to discover he was still puzzling over the first, extremely simple question on the page.

"How the f***ing hell do you do these fractions?" he asked. As the paper got decidedly harder after that first question, I spent the next few minutes chuckling away to myself. None of us were in the least surprised when Nobby failed to surface for the following week's Maths lesson.

From Horror to Beauty Queen

To my knowledge, only Nobby Stiles and Frank Spraggon suffered with poor eyesight during their playing days with Boro and yet I had reason to question the eyesight and judgement of several team-mates during the 1972-73 season when we spent a few days at Bisham Abbey in preparation for an important game in the capital.

On the evening we arrived, who else should be booking in but the England Ladies football team? I think it's fair to say they weren't the prettiest girls we had ever seen so the dialogue went along the lines of: "Oh my god, look at the thighs on her!" and "My god, what a horror she is."

By the Monday evening, after two or three pints of the local brew, our views had altered somewhat. "Heh, she's not bad," and "What a lovely figure," were now par for the course.

By the Wednesday, following another couple of hours at the bar, some of the lads were gagging for it. Needless to say, their critical analysis of the England girls now comprised lines like: "Wow, she's a beauty queen," and "What I could do for that!"

By the end of the week they were all beauty queens. It just goes to show what a few pints of strong ale can do for your eyesight and judgement.

Size *Does* Matter

Little Stan Cummins was perhaps the smallest player ever to pull on a first team shirt for Middlesbrough. No-one, however, can question the impact he had when he first broke into the side as a teenager and he fully deserved to receive a sponsored VW from Ron Turnbull Garages. If I remember rightly, splashed along the side of the vehicle was the line: "Stan Cummins drives a Ron Turnbull car".

Unfortunately, Stan's diminutive size was to prove his downfall on only his second day in the car. Leaving Ayresome Park for Hutton Road, Stan was turning out of Warwick Street but couldn't see over the school railing to his right. As he attempted to make a right turn out of the street, another car hit him side on, causing an enormous amount of damage to his new motor.

The following week, however, us players proved we were all heart by having an impromptu whip-round. With the cash collected, we were able to buy him just what he needed to avoid any repeat of the accident - an 18 inch thick foam cushion!

Hong Kong Souey

Our second World Tour, at the end of the 1976-77 season, will always remind me of just how much Graeme Souness lived up to his play boy image. The tour took in Norway, India, Hong Kong and Australia, but it was during our brief visit to Hong Kong that Souey hit top form - off the field.

During our stay, we played one game but were thankful to have another cancelled, giving us a welcome opportunity to see the sights following a hard English season. On the evening we were due to leave for Australia, our aeroplane developed technical problems so, having been told to pack our bags and be ready to leave on instruction, we made our way into one of our hotel's magnificent bars. In the Dickens Bar, many of the lads quickly got chatting with the bar's second generation dancers. It was close to midnight and we were enjoying ourselves over a few drinks when, to our disappointment, Jimmy Headridge instructed us to go upstairs to collect our bags and to be on the team coach ready for departure in 15 minutes.

Graeme and I made our way up to our room on the tenth floor, collected our suitcases and entered the lift for our descent. As the lift doors closed, I had no reason to suspect what was to happen next. The lift descended to the second floor where, to my astonishment, the doors opened, Graeme picked up his bags and stepped out of the lift.

"I'll see you in three days, Buffalo," he smiled, calling me by his nickname for me. "I'm fixed up with one of the dancers. I'll see you in Australia!" Flabbergasted, there was no time for me even to mutter a response. The doors were shut and I was left alone in the lift as it made its descent to the ground floor.

Once there, I made a sharp exit in the direction of the team bus, only to be spotted by Jimmy Headridge. "Where's Souness?" he enquired.

"I don't know, Jimmy," I lied. "I haven't seen him in 10 minutes."

As I boarded the bus, I shared my secret with Phil Boersma. Like me, he couldn't believe it. But Phil, having witnessed Graeme's approach to the girl in the Dickens Bar, was by no means as surprised as I was. A single guy, good looking and immaculately dressed, Graeme didn't always think with his head so I wasn't surprised that he had got himself fixed up. What did amaze me was his audacity to simply walk out on the team and the way he had concealed his plans from me for so long. I guess Graeme was the Emerson of his time.

Over the next few minutes, Jimmy was given negative replies as he asked different lads if they had seen Graeme. Both Jimmy and Harold Shepherdson, the man in charge until John Neal succeeded Jack Charlton as our new manager, were furious. Then, after no more than five minutes, I was surprised to hear Jimmy shout out: "Come on, driver. Let's go."

At the airport, I rang our hotel room in a bid to speak to Graeme and convince him to catch a taxi and join us. Having witnessed the black mood of Jimmy and Harold, I was concerned he would be in bigger trouble than he had bargained for. Alas, there was no answer in our room and we flew out to Melbourne without Hong Kong Souey.

Rumours abounded during our first training session in Melbourne that Graeme was set to be deported back to the UK for his dismeanour as soon as he caught up with the squad. But, for two more days, there was no sign of him. Then, at five in the morning, there was a knock on my bedroom door. No surprises for guessing whose smiling face should greet me at that unearthly hour.

"Now then, Buff!" he grinned, seeing a combination of disbelief and concern on my face. I could tell by his expression that he had obviously enjoyed his extended stay in Hong Kong.

"You're in for it," I warned him. "I've heard Charlie Amer isn't best pleased with you and I've heard Shep saying you're on the next 'plane home."

With an apparent lack of concern, Graeme dismissed my comments with a shrug.

News of his late arrival soon filtered through to the club's hierarchy and Souey was summoned to see the chairman as I joined the rest of the lads for training the following lunchtime. As I returned to our room afterwards, I could hear Graeme's happy whistling inside and knew immediately he was off the hook.

"Well, what happened?" I asked him.

Completely unfazed, he explained: "Well, Charlie started to give me a bit of a lecture, saying I shouldn't have done that and that I was breaking club rules. But then he said 'Mind you, I was a bit like you when I was your age.' He left it pretty much at that."

"You lucky bugger," I said, shaking my head. "If it had been anyone else in the team we'd have been on the way home."

Fortunately for Graeme, he was very much the star of the side at the time and had yet to sign a new contract with the club. Clearly, the chairman had thought it best not to risk upsetting him too much. In fact, so desperate was Amer to keep Graeme sweet, he offered him the chance to stay on in Australia and guest for a team in Adelaide as an inducement to sign a new contract. Naturally, Graeme accepted an opportunity to spend more time in such a beautiful country and remained in Adalaide when the rest of the squad returned home to England. Unfortunately, the ploy did not work and Graeme joined Liverpool just four months into the new season.

But even from the other side of the world, he proved he could drop me in hot water with my wife, Diane. During our stay in Hong Kong he had bought a Fujica camera and little did I know that after a heavy drinking session he had taken pictures of me naked in our hotel room. Back on Teesside, I returned home from a shopping trip to a rather ferocious reception from Diane. "What's this?" she demanded to know, thrusting into my hands a photograph which quite clearly showed my naked torso from the waist down. On the back of the photo was the message: "Missing you terribly. Wish you were still in Australia with me. Love, Samantha." I recognised Graeme's writing and devilment immediately but Diane refused to believe it was an innocent prank. To my bemusement, she left the picture on the coffee table to be picked up that afternoon by my mother-in-law. Shocked, she enquired who it was in the photo. Rather embarrassed, I snatched it from her and replied: "Nobody you would know."

That particular world tour had begun with a flight out from Newcastle airport to Norway where we took on two semi-professional sides. I scored the only goal of the game in our second game, a thunderous half volley from the edge of the box that nearly broke the back of the net. I couldn't help but think what a waste as the goal had been witnessed by no more than a thousand spectators.

From Norway, we flew to Heathrow to catch a connecting flight to Hong Kong where two games had been arranged during our five-day stay. As it turned out, we had an unscheduled touchdown in Bombay, India, as our aeroplane had developed an oil leak in one of its engines. As we were staying overnight in Bombay, I wasn't going to let the opportunity of seeing a few of the sights pass me by. I was joined by Graeme and director Mike McCullagh in catching a taxi to see the famous Gateway to India. Whilst enjoying a couple of drinks in a plush hotel overlooking the Gateway, I couldn't help but notice the hypocrisy of India. On the way in from the airport, we had seen thousands of mud huts and shanty houses whilst the city centre was full of people laid on the pavement who clearly had no roof over their heads each night. And yet, on entering the heart of the city, it was impossible to miss the plush, modern buildings and sumptuous temples of great wealth. My other abiding memory of the city was a pungent smell which was quite nauseous in the heat of the night.

Next stop was Hong Kong after a few breathtaking moments on our flight into the city's airport. Looking out of the window during our descent, I was shocked to see that we were what seemed no more than 50 feet away from the towering peaks of skyscrapers which were breaking through the cloud on an extremely humid day. My first thoughts were that we were going to crash and it was great relief that we touched down on the landing strip which took us to the very edge of the sea.

Within minutes of booking in at our hotel, Graeme and I were typically out and about, curious to see what the natives looked like. We were no more than 50 yards along a crowded and bustling Hong Kong street when I got a tap on the shoulder. I turned around the see the broad smile of a bearded English guy.

As I looked at him, rather puzzled, he broke the silence. "It's Willie Maddren, isn't it?" he enquired.

Naturally flabbergasted, I asked: "Where do I know you from?"

"You know me," he laughed. "It's Smithy - we used to play football together at John Whitehead Park."

As soon as he spoke those words, I looked past his beard and recognised him as one of many Sunday afternoon players who had put down their coats as goalposts to share games of football on that well worn area of Billingham. Apparently, he was working in Hong Kong for an oil company. I found it quite unbelievable, however, that halfway around the world I had been spotted by someone from my hometown. What a small world it is!

Back in our room, Graeme rather excitedly passed me a small hotel diary showing photographs of many of the Chinese hostesses earning a living in Hong Kong, each with their telephone numbers listed beneath. I was far more interested

Extra Time – The Final Chapter

in getting down for dinner. With its own internal shopping arcade, the hotel was fabulous and its cuisine first class.

However, following a light meal, there was an unpopular decision to fit in a light training session as we had lost 24 hours in our preparations for the following day's game with a Hong Kong XI at the International Stadium. The humidity, even in the evening, was unbearable and it was obvious it would take us a day or two to acclimatise.

The following day, as we left our air-conditioned accommodation to play the friendly, I was shocked by the rush of warm air that met us as we prepared to board the coach to the stadium. It was like opening an oven door. That afternoon, simply during our pre-match warm-up, our white shirts became transparent with sweat. Thankfully, we took a 2-0 lead within the first 15 minutes, after which we found the heat and humidity so hard to come to terms with that the remainder of the game was played at a walking pace. Those two early goals proved enough to win the match but we failed to impress our hosts who subsequently cancelled the game planned for two days later. We received something of a slating in the local press who felt that an English First Division team should have acquitted themselves better. I guess they expected goals and excitement but I felt the criticism was unjustified as everyone gave their best in extremely trying conditions. Still, at least the extra day off gave us more time to enjoy more leisure time among the skyscrapers and bustling shops of that fabulous city.

In Adelaide, we met up with our new manager John Neal for the first time and it was instantly obvious that he was a nice, jovial kind of guy. John was still jet-lagged as he addressed us for the first time in our hotel. But he made a point of saying that he could not believe that a football club would embark on such an arduous tour at the end of a long English season. Although I enjoyed the tour, I had to agree with those sentiments.

One quite amusing feature of the tour was a visit to a small town called Lithgo, about five hours from Sydney. Graeme, in particular, wasn't best pleased and after about three hours on the coach commented that only Middlesbrough would entertain the idea of travelling out to the Australian backwoods to play a Mickey Mouse match against a team we had never even heard of. I couldn't have agreed more. Lithgo had never even hosted an English side before, let alone one of our stature, and I could only assume that the club had been given a reasonable retainer to play the game.

It's a Funny Old Game

The town of Lithgo was like something out of a wild west show, with the step from the street on to the pavement being at least 18 inches high, while the shops were full of outdoor clothing and equipment best suited to lumberjacks. On our first evening there after arrival, we were guests at a civic reception in the town hall building, where the lads occupied seats in a semi-circle looking up to an elevated seating area where the mayor, John Neal and other dignitaries were seated. Meanwhile, the town's folk were at the back of the building behind us. All mayhem looked set to break loose from the moment the Mayor of Lithgo began to address us. His voice was identical to the cartoon character Deputy Dog. On hearing his voice, we looked across at one another and were busting a gut simply to contain our laughter. One thing I made a conscious decision not to do was look at David Mills as I knew one amused glance from him would send me into a fit of the giggles.

As the mayor continued in the same amusing fashion, he told us: "If you get the chance I'd like to show some of you Middlesbrough boys our open spaces." He was referring to the rather rugged terrain which surrounded the town. At that, I had to put my head under the table in a bid to control my laughter. I was immediately joined by Phil Boersma alongside me. I managed to contain myself but I made the fateful mistake of looking across the room where my glance was met by Millsy. That was it. We both exploded with laughter, our infectious giggles echoing around the dome-shaped building and ensuring the rest of the lads quickly followed suit, to the amusement of the locals. You can imagine the embarrassment of John Neal as he looked down on us with disdain.

Having survived that greeting, several of us decided we were hungry and I asked a local taxi driver where the nearest restaurant was. "Just up the road," came his reply. With that, Graeme, Phil Boersma, Alf Wood and me jumped in the cab and asked him to take us there. We had been in the taxi for 20 minutes when, in complete exasperation, I asked the driver how much further we had to go. "Just around the next corner," he replied. What we hadn't bargained for was that the time distance to any inhabitant of Australia doesn't mean quite the same thing as it does to us in the UK. Worse still, the taxi finally came to a halt outside a transport cafe high up in the mountains. What turned out to be a hamburger and a few hotdogs cost me the princely sum of £30 for the taxi fare, as it had been my bright idea to go looking for food.

The game against Lithgo was not a contest. Such was the poor quality of the opposition, we were 11-0 up at half-time and we could easily have surpassed our eventual total of 14 goals had we not eased up considerably in the second 45

Extra Time – The Final Chapter

minutes. What amused me about the game was the pleasure we took in taking the Micky out of our centre-forward Alf Wood, who had failed to score any of those 11 first half goals. As the game went on and our sarcasm increased, so Alf became increasingly poorer. Only when he was pulled back to centre-half to allow me to take a rest did the leg-pulling cease.

The big match of the tour came in Sydney against the Australian national side in one of their final warm-up games before they began their World Cup campaign. There had been suggestions in the local press that a good win over an English First Division team would act as an ideal morale booster but we didn't read the script. Or rather we ripped it up and threw it to the wind. We absolutely tore them apart, beating the pride of Australia 5-0. Playing in midfield, I found myself in opposition to my old Boro juniors team-mate Peter Wilson, who had become captain of his country since emigrating Down Under to start a new life many years earlier. I scored our fifth goal, a left foot volley from fully 30 yards but, again, I couldn't help but think what a waste it was as it was a goal to grace any game. But our overall performance was flawless. Afterwards, John Neal addressed us to say: "I'm pinching myself, I can't believe the quality of the team I have just inherited."

The final game of our tour was back on the same Perth ground where I had suffered those embarrassing diarrhoea problems two years earlier - and this time it truly established itself as my least favourite ground. For the first and only time in my life, I played a match whilst suffering from a hang-over. Recognising that we had won every game handsomely, Souey and I had decided it wouldn't be amiss to enjoy a few drinks the day before our final match. Having spent the afternoon as guests at a cocktail party, we returned to our hotel around six o'clock where I met another friend who I had met on the club's previous tour to Australia. Having heard we were in town, he insisted on taking me out for the remaining hours of the evening.

Oh, how I wish I had resisted the offer of alcohol during the following day's game. Suffering from a blinding headache, midway through the first half I found myself in the opposition penalty area with a right wing cross dropping perfectly for me. "Oh no, I've got to head this damn ball," I thought to myself. I met the ball full-on with my forehead and as the back of the net bulged I stood with my head in both hands in enormous discomfort!

Looking back, those trips to the other side of the world were undoubtedly among the highlights of my playing career as they also offered such wonderful life experiences.

14

On the Coaching Ladder

WHEN their playing careers are over there are many who struggle to make the most of life after football. Like the majority of ex-players, I initially found it hard to adapt to no longer living my life from Saturday to Saturday, game to game. Where I had an advantage, however, was that I have always been something of an entrepreneur while I had always believed I would have a natural aptitude for coaching when my playing days were over. So rather than moping about at home with nothing to do, within 18 months of retiring from the game I found myself with no less than three forms of income. My three working passions were football coaching, a sports retail outlet and a pie shop!

My first move into coaching came in the Northern League with Whitby Town a couple of months after hanging up my boots. When Whitby's manager, my old friend Steve Smelt, asked me to help out with the coaching, I had no hesitation in accepting. Having lost several of the club's better players to Guisborough Town, Steve had inherited what amounted to a Teesside League team and had consequently suffered a few heavy defeats during his first games in charge. However, we rallied and got a few good results towards the end of the season.

After a 1-0 defeat to Tow Law Town one cold March day, however, I was approached by Don Burluraux, one of my former Boro team-mates who was now on Whitby's books. Don was angry and I soon understood why. He showed me the contents of an envelope. Where there should have been his usual match fee of £7.50, there was just £2.50. I agreed to look into the missing money and approached the club chairman Ken Graham and asked why Don had received only £2.50.

"I thought he was a load of crap and that's all he deserves," he responded in forthright fashion. "I took the fiver out at half-time."

Extra Time – The Final Chapter

He was right. Don hadn't enjoyed a particularly good game. But I was shocked that he could be so obstinate. "With due respect, Ken," I replied. "You can't be seen to be doing that kind of thing. We need to sign a lot of new players in the close season and if word gets around that the Whitby chairman docks your wages if you don't play well we won't have a hope in hell of signing anyone."

Thankfully, that summer I was able to help Smelty sign several better quality players but before the new season began I was given the opportunity to get back into the professional game when I was approached by two of my former Boro team-mates, Billy Horner and George Smith, who were in charge at nearby Hartlepool. Having missed the day-to-day involvement with football since leaving Middlesbrough, this was just the chance I'd been waiting for and I didn't have to be asked twice. Following an interview with club chairman Vince Barker, I was offered the position of first team coach, a role I would share with my old pal and best man George. My starting salary was £90 a week, less than half of my basic wage with Boro but the money wasn't important. I was simply delighted to be back in the game and on the first rungs of the coaching ladder.

In terms of players, Hartlepool had a mixture of the good, the bad and the ugly. We had three decent youngsters in Mark Lawrence, John Linacre and Keith Houchen but mainly there was a lot of dead wood to sort out. Over the course of the next year, the three of us began to fashion a reasonable first team and avoided the lottery of re-election by finishing 19th.

But we were to take big strides forward the following year. Like all clubs of that size, the main problem at Hartlepool was that there was no money available to buy new players so a good youth policy was crucial to the club's survival. I watched the club's juniors play on a number of occasions and Ken Sutheran, the guy who was running the team, had a good eye for talent though we were getting beat by the odd goal against the likes of Newcastle and Sunderland. I meant no disrespect to Ken when I expressed my view that with better coaching and tactical know-how we could reverse many of those results and lay the foundations for the club. For the following season, I persuaded Billy, as manager, to take on Steve Smelt as a part-time junior coach. Steve, who had by now left Whitby, was assistant manager of the England schoolboys team and had a wonderful pedigree for coaching youngsters.

Working alongside Ken, Smelty made an immediate impact and by Christmas the juniors were top of the Northern Intermediate League. One particularly pleasing result for me came at Hutton Road where our lads won 6-2 against a Middlesbrough side boasting future first team players like Darren Wood and Stephen Bell. Boro's coaching staff dismissed it as a freak result and claimed our players were final year juniors while their lads were a couple of years younger. That could not have been further from the truth. Six or seven of our players were in their first year and would be eligible to play at that level for another three seasons. Indeed, four of them would go on to play first team football for Hartlepool. Paul Dobson and Kenny Lowe both did well in the lower divisions while two brothers, Andy and David Linighan, played at the highest level during their long and fruitful careers.

Although I was first team coach, I liked to involve myself at an intermediate level and would often spend time watching Boro, Stockton or Hartlepool schoolboys in action. But I felt we had to start looking for talented players at an earlier age so decided to hold a coaching school for under-13's, inviting 30 of the best youngsters from those three areas to attend at English Martyrs school in Hartlepool. It would give me the chance to take a close look at the best young players in the region in an unofficial trial. All the kids seemed to enjoy the three-day course but I knew the crunch would come when I addressed them at the end of the final session. When the time came, I asked for a show of hands from those who would consider letting me talk to their fathers with a view to signing associate schoolboy forms for Hartlepool. To make it worthwhile, I had hoped for maybe three or four hands. What I got was no less than 29 hands going up without hesitation. I was absolutely thrilled. Only one lad did not put his hand up. "Why haven't you put your hand up, son?" I asked. His reply was typically honest for a lad of his age: "Because my dad works on the rigs and you'll be wasting your time coming round."

Among that show of hands were those of a young Peter Beagrie, Mark Venus and another lad called Ian Knight who would go on to win England under-21 caps with Sheffield Wednesday. Over the next couple of months I approached more than 20 families, mainly in the Middlesbrough area, with a view to allowing their boys to sign for Hartlepool. I sold them the idea that it was alright them bragging that their son had gone to Manchester United or Liverpool but they needed to ask themselves how many kids they knew who had made it into the first team at Old Trafford or Anfield. The answer was very few indeed as at the time both clubs had very poor youth development policies. I argued that by letting their boys climb the first rung of the ladder with Hartlepool they would get their first team chance long

Extra Time – The Final Chapter

before they would with any First Division club. More importantly, at that age the quality of the coaching youngsters received was vital and at Hartlepool we had four of the best in Billy, George, Smelty and myself. Almost incredibly, I managed to sign six of the Middlesbrough Schoolboys team that won the national ESFA Shield that year. They were turning down the likes of Manchester City and others to join little Hartlepool.

Although we missed out on the Boro team's two stars, Stephen Bell and Gary Gill, my major coup was in persuading the parents of Peter Beagrie to let him join us. Even at the age of 12, Peter's ability was there for all to see. Although a tiny lad, he had what I called "the Cruyff turn" and was excellent at making a yard or two for himself. With Peter and others, I could see the club creating a wonderful foundation for the future.

That season our juniors became the first side representing a Fourth Division club to win the Northern Intermediate League. Winning the league was normally the exclusive domain of Middlesbrough, Sunderland, Newcastle and Leeds but thanks to the achievements of Steve Smelt and Ken Sutheron we had wrested it from them. This was achieved despite having facilities which could best be described as archaic. It should have been a time of great joy but, sadly, there was disharmony in the camp and it was to raise its head in the ugliest of manners before the first team's penultimate home game of the 1980-81 season.

As the intermediates proudly paraded the championship trophy around the Victoria Ground, Smelty asked me to look at the letter he had just received from the chairman. It read that due to economical circumstances it was necessary to dispense with Steve's services. Incredibly, his thanks for winning the club the league was to lay him off. The reason could not have been a financial one as Steve was on just £20 a week in expenses. When I confronted the chairman, he blamed Billy for the decision. In return, Billy blamed the chairman. I couldn't help but wonder if Ken, who was very friendly with Billy, felt he'd had his nose pushed out with Smelty's arrival. Whatever the truth behind that strange decision, it was the beginning of my disenchantment with the club.

That second season with Hartlepool was a successful one for the first team and we spent the majority of the campaign in the chase for promotion to the Third Division. Having wheeled out the dead wood, we began to make real progress and I felt it was a great environment in which to learn the coaching trade. After my first year at the club, I had thought it wise to take my full FA coaching badge and enjoyed a wonderful two-week course in Durham. Joining me on the course were big football names like Pop Robson, Jim Montgomery, Jim McNab, Jim Ryan and Allan Hunter together with a variety of local coaches. However, doing the learning rather than the teaching didn't come naturally to me. Whilst showing us a defensive situation during a tactical session, the FA's staff coach Keith Wright told us that the golden rule was always to mark "in to out". No sooner had Keith issued those words than, without thinking, I blurted out: "No, that's not right. When the ball is in the opposing full-back positions, I always mark out to in to ensure I am first to the ball when it is knocked in the channels behind my full-back." It was hardly surprising that Keith didn't look too happy. I immediately regretted it and asked myself what I was doing. I was supposed to be passing a coaching course, not conflicting with the people who were about to judge me.

But I couldn't just let it go and was relieved when Keith allowed me to show him what I meant by organising a defensive situation around me using my fellow course participants. By the end of the session the whole group knew I had proved my point while my views were supported by Allan Hunter, the former partner of Kevin Beattie at Ipswich. "Willie's right," he said. "That's exactly how we mark at our club under Bobby Robson."

Fortunately, that matter of principle didn't cost me when it came to passing the written and practical exam at the end of the exam. Indeed, I was told by my old pal Steve Smelt, who was staffing another course, that I had achieved one of the highest marks ever at Durham. Attending as a coach from a professional club, I was relieved to pass as I would have been somewhat embarrassed had I failed. But it did appear that in those days the FA tended to push through many of the ex-pro's at the expense of other coaches from perhaps less privileged football backgrounds. There were several schoolteachers on the course whose knowledge had impressed me and their failure to pass mystified me.

Back at Hartlepool, one of the new boys was a lad called Bob Newton, who arrived at the Victoria Ground after a spell at Preston at Her Majesty's pleasure. But he had used his time in prison well. He had a magnificent physique and was the perfect front man in the lower divisions. Although he enjoyed a reasonable career, Bob could and should have gone much further. Powerful and brave, he possessed a good first touch and could finish in style.

But his poor attitude was his Achilles' heel and he frustrated the hell out of me on the training ground. More often than not he would have been out the night

Extra Time – The Final Chapter

before, had a skinful and be hung over when he reported in for training. Consequently, all the balls he considered not to be good enough would simply bounce off him, making it difficult to involve him in training sessions. I told him in no uncertain terms what I thought of him. On many occasions midway through a training session we would stand nose to nose while the other players looked on. Looking back, I am quite relieved it came to nothing as he was built like the Incredible Hulk. In many respects I liked his arrogance. He was confident and when that was controlled he was some player but he simply didn't look after himself. That bit of dedication could have seen him playing at the highest level.

He and Keith Houchen formed quite a potent attacking spearhead and, for the biggest part of the season, we were in the division's top four. Houchen, who was only a teenager, was still learning his trade but the potential was there. I spent many hours with him and Mark Lawrence on the training ground, drumming it into them that they couldn't afford to be static in the middle of the park. I told them that whenever they played the ball wide, it was their job to race into the middle for the return ball - but never to run in straight lines. I would tell Keith time and time again that he had to threaten to go in one side and then turn and go another way to get on the blind side of his marker. I was delighted many years later to see the penny had dropped with Keith when he scored the winning goal in the FA Cup final with a diving header from a right wing cross, having first played the ball out to the wing and raced into position for the return.

I think it is fair to say that the quality of coaching being provided by Billy, George and me was as good as could have been found at almost any club. We often used to wonder if our methods were above the ability of Fourth Division players. Many was the time when having practiced a particular free-kick all week and seen it worked to perfection on a Friday morning, it would all be forgotten on a Saturday afternoon. It would drive us crazy to see two players stood over the ball, scratching their heads and wondering what they were supposed to do. That was the difference between someone like David Armstrong and players at that level. It was necessary to tell David only once and it was as if it was stored in a computer - it was there forever. But having worked with players like Spike, Murdoch and Souness, who could drop a ball on a sixpence, it was frustrating to realise that the players you were working with could not perform even the basics of the game.

We had combined the potential of our younger players with a couple of older pro's with great success. On Billy's behalf I had approached the former Sunderland midfielder Bobby Kerr and Newcastle defender John Bird and they agreed to join the club to provide some much needed experience alongside the youngsters. For all his experience, Bobby had a tendency to make one very basic error. Rather than stand up to opponents and make himself difficult to beat, he had a habit of diving into tackles, showing his intentions to an opponent from fully 15 yards away. Every time he did so, he came to expect my shouts from the touchline as I barracked him for such a basic error. He would put his arm up to acknowledge what I was saying but would always do it again. After seeing this happen several times, I asked him how he had got away with it all those years. After all, he had played over 400 games for Sunderland. His reply was honest. "Willie," he said. "Exactly what you are telling me now, Bob Stokoe was saying to me 10 years ago." He never did learn.

Behind the scenes, however, was where all the hard work was done - and it was often far from glamourous. At Hartlepool, we had only one apprentice, Barry Stimpson, who was allowed one day's college release every week to further his education. That would leave me and George with the duties Barry normally performed after the first team players had departed. As we mopped out the toilets one afternoon, I couldn't help but ponder the change in direction my life had taken. "Hey, George," I smiled. "If anyone had told me two years ago when I was in Hong Kong with Middlesbrough that I'd soon be cleaning out Hartlepool's shit house I would have committed Hari Kari!" And yet the truth was that I was absolutely thrilled to be back in football at all. I was literally as happy as a pig in shit.

Things began to turn sour, however, due to the increasing interference of the chairman Vince Barker in first team matters. Consequently, I often found myself at loggerheads with him and, though I wasn't the manager, I became increasingly frustrated. Our relationship took a serious downturn after comments I made on local television following a game against Wimbledon at Easter 1981. With four promotion places up for grabs, we were still in with a good shout of going up but I knew we would struggle during the busy Easter period unless we could bring in a couple of new players to cover for the inevitable injuries. Indeed, Billy even had a couple of players in mind, at a total cost of about £15,000. On approaching the chairman, however, the request for transfer cash was dismissed. "Play some of the kids," Barker had said. He knew they were top of the league but what he wasn't taking into account was the fact that the better players among them were only first year trainees and would be well short of the requirements of a Fourth Division player.

That Sunday against Wimbledon, we made a rare appearance on Tyne-Tees

Extra Time – The Final Chapter

Television, only to lose the game 3-0. At the manager's request, I gave an interview with presenter Roger Tames who asked me what had gone wrong. My answer was that the players had done a magnificent job but had taken us as far as we could go. I added that, sadly, a club like Hartlepool did not possess the finances to buy the odd player or two to give us the extra impetus when we had injuries. I was simply stating a fact but Barker took it as a personal slant against him. From that moment, our relationship went downhill all the way.

Things became further strained when Barker rented out two pie shops within the Victoria Ground to me. Such was the success of the shops that his mood towards me became frosty. Consequently, after we had built up a good franchise operation over the course of a season, he refused to rent them to me the following year and the club began to run them again. I have always been a bit of an entrepreneur so I had no hesitation in going into that particular business opportunity with a guy called Fred Appleton, who was head caterer at Stockton and Billingham Technical College and an ardent Boro fan.

However, I will never forget our first matchday in business. There was just half an hour to kick-off at the Victoria Ground and I was about to hand in our team-sheet to the referee when I was faced with Fred with his head up against the wall in apparent despair.

"What the hell are you doing here, Fred?" I asked in surprise.

The guy was in a real panic. "I've just locked myself out of the friggin' hut," he gasped. "All the Bovril will be boiling over and the pies are probably catching fire."

I looked at him in disbelief. "What the f*** do you expect me to do?" I asked him. "I'm putting in the team-sheet."

He was actually hoping I would go over and knock the door down to save our pies. How he expected me to explain to the referee that the team-sheet was in late because I was rescuing our pies, I will never know. I can just picture the headlines in the press: "Hartlepool's team-sheet late and club faces fine because Willie's pies and Bovril were overheating!" In the event, Fred did go back and sort out the problem himself and I, thankfully, was able to hand in that team-sheet. God bless you, Fred.

By that time I was also official kit supplier to the club, having opened up my own sports retail outlet some months before leaving Middlesbrough. I provided all training shoes, boots and other incidentals to the club at a huge discount. Even so, the chairman had not paid me for more than three months and the bill was topping

£3,000. Despite many personal confrontations, asking him to sort the debt out, there was never a penny forthcoming, until eventually I had to send my own club chairman a solicitor's letter. Without a response, I told him I wouldn't be renewing my advertising board behind the goal the following season. That was a move which did receive a response. Within an hour, the whole of the board had been painted out.

Things came to a head when I told Barker that he must sign one of our trainees called Paul Dobson on a professional contract. Dobson had scored 50 goals in helping the intermediates win the league and yet still wasn't on the books as a full-time player. I warned the chairman than unless we signed him we would lose him to another club, many of whom had seen his ability at first hand.

I was not prepared for his answer. "I'm not signing him - he's a lazy bastard," he replied. "He reminds me of that Jimmy Greaves."

I looked at him and wondered if he was serious. When I realised he was, I could see it was pointless continuing the conversation. I walked quietly out of the room and closed the door behind me. That was followed by the unbelievable decision to end Steve Smelt's association with the club. Despite all the talented youngsters we had, I knew the chairman was strangling the club. I had helped build a strong foundation but Hartlepool would never have a future whilst we had a chairman so lacking in long-term ambition. He also refused to invest in improving the ground and that had further detrimental effects. As long as the club looked like the arse-end of the world, we had no chance of attracting players to take it forward. Consequently, on the odd occasion when we did attempt to sign a player, it was suggested we would meet them in Middlesbrough or Stockton beforehand and try to get them to sign on the dotted line *before* they saw the ground.

Just a month into the 1981-82 season, I could take no more and resigned. I was a little bit disappointed with Billy Horner as I felt he had allowed the chairman to interfere too much. I had only a one-year contract but Billy's was for seven years and he knew Barker could not afford to sack him so I felt he could have stood up to him more than he did. Even so, I liked Billy who was a nice guy, perhaps too nice. Despite the bitter taste I had on leaving Hartlepool, I had enjoyed my time there and the experience of working alongside Billy and George was a good one. More importantly, working with a shoestring budget was to hold me in good stead in the years which followed.

15

Back at the Boro

I GUESS it was my destiny to return to Middlesbrough. The football club was my life from the age of 16 to 27. It was a love affair and it is impossible to simply turn your back and forget that type of devotion, no matter how bitterly and tearfully it ends. I had loved being one of the club's star players and a hero to the fans and knew I was held in high esteem by Teesside's football followers.

My departure from Hartlepool was followed by over two years out of the game, building up my own sports retail business but missing the game terribly. With the shop flourishing, however, I was tempted by an advertisement which appeared within the pages of the local newspaper, the Evening Gazette, that Middlesbrough were looking for a physiotherapist. Although I had only passed my preliminary badge as a physiotherapist, I also had the benefit of long hours spent in the treatment room over the years, seeing various physiotherapy techniques at close hand. I saw the vacancy as my long-awaited chance to get back into the game.

I was delighted when Boro manager Malcolm Allison returned my letter and granted me an interview. During the interview itself, Malcolm explained to me that the club had a veteran physio called Lew Reynolds who, whilst talented, was getting on in years and could no longer travel with the team to their busy schedule of away fixtures. He wanted the incoming physio to learn from Lew and eventually replace him. After an amiable chat about my qualifications and background, Malcolm offered me the job which I had no hesitation in accepting. It was October 1983 and I was back at my beloved Boro. And yet it was ironic to think that I was still only 31 and, had fate not dealt me such a cruel blow, I could so easily have been playing for the club with many more years left in me.

In the first and only game I attended as the club's physio, against Blackburn at

Back at the Boro

Ayresome Park, I treated striker Paul Sugrue in the penalty area in front of the Holgate End. As I approached Sugrue, who was writhing in agony, the crowd began a chant which was music to my ears after so long away: "Maddren for England!" With Suggie prostrate on the floor, my face had a smile as wide as the River Tees and I acknowledged the fans' support with a wave of my magic sponge, the water trickling down my arm. The player eventually resumed play and I enjoyed much banter with the supporters as I walked around the ash track back to the dug-out.

A week later, Malcolm asked me if I would work with the club's intermediates. Their previous coach, George Heard, had left and I believe the junior side was being run by a part-time coach. I immediately accepted the manager's request to supervise daily coaching sessions and their Saturday morning fixtures. It was an easy transition as I felt far more comfortable coaching players than I did treating them for knocks and strains. But I was astonished to find the club's juniors struggling towards the bottom of the Northern Intermediate League as we had always had a great youth policy. At that level, developing skills is far more important than winning games and trophies but Middlesbrough had always had a knack of doing both.

Treating Boro reserve Andrew Strong during my brief spell as Middlesbrough's physiotherapist.

Extra Time – The Final Chapter

I worked on the lads over the course of six months, training morning and afternoon, and slowly but surely we began to develop an understanding and climbed the table to eventually finish runners-up to Newcastle. Whilst we did not have talent in abundance, four of the better players were Peter Beagrie, Colin Cooper, Alan Kernaghan and Mike Heathcote. None stood out more than Beagrie, who had by then made the switch from Hartlepool. He had been used as a left-back in the reserves but I pushed him further forward to occupy the left or right wing where his skills could be used to greater effect. Beagrie's defensive ability could best be described as naive and he was never going to make the grade in that position, but he immediately began to look like a potential first teamer once he was pushed forward. He had that little bit of arrogance that I liked in a player though I questioned his infuriating habit of wanting to beat an opponent a second time. I spent long hours trying to drum home to him that, having beaten a player and created a yard or two of space, it was his duty to cross the bleedin' ball, not go back and try to beat the damn player again. As such, all advantage was lost as defenders had a chance to prepare for the cross when it finally came.

Colin Cooper quickly began to look the part at junior level. He was a terrific reader of the game, always dropped off early, gave himself plenty of time on the ball and had a first class attitude in training. The only question mark I put against him was his physique as, at 17, he wasn't the tallest of boys and was very lean. But he more than made up for that with a big heart and was always likely to go far. I occasionally used Alan Kernaghan at centre-forward but many times as a centre-half. I always felt he had a good chance of making it as he was comfortable on the ball when playing at the back, though he lacked a bit of pace.

Mike Heathcote lacked Alan's ability but if I had asked him to run through a brick wall he would have done so, such was his determination and will to succeed. Later, when I became the club's manager, I had to make the sad decision to release Mike, though I told him that although I didn't think he had the ability to play at the highest level, I felt he would always make a living from the game, perhaps in the lower leagues. I hoped he would prove me wrong and for a time it seemed he would as, after a spell with Spennymoor, he was snapped up by Sunderland and played the occasional game for their first team. But, as I had predicted, he went on to spend the majority of his playing days at a lower level with Shrewsbury, Cambridge and Plymouth.

Up front, we had a guy called John McMahon who was fast enough to catch pigeons. Without the overall ability to pass the ball around, I decided to revolve our tactics around John's explosive speed and the ploy worked a treat. John had an outside chance of making it but I always felt he needed to be a bit braver in the box to match his electrifying pace. Too often he would infuriate me by allowing the opposition centre-back to have free headers, giving them time to compose themselves and head the ball back over our midfield into the heart of our defence. I worked with him for hours trying to get across the idea that if he couldn't win the header, then he should back into the defender and make him spill or mis-head his clearance. Had he applied that to his game, he may well have made it but John couldn't grasp what I was trying to teach him. About a season after I became manager, I decided to give McMahon a free transfer and Cyril Knowles played him for Darlington in a Freight Rover match. Incredibly, John scored five goals that night and the following morning my chairman Mike McCullagh asked me if I was sure I hadn't made a big mistake in releasing him. To be quite honest, I wondered about it myself. Before long, however, Darlington had released the lad and, sadly, he never made his mark in the professional game.

That season we reached the NIL Cup final against the champions, Newcastle. After winning the first leg by a single goal, we lost 3-0 in the return at Benwell. Despite the defeat, Beagrie performed particularly well on the night but one Newcastle player was on a higher plain from all the rest. Playing behind their front two, he destroyed us with his all-round skill and passing ability and it was obvious with talent like his, the sky was the limit. It was my first glimpse of Paul Gascoigne.

My role in charge of the intermediates eventually became full-time while I was also given responsibility for the reserves home and away. The second team team duties had previously been covered by first team coach George Armstrong but he was quite happy for me to share the burden. Unfortunately, my first game in charge of the reserves will forever remind me of the demise of Kevin Beattie, a defender I had once rated the best in the country. At the time, I was still assisting George and travelled with him and the team for an evening game at Notts County. As he lived away from Teesside, it was planned that Kevin would join up with us on our arrival at Meadow Lane. As the team bus pulled up outside the ground that night, their chief steward handed a note to George informing him that Beattie's car had broken down and he would not be able to make it to the match. I had the utmost admiration for Beattie as I believe he would have been an all-time great had he not suffered injury problems, but I couldn't help but wonder why he was still being paid by the club. After all, here was a player who I had not seen around Ayresome Park in the two months since I had returned to the club.

Extra Time – The Final Chapter

On reading the note, George wisely said: "Willie, you can take the team tonight and I'll watch from upstairs. It will be good experience for you." George was right - it was good experience. Mission Impossible would be another way of describing it. Beattie was to have been our only experienced pro in a side comprising four 16-year-old triallists, four first year youth trainees, a triallist goalkeeper and one apprentice. It was the most inexperienced reserve side I had ever clapped eyes on, a team of babies. Although they were a top flight side at the time, Notts County were operating with only 16 professionals which meant eight or nine first team players, including John Chiedozie and Andy McCulloch, appeared for their reserve team that night. I was delighted to get away with a 9-0 thrashing because, in all honesty, we were lucky to get nil. Afterwards I told our young lads that there was no disgrace losing like that to a side boasting nine first team professionals.

But I found my role with both the juniors and reserves an absolute joy and was continually looking at young lads in the local leagues who might have missed the boat originally but were now worth taking a second look at. We would occasionally use Northern League players to add a bit of steel to our young reserve side. One of the lads we looked at was a certain Gary Pallister, but more of him later. Another I thought might have half a chance was a striker called Charlie Butler who we used on several occasions. Charlie was a prolific goalscorer at Northern League level for many years but I felt he fell just short of the mark in terms of the professional game. I also gave a trial to Paul Dobson, the lad Vince Barker had likened to the "lazy" Jimmy Greaves at Hartlepool. Unfortunately, injury meant Paul hadn't played for three weeks prior to the game and I think that lack of match fitness may have cost him. Although he made by far the best attempts on goal over the 90 minutes, Malcolm Allison didn't fancy him as a player.

I enjoyed my experience under Big Mal immensely as he never interfered and I was left largely to my own devices. To be honest, I didn't see an awful lot of him on the training ground, although when I did see him at work, it was obvious he was an exceptional coach. The only thing that I questioned about his methods was that at times he tended to experiment too much. It baffled and intrigued me that most weeks the first team still hadn't seen a football in training by Wednesday morning. Believe it or not, a typical Monday morning training session revolved around table tennis tables in the club's recreation room. It was usually supervised by Lenny Hepple, a balance expert whose principles were geared towards achieving sharper reactions and greater balance. Quite often it was a table tennis ball rather than a football that the first team practiced with on Mondays as Lenny believed this was the ultimate reaction sport. If that was not strange enough, Tuesdays under Big Mal were even more off the beaten track. That was the day for Roger Spry to visit. Roger was some kind of martial arts-style fitness instructor and, watching his sessions, I observed plenty of high kicking, stretching and dancing to music.

But Mal's methods weren't restrained to the training ground. There was room for them in the dressing room too, as I witnessed before our game against Blackburn for my first match back at the club as physiotherapist. Malcolm had instigated a pre-match routine whereby the first team players would form a circle, join hands and, rather like basketball players do today, rouse each other up by chanting in unison: "We're gonna win, we're gonna win, we're gonna win..." That afternoon they lost. As they did the four games on either side of that fixture. Indeed, Jim Platt, who had been released soon after Big Mal's arrival at the club, later told me how he had witnessed that same chant before the previous season's home game with Blackburn. On that occasion Boro were stuffed 5-1. I observed all this from the back of the dressing room but resisted George Armstrong's invitation to join in.

To be fair, I don't think anyone could blame Malcolm for the club's slide from the heady days of top flight football during my playing days. The downward spiral was already spinning out of control long before his arrival and he had no money to spend in trying to turn our fortunes around. The problems went back to an FA Cup quarter-final defeat to Wolves in 1981 which had signalled the departures of talented stars like David Armstrong, Craig Johnston, David Hodgson and Mark Proctor.

I liked Malcolm and was grateful to him for giving me the chance to get back into football. Although I felt the club was struggling in terms of the quality of first team personnel, I was happy to get on with the challenge of providing a future foundation with the development of the stars of the future. I wasn't too interested in the internal politics of the club, preferring to keep my head down and do my best, but when results went from bad to worse I did begin to worry that I might soon find myself back out of football as a new broom often sweeps clean.

Results weren't exactly going our way and crowds were down to a bare minimum of just over 5,000. Only one win in nine games during February and March of 1984 increased the pressure on Malcolm who was coming under more and more pressure from the board to sell some of the club's star players to bring in much-needed finance. But rather than buckle, he issued a controversial statement that it was better for the club to die than linger on. What he actually wanted the club to do was to go into receivership to clear the debts, which is what happened under the instigation of Steve Gibson two years later. There was no likelihood of Mal getting money to spend and maybe he saw receivership as a way of making a new start for the club. However, his statement did not go down well with either the supporters or the club's chairman, Mike McCullagh.

Following a 2-0 home defeat to Fulham, Malcolm summoned me, George Armstrong and his chief scout Ted Davies to his office where he informed us that there would be some bad news and then some good news. I don't know what he meant by that. I can only assume that he had a consortium in the wings, ready to take over the club but if that was the case nothing ever came of it. The next we heard was an announcement that Malcolm had been sacked. Personally, I was sad to see him go. After all, I knew my job may well go with his.

However, shortly after the dismissal of Big Mal came the appointment of Big Jack. My former boss Jack Charlton was back at the Boro, at least until the end of the season. Even so, I wasn't complacent enough to think my job was safe. I knew him well enough to know that he wouldn't feel he owed me any loyalty simply because I was a former player of his. I was naturally nervous, therefore, when Jack summoned me and George to the manager's office during his first morning in charge. Personally, I was surprised Jack had come back as he had not been linked with any other jobs since leaving Sheffield Wednesday a year earlier. But it seemed that he had agreed to steady the ship as a favour to Mike McCullagh as they were long-time friends.

After greeting us and asking us to take a seat, Jack got on with what he had to say. "I know you, Willie, and trust you," he began. "So from now on you will work with me with the first team. You, George, can take the reserves and kids until I find out if you've got any passion for this club."

Don't ask me why, but at that very moment I knew that my destiny would be to leave my secure job with the reserves and juniors to get the manager's job, only to get the sack. In an instant I knew that Jack would not fancy the job long-term and that I would be in the hot seat in the not too distant future. In the meantime, I knew that if anyone could turn things around then it was Jack. Malcolm had always had a wonderful knack of telling the media about the good young team he had but it was only on Jack's arrival that people realised we were in trouble and could still

Back at the Boro

actually face relegation to Division Three. But I knew Jack would identify the problem areas very quickly.

With no time to get to know his players, Jack allowed me to pick the team for his first game in charge, against Oldham at Ayresome. So my first Boro side lined up as:

1. Kelham O'Hanlon
2. Darren Wood
3. Tony Mowbray
4. Paul Ward
5. Mick Baxter
6. Irving Nattrass
7. Stephen Bell
8. Mick Kennedy
9. Heine Otto
10. Paul Sugrue
11. Gary Hamilton
12. David Currie

Jack had not previously seen the team play and was shocked by the poor standard. After about 20 minutes he turned to me and said: "I can't believe this crap. We haven't got a player. I can't believe the fans used to criticize my team. Our team was on another planet compared to this load of crap."

Although we went 1-0 up, Mick Baxter, our big centre-back, was getting knocked from pillar to post by Oldham's Mick Quinn. As the match went on, Jack became more and more aeriated about Baxter's inability to give Quinn a hard time and eventually turned to our sub, David Currie, and asked: "Can you play centre-half?" David, a striker, couldn't defend to save his life and looked frightened to death at the prospect. Before he had chance to answer, I interrupted: "Don't be stupid, Jack - no, he can't."

Knowing Jack as I did, I asked him not to be too hard on Baxter at half-time as he was not the type of lad to respond to a bollocking. But my advice fell on deaf ears.

Back in the dressing room, the first person Jack approached was Baxter. "Are you OK?" he asked.

Extra Time – The Final Chapter

Mick started to reply: "Well, yeah, I've just had a bit of a cold all week..."

Jack didn't wait for him to finish his sentence. "Well start winning some f***ing balls in the air, otherwise we're going to lose this f***ing game through you!"

That was about as diplomatic as Jack could be. Poor Mick had never come across that style of management before and I could see his chin was on the floor. As Jack moved on to talk to one or two of the other lads, I told Mick not to take any notice of him. "Don't worry about Jack," I said. "Me and Boamy were on the end of many a bollocking like that."

At the end of the game, which we won 3-2, Jack expressed to me his alarm at the players' overall lack of fitness. He told me he had commitments with the army the following week but that I should "run the balls off them" on Monday morning. I thought: "Cheers, Jack." It would be my first time in charge of the first team and I knew a hard training session would go down like a lead balloon. Normally in the end-of-season run-in, it was important to conserve energy and stay clear of fitness training but I knew Jack was right, having witnessed countless balance, reaction and dance exercises over the previous months.

My announcement on Monday morning that we would be concentrating 100 per cent on physical exercise was met with the moans and groans I had anticipated. The players couldn't understand it. Even so, all but one got on with it and worked hard.

The only one to question my authority was Paul Sugrue. "I can't f***ing believe this," he moaned in his whining Cockney accent. "Having to do a physical at this stage in the season."

"You do it whether you like or not," I told him. "Because you're not f***ing fit." I didn't use Jack as my excuse. If I was going to survive at that level, I had to do so on my own steam.

I ended the session with a game of five-a-side which appeared to be a popular decision. I told them that, providing the game was competitive, we would play it for the last 20 minutes. After about 10 minutes, however, someone hit a shot about a yard wide of the marker cone. "Goal!" shouted Sugrue. "Goal kick," I replied, the result of which was a remonstration about my decision by both Sugrue and Mick Kennedy. I wasn't going to be questioned on my first day in charge. I told all the lads to finish the five-a-side there and then. Instead, we would do two fast laps of the field, courtesy of Sugrue and Kennedy. With that, I heard them say that they wouldn't do the laps. On hearing their whispers, I told them anyone who didn't complete the laps in less than one minute 30 seconds would be back for extra training that afternoon. Thankfully, both of them completed the laps in the allotted time.

Sugrue was the biggest moaner. I knew he was trying to test me out and see how far he could push me in my first time in charge. After training, I pulled him aside into the referee's room. "I know what you're about," I told him. "But I've played with far better players than you in my time. If you don't toe the line in terms of discipline, I'm big enough to put you through the wall."

To be fair to the lad, he acknowledged that he had been out of order. He knew as well as I did that he had been trying it on.

The following week, Jack still had engagements with the Army in Germany so I took charge of a first team match for the first time, taking George Armstrong as my assistant for our tough away match at promotion-chasing Blackburn. Rovers' Simon Barker scored a 35-yard belter in the opening 10 minutes and I thought we might be on the end of a hammering, as they were a good side at the time. As it turned out, we were unlucky to lose to that single goal but I was disappointed not to have taken at least a share of the spoils in my first game in charge.

A couple of draws followed, before we faced Howard Wilkinson's table-topping Sheffield Wednesday, who were, of course Jack's former club. In those days, Howard played a rigid off-side trap, a flat back four pushing up almost to the half-way line. But, once again, Jack proved to me what an astute tactician he was. All week he had the lads working on a tactic which was similar to the one he had employed involving Alan Foggon 10 years earlier. Every time the ball went forward, our front two were to make runs, not towards the opposition goal, but towards ours. This ensured they stayed onside with midfield runners coming from deep positions to get on the end of long passes. The tactic destroyed Wednesday. We created chance after chance and eventually won the match 2-0.

We felt four points from the final four games would ensure the club's safety from the drop zone. However, we were made to wait for those points. Swansea, who were already doomed to a second successive relegation, beat us 2-1 at the Vetch Field. It was after that game, back in our hotel, that Jack revealed he was recommending me to succeed him as manager of the club. Given what had gone before, the news didn't come as a complete surprise to me. What I was shocked about was the dire financial situation the club now found itself in. A £1.3 million debt and a ground in desperate need of repair were clearly priorities before any cash could be freed for new players. In fact, there would be pressure from day one to sell our best players.

I had to smile when he finished giving me the bad news with the line: "I think it's an impossible job. Oh, and by the way, I've recommended you for it!"

Jack told me he had already made his sentiments known to Mike McCullagh and the board but I knew they wouldn't let him go lightly. That night one of the directors, Keith Varley, offered Jack a king's ransom to manage the club on a permanent basis but he was having none of it. I was later to discover that Jack was a wise man to turn down the offer.

But this was my chance to manage my hometown club. How could I refuse? Being one of them, I felt for the supporters who had seen the club plummet from the top flight to the brink of the Third Division in a matter of a few years and I was desperate for an opportunity to bring about a turn in our fortunes. Now, thanks to Jack's support, it seemed I would be given that very chance.

I got to know Jack well during our brief association as manager and coach and found him to be a far more amiable, relaxed guy than the man I had known during my playing days. I had never seen the warmer side to his personality. Mind you, I don't think any of those players we had in that team of '84 still believe he has a warm side to his nature. After Malcolm's softly softly methods, Jack's abrasive approach to training and management came as something of a culture shock to them.

The following week, we made absolutely sure of our survival for one more season with a 1-0 home win over Charlton Athletic. Once again, Jack had made a promise to be with the Army, leaving me in charge and I was relieved to be able to guide us to safety. I know people may question Jack's frequent absences when he had agreed to help the club out but it was not a case of him abusing his power. In fact, he did not take a penny off the club for all his time and effort during his spell as caretaker manager. He came back only as a favour for the chairman and for his love of the club and its supporters.

The next day we travelled to Brighton for our penultimate match, a Bank Holiday Monday fixture. On the Sunday evening, I received the call I had anticipated from Jack. "Well done, yesterday," he said. "It was a great result. There's no need for me to come down for the game tomorrow."

I acknowledged the fact, though I realised I would have my work cut out in his absence. As I had travelled to the south coast with just myself and 14 players, it meant I would be manager, coach, trainer and physio. The club could not afford the staff so I had been acting as physio at our away games in any case, but this time I really had my hands full. Having tended to an injured player late in the match, I was still making my way back to the dug-out when an almighty roar went up around the ground. As I turned back to the pitch, I saw that Mick Kennedy had been shown a red card. Returning to the dug-out, shaking my head, I asked sub Garry MacDonald why Kennedy had been sent off. "I don't know, boss," he replied. Garry was trying to avoid dropping his team-mate in it, as I later discovered the dismissal was for elbowing an opponent in an off-the-ball incident.

Whilst the club's survival was of the utmost importance, I had a second reason for being grateful that we were safe from relegation before the last match of the season. For, 12 months earlier, I had pencilled in the date of May 12th as my wedding day to my beloved Hilary. It was with much relief that I was able to attend my wedding and leave the matchday duties to George Armstrong. We drew our last game 0-0 against Huddersfield in a quite uneventful and, I believe, forgettable game. To quote a pun, the main match of the day involved two players called Willie and Hilary in a small church in Eaglescliffe.

I left for my honeymoon with Hilary without having had confirmation from the board of my appointment. However, I was determined to forget all about the pressures of football and enjoy a wonderful start to our marriage. We spent the first week of our honeymoon in Rome, as I had fantastic memories of the scenery from my first visit as an 18-year-old. However, I now found the city's pollution and traffic to be a bit claustrophic and took far more enjoyment from a peaceful second week when we stayed in a beautiful hotel in Sorrento overlooking the bay of Naples with Mount Vesuvius in the background. Little did I appreciate that it would have been easier to climb Vesuvius in its explosive hey-day than to succeed in the job at Middlesbrough.

Returning home full of enthusiasm for the challenge ahead, I soon became perplexed when a week later I had still not had contact from the football club. I found this frustrating as I felt I needed to be at the club organising personnel for the new season. I knew I would have to work through the club's retained list and players would be anxious about their future. Of course, without having heard confirmation that I had the job, all sorts of things began to go through my mind and I started to wonder if they had decided to disregard Jack's advice and look for a more high profile manager. Eventually, five weeks after Jack had told me he had recommended me for the job, I rang him to ask what the hell was going on. Like

Extra Time – The Final Chapter

me, he was annoyed that nothing had yet been done about my appointment and promised to ring Mike McCullagh to find out what was happening. Within a couple of hours, the chairman rang me and asked me to meet him at his offices at Marske Machine Co. the following morning. He assured me an announcement would be made following our discussion. I had known Mike for many years, since his time as a club director during my playing days, and I felt I could trust him. He had built a very successful business in the engineering industry and was well respected by his workforce.

At 10 o'clock the next morning, Mike repeated Jack's story of some weeks earlier about how the club was in such dire straits and needed to be run on the tightest of budgets with huge financial constraints for at least the next 12 months. He outlined to me that there would be no hope of making cash signings and that a maximum salary for those I picked up on a free transfer would be £250 a week - £300 if I really had to go that far.

"What does the top earner at the club take home?" I asked.

"£550 a week plus bonuses," he replied.

I spelt it out to him that with such constraints we may only get the dregs from the free transfer list as the better players would obviously be tempted by higher salaries. "Recognising also, Mike, that I've got to sell two of our best players to keep the bank happy, where are you expecting us to finish in the league?" I queried.

Thankfully, his reply was realistic. "If you finish out of the bottom three, I'll be delighted."

It didn't need saying that the job was mine. But Mike was rather embarrassed to discuss my salary. As coach for the club's juniors, I had been on £10,000 a year. My new salary as manager would be £12,500, though he hastened to add that I would receive expenses whilst using my own car. I recognised in an instant that this was surely the worst salary for any manager in the Football League but I didn't bat an eyelid. For me, the job wasn't about money. I had a burning desire to take the club back to its former status and to give back to the people of Teesside a pride in their team.

16

Just about Managing

I DOUBT I made many friends in my first few weeks as manager of Middlesbrough. But then I wasn't there to make friends. I was there to try to build a team good enough to keep us out of the Third Division. Anything after that would be a bonus. But I was soon to discover that I was being asked to turn very cloudy water into wine.

I was full of boundless enthusiasm in my first days in charge of the club. Although, at 33, I was very young to be a manager, I was far from overawed about the prospect. I welcomed the challenge and had much confidence in my own ability to put things right tactically and to analyse the opposition's strengths and weaknesses. I was confident too that I could put together a team capable of achieving at least a mid-table spot in the Second Division. But, boy, did I underestimate the job in hand.

Before I did anything else, I knew I had to do a job no-one enjoyed - telling players and other staff they no longer had a future at the club. The day after my meeting with Mike McCullagh, it was made public that I was the club's new manager and the two of us chatted with a handful of local reporters at Ayresome Park. It was a far cry from the all-singing, all-dancing press conferences held to announce new appointments at the Cellnet Riverside Stadium nowadays but I made it clear that I believed it would take three years to turn the club around. After all, we had no money to buy players so I would have to rely on our talented youngsters who I felt were at least two years away from being able to handle regular first team football. As I walked back to my office after that rather unspectacular beginning, Ted Davies, the club's chief scout, congratulated me on my appointment. Unbeknown to him, Ted was to become the first casualty of my

Extra Time – The Final Chapter

retained list. Appointed by Malcolm Allison, Ted had given me several reasons to mistrust him and I had no intention of keeping him on as part of my team.

The previous week I had heard him talking to the Manchester United pair of Harry Gregg and Lou Macari who were interested in taking the Boro job as a partnership. They asked Ted to keep them informed of any developments. Ted knew I was getting the job but, instead of telling them that was the case, he kept them on the hook, perhaps in the hope that the chairman might change his mind.

I think he was quite shocked when I asked him there and then to clear his desk, taking with him only what belonged to him. I think perhaps he looked at me, just 33 years old, and thought I was a bit green and probably hadn't noticed what he was up to. Accepting that it was my decision and he had no choice in the matter, he left the office quietly with barely a word.

That was only the first of many unpleasant duties I had to perform during my first two days in charge. The chairman had made it perfectly clear that I had to prune the playing staff considerably. I had turned down his offer to play the hatchet man, insisting that if there was dirty work to do then I had to be the one to do it. As it was the close season, I called in all the players and let them know where they stood. However, I knew I had to be aggressive with the clear-out and decided to release nearly every reserve and intermediate.

The hardest one to say goodbye to was young Mike Heathcote, whose commitment could not be questioned. Striker Garry MacDonald was a borderline case but I knew I was right to release him and he went on to play regular football in the lower divisions with Darlington. I had watched Garry play many times and, although he held the ball quite well, he didn't use his weight for such a big lad, wasn't dynamic enough and didn't score enough goals.

Mick Baxter was another casualty of my clear-out. Only three years earlier he had been a club record £425,000 signing from Preston. God bless him, he was a lovely lad, but in comparison to the likes of Stuart Boam, he had nowhere near the type of aggression I wanted to see in my central defenders. Rather, he was a gentle giant. But the biggest factor in my decision was Mick's salary - he was one of the top wage earners with, I believe, a loyalty payment built into his contract which meant that if we were to offer him an extension we would have had to fork out a considerable sum of money just to retain his services. Mick had to go, as a new club policy was that no signing on fees would be paid to players. He eventually joined Portsmouth on a free transfer. It saddened me deeply, however, when Mick tragically died of cancer at the age of just 33, without ever playing another game.

The truth of the matter is that there were other players I would have liked to have shifted out but the club could not afford to pay off their contracts, so for the time being we were stuck with them. Whilst releasing players would save on the wage bill, our rising debts meant there was also pressure on me to raise money with the sale of one or two of my better players. Both Sheffield Wednesday and Portsmouth were interested in midfielder Mick Kennedy whilst Chelsea and Portsmouth made enquiries about our young defender Darren Wood. Kennedy was the sort of player I could ill afford to lose. Although I thought he could be a bit of a head-banger, he was a winner. He was the sort of lad who would crudely put his foot in and intimidate opponents and there wasn't enough of that type of player at the club. But I knew I would have no option but to sell him if we received the right offer. I felt he was worth £150,000 of anyone's money so was pretty disgusted when Portsmouth made a paltry bid of £80,000. But people were aware of our predicament and knew we were under pressure to sell. Such was the pressure on us from the bank, Mike McCullagh told me that we would have to snap their hands off if I could squeeze another £20,000 out of Portsmouth. Sure enough, we settled on a fee of £100,000 and Kennedy made the move to Fratton Park. That kept the bank happy for a while but not me - and certainly not the club's supporters who viewed the deal as another case of us selling one of our best players for financial gain. Little did they know that the club was so close to financial ruin.

Turning to the important business of introducing new blood to the club, I had naively believed that, like me, other managers were already worrying about their squads for the new season, two months before the campaign got underway. But, as with most players, every other manager was away on holiday and there was no chance of making any progress on the transfer front for the next few weeks. Indeed, experience was to teach me that most deals are transacted from mid-July onwards.

But I was also to suffer a rude awakening in terms of Boro's financial clout - or rather the lack of it. The chairman had appointed a "trouble-shooter", David Gaster, who would act as the club's financial controller for at least three months. I would have to check and agree with Gaster before doing anything with a financial cost. It was to prove a frustrating arrangement.

When July came around, I received a Football League list of all the players who had been freed by their clubs. I systematically went through the list, highlighting the names of the better players and drawing up my own list of targets. My first

Extra Time – The Final Chapter

target was a guy called Joe Waters who had been given a free transfer by Grimsby Town. I needed a midfield play-maker and Joe, an experienced lad and recognised as a good passer, fitted the bill. He was keen to join us and I explained to him that my long-term policy would be to weed out the players with no passion for the club whilst gradually introducing talented youngsters. I wanted him to provide the experience and good example for the younger lads.

Joe was all set to sign but the stumbling block was his terms. He had been on £300 a week at Grimsby and assured me he would join us if we matched that salary and gave him a £5,000 signing on fee to cover his moving expenses. I found it irritating when Gaster told me I could offer him £250 a week and no more. For heaven's sake, the guy had been playing for little Grimsby Town and we couldn't even match his wages. Given Middlesbrough's history, it was a measure of just how far we had fallen. I went back to Gaster and he agreed to go up to the £300 mark but there was no chance of a signing on fee. When I finally rang Joe back, he told me the ex-Birmingham manager Freddy Goodwin had been on the phone from America. Freddy was willing to fly Joe and his wife out there for seven days to take a look at the set-up they had in the North American Soccer League. I knew that was the end of the story. In fact, I was surprised when, out of courtesy, Joe rang me on his return to say that, although he really fancied coming to Boro for the challenge, the package of a house, car and double the wages we were able to offer him was just too good to turn down.

My next target was John Trewick, a former WBA midfielder who had been freed by Newcastle United. John appeared to be interested in joining us until we discussed salary. I was hugely disappointed to discover Oxford United - newly promoted from the Third Division and another club I had always considered to be a minnow in comparison to Boro - had been able to make him a far better offer. He naturally joined Jim Smith at the Manor Ground.

I was now beginning to realise just how naive I had been. I had been confident of achieving reasonable success on the pitch by wheeling and dealing in free transfers. What I hadn't realised was that to get the better players, even off the free transfer list, would require me being able to offer higher salaries than I was able to. Eventually, after much frustration, I signed Mick Buckley from Carlisle. I was desperate for an experienced midfielder who could join things up in the middle of the park and Buckley had been capped by England at under-23 level during his days with Everton. It is fair to say, however, that he wasn't exactly my first choice.

My second signing was a player whose honesty and character I knew inside out - a man I could trust on and off the pitch. He was my old friend and Boro team-mate David Mills. Having left Boro as the country's most expensive footballer five years earlier, I was now able to bring him back to Ayresome Park on a free transfer, but I knew he would guarantee me 15 goals a season. I had watched him in action for Newcastle several times in the previous couple of seasons and, even at 32, he still had that extra yard of pace. More importantly, he hadn't lost the desire to chase lost causes and go in where it hurt. David was surprised at having to take a huge wage reduction in joining us but I promised I would look after him if things went well. Some months later, Millsy asked for a transfer as he was so disappointed that other players who had been with the club for some time were on so much more than he was. I had a lot of sympathy for him but the financial constraints I was working under meant I could nothing about it.

But my pre-season problems were not confined to my playing squad. Requiring enticements for players, I approached local garage owners in an attempt to find vehicles for their personal use. Both Lookers of Billingham and the local Mitsubishi dealer initially agreed to sponsor three cars but, to my huge disappointment, the latter withdrew his offer on learning that Lookers had matched his deal. Incredibly, he wanted exclusivity as the club's car supplier. I angrily told him that if he wanted exclusivity then he would need to sponsor all 11 first team players.

As the new season approached, I found myself in confrontation with David Gaster, who was dogmatic about the club's finances, keeping a careful check on every last penny. Remembering the success of our pre-season visit to Largs in Scotland during my playing days, I felt a similar trip would be good for team spirit as we prepared for the new campaign. I was shocked when Gaster refused to even consider funding such "extravagance". Rather than accept the decision, however, I contacted Hibernian, Morton and Motherwell, who each agreed to cover our hotel expenses in return for us playing pre-season friendlies against them. Having done so, however, I was still short of the cash to cover our travel expenses of about £1,000 for the week. Thankfully, Appleyard van hire kindly agreed to supply to the club free of charge a 12-seater mini-bus on the condition that we insured it for the week. As we could not afford to hire a driver, our new signing David Mills was the man behind the wheel whilst two cars followed behind carrying the remainder of our small first team squad.

Despite those ridiculous restraints, that week's training was magnificent and it

Extra Time – The Final Chapter

was clear there was plenty of enthusiasm among the lads. The day before the players had returned after their summer break, I was brassed off when George Armstrong - my only coach - had told me he was joining QPR as their youth team coach. In his absence, Millsy and Irving Nattrass, my two most experienced players, shared training duties with me. However, during the half-time interval of our first friendly, at Motherwell, I gave Millsy perhaps the biggest rollicking of his life. In trying to set an example for the others, he had taken throw-ins, free kicks, and as a result of his enthusiasm been caught offside umpteen times. Looking back, I might have gone a wee bit over the top as I well and truly bawled him out. But I wanted to impress upon the other lads that, although Millsy was helping with the coaching and was an old friend of mine, I would have no favourites when in came to spelling out what was needed tactically. Being the good pro that he was, David took my words in the way they were intended and did not retaliate. Indeed, by the end of the game I felt more than a little guilty as he had played in a far more controlled manner and scored both goals in giving us a 2-0 win.

After that morale-boosting start to the tour, we lost narrowly to Morton, who were then in the Scottish Premier Division. They offered us our sternest test and gave me a good idea about how we were developing. Our next match was against Hibs, a game I was particularly looking forward to as they didn't usually finish too far behind Celtic and Rangers. However, I was embarrassed for anyone from Hibs to see us turning up for the match in a hired 12-seater mini-bus so gave Millsy instructions to park round the corner from the ground. From there, young Peter Beagrie and John McMahon were told to carry the boots and kit the remainder of the journey. I was over the moon with a goalless draw on the night as it was a defensively sound performance, though I did have a few doubts about our left-back Geoff Scott who appeared to be defensively naive for all his experience. Having been released by Charlton, Scott had joined us on a month-by-month contract but was clearly struggling. My problem was that my squad was wafer-thin so I was in no position to be fussy.

Our final pre-season friendly was against Newcastle United at St James' Park. Their manager was Jack Charlton, who had surprised me by taking on the job. Football management had seemed the furthest thing from his mind when we had parted at the end of the previous season and he had appeared happy to concentrate on his TV career. When I rang him to ask why the change of heart, he admitted he still wasn't sure if he had done the right thing. He revealed his uncle, the great Jackie Milburn, had talked him into it. I was pleased he did because it meant we faced high quality opposition including a young Chris Waddle and Peter Beardsley. Midway through the second half of a 2-2 draw, I was busy screaming instructions to my players when Jack shouted across from his dug-out for me to be quiet. As I looked across to him he had a wry smile on his face. Perhaps he could see in my raw enthusiasm something of himself a few years earlier.

On the Wednesday before our opening fixture at Portsmouth, I supervised training before swapping my manager's hat for a chief scout's hat and catching the one o'clock train to the south coast to catch Pompey in a friendly with QPR. Without the luxury of an assistant to accompany me, it was quite a lonely trip. On arriving at Fratton Park, who should be the first person I bump into but George Armstrong who, rather embarrassed, asked me how I was doing. Having spent a reasonable amount of money during the close season, Portsmouth were among the promotion favourites but, as I jotted tactical notes into my note book that evening, I didn't see anything to frighten me. Alan Ball had two good players in a young Neil Webb and the prolific Alan Biley - not forgetting their recent acquisition, Mr Kennedy - but I left for home confident that we could come away with a result if we organised well that Saturday.

Whilst the squad was wafer-thin in terms of experience, I was reasonably happy with it and believed the arrival of Mills and Buckley would compliment and help the young players I already had. Those young pro's were going to be on a steep learning curve but I hoped the more experienced pro's would help bring them on. Among those I had high hopes for were Stuart Ripley, Colin Cooper, Peter Beagrie, Alan Kernaghan and Gary Hamilton. As the club's youth team coach the previous season, I had given Ripley his first chance at that level while he was still a schoolboy and I felt he could possibly be the first of the few that would prove to be good enough. Physically, he was better equipped than any of his counterparts as, at 17, he was already a man in stature. I knew too that Colin Cooper had a good chance but his slight physique meant it was too early to push him into the first team fray. I felt I could shape Beagrie into a good player, Kernaghan was showing promise and Gary Hamilton, though still naive, looked as though he might make a player.

That opening fixture with Portsmouth was the usual south country hot weather start, with the temperature soaring to almost 80 degrees by the time the clock struck three. It being my first game officially in charge of my hometown club, I was naturally apprehensive prior to kick-off. My team for that nail-biting first match was:

Extra Time – The Final Chapter

1. Kelham O'Hanlon
2. Darren Wood
3. Paul Ward
4. Mick Buckley
5. Tony Mowbray
6. Irving Nattrass
7. David Mills
8. Gary Hamilton
9. Heine Otto
10. Paul Sugrue
11. David Currie

We gave as good as we got during the first 45 minutes and should have gone in a goal up. A minute before the interval, we won a right wing corner which presented us with a chance to take the lead at the perfect time. In training we had worked on a fast delivery with a low projectory head height for a thin touch with a near post header on to the back post. Striker David Currie was positioned on the back post that day in what I always call the glory position. But there was to be no glory for David. The delivery was perfection, the near post flick equally good, to find Currie two yards out with a free header. All he had to do was put his head forward on to the ball and its pace would have taken it over the line. I can still see him pulling his head back to bullet a header into the net. By the time he had completed the follow through, he caught the ball too thinly and it flew past the post.

I thought it was a bad miss but David was to eclipse even that later in the season when the ball went across the face of the goal to present him an absolute sitter. But he took his eye off the ball and sliced it wide of the post from just two yards out. But those missed chances were exceptions as "Kid Currie" was the most composed finisher in the club at the time.

Back in the Portsmouth encounter, there were 89 minutes on the clock and I was looking expectantly at my watch, believing we were about to achieve a tremendous result. With the seconds ticking away, a hopeful up-and-under from their right wing put the ball in flight for at least three or four seconds. When it eventually dropped, it did so between Darren Wood and Alan Biley, level with the back post and six yards out from goal. Defender and striker rose to head the ball in unison. The loose ball dropped between them and Biley toe-poked it agonisingly over the line for a late, late winner. I was particularly disappointed with the goal as I felt 'keeper Kelham O'Hanlon had had more than enough time to come and take the cross.

But I was absolutely gutted with the defeat. Having gone to such lengths to get things right and come so close to see it all go to plan, falling short in the last minute was hard to take. After the game, Mick Kennedy said he felt we had played well and were unlucky but that was no consolation to me. But I knew it was just one game and there were many more to come. In the dressing room I told Kelham I felt he should have taken the ball but, by and large, I congratulated my players in an attempt to lift them as they were clearly as disappointed as I was.

My post-match team talk could not have been any different four days later. In the dressing room of Valley Parade, I went ballistic with the players after a 2-0 League Cup defeat to Third Division Bradford City. A certain John Hendrie - later to become a huge Boro favourite - did the damage that night, enjoying an excellent game on their right flank and providing the ammunition for their goals. But if you don't match the aggression of a lower division team from the start then you will struggle, and I felt our performance lacked passion. But if I was disappointed about our opening two displays, then it was nothing compared to my first home game in charge against Grimsby the following Saturday.

At the risk of supporters who saw that match suggesting it was like pulling teeth, I have to admit I paid a visit to the dentist's the previous afternoon to have a tooth removed from the lower left hand side of my jaw. After tugging at the tooth for about 15 minutes, the club's dentist Harry Dredge realised it wasn't going to come out so sent me to Middlesbrough General Hospital to have it surgically removed. I arrived at the hospital mid-afternoon and was still there at seven o'clock that night, having received many inquisitive glances from supporters surprised to see the Boro manager in a side ward of a hospital on the eve of our opening home game. Not until 7.30 was I wheeled into the operating theatre where a piece of my jaw was removed to take out the long root of that damn tooth. By the time I left, I was in absolute agony and the side of my face was badly swollen.

I took the following day's pre-match team talk in extreme discomfort and with my face still swollen. In my talk, I drew my players' attention to Grimsby's attacking pair of Kevin Drinkell and Paul Wilkinson, informing them that they would both be a handful in the air. It was imperative therefore that we denied them

Extra Time – The Final Chapter

quality service from the flanks. After 20 minutes we were 4-0 down. I'll leave you to decide if the team heeded my advice. Two free headers from corners put them on their way while the young Wilkinson - another future Boro star - hit their third, running free as we were caught trying to play Grimsby offside. We were an absolute shambles. All the understanding and good play we had worked on in pre-season had gone right out of the window. Imagine the feeling I had as I watched helplessly from the dug-out. I was in utter disbelief. Like me, I think our fans were shell-shocked at such trauma in our opening home fixture.

Half-time couldn't come too soon, though I knew it would be a case of damage limitation and simply showing some pride during the second 45 minutes as the game was long lost. I tried to install some semblance of discipline in the defence as I knew that had we chased the game willy-nilly we might have ended up losing by eight or nine. To that effect, I had a real go at my two centre-backs, Irving Nattrass and Tony Mowbray, as they had allowed Grimsby's twin strikeforce to break free time after time. Thankfully, we coped far better in the second half but the damage had been done in that first 20 minutes. Having lost the game 5-1, I really let rip back in the dressing room and dished out a severe bollocking to the whole team.

Collectively, everyone was to blame, not just the defence. But in the post-match inquest with the press, I was particularly critical of Nattrass and Mowbray. Obviously Grimsby's forwards had wreaked havoc but more importantly I felt Nattrass had tried to force his own tactics on to the game. In pre-season, I had worked on the team defending a little bit deeper than usual to eliminate balls being played in behind our defence but Nattrass, who was a vastly experienced player, had influenced young Mowbray to push out of defence quickly. It had left Tony in two states of mind in that he didn't know whether to come out or stay back, to stick or to twist. Although prone to injuries, I had high regard for Nattrass as an excellent defender but I needed to make it clear from the start that he had to follow my instructions.

On the Monday morning following the debacle, Irving came to see me in my office. He told me that never in his whole career had he been personally criticised in the press and he found it unacceptable. We had a definite disagreement over it as I was adamant that he had tried to impose his own tactics on the game which were in direct conflict with my orders. Irving had little choice but to accept what I was saying and he did knuckle down over the months which followed.

On the Sunday after the mauling by Grimsby, Hilary and I took a drive out to

Just about Managing

High Force but, far from enjoying the fresh air and beautiful scenery, I was a million miles away, wondering what the hell had gone wrong the previous day. I was depressed and embarrassed that a team of mine could lose so badly in front of our fans. In truth, I had already started to heap far too much pressure on myself.

We were level at 2-2 with only minutes left to play in our next match at Notts County. But I was again dealt a blow and left to ponder what might have been. As the seconds ticked away, we should have simply been playing the game out to the final whistle but Heine Otto made a fateful error. Tracking an opponent on the touch-line, he made a wreckless challenge despite the fact that this guy was going away from our goal. From the resulting free-kick, Notts County scored the winner. I couldn't believe it. Instead of having our first point of the season, we were left to travel home having made it three league defeats out of three - and all due to a naive mistake from an experienced player who should have know better. I was hugely disappointed with Heine and told him so in no uncertain terms back in the dressing room.

We finally secured our first point of the season with a 1-1 home draw against Wolves, though I was again left thinking that we had thrown points away as we dominated the match. Three days later we faced Wimbledon at Ayresome Park and actually did very well against a side on its amazing rise from non-league football to the top flight. But an individual error was to cost us dear yet again. We were a goal up in the closing minutes of the first half when a clearing header by our defence fell at the feet of David Currie. Receiving the ball close to the halfway line, David would have had a free run at goal and a great chance of scoring if he had simply turned. Instead and quite inexplicably, he decided to pass the ball back to Kelham O'Hanlon in our goal, attempting to play the ball through a crowd of players. Sure enough, the ball fell well short of the 'keeper to the feet of Wimbledon's striker, who gleefully turned and fired in their equaliser. David's actions left me in a state of disbelief but I couldn't even bollock him. He knew exactly what he had done and was almost in tears at half-time. Sadly, his error proved to be the game's turning point. Wimbledon dominated the rest of the game and we crumbled to a 4-2 defeat.

On top of all this, I had to contend with press speculation linking John Bond with my job. I doubt very much it was anything but a wild rumour but it was unsettling all the same. But there was, however, light at the end of the tunnel. It came in the form of a first win of the season at the ninth time of asking. Currie scored twice and Mills another in a 3-2 home success over Cardiff City, though the

Extra Time – The Final Chapter

visitors scored their second with about 10 minutes left so, instead of coasting to what should have been an easy win, I was left on the edge of my seat and pleading for the final whistle to blow. The relief of hearing the sound of that whistle was immense. I had been putting myself under a ridiculous amount of pressure because I so much wanted to give the people of Teesside a winning football team. Now I had finally got my first three points under my belt and it lifted a huge weight from my shoulders.

After our awful start, we began to put a decent run together and climb the league. That win over Cardiff was the first of four victories in five games, including an excellent 3-0 success at Sheffield United. I had watched United before our game at Bramall Lane and felt their centre-backs were a little bit slow and cumbersome. As a result, our training in the days before the match concentrated on dropping balls in behind the two centre-backs for Millsy to run on to, while Currie was to pull the defenders further out of position by making decoy runs back towards our goal. In my pre-match team talk, I emphasised the need to keep things tight at the back and not concede any goals in the early stages because - as Jack Charlton had proved in Boro's game at Leeds many years earlier - the Yorkshire crowd were prone to turning hostile on their team if things didn't go to plan. Both tactics worked a treat. We kept it very tight early on whilst creating a number of openings at the other end. Just as I had predicted, United's fans turned on them, serving to make their players more nervous and to attack with less discipline than they normally would. That, in turn, helped to create even more chances for us. We absolutely murdered United that day, creating one chance after another with balls over the top of their defence. A penalty by Currie was followed up with further goals from Bell and Mills. But such was my knowledge of our ability to mess things up for ourselves, not until we were in the final minute did I turn to Steve Smelt to say: "Smelty, I think we're going to win this one!" For the first time, I was really beginning to enjoy life as a manager.

We continued on that positive theme with a third win on the bounce at home to Manchester City. We were 1-0 down at half-time but still felt confident of winning the game as we had played into a gale force wind through the first half. For the remainder of the match, we would have the wind behind us. Sure enough, we penned them into their half throughout the final 45 minutes and came back to win 2-1 through two goals from Millsy, taking his tally to seven in just 11 games. His value to the team could not be questioned and he was proving a fantastic free transfer signing.

Just about Managing

But whilst we had such a small squad with absolutely no cash with which to strengthen it, the good times were unlikely to keep rolling. The points again became hard to come by and we went into a Boxing Day clash at Carlisle on the back of just one win in nine games. Our desperate financial position was perhaps best summed up by the venue for our pre-match meal that day. Due to the club's ever-tightening purse strings, I had just £100 in expenses for the entire squad so we duly descended on The Little Chef between Hexham and Carlisle where tea, toast and jam was the maximum we could afford. It was hardly the ideal preparation for such an important match though we went on to win 3-0 against all the odds.

It was a far cry from the present Boro set-up who often enjoy the luxury of flying to away games of any distance whilst staying overnight at four star hotels. In contrast, I had reluctantly agreed with David Gaster to eliminate overnight stays when playing any clubs further north than Birmingham. Their ground, St Andrew's, was some 180 miles away from Middlesbrough and getting there involved a journey of up to four hours but the decision had been made that if our game was in the West Midlands or closer then we would travel on the day of the match itself.

By that stage, I had made two new additions to the squad - though I was forced to fight tooth and nail to get the board's go-ahead on both players. The pressure to sell another player had become a day to day aggravation and I knew that sooner or later Chelsea would come up with the money for Darren Wood. I knew that when they did I would be forced to sell him but I was determined to come out of the deal with something. Therefore, when they did come in for Darren, I insisted that former Boro defender Tony McAndrew be included as part of the deal. With Wood valued at £100,000, we received Tony plus £40,000 in cash, a deal I personally was delighted with despite having lost one of my better players.

Soon after signing McAndrew, I told the board I wanted to bring in another centre-back and ear-marked the former Luton player Mick Saxby who was available on a free transfer from Newport County. Saxby, who had been transferred for a fee of £200,000 just a few years earlier, was now available for nothing but I still had to battle with the board before being given the go-ahead to sign him. The directors couldn't understand why, having just signed McAndrew, I felt I needed another central defender and we had a long discussion as I tried to get across to them that it was such a crucial position and that it was essential I had cover for McAndrew, Nattrass and Mowbray. This was particularly important as I was keen on playing a system of three central defenders with one acting as sweeper. After much discussion, I was eventually given permission to sign Saxby and felt at the time he was a good acquisition.

When not involved in transfer activity, I was usually working hard behind the scenes in a search for new players. I realised that the squad was still well short of the one I needed and continued to look high and low for good players who would be available on the cheap. But I was acting as manager, scout and chief bottle washer in terms of my duties for the club. As I had no assistant, I was out on my own most nights watching games the length and breadth of the country in the hope of spotting a player who might not only be available for a small sum but could strengthen the squad I had. I would watch first team games, reserve team games and Northern League games at every available moment.

One player I spotted whilst on my travels was a teenage striker called Robbie Wakenshaw who I saw play for Everton reserves. On the night in question, I set off in my car in driving snow. Such was the ferocity of the snow, I almost turned back at Ferrybridge as I questioned whether any game could be worth driving through such atrocious weather. But I drove on to complete the three-hour journey and was, unsurprisingly, the only representative of any club sat in the Goodison Park directors' box that night.

On seeing me, a rather surprised Everton boss Howard Kendall asked: "What the hell are you doing here on a night like this?"

Quite matter of factly, I replied: "Howard, I have to cover all games as I desperately need new blood in my team."

Wakenshaw, however, made the journey all worthwhile. He was a revelation, scoring six goals. That night as I drove home, I was excited about the prospect of signing the talented young player I had just seen and wondered whether Howard Kendall might be prepared to sell him. After all, he was hardly struggling for strikers, having the likes of Andy Gray, Adrian Heath and Graeme Sharpe on his books. I would have been prepared to pay up to £50,000 for a player of his ability - if I'd had that sort of money - even though he was yet to make his first team debut. I rang Howard the following morning but was disappointed, if not exactly surprised, to hear him reply: "Willie, I am under no pressure to sell any of my players, let alone one who is an England youth international who I plan to put in the first team before long." Ironically, as Everton strode on to win the championship, Wakenshaw failed to fulfil his massive potential and eventually played only a handful of games in the lower divisions with Carlisle, Rochdale and

Crewe. That night, however, I know I saw a lad with truly outstanding potential and I cannot imagine how he failed to set the game alight with such ability.

Another player I enquired about after spotting him on another scouting mission was Jimmy Quinn, a striker who was to go on to become Northern Ireland's all-time top scorer. I saw Quinn in action for Blackburn reserves against Newcastle at St James' Park and the lad looked tremendous, scoring two thumping headers. Tall and lean with an eye for goal, he looked like just the sort of goalscorer I was looking for. Alas, when I enquired about Quinn with Blackburn the following day, I was left in no doubt that they weren't interested in selling him.

But while I was looking to bring in an extra striker, I found myself one short when I made the decision to release Paul Sugrue. With such a small squad, I could ill afford to lose any player but I made an exception with Sugrue. Currie and Mills were my two regular forwards and Sugrue wasn't happy about being left out of the team. One of Malcolm Allison's signings, he was good on the ball but there was rarely an end product as he wasn't a prolific goalscorer, whilst I felt he lacked any passion to do it for me at the club. But his biggest drawback was his rather arrogant personality. Tiring of reserve team football, Sugrue came in to my office one afternoon and asked for a transfer.

"Yes, providing the board agrees to it, you can go," I replied, without a moment's hesitation.

Rather cockily, he asked what kind of fee I would be looking for.

Raising my eyebrows, I looked at him across the desk and told him: "You'll be going on a free transfer. I doubt we could get anything for you."

Sugrue had a naturally high opinion of himself and I'm sure my words brought him down a peg or two. They certainly bruised his rather inflated ego. On my recommendation, the board were happy to agree to let him go and Portsmouth eventually took him on a free transfer. Within a month, however, their chairman, Mr Deacon, called to ask me to take him back. Surprised, I asked him why. Deacon explained that he had given Sugrue about £1,000 to help pay for his moving expenses but he had rarely been away from his door since, constantly asking for more financial assistance.

"Quite simply, I've had enough of him," he concluded.

But I wasn't remotely interested in taking back a player who had been a disruptive influence throughout my time as manager. "With all due respect, Mr Deacon, we've washed our hands of him," I replied. "He's your problem now."

Extra Time – The Final Chapter

Back on the pitch, we suffered FA Cup embarrassment at the hands of Darlington, our neighbours from up the A66. Listening to the draw on the radio as we travelled home from a league match against Birmingham, I commented: "That's the worst draw possible." It was a no win situation for us. While we were fighting for our Second Division lives and close to going out of existence, little Darlington were top of the Fourth Division and playing with great confidence under former Boro and Spurs star Cyril Knowles.

To make matters worse, by the time the tie came around we were slap bang in the middle of a mini injury crisis that left us desperately short of players. We did, however, have home advantage and before the match I impressed upon my players the importance of matching Darlington's commitment. If we did that, I told them, then our superior skill would take us through. As the pitch was heavy, I made it clear it would not be a game for purists - the ball needed to be hit to the front men early and nobody should consider trying to pass the ball through the middle. Darlington had the better of the first 45 minutes though neither side looked like scoring and we reached half-time with the game still goalless.

As we headed for the dressing room, I was amazed to hear Gary Hamilton say to a team-mate: "Jesus, Sinksy nearly halved me in two in the first couple of minutes." Gary was referring to Mike Angus, a former Boro player, who was naturally keyed up for the game.

Gary was the type of player equipped to go in hard when the situation required it so I was shocked that he could be surprised by Angus's physical approach. "Hey, Gary," I interrupted. "It's a war out there. You don't think he's going to do you any favours, do you? The boy wants to win and I expect you to get back out there and return the compliment."

We eventually escaped with a goalless draw. Both sides had chances to win the game in the last 10 minutes I was happy to get away with a draw. It was my belief that over two games we would prove to be the better team.

The replay at Feethams was played on a bone hard, frosty pitch. Again, my instructions were to play the ball forward quickly and not to risk getting caught in possession by dwelling on it. With their pride stung from the initial game, the players were ready for this one and we enjoyed the lion's share of the possession during the first 45 minutes. Everything went to plan and we narrowly missed going ahead on several occasions. Midway through the second half, there was nothing to suggest we would not go on to win the game. Then, disaster. From a harmless looking cross into our box, McAndrew killed the ball and waited for O'Hanlon to claim it. He didn't. During that moment's indecision, Garry MacDonald nipped in between the two to poke the ball over the line from no more than six yards. It was sweet revenge for Garry, who I had released the previous summer, but I was livid with my defender and goalkeeper. The ball was there for Kelham to claim but Tony, with all his experience, should have known not to take chances like that and should have swept the ball out of the ground if necessary. Having gained a psychological advantage, Darlington scored a second soon after from a near poster header.

Then, with just five minutes remaining, scores of Middlesbrough fans invaded the pitch, causing the referee to send the players to the dressing rooms until order could be restored. During the 10 minutes we spent back in the dressing room, I tried to instill in my players a belief that all was not lost and that we had to go back out there and give it our all. As it turned out, McAndrew pulled a goal back but Darlington held out for the win. At the time, the sound of the final whistle was the lowest point in my life. I can't even begin to describe the hurt and humiliation I felt that my Middlesbrough team had been beaten by Darlington. I had known the pain of defeat as a player but as manager the highs and lows were increased 10-fold.

It was hard to face the club's directors after the game. It crossed my mind to offer my resignation. But I was never a quitter and decided that if they wanted a change then they would have to sack me. Though my morale was at an all-time low, I knew I could not afford to let anyone see I was down. Though I was putting myself under enormous pressure and the job was at times killing me, I had to continue to motivate the players so the only person who ever saw me looking depressed was my wife.

The poor results were hurting me enormously. I had enjoyed a wonderful rapport with the Teesside public from my playing days and it worried me that it might all go down the drain as a result of my lack of success as a manager. Fortunately, they were giving me every chance and, while attendances had dropped to little more than 4,000, I had heard very little dissent from the die-hards who turned out to watch us week in and week out.

The goals which had flowed from Mills and Currie during the first half of the season had dried up. Of the 25 league goals they shared that season, all but three of them came in the first 21 games. It was clear we lacked a target man as neither was the type to win high balls. After getting through to Mike McCullagh and the

Extra Time – The Final Chapter

board that a new face was needed to add impetus to our quest to avoid the drop, I approached Southampton boss Lawrie McMenemy about one of his reserve team strikers. I had seen Ian Baird playing for Newcastle whilst on loan from The Dell and he had impressed me as the type of player we needed to lead our front line. Having agreed a £50,000 fee with Southampton, I met the player midway at Leicester Post House in an attempt to persuade him to join us. I felt our talks went pretty well, though I knew he was concerned at the prospect of dropping from the First to the Third Division in a matter of months as we were just one place off a relegation position. Although I tried to pin him down to a decision there and then, he was insistent on discussing the move over with his father and promised to ring me the next morning. The following day, I got the call I had anticipated - he did not fancy the move. Lawrie McMenemy rang me an hour later to say he was disgusted with the boy as it was unlikely he would play in his first team and he felt he had shown a distinct lack of ambition. Five years later, my decision to go for Baird was, however, vindicated when my successor Bruce Rioch paid Leeds United £500,000 for him.

Disappointed to have missed out on Baird, I switched by attentions to Brighton's Terry Connor, a front man who had always caused problems for our defence. Although not particularly tall, he was good in the air and always got 15 to 20 goals a season. Having been tipped off that Connor was homesick for Leeds and wanted to return north, I contacted Brighton's manager Chris Catlin and settled on £50,000 - a fee later confirmed by the clubs' two chairmen - but I was again to be frustrated in my efforts to strengthen our forward line. I was invited to Brighton for their Tuesday night fixture with top-of-the-table Blackburn to complete the formalities of the move. Though I had asked for Connor to be left out of the team, Catlin insisted that he was needed for such an important fixture when the player had yet to agree terms.

Having travelled to Brighton from Teesside by rail that afternoon, I arrived at the Goldstone Ground shortly before kick-off and did not have chance to talk to Catlin before the game. I was, however, warmly greeted by the Brighton chairman and his fellow directors and ushered into the boardroom before taking my seat for the game. From that moment on, it was downhill all the way as far as any potential deal was concerned. Brighton won the match 3-1 with Connor scoring twice against the league leaders. That only served to convince me he was just the man we needed but, as I waited in the boardroom, I became increasingly irritated as the minutes past by without sight nor sound of chairman, manager or player. When three quarters of an hour had passed since the final whistle, I was becoming concerned that there might be a problem. Finally, the chairman appeared and asked if he could have a quiet word. Clearly embarrassed, he rather apologetically told me that the manager had changed his mind over the deal due to Connor's performance that night. I was furious and demanded to see Catlin, who, on his appearance, rather sheepishly gave me the same story, insisting he did not dare let the transfer go through as he would be pilloried by the fans.

Having been dragged several hundred miles on the assurance that the deal would go through providing I could agree terms with the player, I could hardly believe what I was hearing. Shaking with anger, I told Catlin: "You are a disgrace to the game. In all my time in football I have never experienced such total lack of professionalism from a manager and club chairman." I asked to speak to the player to inform him what was going on but they insisted that would be futile as their decision, though regrettable, was final. I walked out of the Goldstone Ground in utter disgust. I was also thankful that my chairman knew that the deal had been agreed prior to my visit as otherwise it might have appeared that there had been no foundation to my trip. Travelling home the next day, feeling very frustrated, I wondered what kind of profession I was involved in when people could conduct themselves in such a shoddy manner.

As there were no signs of the financial situation improving, I was not surprised when Mike McCullagh resigned as chairman to be succeeded by Alf Duffield. Although he remained on the board, I was sorry to see Mike relinquish the top role within the club. Before hitting up our working relationship, I had always found him to be a warm and friendly sort of guy with a bubbly personality. But our previous friendship had been put under great strain during our time as chairman and manager. Thankfully, I'm pleased to say we remain friends to this day.

The new man, Duffield, was not so easy to get on with. On his appointment, he called me to his office at ITM Offshore in Middlesbrough town centre. We had never previously met but our 20-minute chat in the ITM boardroom confirmed in my mind the accuracy of his reputation as abrasive and dictatorial. Indeed, he gave me good reason to doubt whether I could work with him.

Although there would be cash available for new players, Duffield suggested I was too young and inexperienced to be the club's manager and sounded me out about his idea to bring in a more experienced man for me to work under.

"If that's what you feel then you'll have to sack me," I told him. "I've worked

Extra Time – The Final Chapter

my balls off to get this club where it is. There's no way I'm just going to hand over the reins for somebody else to come in, have the benefit of financial backing and take all the credit."

We parted with the mutual understanding that we would give it a few weeks and find out more about one another before making any decisions. It was hardly surprising, therefore, that our relationship remained tense and cool - until things came to a head the day we played Manchester City at Maine Road. The catalyst for a heated dispute was a young man called Stephen Bell.

I have never seen a more outstanding player between the ages of 13 and 17 than Bell. I had seen him help Boro win the English Schools Shield some years earlier when he had looked the most exciting prospect in the country. Though only very slight in build, he had more natural skill than most players could even dream about. Had he continued to progress as one might have expected, international football would have been a formality and yet he was to waste every last bit of that magnificent potential. Having become only the second 16-year-old ever to play for Middlesbrough's first team, he had been a shining light under Malcolm Allison, but his young career was already threatening to come off the rails long before my arrival at the club. Keen to ensure he remained with Boro rather than moving on to a bigger and more ambitious club, Malcolm had given Bell a contract better than most of his more experienced team-mates. That was a mistake. It was the ultimate case of being given too much too soon. They had given this working class kid more money than most people could dream of but had given him no advice on his finances. He had needed a father figure and the sort of protection Alex Ferguson offered Ryan Giggs during his formative years. Despite being a top earner, at the age of 19 I believe he had already had his house re-possessed. I can only assume this was a result of his gambling and excessive socialising. I was getting much feedback that Stephen had been spotted nightclubbing on a Thursday evening absolutely blotto on alcohol. I found that very disappointing because much time and effort had gone into trying to rehabilitate Stephen and put him back on the right track.

Some months earlier I had persuaded David Gaster to let me bring in my old friend Steve Smelt to operate as the club's physiotherapist and youth coach during weekdays, with two volunteers, Keith Scurr and John Barry, taking the juniors on Saturdays. Meanwhile, a preliminary coaching badge holder called Alan Gallafant ran the club's new Centre of Excellence. The football club remains indebted to those three people as they gave their time up with no financial reward whatsoever.

Bell had been the star of the Middlesbrough Boys team which Smelty had led to English Schools Cup success some years earlier and I knew Stephen retained great respect and admiration for his old coach. If Smelty and I could work on Stephen both physically and psychologically, I thought we might just see him fulfil his early potential. Smelty and I had numerous discussions with Belly and he appeared to listen and take on board the advice we were offering. Unfortunately, he wasn't a strong character and was easily led by those he spent his time with away from the football club. Whenever he stepped out of line or broke a club rule - more often than not being out boozing within 48 hours prior to a game - I tried to hurt him by fining him a week's wages but it had little effect. Within a couple of weeks, I would hear that he was back to his old habits.

Inspecting a snowbound Ayresome Park pitch with match officials. I personally helped to shovel snow off the pitch.

Most worrying was the fact that Stephen was no longer looking after himself physically and had lost the extra yard of pace which had made him such a threat to opposing defences a couple of years earlier. Instead of showing determination to go past defenders, he was rarely beating his man and was tending to wait to get hit and win a free-kick. Under normal circumstances I would have bombed him out and left him to think over the error of his ways in the reserves but I often had no option but to play him, so thin was my squad.

That was the case on the afternoon of March 9th 1985 when we paid a visit to Maine Road to take on promotion-chasing Manchester City. Such was the length of our injury list that day, I was forced to play Bell and name David Mills as sub despite the fact that he was suffering with groin and Achilles' tendon problems. Going into the match on the back of 11 games without a win, I was under immense pressure and was less than happy when Alf Duffield and his fellow directors decided to travel with us on the team bus. We didn't get off to the best of starts,

Extra Time – The Final Chapter

falling behind midway through the first half, and my immediate thought was: "Here we go again - this could be an avalanche." That wasn't to prove the case as resolute defending meant we were still just a goal down with 20 minutes left, though we had never really threatened to score ourselves. Recognising that Bell had not gone past an opponent all afternoon and had contributed little to the game, I asked Millsy if he thought he could play the last 15 or 20 minutes. I thought his reputation might at least cause a bit of a stir in their defence, particularly as he had scored twice against them earlier in the season.

I knew before holding up the number 11 card that substituting Bell would not be a popular choice among the directors. Stephen had been bending the chairman's ear in Duffield's town centre nightclub, telling him he was getting a raw deal from the manager. At the same time, certain directors had told Duffield how good Bell used to be. Deep down, however, I knew that if I did not make that substitution I would be cheating not only myself but the club and the supporters too. So, off came Bell and on went Mills, sadly to no avail as City held on to their slim advantage.

I was just finishing my post-match pep talk to my players when the dressing room door burst open and in barged Duffield accompanied by his predecessor, Mike McCullagh. Alf's expression looked like thunder. "Can I have a word with you?" he asked.

I was in two minds whether to tell him to get out there and then. For some reason I walked across to the door and ushered them outside into the corridor. "What's all this about?" I asked.

"I need to know why you took Bell off," said Duffield.

I was infuriated to have my authority on football matters questioned in such a way. "Because I am the manager of this football club and I am entitled to do what I think is in the best interests of the team," I answered, barely containing my anger. "In my opinion he had not contributed anything positive in 70 minutes."

As we continued to debate the merits of my substitution, we became aware of the many inquisitive glances from people milling about the corridor. "Can we go somewhere a little bit quieter?" asked Alf. The three of us made our way upstairs into Maine Road's main stand where we sat overlooking the pitch not a hundred yards away from the press box which was still occupied by national and local journalists, busy filing their match reports for the following day's newspapers. Little did they know that a potentially explosive story was unfolding so nearby.

Before Alf could continue the debate, I said: "What you just did, barging into the dressing room to confront me in front of my players was totally unprofessional. You would never have pulled Jack Charlton or Malcolm Allison like that and you are not f***ing doing it to me either. As a matter of fact, Mr Duffield, you can shove your job up your arse."

McCullagh was shocked with my harsh words. "Willie, you can't talk to the chairman like that."

Turning to Mike, I continued: "What he has just done in front of my players is unforgiveable." I looked back at Alf: "If you want to pick the team you can damn well get on with it." At that I stood up. I was ready to walk away not only from my seat but from the club. I wasn't prepared to tolerate such interference.

"Willie, sit down - please," said Duffield. I did so reluctantly and he went on to say he was concerned that it appeared I had a personal grudge against Stephen Bell. He wanted to make sure that was not the case. My response was that Bell's behaviour was making the club a laughing stock. "Quite honestly, I've had enough and I'll be considering my future with the club over the weekend," I added. As he pleaded with me not to be so hasty, I made my way down the stairs and back into the stand.

On my walk back to the dressing room, I felt sure it was time to leave the club. More immediately, I had no intention of travelling back on the team coach with the chairman and his directors. Instead, I began to look for another director, Dick Corden, with whom I enjoyed a good relationship and I knew had travelled to Maine Road by car. Frustratingly, Dick had already left the ground and I boarded the team bus to a quite solemn atmosphere. On the way home, I told Steve Smelt it was my intention to resign over the weekend and he spent the next two hours giving me every reason why I shouldn't. But my mind was made up. The job was hard enough without interference from an amateur.

On our return to Ayresome Park, I popped in to my office to collect a few things from the referee's room. I was followed down the corridor by the chairman, who was insistent that there had been a misunderstanding. I was having none of that. I gave him my home telephone number and told him to ring me the next day by which time I would have talked the situation over with my wife and would give him my decision as to whether I would be remaining in the job.

After pondering the situation over throughout Sunday and talking it over with Hilary, I felt the position was intolerable. But Alf wasn't as daft as I thought and the call he had promised never came. He knew full well what my answer would have been. However, I proceeded to write a resignation letter and took it with me to the club on Monday morning. Ringing ITM's offices to speak to Alf, I was informed that he wouldn't be in that morning.

Worse still, a meeting with the Mayor and Mayoress had been arranged for all club personnel at the town hall that lunchtime. It was the last place I wanted to be but I made my way there with my resignation letter tucked in my pocket. Across a crowded room, I caught the eye of the chairman and began to make my way over to him. I was desperate to catch a word with him and do what had to be done but every time I made a move in his direction someone would engage me in polite conversation. By the time I made my move, he had gone.

Back at Ayresome, I rang his office and finally engaged him in conversation. He agreed to see me immediately in his office. As I walked in the room, I took the letter from my pocket and planted it firmly in front of him. "You have my resignation," I said.

"I do not accept it," he responded. "I've done a bit of homework over the weekend and what you told me about Stephen Bell appears to be correct. All I was concerned about was that it wasn't a personal thing." Over the hour which followed, we talked constructively and Alf assured me that he would not interfere again with the playing side of the job.

I told him that would be the only condition under which I would be prepared to consider withdrawing my resignation. The discussion which followed was a turning point in our relationship. Alf had recognised that, although I was only a tender age for a manager, I was not to be dictated to or pushed around by anyone. Our working relationship improved in leaps and bounds from that moment on and I was to receive much support from him.

Even so, I was being quite unfair on myself by heaping ever increasing amounts of pressure upon myself. In my spare time - or what little of it I had - I would perhaps watch TV without ever really appreciating the programme that was on, my thoughts lost in a world of tactics and training methods. Within an hour of a defeat I would be working out in my mind how to juggle the pack - always the same pack - of players to find a winning formula and what Monday morning's training would entail. I would discuss the team selection with Steve Smelt or John Coddington, a former Boro coach who I had brought back on a part-time basis, but the final decision was mine and I would mull over what limited options I had for hours on end. Most nights were taken up watching future opposition or on the look-out for potential bargains. I ate, breathed and slept Middlesbrough Football Club. I just could not switch off. It was hardly surprising therefore that it reached the point where I was nearing total burn-out. On one occasion, Hilary wallpapered the hall, stairs and landing of our house while I was at a Saturday away game but I didn't even notice the change until she pointed it out to me the following Tuesday. I was in my own little world.

Told I had £50,000 to spend on a new player or players, I was becoming increasingly worried that I might have to battle on for the remainder of the season with the squad I had as we were fast approaching the transfer deadline. Then came a much needed change of luck on the transfer front. In a matter of days I was able to bring in two new players thanks to my network of contacts within the game. I had developed a good relationship with Leeds United's chief scout who knew I was looking to improve the team in both full-back positions. Having lost Darren Wood to Chelsea, I tried out a long succession of players at both left and right-back without great success. Tony Forthrop at Leeds told me he had heard a whisper that Brian Laws might be available from Huddersfield. I had seen Laws in action on several occasions - indeed, he had scored against us that season - and he had always impressed me as a good attacking full-back, though he was perhaps a bit naive defensively. However, I knew that would be less of a problem as we were playing with wing backs and three central defenders.

On contacting Huddersfield boss Mick Buxton, I was told Laws was available at £30,000. That made me suspicious as I knew he was worth at least twice that figure. Keen to find out more about his character and what made him tick, I arranged to meet Laws in The Swallow Hotel in Leeds where it quickly became apparent I had nothing to worry about on that score. He came across as a pleasant guy, ambitious and not unintelligent. However, he was hedging his bets as First Division Southampton were showing an interest in him. I knew I couldn't hang about so when a couple of days passed by without a decision, I forced his hand by telling him he either wanted to join us or I would have to turn my attentions elsewhere. Thankfully, Laws travelled to Ayresome Park and we agreed a deal without any hiccups. In my opinion, I now had the best attacking right full-back in the league. Laws was to go on to fulfil his full potential in Brian Clough's highly successful Nottingham Forest team of the late '80s and early '90s.

Though I had only £20,000 left to spend, I now turned my attentions back to bringing in a player to lead the front line. As Nattrass, Mowbray and McAndrew were performing well in central defence, we were conceding very few but by mid-

Extra Time – The Final Chapter

March we had scored just five goals in 12 games and I knew it was imperative I brought in a target man. I contacted my old Boro team-mate Terry Cooper, then at Bristol City, to ask him if he knew anyone in the target man mould who would score his quota of goals. Terry owed me a favour, as some years earlier he had picked my brains about a former Boro reserve called Alan Walsh, who was playing up the road at Darlington. Terry had asked me if I thought he was worth £15,000, to which I had advised him that he was worth £30,000 of anyone's money as he would get him at least 10 goals a season from free-kicks alone as he could hit them like shells. Over the next few years, Walsh fully justified my recommendation by scoring over 100 goals for City. Terry returned the favour by recommending to me a centre-forward at City's local rivals, Bristol Rovers, who he said wasn't afraid to rough it out when the going got tough. It was to be the only occasion I signed a player without watching him myself. In my place, I sent to watch Stephens a man whose judgement I trusted, Barry Geldart, who was impressed enough to believe he wouldn't be a gamble at £20,000.

Like a lot of clubs at the time, Rovers were in a tricky position with their finances and were prepared to let him go. Having agreed terms with his club, I arranged for Stephens to travel to the north-east to complete the deal on a Friday evening, the night before we were due to play Sheffield United in a vital league game at Ayresome Park. Never having seen him, I arrived to pick up my new centre-forward from Darlington Railway Station expecting to see a big brute of a guy. I was a wee bit surprised, therefore, when I came face to face with him. Lumbering towards me was the rather stocky frame of a smiling, scruffy, blond-haired man who hardly resembled the way I had pictured him. I drove Archie to the Stork Hotel in Stockton, where I knew owners Eleanor and John Pole would look after him well, as they often did the club's triallists. During an hour's talking to Archie, he downed three pints and succeeded in wiping from my mind any lingering doubts I had about him. He was hungry and felt a move to Middlesbrough would be a big step up the ladder. I knew he was my type of player.

Such was my confidence in Archie, I conducted the following day's pre-match team talk rather anxiously as I knew I had left him with Alf Duffield to agree personal terms. I couldn't help but wonder if Alf's rather abrasive manner would put him off the idea of a move to Teesside. It was with huge relief, therefore, that I discovered at half-time that Archie had agreed terms with the chairman and was now a Boro player. To make matters even better, our young centre-forward Alan

Kernaghan scored the only goal of the game against Sheffield United to give us three valuable points - our first win in almost three months. Having offered my resignation only a week earlier, things had quickly turned around in terms of my relationship with the chairman.

I will never forget the first training session Archie attended as a Middlesbrough player. Never having previously heard of him, like myself, the players were perhaps expecting to be introduced to someone well in excess of six feet and were surprised to see Archie's less than imposing figure. Much p***-taking ensued and when Archie scuffed a shot, it was met with guffaws from the players who were clearly wondering who the hell I had bought to save our season. But Archie had the perfect answer to their leg-pulling. As a free-kick was curled into the box, he rose like a salmon, elbows flaying wildly, to thump a header past Kelham O'Hanlon from fully 15 yards. In a flash, the ball was in the back of the net and in that split second the whole squad knew what Archie could do for us. It's a funny thing in football that all it takes is one incident like that for an outsider to be accepted. From then on, he became a most popular player among team-mates and fans alike. He was the sort who would live hard and work hard.

Meanwhile, Alf's funding had offered me the opportunity to bring in a full-time first team coach in the shape of Richard Dinnis, who had previously managed and coached Newcastle United. Although not regarded as a number one, Richard had a good reputation as a first class coach and his arrival helped relieve me of some of the stresses and strains of trying to do all the management, coaching and scouting. Although on the surface I had maintained a calm outlook, my batteries were running low and Richard helped to share some of the burden.

Archie scored his first goal in his second game, a 1-1 draw at Wimbledon, before we took on one of our fellow strugglers, Carlisle, at Ayresome in a true six-pointer. With the scores level at 1-1, we were looking the more likely to win. But then came a truly horrific miss that was the worst I ever saw throughout my days as player or manager. From a right wing cross, I can still see the ball bypassing the goalkeeper on the near post to arrive at the feet of David Currie no more than two yards out. With the goal at his mercy, David had only to tap the ball over the line and yet he somehow contrived to miss the target altogether. Perhaps believing he could not miss, David took his eye off the ball and got only the thinnest of touches to deflect it past the far post. It was almost impossible to miss but somehow he did. No-one misses on purpose, of course, but if I could have gone on the field at that moment, I would have choked David! He was a lovely lad and, sadly, I think he

Extra Time – The Final Chapter

may have lost confidence from that day on until he left the club, as the crowd perhaps never forgave him. What compounded our misery was that almost immediately Carlisle took the ball to the other end of the field to grab an unlikely winner.

With our new-found confidence knocked sideways, we lost 1-0 at Jim Smith's promotion-chasing Oxford in our next match, though it was difficult to believe that United were top of the league as we tore them apart in the first 45 minutes without getting the vital goal. With Stephen Bell - in for the dejected Currie - tormenting their left-back to enjoy perhaps his best 45 minutes for me, Archie was desperately unlucky not to put us one-up. Such was the ferocity of his header that it hit the crossbar from 12 yards before rebounding back out to the D outside the penalty area.

Maximum points from our next two home games helped steady the ship and with Cardiff, Fulham and Notts County below us, I felt we would need six points from our final three games to guarantee us safety. We looked on course for a well deserved point at Crystal Palace over Easter, only to be denied by a late winner from Ian Wright. We now had two games to save our season.

For our final home game, against second placed Birmingham City, I decided it was time to introduce one of the talented youngsters I had been nurturing. Enter 19-year-old Peter Beagrie for his league debut in place of Alan Roberts, who appeared to be suffering from a lack of confidence. Having impressed me in training, I called Beagrie to my office and asked him if he would be up for playing against Birmingham. There was a sparkle in his eyes as he gave me a most positive reply. I took what might have appeared to be a gamble in playing Peter that day, though I knew he wouldn't suffer from nerves as he was naturally confident. I felt that if we could get enough balls out to him on the wing then he could cause City problems with his ability to twist and turn and create that extra yard for crosses. I was proved right as he had a super game and we fully deserved a goalless draw against our high flying visitors. Peter very nearly grabbed the all important winner late in the game with a terrific left foot shot which their 'keeper turned around the post at full stretch. As we trooped back to the dressing room, however, my thoughts turned to how our fellow relegation strugglers had done in their games. I was hugely relieved to discover that our destiny remained in our hands. If we won at Shrewsbury in our final game then our Second Division survival was guaranteed.

Just about Managing

Winning at Gay Meadow was by no means a foregone conclusion as they had murdered us at Ayresome earlier in the season when we had been fortunate to escape with a 1-1 draw thanks to a late own goal. Recognising the importance of the last fixture, I asked Alf Duffield if he could find the funding to allow us three days' training at Lilleshall prior to the game. Thankfully, for the first time all season, I was afforded the luxury of the best possible preparation for a game. Having said that, such preparation had been considered the norm in my playing days and we would probably have been away for a full week for such an important game under Jack Charlton.

Training away from the attention of the media was very relaxed amid facilities which were out of this world compared to our usual surroundings. The Lilleshall pitches were like bowling greens in comparison to the "ploughed fields" of Hutton Road and Hall Drive which I had been forced to subject the players to all season. I allowed them the luxury of a few drinks on Wednesday evening but there was a strict curfew on Thursday and Friday with all players under orders to be in bed by 11 o'clock. I avoided any training which was too physical as I could see the lads were ready, simply by witnessing how competitive they were in our five-a-side games. In fact, I was frightened one or two of them might suffer injuries and had to call a halt to some sessions before they did themselves damage.

The mood in the camp was first class but the one thing which did worry me - and it had worried me all season - was that we were operating with only one goalkeeper, Kelham O'Hanlon. As Kelham was the only 'keeper on the club's books with first team experience, I rarely allowed him to take part in any ball handling or shooting practice in Friday training sessions in case he put a finger out or got injured in some other way. By that time, of course, it would be too late to sign a replacement on loan and I would have been forced to pitch in the intermediate team 'keeper who was well short of being ready for such a challenge.

The atmosphere in The Shrews Hotel on the Friday evening was, strangely enough, one of great anticipation rather than anxiety. I personally was a wee bit nervous though I had a good feeling about the game. I knew there was no need to motivate the players. In fact it was more a question of calming them down as I could sense they were all champing at the bit to get the job done.

Even so, we arrived at Gay Meadow armed with radios to take with us on the bench, to allow us to convey to the players just what our fellow relegation strugglers were doing. We knew a draw might well be good enough but I impressed on the players that we should go for all three points to ensure our Second Division status remained in tact no matter what. Earlier in the week, I had phoned Wimbledon manager Dave Bassett to tell him they could do us a favour by beating Cardiff that day. "We always beat Cardiff," he replied. "And I'm sure we'll do you a favour on Saturday, Willie."

I didn't pay too much attention in my team talk to the quality of the opposition, apart from mentioning what free kicks they might employ against us. It was all about how we played. I was taken aback by the deafening roar from our supporters which greeted our arrival on the pitch. Middlesbrough fans had taken over a whole stand behind a goal to our right and created the sort of noise I hadn't heard since my own playing days. The game itself couldn't have started better for us and we went 1-0 up early on. Showing the sort of form which had tempted me to buy him in the first place, Brian Laws won the ball in the tackle about 40 yards out, advanced forward and hit a first time shot from fully 30 yards. It was a goal from the moment the ball left Lawsy's boot. It flew into the far corner of the net to an explosion of noise from the far end of the ground. Yours truly leaped about six feet into the air a split second before the ball hit the net.

The goal set the tone for the rest of the game. We tore them to ribbons over the next 15 minutes though it concerned me that we failed to convert territorial advantage into a second goal. Archie missed two one-on-ones with the 'keeper while we had numerous half chances but that second goal just would not come. Then over the radio came the sort of news we had dreaded - Cardiff were winning 1-0 at Wimbledon. But this was a game in which we held all the aces and young Peter Beagrie rewarded my faith in him with a tremendous first 45 minutes during which he looked like he had been a first team player all his life. Creating space for himself, he scored the all important second goal with a crisp shot from just inside the box. To go in 2-0 up at half-time was more than we could have hoped for. The back three of Mowbray, Nattrass and McAndrew had been magnificent in keeping Shrewsbury's strikers under tight wraps. The excitement in the dressing room was bubbling but I reminded them that the job was only half done and told them to continue playing with their heads as well as their hearts.

It was important that we didn't simply try to defend the lead as I knew that if we dropped too deep their centre-forward was exceptionally good in the air and would exploit any crosses we allowed them. But no matter how you try to impress on players not to do so, in such situations they instinctively tend to defend deeper. That, combined with what must have been a hell of a bollocking from Chic Bates to his Shrewsbury players, served to ensure the second half was a totally different game. I was amazed that, although they had nothing to play for in terms of their league position, they took on a physical approach to the second half and proceeded to kick lumps out of our players. This halted our flow of attacks and the game became fragmented. Although our goal was rarely threatened in the first 15 minutes, there was a new intensity about the game. With about 20 minutes left, Gary Hamilton was sent off for what the referee saw as too fierce a tackle. It was perhaps only retribution from Hammy for what had gone on before but his dismissal put a whole new light on the tactics of the game. Reduced to 10 men, we left Currie on his own up front and got Stephens to drop back to add numbers to the midfield. Our attacks became less frequent and we were forced further and further back as they launched attack after attack.

With 15 minutes left we lost another player. Beagrie had been kicked in an off-the-ball incident but as the referee turned around he saw only Peter retaliate by using his fists. Their player had clearly taken advantage of young Peter's inexperience and now we had only nine men to play out what was left of the game. Incredibly, we were lucky not to be reduced to eight players as, just a couple of minutes after Peter's red card, Paul Ward took out one of their players with a thigh high tackle which was by far the worst of the game. I was thankful to see the referee produce only a yellow card as playing out those final minutes with only eight men might have proved too much.

Shrewsbury were camped in our half from then on and the tension was unbearable. To add to the pressure, the referee added on almost 14 minutes of injury time due to the sendings off and the lengthy period of injuries. As the minutes and seconds ticked away, the tension increased to breaking point. Having heard that Wimbledon had equalised against Cardiff, I knew that the draw might be good enough but I took nothing for granted and spent the final minutes screaming at the ref and linesman to end the game, whilst our fans made a deafening noise as they whistled for the match to finish.

When that final whistle finally sounded, I was ecstatic and a floodgate of emotions opened. Players hugged one another and danced with delight before lifting me shoulder high as I made my way across the pitch to acknowledge the support of the fans. A smiling Millsy, who had missed the final weeks of the season with an Achilles injury, half danced and half hobbled across the pitch, a plaster on his leg and a walking stick in his hand. We had secured our own destiny and I was finally able to experience relief in my job - not to mention immense satisfaction.

Extra Time – The Final Chapter

Now I finally knew how rewarding the job could be if I could achieve success. Back in the dressing room, there was a feeling of absolute euphoria. At one point I felt certain I was about to pass out. Whether it was just the tension of the season combined with the excitement of the day, I don't know, but I had to sit down and calm myself. Directors and friends came in and bashed me on the back to congratulate me.

Finally, I got some harmony and quiet and told the lads: "Let that be a lesson learned. Never again subject yourself to having to achieve a result like that in the final game." Ironically, they would have to do the exact same thing a year later on the same ground - but by then a new name would be in charge of Middlesbrough Football Club.

With Cardiff having lost their game at Wimbledon, 2-1, this was the final league table:

	P	W	D	L	F	A	Pts
18 Sheffield U	42	10	14	18	54	66	44
19 Boro	42	10	10	22	41	57	40
20 Notts Co	42	10	7	25	45	73	37
21 Cardiff	42	9	8	25	47	79	35
22 Wolves	42	8	9	25	37	79	33

In the boardroom, a smiling Mike McCullagh bought me a pint of lager. It was despatched with great ease and speed. I drank another two before I left Gay Meadow. Such was the buoyant mood on the way back, we stopped off at a pub for half an hour for more celebrations. When I finally got home, Hilary was happy to join in the party mood though, with her not being a football fan, I was relieved that she didn't ask me too much about the game. I was physically and emotionally drained and I was happy to sit in almost total silence as we enjoyed a quiet drink together. She had seen in me in a zombie like state so

A hug for Tony Mowbray after we had avoided relegation.

281

Just about Managing

Magic moments: chaired from the pitch after our vital final day win over Shrewsbury in 1985. The players pictured are (from left): Heine Otto, Paul Ward and Brian Laws.

Extra Time – The Final Chapter

many times in the previous weeks and months but this time the usual look of anxiety was replaced with a beaming smile.

The following morning as I looked in the Sunday newspapers to see us fourth bottom in the league table, it was only a minor distraction from my thumping headache, a reminder of the previous night's celebrations. But, deep down, my mind was already focusing on the new season when the challenge would be there to do it all again...

17

Building Boro's Future

AFTER the close escape of the previous season, the 1985-86 campaign was always going to be make or break time, both for Middlesbrough F.C. and Willie Maddren. And that's exactly how it proved to be. But there were to be many twists and turns along the way in a season which I now look back upon with a strange combination of pride and frustration.

That I can recall those days with pride is a direct result of my success in making several astute signings whilst developing young players who were to go on to become footballers of the highest quality. After coming so close to going down the previous May, I knew we would have to strengthen the squad if we were to have any hope of progressing. I was grateful that on becoming chairman Alf Duffield had agreed to sanction £200,000 for me to spend in the transfer market. Nowadays, that is a laughable sum. Even then, it was hardly a king's ransom. John Neal had spent well over twice that figure on Irving Nattrass six years earlier whilst Terry Cochrane, Mick Baxter and Joe Bolton had all been purchased for individual figures in excess of £200,000 before my arrival at the club. But that £200,000 offered me a lifeline which meant I would no longer have to rely solely on free transfers.

Following a fortnight's holiday in Rhodes with Hilary, I got down to the task of sorting out the wheat from the chaff, the good from the bad, as I began to prepare early for the new season. Looking back on the previous campaign, I had reason to be pleased with many of the players but felt others had let me down or for some reason never quite performed as I knew they could. I was particularly disappointed with certain senior players. I did not feel Mick Buckley, for instance, had shown me any loyalty considering I had picked him up off the soccer scrapheap, and made the decision to release him.

Extra Time – The Final Chapter

Two others who didn't always do themselves justice were Irving Nattrass and Tony McAndrew. Irving was probably the most talented player at the club but I was always suspicious of him. Though he was carrying an injury, I often thought he played within himself and couldn't see him going through any brick walls for me or the club. He was already a wealthy guy and I didn't feel he had the hunger for the game he had once had. Having said that, after our early disagreement, he had shown reasonable consistency in my first season but I never saw him as a long term answer in central defence. Indeed, I took the club captaincy off him as I was disappointed when he refused to attend a social event on Teesside. He lived about 40 miles away in Chester-le-Street and felt it was too far to travel to Teesside. I wanted a captain who was committed to the cause so replaced him with Brian Laws. Unfortunately, Lawsy never got much backing from the club's senior players. They set their stall out to make it hard for Brian, so much so that I eventually took the captaincy off him as I felt he wasn't strong enough to handle some of the older lads.

There was no love lost between Irving and Tony McAndrew, possibly as a result of previous encounters when they had been team-mates under John Neal. I would often hear Tony calling Nattrass "Irv the Swerve", a reference to the fact that some believed Irving tended to pick and choose his games. McAndrew was nowhere near the player he had been when he had left Boro for Chelsea a few years earlier. But, whilst I had no doubt in Tony's commitment on the field, I was frequently disappointed with his whinging attitude on the training ground. He was often sarcastic and whined about decisions. The job was hard enough without that and I felt, as a former team-mate, he should have been backing me up when I had to give players a bollocking. Instead, he would be conspicuous by his silence. It seemed he was keener to make himself popular with the players than do the job I had brought him in to do. I wanted him to shake his fist and gee up the younger players as he had done during his time under John Neal. I had hoped Tony would keep his team-mates in line when they needed a kick up the backside.

As a result of his sarcastic attitude on the training ground, I was never sure if Tony was 100 per cent behind me. One day I pulled him into my office to tell him so. "But I've always been like that, Willie - ask anyone," he replied. "It's nothing personal."

Whilst few fans would have missed Buckley, I know many questioned the wisdom of allowing Heine Otto to leave on a free but perhaps I should explain why he had to go. If I recollect, I think his contract stated that we had to offer him a substantial signing on fee if we wanted to renew it. If we couldn't pay it then Otto was allowed to leave as a free agent. Given our financial predicament, there was no way we were in a position to pay the fee so Otto made a decision to return home to Holland. But for that clause, I may well have wanted to keep him though Heine was not necessarily the sort of player we needed at the time. A lad with a terrific personality, he was a player of immense technical ability and would have been a great player in a good side. My concern was that he tended to be conspicuous by his absence when the going got tough - and I knew the months ahead were unlikely to be easy.

I sacked Stephen Bell at the end of the season. He had stepped out of line once too often and I felt he was simply too far gone to rehabilitate. I had given him chance after chance but it was all to no avail, though dismissing him gave me no pleasure. It was such a waste of a great talent, such a tragedy. Eventually, Alan Ball took up his registration at Portsmouth and I remember reading that Alan was going to put him back on the right track and restore him to his former glory. Within weeks 'Belly' was back on Teesside, having left Portsmouth. He did play a few games for Darlington the following season but he played his last league game at the age of 22 and was playing for the likes of Hemlington Social Club long before his mid-20s. In an interview in the Middlesbrough Supporters South magazine, Stephen later admitted: "I was taking home girls virtually every night and going to bed at three or four o'clock in the morning. You can't do that if you're a professional footballer. I honestly never went out on the town on a Friday night if I had a game on the Saturday, but the rules were you were supposed to stay in on Thursday nights as well and I ignored that. I was burning the candle at both ends". Wasting his talent like that must surely haunt him now. Many years later I saw Stephen in a pub and was surprised when he offered to buy me a drink. Perhaps he realised that only he, no-one else, was responsible for his downfall.

Another disappointment was the departure of my new coach Richard Dinnis who announced he was leaving to chase the big money as a coach in the United Arab Emirates. His timing was particularly unhelpful as it left me, once again, without a full-time coach throughout pre-season training. A couple of weeks after leaving, Richard rang to say he had made the biggest mistake in his life and could he come back. Although I hadn't appointed a replacement, the answer was a firm "no". He had burned his boats with me and there was no going back. To compensate, I asked John Coddington to come in full-time as I thought better the devil you know. I paid John a full-time salary and he left his wife to look after the

Extra Time – The Final Chapter

tenancy of the pub they owned in Normanby. Looking back, it probably wasn't a good arrangement. I trusted John and he was a good coach who was strict on discipline, but I just felt that at times the pub was a bit of a distraction for him. I was still travelling alone to watch evening games when normally a first team coach would have accompanied me.

Another player who left the club, again without a fee, was our only experienced goalkeeper, Kelham O'Hanlon. Kelham was a chirpy character in the dressing room and I liked him but I always felt he was short at that level. Unfortunately, I think he suffered from having no opposition for his 'keeper's jersey but I made the decision to make it my priority to strengthen that vital position. Meanwhile, both Mick Saxby and David Mills were two players denied me by injury and neither would ever play for me again. Saxby spent a full year on the sidelines and was eventually forced to retire from the game with a cartilage injury after playing only 15 games for the club. With 14 goals, Millsy had made a marvellous contribution to our successful efforts to avoid the drop the previous year - quite apart from the help he had given me in coaching the club's juniors. He had lost a yard of pace from his peak but at that level he still had the ability to cause defences problems and a similar contribution from him in my second year in charge would have assured us of a mid-table finish. Instead, having ruptured his Achilles' tendon late in the previous season, I knew I would be without him until at least the midway point of the 1985-86 campaign. As it turned out, he would not even manage that.

Without O'Hanlon, Buckley, Otto, Bell, Saxby and Mills, I knew I needed to bring in four or five new players and got Alf Duffield's approval to start trying to push through a few deals with the £200,000 he had publicly sanctioned. My number one target was Stephen Pears, the reserve team goalkeeper at Manchester United who had played on loan with Boro under Malcolm Allison. It didn't take a genius to see that he had exceptional ability so, having read in the press that he wanted first team football, I made contact with him about moving to Middlesbrough - and was delighted to discover he was as keen as mustard to return home to the north east. I was also keen on one of United's reserve team midfielders, Alan Davies, a young lad who had made a name for himself in the 1983 FA Cup final against Brighton. A full Welsh international, I had seen him playing for United's first and second teams and he struck me as an accomplished midfield play-maker.

The problem I had was that United boss Ron Atkinson was on holiday in

Marbella. I rang Big Ron at his holiday retreat and enquired about his two players. Initially he was talking in terms of £100,000 for Pears but after a bit of haggling we settled on a fee of £80,000 plus a further £35,000 for Davies. Ron told me to ring United's chairman, Martin Edwards, and tell him he had agreed those figures with me and that I had permission to talk to both players. If Martin wanted confirmation, he should ring him in Marbella. I was ecstatic and, having dealt with the formalities with Edwards, rang both players and told them to be at Ayresome Park for noon the next day. I couldn't contact Alf initially but eventually got in touch with him at nine the following morning and informed him I would hopefully be pushing both deals through that day. I was horrified when he revealed he didn't have the money.

"Hang on," I said. "Not only have you told me personally I can sign new players, but you have also announced it publicly."

"Yes, that's correct," he said. "But I haven't got the money at the moment. Just show them around the ground and put them off for a fortnight."

I was flabbergasted. "I can't do that, Alf. That's totally unprofessional. United will wonder what the bloody hell is going on, having already agreed the fee."

"I'm sorry," he replied. "But that's the situation."

"What's more," I continued. "Lawrie McMenemy takes over as Sunderland manager tomorrow. Chris Turner will almost certainly go to Man United on a free transfer and, without a shadow of doubt, Lawrie will fancy Pears as his replacement. If I don't sign him today, you are putting the whole deal in jeopardy."

"Willie, that's not going to happen. There's no way Turner will go to Man United to be number two to Gary Bailey."

At 11 o'clock that morning, just an hour before the two lads were due to arrive, I jumped in my car and drove across to Alf's HQ to confront him. In his office, we had a lengthy discussion and I insisted that, if nothing else, I had to sign Pears that day. Finally, he gave in to my request and promised to find the money for Pears but insisted I was to put Davies off for the time being. As we climbed into our cars - Alf on his way to Pontefract races - it came over the radio that Chris Turner had signed for Manchester United. I took great pleasure in shouting across to Alf that what I had predicted had materialised.

Back at Ayresome Park, it didn't take two minutes to get Pears to agree to join us. First team football, not financial reward, was his priority. Somewhat embarrassed, I discussed terms with Davies and we appeared to be OK on that

Extra Time – The Final Chapter

front. During our chat he revealed to me that he was about to embark on a fortnight's holiday so I told him to go away for the two weeks, think about the move and let me know of his decision on his return. Surprise, surprise, Middlesbrough were no longer in the running by the time he had returned. Several other clubs had approached him and he eventually opted to join First Division Newcastle.

However, I was over the moon to have signed Pears. He cost well over a third of my budget but I had no doubts that he would go on to become one of the country's top goalkeepers. Indeed, I still regard his signing as being of equal importance to those of Bernie Slaven and Gary Pallister. A quiet, introverted guy, he was a total professional on the training ground and would get angry not only if a team-mate beat him to score but even if he simply spilt the ball and failed to hold a shot at the first attempt. In terms of reactions, he was one of the sharpest 'keepers I've seen and was exceptionally brave. Possibly the only weakness in his game was that his lack of height meant he didn't always command his area in terms of crosses.

Pears was an important piece in the jigsaw, though one or two other defensive pieces were never quite put in place. My long term plan was to play young Colin Cooper as a sweeper alongside two markers in Tony Mowbray and a young man called Pallister, whilst I came agonisingly close to having the two finest attacking wing backs in the country in Brian Laws and Neil Pointon. That would have been some defensive line-up and one which would have given the club a solid foundation for many years to come.

That I missed out on Pointon still rankles with me. Having signed Laws at right-back, I pursued an interest in Pointon at the end of the 1984-85 season. At the time, he was playing in the Fourth Division for Scunthorpe United. Although still a teenager, he had already played in excess of 150 games and, on another tip-off from Leeds' chief scout, I decided to take a closer look at him. Barry Geldart and I went along to Scunthorpe unannounced, paid for tickets and stood on the terraces with the fans as we didn't want to tip anyone off that we were interested in Pointon. I was impressed, as I was on each subsequent occasion I watched him. He had pace, tenacity and a long throw which could almost reach the far post.

I made contact with Scunthorpe and was told he would be available for £35,000. I told Alf that if we could get him then we would have the two best young full-backs in the league. I was surprised, therefore, when he told me to offer

£27,500. Alf insisted they would snap our hands off though I had my doubts as I knew he was worth more. Sure enough, our offer was turned down. Alf told me to bid £30,000 - and, again, the bid was met with some derision. Then, after seeing him in action in a friendly against Leicester, I put in an increased bid of £32,500. On speaking to the directors at the Old Show Ground, they insisted that they would hold out for £35,000.

Throughout this time I was becoming increasingly agitated with the chairman's insistence on going up £2,500 with each offer and felt we should just pay Scunthorpe's asking price. I could see the value in trying to get him a bit cheaper, as nobody puts in their top value with their first offer, but could sense their frustration and was concerned that another club might see what I had seen in him. Knowing we were close to a deal, I told Scunthorpe's chairman that I felt I could persuade Alf to go to £35,000 but first I wanted to speak to the boy to see what made him tick, what ambition he had and if we could agree personal terms. Our meeting at Ayresome Park went well and Pointon came over as a super lad. We had no problem in agreeing finances and we parted believing that completing the deal would prove a formality. After speaking to Alf, I rang Scunthorpe's chairman and told him we were now prepared to go the whole hog and offer £35,000. I was appalled by his response.

"We've now put a higher value on him," he said. "We are now looking for £40,000."

"That is not the way to conduct business," I told him, infuriated. "I'm hugely disappointed with your attitude and will be dropping my interest in the boy if that's how you go about things at Scunthorpe."

As frustrating as it was, we had dragged it out and they now knew how keen I was to push the deal through. I did drop my interest as a matter of principle though I told Pointon that if he wanted a move he could cause trouble at the club and insist on a transfer. But he simply wasn't that type of lad and the move never transpired. It irritated me, however, when six months later Everton manager Howard Kendall signed Pointon for £50,000 and put him straight into their championship team, winning rave reviews about his ability to spot such talent in the lower divisions. Meanwhile, I would struggle through the season with a mish-mash of left-backs, none of whom fitted the bill.

Having missed out on Davies, I was still short of a midfield playmaker and turned my attentions to Carlisle captain Don O'Riordan, an exceptional long range

Extra Time – The Final Chapter

passer who was totally comfortable on the ball. Equally at home in central midfield or as a sweeper, he had scored about 15 goals the previous season so I was delighted when a few minutes of haggling saw Bob Stokoe reduce his initial valuation from £50,000 to £40,000. We had a deal and, on meeting O'Riordan, I found him to be a very personable, ambitious guy who saw a move to Middlesbrough as a step up the ladder. Although I later made him captain, he never scored the goals I hoped he would get and moved on after only one season with the club.

Knowing I would be without Mills for much of the season, I still lacked a potent goalscorer to compete for the attacking positions with Stephens and Currie. Whilst he had a terrific left foot and remarkable dribbling ability, Currie had yet to appreciate the idea of being a team player and was very much an individual who was difficult for his colleagues to read. But he always looked as if he could develop into a reasonable player and I was amazed when, after my departure, Bruce Rioch gave him a free transfer. I could have sold him for anything up to £50,000 as I often received enquiries from other clubs about him in the region of £30,000 for him.

Sheffield United's Keith Edwards fitted the bill perfectly in terms of what I was looking for. Keith was Teesside-born - indeed I had played in the same Stockton district boys side as his brother Lennie - and, when I spoke to him, it was clear he was keen to join us. But my enquiries came to an abrupt halt the moment United boss Ian Porterfield quoted an asking price of £200,000 - my entire transfer kitty for the season!

Recognising Edwards was way beyond my limits, I got in touch with Norwich City about Gary Rowell, a player who had been a consistent goalscorer up the road at Sunderland. Having struggled with injuries, Gary was out of the first team picture at Carrow Road but stalled on a deal with us as he wanted to see if any First Division clubs came in for him. Frustrated, after several days I gave him an ultimatum - either he committed himself to Boro or he could forget the deal altogether. He subsequently signed for us for £10,000 down with another £10,000 to follow after a certain number of appearances. I don't think that second figure was ever paid. Knowing what Rowell had been capable of in his Sunderland days, I didn't feel he could have deteriorated too far over the previous couple of years and felt he would give me 15 to 20 goals in a full season, such was his composure in front of goal. Although a confident guy, Gary was a bit of a loner and didn't socialise with the other players though he never gave me any trouble in terms of his temperament. Rowell was the fifth player I had signed for a combined total of just £180,000.

I always felt Rowell was a good pro and measured that in terms of the fact that, although already a good finisher, he was always keen to stay back to work on his goalscoring after training had ended. Other players at the club were not so committed to improving their game - as was demonstrated when I introduced a piece of equipment to help the lads practice their free-kick technique. "Willie's Wall" was a wooden construction built by Mike McCullagh's firm, Marske Machine Co., and designed to resemble a defensive wall, with five smiling faces painted on it to represent each opposing "defender". Although something similar had been used by the Brazilians to practice their famous free-kick skills, it was quite revolutionary in this country and caused quite a stir among the players when I first wheeled it on to the training ground. It disappointed me, however, that after a couple of months the novelty wore off and, though the players had initially voluntarily stayed back on an afternoon to practice the skill of bending the ball over the top, in time the wall was no longer used. It displayed a lack of dedication. In my time, players would have spent long hours working with such a tool but my players soon stopped.

Even when Willie's Wall was in use, I would become frustrated by the half-cocked attempts from even my most experienced players who it seemed lacked the confidence and ability to bend the ball over the wall. The wall was battered and I would constantly bellow a reminder that the object of the exercise was to miss the damn thing. Baffled by their inability, I would show them how to do it and more often than not would bend the ball over the wall and into the net - using my left foot as I could hardly kick with my once favoured right foot, such was the pain in my knee. I could see the players looking at me as if to say "What a clever dick" but I felt they should have been able to do it too.

Things were no better with other set pieces we worked on. Time after time I would be able to put the ball just where I wanted it but became frustrated that my players couldn't do the same. I worked on a free-kick which was meant to confuse the opposition but too often it just confused us. Two players would stand over the ball with another standing parallel to them some five or six yards away on the left. I gave the players instructions to abort the first attempt and then pretend to argue in an attempt to fool the opposition and the crowd that the move had gone wrong. In the heat of the discussion, the defensive wall and goalkeeper would hopefully be lulled into a false sense of security. The ball would then be toed between the legs of one of the guys to a team-mate standing parallel on the opposite side of the wall.

Extra Time – The Final Chapter

He would then put his foot on the ball to kill it dead for a left-footed player to run in and bend it around the opposite side of the wall, hopefully with the 'keeper stranded at the wrong side of the goal. We tried this on several occasions during games, only to hit the side netting and near post, never the back of the net. For those readers up-to-date with the modern game, Manchester United's David Beckham scored a similar goal in his team's memorable 5-3 win over Chelsea during the 1997-98 season. I ached for a David Armstrong to provide the quality execution as 'Spike' would have had an 80 per cent success rate with that type of free-kick. When set pieces which you have worked on in training do come off it gives you huge satisfaction as coach but, sadly, I didn't have enough quality at the club.

Irving Nattrass with "Willie's Wall" – my own version of a Brazilian invention.

I wanted corners belted in with a lot of pace with a man pulling off the back post hopefully for a free header. But I became increasingly disillusioned when in games players would float the ball in, making it easy for the 'keeper to catch it unchallenged. Perhaps it was through lack of confidence but that in my opinion was the easy way out. Sometimes, when you're having a bad time, it takes much moral courage to have a go at something like that, especially when you know it might go behind for a goal-kick without even reaching the penalty box.

I was down to the bare bones in terms of the first team squad right from the opening day of the season. Paul Ward's final day booking at Shrewsbury, combined with the dismissals of Gary Hamilton and Peter Beagrie, meant I was forced to play Irving Nattrass despite the fact he was struggling with a back strain. There were five new faces in the starting line-up to face Wimbledon at Plough Lane

Building Boro's Future

and only Nattrass and Mowbray retained their places from the previous season's opening day fixture. This time I named the following team:

1. Stephen Pears
2. Brian Laws
3. Steve Corden
4. Gary Pallister
5. Tony Mowbray
6. Irving Nattrass
7. Alan Roberts
8. Don O'Riordan
9. Archie Stephens
10. Tony McAndrew
11. Gary Rowell
12. David Currie

The 3-0 defeat which followed was probably an accurate reflection of the game against a side which was to win promotion to the top flight that season. That day Pallister and Corden made their debuts alongside one another and yet their futures were to take such differing tracks that poor Steve must wonder what might have been. To be fair, I only picked Steve at left-back because of suspensions to other players though I did feel he might have a future in the game, thanks to his great attitude. He was a workmanlike player with lots of aggression though a little bit short technically. Unfortunately, in a first half tackle he twisted his leg in what looked an innocuous challenge but it was immediately obvious he was in enormous discomfort. It transpired he had broken his leg. It was a terrible blow for the lad and, sadly, he was never to play again at that level.

We all know, of course, what Pallister has gone on to achieve in the game and I thought he did quite well on the day, though he was tripping over his tongue in the last 20 minutes. Things were very different three days later when we lost 2-0 to Third Division Mansfield in the Milk Cup. At half-time, I blew my top with the majority of the players and had a particular go at Pally. His first half performance was a nightmare. Every aspect of his game was wrong - he wasn't physical enough, struggled to concentrate and generally allowed opponents to boss him and push him about. I knew he was better than that and told him so. "You played out there

Extra Time – The Final Chapter

as if you don't feel you belong," I said. "You are in the team on merit. You need to recognise that and start playing with some sort of belief."

To be fair, Gary had been playing local league football until just a few months earlier and it was perhaps too early for him to be playing at that level. He was 20 years old but was built like a beanpole and needed to spend some time on the weights. Pally first came to my attention two years earlier whilst playing for Billingham Town in the Northern League. I decided to give him a try out in the reserves after our scout Barry Geldart had received a number of good reports on him. At 18, he probably thought he had missed the boat in terms of a professional football career but I thought he might be worth taking a closer look at. During the first 20 minutes, I could see he was finding the pace of the game very hard, just as I had when making the transition from junior to reserve team football many years earlier. With his long, lean physique, he reminded me of a young foal but while he was clearly struggling with the physical side of the game, I noticed that he was always comfortable on the ball and had a good range of passing. I also noted that he attacked the ball well for a big lad - strangely, many big guys don't have a particularly good leap and tend to just stand and head the ball - but Pally was commanding in the air. Gary was hardly encouraged by Boro's ex-Scotland international John Brownlie, playing at right-back that night, who apparently criticised the lad throughout the match.

As he trooped into the dressing room after the game, Pally looked red-faced and hot under the collar. He also wore a look of complete dejection and I could tell he thought he had blown his chance. "I've had a f***ing nightmare," he blurted out. When I had finished addressing the players in my then role as reserve team coach, I had a quiet word with Gary to let him know that we would have another look at him at a later stage. Many years later he admitted that he thought I was only being kind but I had seen enough in the first 20 minutes to suggest that he might make a player. I told Barry Geldart that the lad needed to go back into the Northern League to toughen up a bit and develop physically. Meanwhile, we would keep close tabs on him.

Soon after my appointment as the club's manager, Billingham Town's coach Ray Halliday and secretary Tommy Donnelly got back in contact with Barry to say they thought Pally was worth another look. In response, Barry and I took in one of Town's next fixtures at Bedford Terrace and Pallister enjoyed a most accomplished game. We decided to take a closer look at him and invited him to play in two or three reserve team fixtures. His opponent in one of those games, against Grimsby

Building Boro's Future

Town at Ayresome Park, was an England under-21 international called Gary Lund. Pally hardly gave him a kick of the ball. His potential was there for all to see.

I immediately made an approach to my board of directors with a view to signing Gary, but I wasn't prepared for their answer. The bank was already concerned at the lack of inroads the club was making into our financial plight so if a player was to be added to the squad, then another player must in turn be sold. Rather than give up, I decided to pursue my efforts to make Gary a Boro player down a different avenue. Dick Corden, of Industrial Scaffolding, was a local businessman I had known for several years and he had previously sponsored a young triallist called Scott Johnson who unfortunately had not made the grade. I went to see Dick in his Portakabins within the grounds of Grayson, White & Sparrow on Stockton Road, where I told him I had seen a young lad of outstanding potential. I asked him if he would consider paying his wages until such time I could persuade the board that he would make a good player. Dick asked me what sort of money would be involved. I knew Pallister was out of work so we wouldn't have to pay him a huge amount of money to persuade him to sign for us so I told Dick it would not be in excess of £80 a week. He had no hesitation in granting me my request and I duly signed Gary on a month-by-month contract on the princely wage of £60 a week!

I remember Gary walked into my office wearing a smile as wide as his face but his jaw hit the deck when I told him the terms I was able to offer. Bless him, I knew he would be better off financially on the dole and doing a few guvvy jobs but here was an opportunity to break into professional football just when he thought the chance had passed him by. Sure enough, he signed on the dotted line though his mood was not so bouyant as he left the office. On the other hand, I was absolutely delighted to have secured his registration, albeit on a slender thread. To complete the deal, the club's young director Steve Gibson bought Billingham Town a new team strip as their "transfer fee". I believe I am right in remembering, therefore, that Gary Pallister cost Middlesbrough a grand total of £300. Not bad for a player who would later join Manchester United for a British record fee of £2.3 million!

About three months later I received a telephone call from Ken Brown, manager of First Division Norwich City. He said his scouts had been impressed with what they had seen of the young Pallister. If I would consider letting him go down there for a couple of weeks, they would be prepared to pay us £30,000 if he looked the part. That really set the alarm bells ringing in my head. At the time, Pally had only one week left to run on his latest monthly contract but I gave no hint to Brown that

Extra Time – The Final Chapter

we held his signature almost by default. I bluntly turned down his offer, saying that Pallister would figure in my first team plans in the not too distant future. I was thankful that he did not pursue the lad via the back door as they would have been able to offer him considerably more than his weekly salary at Middlesbrough.

At the next board meeting, I quite arrogantly informed the club's directors that I had turned down a bid of £30,000 for Pallister. There was a look of amazement and embarrassment on the faces around the table. Thankfully, common sense prevailed and it was agreed by all concerned that we had to give him a contract of at least 12 months. I think I doubled Pally's salary to about £120, with the extra incentive that he would earn considerably more when he was playing regular first team football.

It wasn't all sweetness and joy between Pally and I, however. He often found himself on the wrong end of a bollocking from me as a result of half-hearted performances for the reserves. On the night which saw Bernie Slaven on trial against Grimsby, I felt Pally did no more than go through the motions. I had high hopes for him but he simply didn't do himself justice that night. He was naturally laid back but I wanted him to be a bit more forceful. He seemed to be quite happy to be the last one on to the training ground and the first one off it. He was so laid back, he made Perry Como look like a nervous wreck. In other words, he was a big, lazy sod.

To keep him on his toes, I would often keep him back for extra training, when I would spend hours whacking the ball at him to control with his feet or chest to develop his first touch and accuracy in passing. He seemed to respond to that type of work and it quickly became evident that he had a super touch for a big lad. In fact, I felt it was only a matter of time before he was ready for the first team.

After that gruelling game against Mansfield, however, I made my mind up that he needed toughening up. He was in need of league experience but I didn't think I could afford him the luxury of learning in our first team as it may have proved too costly for us in terms of league points. Instead, I arranged for him to spend a month in a lower division, on loan with Darlington. I watched him twice that month and, without doing anything spectacular, he looked far more confident and played with a great deal of composure. At the end of the month, Darlington boss Cyril Knowles tried to pull a fast one by offering me the princely sum of £5,000 for Gary.

I gave the offer the response it deserved. "Knowlsey," I said. "You've always had a good sense of humour and been a cheeky bastard but I'm not as daft as you

Building Boro's Future

think I am. Pallister will come back to Middlesbrough and I thank you most sincerely for giving him much needed first team experience." Cyril knew as well as I did that Pally was a damn good player in the making.

One particular incident stands out in my memory in the development of Pallister into a truly special talent. It came in one of my final games in charge of the club, against Norwich City in January 1986. A high ball dropped out of the sky towards him, with City's Kevin Drinkell, a big burly striker with a huge physical presence, bearing down on him ready to break him in two. Before the ball dropped to the ground, Pally cushioned it with the top of his foot and in the same sweeping movement made a sharp swerve a couple of yards to his right, leaving Drinkell kicking at fresh air. At that moment, I realised Gary Pallister would make an exceptional player. He had all the ingredients needed as he had good control, was strong in the air and was fast. All that he lacked was good concentration but I knew that in time that would come.

Several years later, as a Manchester United player, Gary would often pay me visits at my sports shop on Teesside Park but I found it hard to get out of the habit of talking to him as if I was still his manager. A typical conversation would go something like: "I saw you playing against Everton on TV on Saturday and that Pat Nevin turned you and left you for dead time after time. Why are you still dangling that leg in and finishing on the wrong side of a player?"

The poor lad had only called in to see me on a social visit and would say: "Leave it out, Willie."

But I would go on: "Don't you do extra training in the afternoon?"

"No," he would reply. "I go home for a kip."

"Don't you want to be the best central defender in the country?"

"But Willie, no-one brings us back for more training."

"Well, get hold of one of the apprentices and someone like Mark Hughes to play up against you. That would be the best possible practice you could have."

"I'll think about it, Willie."

"You're still lightweight on your upper body. Why don't you do some weights?"

"You sound like Alex Ferguson now," he would sigh.

Another bugbear of mine was that he would only score maybe one or two goals a season. With his height and ability I felt he should have been scoring eight or nine. I would watch him on TV, making defensive headers and sweeping everyone out of sight but it frustrated me to see him attacking headers in the opposition box like a gentle giant. "I see that Steve Bruce pushing everyone out of the way and grabbing all the headlines with his goals," I told him. "You should be pushing him out of the way and getting yourself on the end of corners."

As he progressed to each new level, Gary always needed time to settle down and find his feet, with one notable exception - at international level. I was nervous for him, watching his international debut for England against Hungary whilst still with Middlesbrough. But that afternoon, my chest swelled as Gary looked as though he had been in the England team all his life and should have marked his debut with a goal. In fact, it mystifies me why he has not won many more international caps. Pally and Tony Adams of Arsenal remain by far the best English central defenders and it is my opinion that Gareth Southgate and Sol Campbell are not good enough to lace Pally's boots. But then, I'm biased.

In one of our conversations over the telephone he hinted to me that one day he would love to return to Boro. I have to admit that I would love to see him wearing the red and white shirt of Middlesbrough once again. If he does return, I hope I might still be fit enough to watch him at the Riverside. I would still feel immensely proud to think back to the day we signed him on a wage equivalent to the price of cheap suit.

Whilst Pallister's spell with Darlington ended after just a month, two of my players went to Feethams on a permanent basis early in that 1985-86 campaign. One of them was Alan Roberts, whose final game in a Middlesbrough shirt came in that defeat at Mansfield. He was a very good crosser of the ball but he lacked consistency and rarely did anything away from home. The other was Paul Ward, an honest player who I knew was capable of making a living in the lower leagues but didn't quite have the ability for the Second Division. I allowed both players to join Darlington, receiving Mitch Cook and £5,000 in exchange. Being an orthodox left-footed player, I felt Cook offered me a better balance in midfield though he never developed the early potential I saw in him.

That £5,000 enabled me to sign Pat Heard, a player who turned out to be the most disappointing acquisition in my time in charge of the club. Having previously been with Everton, Aston Villa and Sheffield Wednesday, I had seen him play many times and watched him in action for Newcastle's reserves in the Central League. He actually scored that night and, although he played left midfield, I knew he would be comfortable at left-back. After reassurances from Jack Charlton that he was a typical bread and butter type player, I took him on a month's loan and he played out of his skin every match, starring in a 1-0 win over Sheffield United, when he made a left wing run late in the game before playing Rowell in for the winning goal. That made my mind up that I should make the move permanent.

I have good reason to remember the day I signed Heard. We were sat in my office haggling over terms when Hilary rang from North Tees Hospital to say she had started premature labour and asked me to go home to get her toiletries and nightwear. I jumped up out of my seat and told Heard: "My wife is having a baby so I'm going now. You can either sign the contract or go back to Newcastle." Worst luck, he signed the contract. It was all downhill from that moment on as his attitude and commitment was always poor once we had given him a contract. He was a huge disappointment. Many people questioned why I suffered him for so long but I had few other options as I was determined not to throw in the kids and jeopardise their careers.

By mid-September, I was starting to see a bit of shape in the team and one of our local lads, Gary Gill, was doing a great job in a midfield holding position, disputing possession as a marker in the middle of the field. Although not an obvious crowd pleaser, Gary was invaluable in that much of his work was unseen by supporters but greatly appreciated by me. I thought the balance of the team was starting to look much better. But luck was not on our side. A goal up and coasting with about five minutes left at home to Stoke City, a long pass saw Rowell clean through with defender George Berry in pursuit. As Gary raced into the box and pulled back his right foot to shoot, Berry hacked him down from behind. It was as blatant a penalty as you could ever wish to see and everyone in the ground knew it. Everyone, that is, apart from referee Trelford Mills who waved play on. The Stoke 'keeper kicked the ball downfield and a defensive header fell at the feet of one of their midfielders some 40 yards out. Advancing about five yards, he hit a speculative shot with no pace on the ball. It was never likely to trouble Stephen Pears - normally. This time, Pearsy uncharacteristically fumbled the ball and it dropped agonisingly over his head and trickled over the line.

At that moment I had an overwhelming feeling of inevitability about my future as the club's manager. Turning to Steve Smelt beside me in the dug-out, I said: "It will never happen for me at this club. You need to be lucky - and I haven't got that luck."

"Don't be so daft," said Smelty. "It's just one of those things."

Extra Time – The Final Chapter

But I have always been a great believer that you do need that bit of luck and mine clearly deserted me that night. Having dominated the game, losing two valuable points so late in the match was a bitter pill to swallow and real doubts began to creep into my mind. I was not prepared, however, for the ridiculous comment made by Alf Duffield after the game. The chairman told me I should drop Pears for his error. I told Alf that Pears would never concede another goal like that in the rest of his career. And I don't think he ever did.

Whilst my faith in Pears remained, I was not so happy with my strikeforce of Rowell, Stephens and Currie. After 11 league games, I was bitterly disappointed with our output of just four goals - three of those from Rowell. I guess Rowell wasn't a team player but you couldn't argue with his goalscoring record throughout that season. Quite why Bruce Rioch later chose to discard him, I don't know, but I suspect he might have been close to achieving the number of appearances whereby a second installment on his transfer fee would be required and maybe Middlesbrough couldn't afford to pay it. A goal from Archie had clinched our first league win of the season over Fulham but he had then suffered a dramatic loss of form. Whether it was a confidence thing, I don't know, but the situation became so bad that I later considered trying to sell him. Having witnessed his initial contribution the previous season, I knew that he was capable of so much more but I was never to get the benefit of Archie in consistently good, aggressive form. At the same time, the goals from Currie had dried up too.

It was quite clear I needed another striker, but as always, I would have to look around the bargain basement end of the transfer market. I did quite fancy the former Coventry striker Mick Ferguson, who was with Brighton at the time, but then, out of the blue, my attention focused on a player who was to become one of Middlesbrough's all-time top goalscorers. As I sat sifting through paperwork in my office one late September afternoon, Barry Geldart knocked on the door and came into the room holding a letter from a guy requesting a trial. Every football club receives literally dozens of such letters each week from people of all ages and abilities asking for the chance to make their name in the professional game and it is a question of selecting the wheat from the chaff. But something in Barry's voice told me this one was a bit different. He explained that this particular guy had scored goals for fun in Scotland the previous season and that he might be worth taking a closer look at. I read the contents of the letter:

Building Boro's Future

Dear Sir,

Last season I was the top scorer in Scottish senior football with 31 goals for Albion Rovers in the Second Division.

At present, I am on 'Freedom of Contract'. I have no intention of returning to Rovers.

I am keen to sample full-time football at the highest level, and wonder if you might consider signing me.

I would be willing to come to your club on a trial basis, as I am desperate to get back into the game.

I honestly feel I have the ability to play for your club. Although I have not played since I took up 'Freedom of Contract' at the end of last season, I have kept fit during the summer training on my own every day.

I am 24 years old, and hope that you will at least think over the approach.

Yours sincerely,

BERNIE SLAVEN

I must admit I had never heard of Slaven but knew we were in no position to turn down any decent player without looking at him, let alone someone who had scored 31 goals the previous year. "Do you want me to get him down here?" asked Barry. "Yeah, let's do that," I answered. "Invite him through and we'll play him in the reserves at Grimsby next week."

My first sight of our new triallist came at a sportsmen's dinner in the Billingham Arms Hotel the night before the Grimsby game. "This is Bernie Slaven," said Barry, who had arranged for him to have a short trial with us. "Hello, Bernie. How are you?" I asked, before asking him about the contents of the glass he held in his hand. It looked suspiciously like a Bacardi and Coke.

"Och, it's just a Coke," he replied, in a broad Glaswegian accent. "I'm tee-total."

I have to admit I was surprised. He was the first Scot I'd ever met who didn't drink. But as I scrutinised our healthy living Scot, I couldn't help but notice his long, scruffy hair and rather unshaven look. On first impressions, I wasn't particularly enamoured with Slaven and was far from convinced he would be the answer to our problems. However, the success of Alan Foggon some years earlier

Extra Time – The Final Chapter

had taught me the lesson never to judge a book by its cover.

The following night I travelled with Barry to watch Slaven in action for the reserves at Grimsby's Blundell Park and quickly began to change my opinion of the man. Although he had told me he had kept up a reasonable fitness by training on his own in Glasgow parks, the lad hadn't played competitive football for five months so I wasn't expecting too much in that first game, believing he would lack sharpness. Over the next 90 minutes, however, I saw a very special talent on view. In a team which included the developing talents of Gary Pallister, Stuart Ripley, Colin Cooper and David Currie, Slaven stood out a mile and was light years ahead of the rest in terms of his thinking, passing and all-round contribution to the game. He must have had nine or 10 attempts on goal whilst Alan Kernaghan alongside him didn't have a shot worthy of the name. Although he didn't score, Bernie succeeded in making a huge impact on me with his ability to gamble on being in the right place at the right time and getting into great goalscoring positions. Had the ball been delivered to him more accurately, I'm sure he would have scored three or four that night.

Thanks to Bernie, I was bubbling with enthusiasm on the journey back to Teesside. Whilst I had been forced to rollick Pallister for his truly lack-lustre performance, Slaven gave me reason to believe that we might still have a chance of pulling away from the relegation trapdoor. My batteries had been running down in the previous weeks but in Slaven I had seen something so special it rejuvenated and excited me.

Despite his obvious talent, I was suspicious of Slaven. I wondered why he was in dispute with Albion Rovers and whether there was some kind of flaw in his attitude. I wanted to find out more before making any final decisions so asked him to return to Teesside the following week for a longer trial. Bernie left Ayresome Park for Scotland promising to return for the trial. But I was left dumb-founded when, on returning home one night, I listened to a message from Slaven on my answer phone, informing me that he wouldn't be coming back after all. He was concerned that he might spend a full week away from his gardening job only to fail with Middlesbrough and return to Glasgow to find he had lost his full-time job. The following day, I got Barry to phone him to say we wouldn't insist on him staying for a full week but would simply like to take another look at him in the reserves.

I was relieved to see Slaven back on Teesside the following Wednesday when

I picked him in a reserve team line-up to play Bradford City at Ayresome Park. Once again, there was nothing to suggest his character would be a problem. More importantly, his performance against Bradford was the nearest thing to a one-man show you can get. That night he was amazing, scoring two and setting up another brace for Archie Stephens in a 4-0 win. The clinical finishing missing the previous week was evident for all to see and the small crowd who saw his display must have gone home as excited as I was.

Indeed, the very fact that Slaven was so impressive made me uneasy. I knew representatives of other clubs may well have been in the crowd and witnessed his display and I was concerned they might try to tap him up at the end of the game. I gave Steve Smelt orders to tell the night watchman, Bert, to lock the ground's iron gates and make sure no-one was hanging around outside. Meanwhile, I went to my office to make an urgent phone call to Glasgow.

Frustratingly, I couldn't raise the Albion chairman Tom Fagan and, at about 10 o'clock, told Slaven that, although I was impressed, I couldn't give him a decision until I had spoken to his chairman about a fee. With great reluctance, I had to tell him to come back in the morning. But I knew the deal had to be agreed that night to avoid the risk of other clubs getting to Slaven. Unfortunately, Alf Duffield was away on business and wasn't due to return for another two days. In his absence, I rang Steve Gibson, the club's young director who had been on the board only a matter of months. I told Steve I had seen a performance that night the likes of which I had not seen for some time. I explained that I would be looking to try and sign Slaven for £25,000 and asked him to back my judgement and grant me permission on behalf of the club to agree to that fee. I was delighted when Steve agreed to put his own neck on the line, as well as my own, by backing me 100 per cent.

It was approaching midnight when Tom Fagan finally answered his telephone. He had been watching his beloved Rangers and I could tell he had enjoyed a whisky or two to celebrate a good win. I quickly got down to the nitty-gritty and asked him what value he would put on Slaven.

"I think he's worth £50,000 of anyone's money," he said.

I knew he was right but that sort of fee was way beyond our means. "Oh, come on, Mr Fagan, I know you've had a good night but you've got to be realistic," I bluffed. "If we go to a tribunal with this boy, we'll offer no more than £5,000. From my experience, they'll settle on about £15,000. They always err on the side of the

Extra Time – The Final Chapter

buying club. The lad has an awful lot to do in terms of adjusting to the pace of English football."

It was all said tongue in cheek with both fingers crossed but I knew I had to keep up the facade. "Let's be sensible," I continued. "I'll pay you £15,000 down with another £10,000 after 20 appearances. That will save us all the aggravation and embarrassment of a tribunal."

There was a long pause at the other end of the phone as he considered my offer. "Och, I've had a good night, the Rangers have won," he responded. "We'll consider it a deal and sort out the forms in the morning."

I tried to remain low key but struggled to contain my excitement over the phone. During the following exchange of pleasantries, Fagan offered me another of his players - a winger - but I was too busy trying to play down Slaven to sound interested. When I finally clicked down the receiver, I was ecstatic and left Ayresome Park, deserted but for Bert, the night watchman, thrilled with my night's work.

The following morning, Bernie happily agreed terms. He had been on £70 a week with Albion Rovers and my offer of £240 a week represented a huge rise for him and he readily put pen to paper. Bernie Slaven was a Middlesbrough player. Two days later, however, he was back in my office where he told me that he thought he could perhaps have secured a better deal. Remembering how delighted he had been with his contract when he had left my office, I asked him if someone had been talking to him. He revealed one of the club's senior players had told him he might have got a better deal for himself. I have my suspicions as to who that player might be and to this day remain disgusted that he chose to convince Slaven that he hadn't done well for himself. But I wasn't about to change my mind. I told Bernie that he still had to prove himself and reminded him he was already on more than treble his wage at Albion. Until he could prove he was worthy of a better deal, he had to consider it a generous offer.

On returning from his business trip and hearing that I had signed Slaven without his approval, Alf Duffield rang me to ask what the hell was going on. "You have no right to sign any player without my consent," he said.

"The deal needed to be pushed through quickly," I explained. "I sought and received Steve Gibson's backing."

In response, he told me he had contemplated giving me the push. It was the first time Alf had mentioned the word "sack".

"I don't care whether you sack me over this," I insisted. "If you did that, my judgement in the player would only embarrass you at a later date."

At a subsequent board meeting, George Kitching, who had been a director for many years and had even had a spell as chairman, stood up and asked how much we were paying Slaven. I told Kitching I didn't think he had any right to even ask such a question in view of the fact that he had been party to the signing of many players on twice the salary, some of whom weren't even half as good as Slaven. To his credit, Alf supported me by telling Kitching to sit down. "Willie's right, George," he said. "When I consider some of the players who have been signed by this club on ridiculous salaries over the years. Time will tell with this lad."

I gave Bernie his first team debut two days later at Leeds United. That day, in a game we lost by a single goal, he missed a chance that I can still picture to this day. It was a volley that he ran on to without breaking stride - the type of chance he would despatch with contemptible ease as his career developed - but this time the ball zipped narrowly over the bar. Slaven was an exceptional finisher who was to go on to score almost 150 goals for the club - something of a bargain at £25,000 - but I think it is fair to say that, for me, his return of goals never mirrored the promise I saw each morning on the training ground. It took him a while to adjust to English football but even on the day I was dismissed I knew he would prove me right. He had close control, an accuracy of shot unparalleled at the club and an ability to gamble on deflections or mistakes to be in the right place at the right time. Given those attributes, his goals return over the months which followed was mediocre.

Missing from the team for Slaven's home debut, against Bradford in mid-October, was a young lad who would go on to become a huge crowd favourite and club captain. At the time, I was experimenting with a new defensive formation using three centre-backs and Tony Mowbray was in my thoughts along with three other players, McAndrew, O'Riordan and Nattrass. In training two days before the game, I played three 20-minute sessions, giving each permutation a chance. When training had ended, I felt the trio of McAndrew, O'Riordan and Nattrass gave us the best balance and decided I would leave Mowbray out of the team. As it turned out, however, McAndrew suffered a hamstring strain so Mowbray's name was on the team sheet which I pinned up on the dressing room wall after Friday's training session.

By that time, I think Tony had already come to the conclusion that he wasn't going to be selected and he was to respond in a way I found hard to come to terms with. On seeing the team sheet, he came to my office where he told me he didn't feel in the right frame of mind to play against Bradford. I was shocked that a young player could say that. Like many players, I had been dropped during my career but never would I have even contemplated saying such a thing. In a fit of temper, I blasted Tony, yelling: "As long as I'm Middlesbrough manager, you'll never play for this football club again. Now get out!"

I didn't, and don't, regret those words though I know I might well have expressed my anger another way. In the heat of the moment, I felt I was fully justified by what I said but, with hindsight, perhaps I could have chosen my words more carefully.

The truth is the reactions of both Tony and I probably weren't helped by an ongoing dispute we had over his salary. Some months earlier, his father had come in to see me to try and negotiate a new pay deal for him. I was surprised that, at 21, Tony wasn't handling his own negotiations as I had dealt with my own since the age of 16. Mr Mowbray explained that he felt Tony had been ripped off under Malcolm Allison and didn't want the same thing to happen again. He went on to ask me for the sort of contract which Stephen Bell had been awarded. I had to remind him that we had only narrowly missed relegation to the Third Division the previous season and were averaging home gates of only 5,000. "The wage bill here won't reach those dizzy heights again for some time so I'm afraid Tony has missed the boat in terms of that sort of big contract," I explained. Eventually I offered Tony, through his dad, the sort of wage most Middlesbrough players of his age were getting, though it was well short of the sort of salary an experienced player was on. I actually offered to more than double his basic wage which, to be fair, wasn't a huge amount but it was the maximum I was allowed given the financial constraints I was working under. In response, I can vividly remember Mr Mowbray insisting that Tony could earn a similar salary at Darlington. I was hugely disappointed, however, when he said he would be advising his son not to sign a new contract.

We remained in dispute over his contract throughout the months which followed and there is little doubt that the relationship between Tony and I suffered as a result, culminating in our bust-up over the Bradford game. I know Tony has claimed that I often ignored him when I passed him in the corridor but I have to say I never did that intentionally. Things were always cool between us after our clash but he remained a major part of my plans. I know "Mogga" has always been a super lad and to this day remain disappointed that we never enjoyed a better relationship. I can't help but think he was being misled somewhat. Tony was still learning his trade and was perhaps a bit green at the time so I would occasionally have a go at him but it was always done constructively. I particularly remember telling him not to wait for the perfect ball on corners but to try and shake off his marker and get in there. I wasn't surprised when he went on to score quite a few goals by attacking the ball in that way as he always tried to put into practice what I preached. Perhaps because I didn't pat him on the back every week, he felt I didn't rate him. That was far from the truth as he remained part of my long-term vision of a defence which would include Mowbray, Pears, Cooper, Pallister, Laws and A N Other at left-back.

After the Bradford game, Tony spent a month or so in the reserves but his commitment remained first class. Players with more questionable attitudes than his might have packed in altogether given my rebuke but, to his credit, Tony was still working hard. Indeed, he obviously impressed Oldham manager Joe Royle during a second team game at Boundary Park as Royle rang me the next day to offer £30,000 for his services. I told Joe he was not for sale - even when he upped his bid to £35,000. Perhaps that went against every word I had uttered on the subject at the time but deep down he always remained part of my long-term strategy.

Eventually we got together with the chairman and held clear the air talks. Alf pointed out to Tony that he had tied my hands in terms of what sort of contract I could offer. Even so, Tony refused to sign a new contract and remained in dispute with the club throughout the rest of my time there. Had I accepted that £35,000 offer, however, perhaps Middlesbrough may not have risen from the ashes as it did as Mowbray was undoubtedly the driving force behind that rise.

Back in the league, we clinched a third win in four games with a 2-0 home derby success over Sunderland. I took some comfort from the fact that we had spent most of the season above our Wearside rivals, especially considering Sunderland had been looked on as promotion favourites under Lawrie McMenemy. Then, on January 1st 1986, we faced Huddersfield at home in a game which we knew would take us to just below mid-table if we won. Sadly, we were atrocious. I couldn't believe two consecutive performances could be so different. Even then, we could have won it, if only luck was on our side. Just before half-time, Bernie Slaven played a one-two with Rowell, took the ball past the final defender and toe-ended it past the Huddersfield goalkeeper. It was a great goal. Never in a million years was Bernie offside - it was impossible - but that's what the ref gave.

Extra Time – The Final Chapter

Again, I turned to Smelty and said: "I've told you, it won't happen for me here. That was a perfectly good goal we've just had chalked off." We had been awful throughout the first half but if we had gone in 1-0 up I could have given my players an almighty bollocking without demoralising them. Instead, the game was still finely balanced and I had to concentrate on lifting them for the second half. As our luck would have it, Huddersfield left Ayresome Park with a 1-0 win.

If we had won that match, the players would have stopped thinking of themselves as relegation material and started to believe in themselves a bit more when they realised they were just below mid-table. The effect that can have is that shots which would have hit the post start going in - luck seems to be on your side. But I was so downcast with our performance against Huddersfield, it prompted me to state publicly that if the players didn't do it for me over the next few games then I would have to consider resigning. "We will find out what they think about me by their level of performance," I said. Our next four fixtures were away to league leaders Norwich City, followed by another trip south to Brighton, who were also doing well, a third away game, at promotion-chasing Portsmouth, and finally at home to another of the top sides, Charlton Athletic. I couldn't have made my ultimatum at a worse time...

18

Mission: Impossible

THOSE crazy enough to go into football management do so in the knowledge that one day they will be sacked. Dismissal is inevitable in a business where success and winning games is everything and loyalty is barely worth a mention. Getting the sack is part and parcel of the game, whether you are a success or a failure. So when it finally happened to me, it did not come as a surprise and I did not feel sorry for myself. What I felt was great sadness that I had not been able to give the people of Teesside a successful football team. And yet I would defy even Alex Ferguson, Bob Paisley or any other management legend to have turned around the fortunes of Middlesbrough Football Club as they spiralled towards disaster during the mid-1980s.

By the time I took charge of team affairs during the summer of 1984, the club had been going downhill for at least five years and I believe my efforts broke the speed of the deterioration. It hurt me to the core that I was unable to bring a halt to Boro's decline and it bruised my pride that for the first time in my career I had failed. For too long I was very hard on myself over my time as Middlesbrough's manager and didn't return to Ayresome for more than five years. That wasn't out of bitterness as so many believed. Embarrassment, perhaps. A defence mechanism to avoid too many painful memories being rekindled, maybe. But never bitterness. For 18 months, I put my heart and soul into Middlesbrough Football Club and even in the darkest hour, even at my last game, never did the fans hound for my blood.

But deep down, I blamed myself. I felt I had made mistakes and perhaps someone else could save the club. I was wrong. Only in recent years have I realised that I did not have a cat in hell's chance of being successful. Now, rather than dwelling on poor results and disappointments, I look back with pride on the fact

Extra Time – The Final Chapter

that I helped to shape the club's future which was to see a rise from the ashes to the massive institution it is today.

My final weeks as manager of Middlesbrough were so bad that when the inevitable finally happened, I was relieved it was all over. My health was beginning to suffer as a result of the pressure - most of it self-induced. I would often sit at home watching TV without even taking in what I was seeing or hearing. I was on another planet. I would be picking the team for the next match or deciding what our next training session should comprise. I just couldn't turn off and that can't be good for anyone.

It dawned on me that the job was giving me a form of unhealthy tunnel vision in the build-up to our game against Norwich City at Carrow Road. As I finished filling in our team-sheet about 50 minutes before kick-off, I turned to Steve Smelt and asked him what the date was. "It's January 11th," he replied. With a wry smile, I told him: "Do you know what, Steve, it's my birthday today - and I had totally forgotten about it."

Thankfully, Hilary was immensely understanding during those early months of our marriage. But sometimes she must have wondered if my mind ever left the football club and focused on our life together. One particular instance when Hilary asked me to go to the local shops for a bottle of milk highlighted just how bad the situation had become. At the time, we were living on a new housing estate on Park View, opposite Preston Park, so I jumped into my car, intending to drive to the supermarket a mile away in Eaglescliffe. I think I must have been picking the team again because I drove out of the estate and turned left towards the A66 instead of right towards Eaglescliffe. It wasn't until I got to the A66 that I realised what I was doing and turned around. The truth is I was on automatic pilot and was making my usual journey to Ayresome Park. But even that didn't jolt me back to reality. Rather than driving on to the supermarket, I turned back into our estate. Instead of concentrating on driving to the shops, I was thinking: "Drop him, put so and so in that position..." I had actually parked up outside our house and was about to climb out of the car when I realised I still didn't have the milk I had gone out to get. At that moment, a neighbour engaged me in a 10-minute conversation but I eventually made it to the supermarket for that damn milk. Arriving back home, Hilary commented on how long I had been. I didn't dare tell her about the journey I had embarked on!

Fortunately, I never did take the stresses of my job out on Hilary. She wasn't a football person and on many occasions didn't even come to our games. I'm sure it

Mission: Impossible

would have only added to the stress had I returned home to face a barrage of questions from her. On one occasion, however, she had had enough of my zombie-like state. That Sunday I was in our living room, as always planning the following day's training session, when the phone rang. Believing Hilary was in the kitchen making Sunday dinner, I answered the phone. "It's Hilary," she said. "I'm just ringing to say your dinner's in the oven."

"Where the hell are you?" I asked, surprised.

"Saltburn," she answered. "I wanted a bit of space." I'm embarrassed to say that I didn't even know she had left the house, let alone that she had driven 13 or 14 miles up the road to the coast.

On her return, we sat down and had a heart to heart when I admitted the job was taking far too much out of me. I promised her that I would make more of an effort around the house and find a hobby to help me turn off from football. Sadly, it remained an unfulfilled promise.

Just as worryingly, it was becoming the norm for me to guzzle my way through a full bottle of wine each day over our evening meal. One morning I looked at the empty bottles and realised that two-and-a-half litres had been consumed, of which Hilary had drank no more than half a litre. The frightening thing was that I didn't even have a bad head. I certainly wasn't an alcoholic but I knew I was drinking in excess as it was the only way I could relax and turn off to any extent.

I couldn't sleep after a game and would often wake up at five o'clock in the morning planning the day's training. With things not going well, I was no longer bouncing into work and was finding it hard to be the bubbly character I had always been. I did wonder if the mask was beginning to slip as I was no longer enjoying the day-to-day routine on the training ground. I began to compromise too much and maybe accept less effort from the players than I would have done in my first six months in the job. In those early months I had been as keen as mustard and would never have let the standard of training drop below the level I would have expected as a player. I did try to keep organising sessions designed to stop us leaking goals whilst attempting to be more productive at the other end of the pitch but when you're not playing well and are losing more often than not, it is easy to put on pretty pretty sessions.

Fortunately, the majority of the players liked me so my relationship with them didn't really suffer, though on the odd occasion I did blow my top. One such instance came during a training session at Hall Drive when, out of sheer frustration, I began shouting and bawling at David Currie. I know my language must have been foul because several people who lived over the road came out of their houses to ask me to tone it down. It just wasn't me to use bad language in such a hostile way and I was most apologetic about it.

During that birthday game at Norwich, we again dominated for the first 45 minutes. Bernie really should have scored but volleyed the ball about an inch wide of the post. Then, just before half-time, Mowbray was adjudged to have pushed Kevin Drinkell in the penalty area despite the fact the City striker was very much the aggressor. Drinkell went down like a bag of tripe but the referee made what I felt was a disgraceful decision by awarding a penalty. It was typical of the way things were going for us as we were truly down among the dead men. Steve Bruce scored a typically brave header to seal a flattering 2-0 win late in the game but I was left wondering what might have been.

It was around that time that I made the decision to find a new full-time first team coach. I didn't think things were working out with John Coddington, who had the time-consuming distraction of running his pub. When I told John I had to decided to advertise the position, I think it came as a welcome relief to him. We duly advertised the post in The Times and The Daily Express and waited for the applications to come in. When I had finished sifting through the applications, I had four good candidates on my short list. They were John Pickering, a former Lincoln and Blackburn boss who, though not comfortable as a manager, was regarded as a good coach; former Blackpool manager Stan Ternent; Peter Morris, an ex-Ipswich player who had managed a number of clubs including Mansfield, Peterborough, Crewe and Southend; and Bruce Rioch, a former Scotland international who had enjoyed an outstanding career before going into management.

Alf told me he would like to sit in on a few of the interviews, which was something I didn't have a problem with. Having tried to fill the role on the cheap in the past, I thought it might not be a bad thing to have some input from the board. That way no-one could blame me alone if the appointment proved to be a bad one.

Of the four I interviewed, I personally felt John Pickering was the right man for the job. Not only did I respect him for his coaching ability but, having spoken to him for well over an hour, felt I would have his undivided loyalty. Ironically, several years later John was to finally get the job of first team coach with Boro but on this occasion he was to miss out. Stan talked the same language as me and I liked Peter too, while there was nothing to dislike about Rioch. He was obviously

Mission: Impossible

the most articulate of those we interviewed and I was impressed by his enthusiasm. I did, however, put one question mark against him. He had been forced to resign from a previous job as manager of Torquay after kicking a young apprentice. Bruce admitted he had just flipped and was ashamed of himself but promised there would be no repeat of it. Prior to the interview, I had only ever spoken to him on a couple of occasions but he had always struck me as a decent guy with a great knowledge of the game.

It was a hugely difficult decision and I would have been happy to appoint any one of the four but Alf, who had sat in only on the Rioch interview, was highly impressed with Bruce. He was a good talker but I honestly think Bruce was too cute for Alf and maybe that is one of the reasons why he felt the need to bail out of the club soon afterwards. With Alf influencing my decision, I plumped for Rioch. It was the only time I ever allowed the chairman to have input in that way. However, I was more than happy with the appointment as I knew Bruce would be able to take some of the day-to-day pressure off me. Having informed Bruce of his success, I rang the other three candidates and I could tell from John's disappointment that he had felt he had a good chance of getting the job as we had got on so well.

The day after I made the appointment public, Darlington boss Cyril Knowles rang me to tell me to watch my back with Rioch. He was concerned that Bruce might be a big threat to my managerial position. My reply was: "Cyril, if I lose my job I couldn't give two hoots who gets it."

With Bruce installed as my first team coach, I was relieved to let someone else supervise training whilst putting my ideas into practice. I needed a bit of a breather and began to spend more time in the office, something which I found hard to do as I was a tracksuit manager and felt almost as if I was cheating on the job. Nowadays, of course, managers at that level have plenty of support staff but I was used to doing pretty much everything and found it difficult to delegate. But I got on very well with Bruce and was suitably impressed with the quality of his coaching.

I told Bruce that I had three games to turn things around, starting with our visit to Portsmouth at the end of January. It was a call for my players to show me how much they wanted to keep me in the job. I felt there needed to be a complete turn-around in attitude and, for once, I was hoping the players would lift me instead of the other way around. We went into the Portsmouth game without goalkeeper Stephen Pears, who had played through the pain barrier during our FA Cup defeat

Extra Time – The Final Chapter

to Southampton when he had been suffering from a broken wrist. I was delighted with Stephen's support on announcing that I would consider stepping down if results didn't improve. "You won't leave, boss, will you?" he asked. "You shouldn't even contemplate it." I will always remember Stephen for those loyal words when I needed to know who was on my side.

Eric McManus, a goalkeeper I had brought in on loan from Bradford, replaced Stephen at Portsmouth, just as he had done in our 3-3 draw at Brighton a week earlier. We were narrowly beaten that day, losing to a goal I felt Pears would have saved if he had been able to play. I felt I'd had a good response from my players but was at my lowest ebb in terms of my drive and enthusiasm for the job. I was becoming increasingly conscious of our league position and began to wonder if having a new man in charge might be the only chance of saving the club from the drop. If so, I wanted to give the new man enough time to turn things around. Throughout all the torment and aggravation, my main concern was always that Middlesbrough Football Club did not drop into the Third Division. Deep down I was desperate for results to turn back in my favour. I wanted to be the guy who created a better future but knew I was losing my previously good reputation among the Boro fans. Throughout this time, Bruce remained supportive. Despite what some people might think, there was no suggestion that he was rubbing his hands together in anticipation of getting my job.

The following game, against Charlton on February 1st, was my last as manager of Middlesbrough. The last Middlesbrough team I selected was:

1. Stephen Pears
2. Brian Laws
3. Tony McAndrew
4. Tony Mowbray
5. Don O'Riordan
6. Gary Pallister
7. Gary Hamilton
8. Pat Heard
9. Bernie Slaven
10. Archie Stephens
11. Gary Rowell
12. Peter Beagrie

Mission: Impossible

That day, from the Ayresome Park dug-out I watched a quite pitiful display from my players against a Charlton side managed by one of my successors as Boro manager, Lennie Lawrence. The final nail in the coffin of a 3-1 defeat was an own goal from Tony Mowbray, though I should say I didn't attach any blame for the result on Tony. He was one of the few players who played with any passion for the club that afternoon. There was a total lack of cohesion and we simply collapsed as a team, leaving us in the division's bottom two. As I watched events unfold, my private thoughts were that I wouldn't be too disappointed if the chairman made me an offer I couldn't refuse after the game. I really couldn't see where I could go after such a lack-lustre performance.

After the match, when I would normally have been in the dressing room yelling at players, I barely said a word. The performance was so poor but I saw little point in saying the same old things again and losing my temper. It was pointless flogging a dead horse. For the first time I allowed Bruce to try and find some words to describe our performance and where we had gone wrong. Inside, I just felt numb.

I didn't have to wait long for the inevitable call from the chairman to go and see him in my office. Immediately, I knew the writing was on the wall. It may sound strange to say it but as I walked up the stairs to my office, half of me was hoping that I would get the sack as I knew it would be a huge weight off my shoulders. At the same time, the other half of me wanted to fight on. I so wanted to avoid being remembered as a failed manager. It was that half of me that still believed and hung on to the idea that there might still be hope of turning things around.

The second I opened the door I knew by the look on the chairman's face that it was all over. Alf was accompanied by the club secretary David Dent. Alf had quite a scowl on his face. I can't remember exactly what he said but the gist of it was that what he had just seen was a load of crap. For once in my life I had to agree with him. "Yes, I can't contest that," I acknowledged. "It was a load of rubbish."

"We can't carry on like this any longer," he said. "Not only I but my fellow directors feel you should stand down."

"I can't afford to do that," I replied. "I can't afford to stand down without some form of compensation. Not only have I devoted 18 months of my life to a thankless task but I have neglected my sports retail business and am in grave danger of losing that too."

Extra Time – The Final Chapter

Alf asked me what I was looking for in terms of compensation. I had 18 months of my contract remaining but, as usual, thinking about the club's predicament, I said I wouldn't hold them to ransom and would settle for half of what my contract was worth. I was in no mood to haggle. The chairman agreed to that, saying he would give me a down payment with the balance to follow over a period of time.

I asked Alf to have an agreement typed out for me to sign and I would be on my way. The 15 minutes it took for the secretary to complete the agreement were long and emotional. It was the saddest moment of my life at the time. For the first occasion I hadn't been successful and that hurt. I considered the endless hours I had put into the job and was almost angry that surely someone who worked as hard as I had done should have a better reward than this. Both Alf and I were extremely emotional and I noticed he had a croak in his voice as he told me he took no pleasure in asking me to stand down and that he felt very sad that it hadn't worked out for me. After some minutes, he nipped out into the boardroom whilst the secretary was away completing details of the agreement. I sat alone in my office for what seemed like an eternity. I was reliving all the "if only's" as I had done on many Sunday mornings over the previous 18 months. And yet at the same time there was a feeling of overwhelming relief that a huge burden had been lifted from my shoulders.

Finally, I collected my copy of the agreement and in an emotional exchange of words and handshakes, Alf and I wished each other luck. As we did so, we were both close to tears. Having said my goodbye's, I descended the stairs and walked out of the iron gates of Ayresome Park for the last time as Middlesbrough's manager.

Naturally, I just wanted to get home and hoped I would not bump into anyone on the way to my car. I thought I had succeeded until Paul Daniel, a sports reporter on the Evening Gazette, shouted to me as I was about to get in my car. I told him I had been dismissed from my job and gave him my thoughts on my departure. Alf had worded it "by mutual consent" but we all know what those words mean - I had been sacked.

When I got home to Hilary, there were no tears. I think news that I'd left the club was as much a relief to her as it was to me. She told me she didn't care and was glad to get her husband back as she had seen what the job had done to me. I was actually quite disappointed when she told me she had cancelled our planned night out at a local Italian restaurant as I thought it would have been a nice

Mission: Impossible

distraction. We opened up our usual bottle of wine but there wasn't too much dialogue. I preferred to silently reflect on the events of the day and the previous 18 months.

Before long, Steve Smelt rang and rather tearfully asked how I was feeling. I assured him I was fine. There was no-one more loyal to me during my time at Middlesbrough than Steve. He was desperately disappointed for me as he recognised how much I had put into the job. He revealed Alf had called him and Bruce into his office after my departure to give them the news. There, Bruce had been offered my job. Steve had told both that he would not have a bad word said against me as he felt they had made a mistake asking me to resign.

Bruce rang the following morning and told me he was sorry I had been dismissed. At the same time, he had accepted the chairman's offer to take over as manager. I understood that and had no hard feelings as he had to work. In fact, I always knew that was what would happen if I was sacked. It was obvious to anyone that Bruce was management material and I'm sure that Alf would have had it in mind that in Bruce he had someone to replace me if necessary.

A third of the season remained when I left the club and I honestly believed that, with a new manager at the helm, the team might just be able to improve enough to pull themselves clear of the relegation zone. Even after my departure I desperately wanted Boro to stay up. Unfortunately, it was a challenge they couldn't meet and relegation came on the final day with defeat at Shrewsbury. That was to prove to be the catalyst for the club going into liquidation and very nearly ceasing to exist. I don't know why but I felt guilty about the situation. I know now that the seeds of that near catastrophe were sewn long before I took charge of the club but at the time I couldn't help but feel in some way responsible. Fortunately, the club survived and, under Bruce's leadership, achieved two successive promotions to return to the top flight after a six-year absence.

Bruce deserves all the credit he got. People sometimes ask if I was envious. Yes, I was. I can't lie about it. I very much wished our roles had been reversed and I had been the one brought in to pick up the threads when the club had almost gone out of existence. The camaraderie and team spirit that resulted from that dire situation was a catalyst in the rise and rise over the two years which followed. But that's not to take anything away from Bruce who clearly did a first class job. Even so, I was delighted to see players I had signed and developed playing such a major role in that successful Boro team. Players like Bernie Slaven, Gary Pallister, Stephen Pears,

Extra Time – The Final Chapter

Brian Laws, Archie Stephens, Colin Cooper, Stuart Ripley, Alan Kernaghan and Tony Mowbray. I drew comfort from their success. I was delighted that all my "major" signings proved me right in the years after my departure as I was hurt to read comments in the Evening Gazette after my dismissal to the effect that I had "wasted" £200,000 in the transfer market.

I have analysed a thousand times the reasons why success eluded me. Perhaps the biggest reason was just sheer bad timing. I didn't have enough support staff, did not have enough money to bring in the players I wanted and had too many players I didn't rate but couldn't afford to pay off. Those were all circumstances which I inherited and had little control over. At the same time, I have to be honest and admit that I was maybe a little naive to believe that I could turn things around whilst working on a shoestring budget. I badly underestimated the enormity of the job.

But for the odd cup game, I never played Ripley or Cooper in the first team and gave Kernaghan only a few outings at that level. My sole reason for that was that I did not want to burden them with the pressure of a relegation battle before they were ready as I was determined not to harm their future development. As early as the cup defeat at Mansfield, Alf urged me to throw the kids in and promised to support my decision. But I felt they were at least 12 months away from being ready. Of course, Bruce made Colin and Stuart regulars in his team and both went on to greater things, as I had known they would. Perhaps if I had done likewise, things may well have turned out differently. When I look back now, I know I maybe should have introduced Ripley into the first team that

Me and Steve Smelt in my office at Ayresome Park. Steve remained loyal to me throughout my time in charge of Middlesbrough.

Mission: Impossible

season. The truth is I considered starting the season with him but then had a change of heart and perhaps forgot about him for too long. Stuart was outstanding in a pre-season friendly with Lincoln and I made my mind up that he would play in our opening league game in place of Alan Roberts. But he had a nightmare in our final friendly at Scarborough and I decided there and then that it was too early for him.

Again with the benefit of hindsight, perhaps I was too tolerant of one or two of my senior players who weren't doing it for me. Perhaps I should have got rid of the dead wood and pitched in the youngsters. But I didn't and I made those decisions because I felt they were right for Middlesbrough Football Club.

I did sometimes make things hard on myself in a bid to keep the peace with players. I always told players the reason why I had dropped them, believing that I would have liked that same courtesy myself during my playing days. But I was simply making a rod for my own back as I would inevitably spend an hour discussing the pros and cons of my decision with the player on the eve of an important match. If I had my time again, I would simply pin up the team sheet and insist that any discussion about my selection took place on the Monday morning. I've often heard people say I was too nice to be a manager and I know people like Bernie Slaven and Brian Laws have said they felt I wasn't ruthless enough but I don't entirely agree with that. Looking back, I was young and naturally inexperienced but I was certainly no easy touch. Bernie and Brian only saw me in my second season as manager, by which time my batteries were almost flat. By then I had stopped losing my temper and was beginning to compromise too much. For too long I tolerated one or two players - the barrack room lawyers, if you like - when I should have got rid of them as soon as they started to give me aggravation.

Despite the fact that success had proved elusive as Boro's manager, in time I knew I had laid the foundation stones for the club's future rise. I knew that all the time and effort wasn't for nothing. I know now that in different circumstances, given the right personnel and right finances, I would have been successful as a football manager. It was sheer bad timing that I should take over my beloved Boro at the lowest ebb in their history when all the odds were stacked against me. But no-one can tell me that I didn't know how to get the best out of players. Or that I wasn't tactically aware. Or that I couldn't coach and develop players. Or that I couldn't spot talent.

But the job took so much out of me that I turned my back on football forever. I

Extra Time – The Final Chapter

left with so few good memories and so many low points. And yet if I had not fallen ill some years ago, I may well have been tempted back into the game. After a few years away from football, I had recharged my batteries and had come to terms with the disappointment of my time in charge at Middlesbrough. Whilst I would not have wanted the pressure of the top job, I may well have considered returning to football in some capacity, perhaps as chief scout or assistant manager. Indeed, five years after leaving Middlesbrough, I was offered the chance to return, to oversee the club's youth set-up. The offer was put to me by Steve Gibson, the director who had approved my signing of Bernie Slaven some years earlier. Steve, who was later to build the club into the force it is today, visited me in my Stockton sports shop, though I was initially rather abrupt with him. I had not been back to Ayresome Park since my departure and had not spoken to a representative of the club in five years. During that time, I had legally pursued the club for £4,000 outstanding to me from my days as manager. I still felt quite bitter that my pursuit of a relatively paltry sum of money had come to nothing.

When my assistant, Julie, told me there was a Steve Gibson to see me, I initially kept him waiting before, after some time, asking her to send him upstairs to my office. On seeing him, I curtly asked: "What do you want?" Steve responded with a question of his own. "Could I just have five minutes of your time? I have a proposition to make to you." What Steve had to say took me completely by surprise. He explained that while Bruce Rioch had done well for the club before his departure, the board had been concerned that very few of the club's youth team players had matured into first team stars since my departure.

"I want you to consider coming back to Ayresome Park to run our youth set-up on a full-time basis," he said.

"Not a chance," I answered.

"Don't say no just yet," he continued. "Even if you won't consider coming back full-time, you could simply work a few days or even a day a week to help you get back into it".

"You couldn't afford me," I responded, refusing to drop my guard. "I'm very much my own man now, with a successful business."

In response, Steve asked me if I would be interested in a salary three times the one I had been on as manager of the club just five years earlier. I didn't give away a thing outwardly but couldn't help but think: "Wow! The club has come on a long way while I've been away."

Mission: Impossible

Steve went on to say that the club wanted me to analyse what was wrong with the intermediates and Centre of Excellence, to discover why they weren't producing players for the first team - and to change things around, as I saw necessary. I would also vet the quality of players joining the club at associate schoolboy and young professional level. "Only now has it been recognised what a good job you did for Middlesbrough in those desperate days," he went on. "The club has reaped the benefits of the quality of your buys and the boys you had a hand in bringing through." Those few words gave me immense pride as, until then, I didn't think the club had appreciated my efforts.

There was even a suggestion that I would be asked to vet the transfer targets of the then manager, Colin Todd. To that, I replied: "Colin would not accept that type of interference - neither would I have done when I was manager." Steve said that was how things would be done at Middlesbrough in future, though I insisted that I would not consider joining a club without the manager's approval.

"Why has it taken you so long to get in touch when things have been so difficult over the money owing to me?" I asked.

"Willie, because of the club's liquidation, we had to do many things that hurt a lot of people, but the object was to keep the club afloat," he said. "That's how it had to be for the survival of the club."

I could see the sense in what he was saying and, from then on, our conversation became a lot more friendly and even jovial. I was extremely flattered that the club wanted me for such a role but I was so advanced in my plans to open a new sports superstore that I couldn't possibly have considered such a distraction. We parted on friendly terms with Steve asking me to keep the offer in mind. That night in bed, I couldn't sleep. I was committed to life in the retail business but was excited at the idea of going abroad to study the youth set-ups at the world's most successful clubs, going to Lilleshall to observe the best coaches and developing the skills of talented young players.

That conversation sowed the seeds in my mind that one day I might return to the game.

Sadly, illness was to rob me of that opportunity.

19

Shop till I Drop

IT WAS the most embarrassing day of my life. And it could so easily have ended in tragedy. Normally it was the prices that went through the floor at my sports retail shop. But this time it was the international all-star cast of Liverpool Football Club, the newly crowned Football League champions. And yet after much hard work in the build-up to the big day things had gone so well.

It was the official opening of Willie Maddren Sports, the new retail outlet I had opened on Norton Road in Stockton. Special guests at the opening were the stars of Liverpool and Middlesbrough football clubs who were due to play each other in an end-of-season clash that evening at Ayresome Park. I had gone into the sports retail business a few months earlier, just before finally accepting that my playing days were over. Knowing that I needed to have more strings to my bow, I had approached the shop's previous owner, Bill Beattie, to ask him to give me first option if he ever wanted to sell the outlet. Four months later, he came back to me with a figure and I went into business with a close friend Peter Hodgson, who had done a great job for me as

Behind the counter at my newsagents shop - selling the news instead of making it.

323

my treasurer during my testimonial year and was also the chairman of the Boro Supporters Club.

On buying the sports shop, I had sold my lease on a newsagents, tobacconists and sweet shop on The Green at Billingham. I had taken up the lease with my brother-in-law, Alex, a couple of years earlier as something to look forward to when I retired but running a newsagents just wasn't me. In fact, I should have known that from the first day when a customer came in and asked for "20 Embassy Regal and 20 More." Never having been a smoker, I took what I believed to be his order down from the shelf and placed two packets of Embassy Regal on the counter! "You silly man," said my bemused customer. "I wanted 20 *More* - the brand of cigarettes - not 20 more!" I did initially consider expanding the venture into an off-licence but thought better of it when the chance to get into sports retailing came along.

Even so, buying the sports shop was a mixed blessing. On one hand, it gave me a new means of income and a new focus, but equally I found being enclosed in a shop, working nine to five, almost claustrophobic. I consequently found myself constantly looking for excuses to get out of the shop, even to do a message or chore. After a career in professional football, I was always likely to find a life away from the game very hard and was thankful that I was in business with a guy as enthusiastic as Peter.

The two of us spent much of the day prior to the opening laying 400 new carpet tiles on the shop's ground floor in an effort to smarten the place up in readiness for being in the limelight. The job actually took us far longer than we had expected and we eventually left our business premises at three in the morning. I think it is fair to say that the two of us vastly underestimated the level of interest that the following day's visit by the Liverpool and Boro stars would bring. I've heard since that the worst ever truancy figures among Stockton school children were recorded that day as youngsters for miles around gathered to catch a glimpse of their heroes.

The queues outside the shop started to form long before the doors opened and when both sets of players arrived the clamber for positions reached the point of frenzy. Eventually, the queue stretched down the high street for almost 500 yards. Graeme Souness, who had kindly arranged the visit after gaining permission from Liverpool manager Bob Paisley, happily posed for photographs with his Liverpool team-mates whilst enjoying the odd glass of champagne to celebrate my proud moment. Meanwhile, we opened the doors to the shop but were well aware of the need to control the crowds in an orderly fashion and as two of three people left the building, the same number would be allowed back in. As a result, even at its peak, there was never more than 150 people downstairs and another 100 on the first floor. Even so, with many special offers on merchandise, we were looking forward to a bumper time in terms of retail sales.

After about an hour, it was time for the Liverpool lads to go but as they made their way towards the door there was a mad rush from customers trying to get last minute autographs. I was casually hanging on to a rail of tracksuits near the front of the shop when, to my horror, the shop floor gave way and an area of about 20 square feet collapsed from the base of the staircase. I was forced to let go of the rail of tracksuits as it, along with several players and customers - probably 15 in all - fell the six or seven feet into the basement below. It was like a slow motion movie of a mini earthquake as people, fittings and merchandise disappeared into this gaping hole amid a cloud of dust and debris. I stood at the edge of this mini cravass in abject horror and complete shock. All around me people were screaming and panicking and as the dust settled I spotted poor Stuart Boam and one of the Liverpool stars, David Johnson or Steve Heighway, picking themselves up and wiping themselves down in the basement.

Amongst all the chaos, there is one vision that stays with me to this day. It is of a young boy down in the hole amid all the mayhem, tapping Liverpool's Alan Kennedy on the shoulder and offering him his autograph book and pen in a last desperate attempt to get his hero's signature!

But the consequences could have been serious. It was a miracle that nobody was seriously injured or killed. A huge free-standing cabinet with 48 glass-fronted drawers had fallen on its end but had thankfully not toppled forwards into the basement. Close by, a perpendicular steel rod, which had been used to prop up the floor, protruded upwards. How easily any one of those falling guests or customers could have been impaled on its rather crude sharp end. Personally, I was dumbstruck and it took me seconds to pull myself together and start to pull people up out of the hole. I was both concerned for the people who had fallen and embarrassed that so many top names had witnessed my personal disaster. Indeed, I often wonder if Graeme was more embarrassed about the event than I was as he rarely spoke to me from that day on.

When the dust had settled and everyone had departed, Peter and I took a quick overview of our lease conditions and terms. Thankfully, all the major structure,

Shop till I Drop

Speaking to reporters on the day my world fell in at the launch of my sports shop.

frames and beams of the building were covered by the landlord, Bill Beattie. We immediately got a leading timber expert in to analyse the damage. On his inspection, he discovered that one of the main joists of the floor simply crumbled away in his fingers. It was riddled with woodworm, damp rot and dry rot, as was much of the basement. Later that afternoon, I informed Bill that we would be seeking compensation not only for the loss of trade that day but for as long as it took to repair the damage.

Television crews arrived on the scene less than an hour after the event, wanting to take pictures of the void in the front of my shop. I wouldn't allow them anywhere near it. But I discovered later that the story of the English football champions falling through a shop floor had made worldwide news. People on holiday in many parts of Europe told me during the months that followed how they had seen the story on TV.

Just as I had thought life would get easier, my whole world had been turned upside down. To be honest, the embarrassment of it all was the worst. But I tried to make light of it, following the old philosophy that any publicity was good publicity. The following week we were back in business and I ran an advert in the local press. Below a cartoon caricature of me falling through the floor was the line: "Prices have gone right through the floor at Willie Maddren Sports". But deep down, I was as sick as the proverbial parrot.

When, soon afterwards, I was approached to take up a full-time coaching role at Hartlepool, it seemed the ideal opportunity to get myself away from the confines of the shop. Peter was delighted for me and I felt quite happy leaving the shop in his hands whilst I would still retain my business interest in it. But my decision to leave Hartlepool two years later was influenced by my concerns that the shop was no longer doing as well as it should have been. In fact, it was in real trouble - we had considerable debts and were two to three months behind in payments.

Extra Time – The Final Chapter

The situation put a strain on the previously good relationship Peter and I had enjoyed and we no longer saw eye to eye with one another. It quickly became apparent that the business could no longer support two livelihoods and I told Peter that either he would have to buy me out or vice versa. I paid off his bank loan and let him keep the company car whilst I paid off about £20,000 from our creditors list. That was the whole of my testimonial money gone in one go. Things became bitter between Peter and I towards the end. I was sad that we parted in such circumstances but it was a hard lesson learned never to go into business with a good friend. Years later, soon after learning I had Motor Neurone Disease, I made a point of going to see Peter. We had been such good friends and I just felt life was too short not to let bygones be bygones.

The months which followed were hard and often worrying as I was concerned that I might have thrown good money after bad. I was now working on my own except for the assistance of a young girl, Julie Marr, but was determined to pull the business back into profit. But first I had to wheedle out a few hangers on. I had been back in the shop for only a month when a certain sales representative came in and enquired as to Peter's whereabouts. I felt this particular rep had taken advantage of Peter's good nature and had vastly overstocked us with his brand of merchandise as we had a centre gondola full of his T-shirts and tracksuits. I let him know in no uncertain terms that Peter was no longer part of the business and advised him to pick up his bags and disappear from view as I reckoned it would take six months to sell the amount of stock he had already sold to Willie Maddren Sports. Needless to say, I never clapped eyes on him again.

Within 12 months, my investment of time and money began to bear fruit and profitability was breathed back on to the balance sheet as the business started to flourish once again. I was particularly pleased with myself because I did all of the book work, ordering and selling myself - a challenging task for any businessman, let alone one who had spent their entire working career in football. I invested in an engraving machine and carried out all the etching of trophies myself, while I was proud to say I was able to put together all the bicycles we sold in a roadworthy condition.

As I was working on my own, I did all the shop fitting myself - a reponsibility which led to a rather embarrassing incident with a female tailor's dummy. Alone in the shop, I began trying to fit a wet suit on to the dummy to promote the fact that we were now selling diving gear. As the model was bigger than the wetsuit and I had no chalk to help, I ended up wrestling with this naked female dummy over a

Shop till I Drop

chair whilst becoming increasingly exasperated. I have to say it was getting the better of me. Having got the leg-ins on, I looked up to see about a dozen faces staring through the window in fits of laughter. No doubt what had initially caught their attention was what must have looked for all the world like a rape scene in the back of Willie Maddren Sports!

But trouble was about to rear its ugly head in the shape of the first of countless run-ins with the numerous rogues, thieves and vagabonds who inhabited Stockton at the time. One winter's evening as I completed an order with an Umbro sales rep called Peter Crawford in my office upstairs, I was alerted by the cries of Jane, our youth trainee, that someone had stolen a badminton racquet and bolted out of the door. I instinctively raced out of the office and took the stairs five at a time. As I bounced out of the front door, I spotted a young Asian boy disappearing around Maxwell's corner with the stolen racquet in his hand. Upon seeing me give chase, he upped the tempo of his run and the two of us sprinted across Bishopton Road and over some waste ground. After about a thousand yards, I was gaining on him considerably and was no more than a hundred yards behind when he panicked and threw the racquet to the ground. I picked the racquet up but continued to give chase, determined to bring the rogue to justice. To be honest, I was so angry that I'm not quite sure what I would have done had I caught him - probably broken the racquet over his head! There was no more than 50 yards between us as we approached the old Radio Tees building but as I followed him into a back alley I was faced with three possible routes and no sign of the culprit. With my chest heaving in the cold air of the day, I gave up the chase and walked back the 50 yards to the main street where I stopped to catch my breath.

As I stood in a sweat, wondering if I was about to suffer a heart attack, I was greeted by the friendly voice of an acquaintance as he walked by. "Hello, Willie - how's your dad?" he chirped. I didn't even have the energy to answer him. Looking down at the racquet I had retrieved, I winced as I noticed its price - £3.99. I had given chase as a matter of principle rather than the money but I still had to wonder about the sense of it all. It took me 25 minutes to walk back to the shop, a distance which had taken perhaps only three minutes in the opposite direction. Sadly, that incident was by no means a one-off.

I got myself into a lot of bother one Saturday afternoon in an amusement arcade less than a hundred yards from my shop. As I walked along Norton Road during my lunch break, I spotted a youth whose reputation went before him sitting in the window of the arcade. He was wearing a distinctive Ocean Pacific sweat top identical to those which had been stolen from my shop during a night time burglary through my skylight the previous Wednesday. Without thinking, I bolted inside and confronted him. There were about 50 teenage boys playing on the machines in the arcade but my mind was focused on the face of this one young rogue sat with a few of his mates.

"Where did you get that top?" I asked him, standing over him.

"What's it f***ing got to do with you?" he responded with dismissive arrogance.

One of his mates chirped up: "He got it from Bill Gates' shop."

Without saying another word, I walked out of the arcade and ran to the nearby Police station for assistance. Re-entering the building in the company of a Bobby a few minutes later, we spotted the same young lad but he was now wearing a totally different top. I explained this to the policeman but it was obvious he couldn't make a charge without catching the youth in possession of one of the stolen tops. I agreed to leave while he made further enquiries with the youths. As I turned for the door, the whole arcade seemed to be consumed in a sense of evil as 20 or 30 of these teenage lads began chanting my name and that I was a tosser. I couldn't believe my ears. It was like something out of Oliver Twist.

An hour later, the Policeman came hobbling up the stairs of my shop to my office. When I asked him why he was limping, he told me that someone had kicked him as he left the amusement arcade. It was only then that I realised how difficult the social problems engulfing Stockton were at the time. Burglaries and petty thieving was something all the retailers had to contend with and the situation would worsen before it improved.

I have to say I didn't spend a single day in the shop during my 18 months as manager of Middlesbrough Football Club. And by the time I left the club, I was in real danger of losing my business. During my first year back at the football club, the shop was run by Beryl Sowerby, a good friend and former neighbour of mine, but due to golf commitments she eventually asked me to find another manager. I returned to the fold several unsuccessful managers later, one of whom was my former school teacher Alan Medd. Having left the teaching profession a few years earlier, Alan had been made redundant from another job when I took him on to run my shop. In hindsight, it was a mistake. He was never cut out for retail. I had idolised Alan during my school days so dismissing him was one of the hardest things I have ever had to do.

Shop till I Drop

On the Monday morning of February 3rd 1986, two days after being sacked by Middlesbrough F.C., I was back working in my retail outlet on Norton Road for the first time in two years. Rather than moping about the house feeling sorry for myself, I decided the best policy was to get straight on with building the business back up again though I knew I faced a task every bit as tough as the one I had left behind in saving the business. That week was one of the hardest of my life. The first week's takings after my return were just £885.

I put my heart and soul into that shop over the weeks and months which followed. I knew that was my only chance of saving it. Despite the temptation to go and watch the football, I disciplined myself to work in the shop on Saturdays as that was the the busiest day of the week, accounting for at least a third of the weekly takings.

After much hard work, things began to get back on the right track and I eventually expanded my retail space by opening the upstairs of the building. There, I sold Marks & Spencer seconds with the intention of eliminating the sports side of the business if it was the success I hoped it would be. The M&S side of the business did well for about four months but then the sports side began to really take off again. Within 18 months, turn-over was up 300 per cent, giving me the confidence to move on to Stockton High Street. Many thought I was taking a big risk moving into the Castle Shopping Centre with its high rent and rates but I have never been afraid to make tough decisions and knew it was a good idea.

Having shut the Norton Road shop at 5pm on a Saturday, we opened up at nine the following Monday morning in retail space previously occupied by Foster's Menswear. All the fixtures and fittings were moved on the Sunday and, at one point, I was convinced we weren't going to have all the merchandise out in time. But some how we made it. I seem to remember catching about three hours' sleep that weekend!

But the elation of opening a new shop quickly wore off with the realisation that the problem I had endured with thieves at Norton Road was intensified 10-fold on the High Street. As the sports retail industry made the transformation from equipment to fashion accessories, shops like mine were becoming favourite haunts for thieves. Having foreseen the problem I might have, I had employed a full-time security man from day one but both of us were inundated with yobbos wandering through the shop, looking to steal whatever they could get their hands on. The two of us walked from one end of the shop to the other, often passing in the middle, as we kept a careful eye on gangs of recognised thieves until they had walked out of the open doors, either on to the High Street or into the shopping centre mall. I personally didn't serve a single customer all day. After that first day experience, I took all the open plan units down and replaced them with old-fashioned glass-fronted millinery cabinets to keep the merchandise protected from thieving hands. Small items like replica team strips had to be kept under lock and key.

I wondered what the hell I had got myself into. The shop was incredibly busy but I knew it would be impossible for me to concentrate on selling and serving with the distraction of so many professional gangs of thieves which were operating throughout the town centre. In addition to the security guard, I decided to employ a bouncer from one of the local nightclubs to ensure the gangs of yobs didn't even make it through the doors on a Saturday. Had they been allowed to do so, I am sure they would have put me out of business.

And yet my confrontations with the yobs were to continue with alarming consequences. Indeed, anyone who saw what I did on the Wednesday night after moving into my new shop might have reconsidered their belief that Willie Maddren was Mr Nice Guy. That night, having worked late tidying up the stock room, I called in at Oxbridge Fish Bar to save Hilary having to make supper. Three teenage lads, perhaps 18 or 19 years old, were stood inside the fish bar. As I approached the counter to get served, I heard one of them say: "There's that Willie Maddren." I decided to ignore the comment but before I'd had the chance to get served, another of the lads shouted over: "Hey, Maddren! It was me that knocked off your shop." He was referring to the fact that my Norton Road shop had been burgled several times.

My blood was boiling that this little git could brag about something that had threatened my business. "What did you say?" I asked, attempting to stay calm. I had heard him perfectly well but wanted him to come closer. Carrying a can of Coke in one hand and stuffing chips into his mouth with the other, he took five or six steps towards me, arrogant as you like. I didn't allow him to even attempt to repeat his boast. Before he had spoken another word, I had grabbed him by the neck and pushed him out of the door on to the street. Coke, fish and chips flew everywhere in the resulting melee as I proceeded to give him a good belting. I just flipped. Having spent thousands of pounds in building up my business, I didn't take kindly to a young upstart like him bragging about stealing things from me. Holding him down on the pavement, I hit him repeatedly until his two friends came to his aid, one of whom hit me as hard as he could on the side of my face. But

Shop till I Drop

I refused to let go as I was determined to make an example of the lad who had thought his taunting had been so clever. Thankfully, a rather frail looking, bespectacled guy came to my rescue as a good Samaritan and between the two of us we fended off the three assailants. As they backed off into the darkness, however, they threatened to burn down my shop and screamed: "You haven't seen the last of us."

People have no conception about the sort of intimidation many shopkeepers were, and no doubt still are, put through in many of this country's inner cities. Mr Nice Guy flipped again the day my shop was visited by seven yobbos, several of whom had been involved in ugly scenes around the High Street. As they walked into the shop from the mall end, I tried to politely usher them out but found myself standing nose-to-nose with a 19-year-old who took great satisfaction from effing and blinding at me. With the aid of my security man and Harry Coltman, a chap of around 60 who worked for me, I managed to edge the gang of lads to the doorway. There, one of them took a swing at poor old Harry.

That was it for me and the three of us began to scuffle with Stockton's lowest members of society. The fracas spilled out on to the High Street where all hell let loose, resulting in me and the 19-year-old grappling on the floor. With his mates and my staff looking on, he initially had me in a headlock on the floor of the busy walkway to the point where I couldn't move. To be honest, I was embarrassed and couldn't help but think that 10 years earlier I would have eaten him alive. With my last show of strength, however, I managed to turn him over and reverse the situation. "You're not so brave now, are you son?" I taunted him

At that, I was astonished to hear a passer-by shout at me: "Leave him alone,

One of my cast-offs! Miss World, if I remember rightly, on a promotional visit to my shop on Stockton High Street.

you big bully." Seconds later I felt a hefty kick on the side of my head from one of the thug's colleagues who realised I now had the better of his pal. The fight ensued for another 30 seconds or so until a police car approached the scene, at which they all scarpered down the nearest side street.

As I stood fighting for breath, my chest heaving, I caught a glimpse of my reflection in the shop window and could see I had several grazes on my face where I had been kicked and punched. "This is silly," I thought to myself. "A man of my age having to put up with torment like this from such social decay." I was 40 years of age and perhaps should have known better than to meet violence with physical force of my own but I was angered that people so young should show such little respect for anyone or anything. Hilary arrived at the shop with our baby Laura about 15 minutes later and was horrified to see the state of me. She became quite upset at the thought that one of the thugs could easily have pulled a knife on me. I made a promise to her that from then on, no matter what the intimidation, I would never again physically take on the yobs. I kept to that promise, though I have to admit it was often a close thing.

Despite the ongoing confrontations with the thieves, my business continued to thrive, enabling me to buy into the sports purchasing group, InterSport. Trade became so good that on an average Saturday we would sell well in excess of a hundred pairs of footwear. Fortunately, for those first two years I had no real competition as the big multiples were still plying their trade in Middlesbrough rather than Stockton. For three full, years Willie Maddren Sports enjoyed huge profits even though rent, rates and service charges were in the region of £50,000 a year. Naturally, I enjoyed that time immensely, though I have much to thank three of my employees in particular - Pauline Gresham, Angela O'Byrne and Julie Marr - who stood by me through thick and thin.

The fun ended the day Instep Sports, a multi-national company, arrived on Stockton High Street with its policy of aggressively discounting all footwear. Such was the impact of their arrival, the number of pairs of footwear I was selling was halved almost overnight. Worse still, Instep were followed into Stockton by another couple of major sports shops and it was clear the town was quickly nearing saturation point. At the same time, I was disappointed to see many of the High Street's quality shops replaced by bargain basement style operations and I began to think it was time to get out of Stockton altogether.

I had already acquired another smaller shop in Coulby Newham which was

Shop till I Drop

doing quite phenomenal business for its size. Indeed, I sold nearly a thousand cycles in one financial year in the late '80s between the two shops. I felt much of the success I was achieving was a result of my policy of selling for serious sports lovers as well as for those looking for fashion accessories. At the time, many of my competitors were concentrating solely on the fashion end of the business. Such was my stock level, I purchased another shop, Bill Beattie's of Billingham, taking my staffing level to well over 20.

Meanwhile, my lease at the Castle Centre was close to its end so I began to carefully consider a move to the new Teesside Retail Park nearby. Having witnessed its initial slow growth, I had looked on Teesside Park as something of a white elephant. I would sit in the car park for a couple of hours studying the traffic flow and noticed that even on a weekend the vast car park was almost empty. There were only about five shops operating on the park at the time though the developers were confident it had huge potential. To find out more, I made it my business to get friendly with the manager of a menswear store that had recently opened there. He gladly showed me turn-over figures which I found quite incredible in view of the quite barren car park outside. I came to the conclusion that if a menswear store could achieve such staggering business then the retail park was more than capable of sustaining a thriving sports shop. I was hell bent on Teesside Park as it was my ambition to build a themed sports retail outlet similar to a mini trade exhibition. Unfortunately, I couldn't afford the larger premises at Teesside Park so settled on a unit of 5,000 square feet and decided to build an upper floor to give me a further 3,000 square feet of retail space.

That was the beginning of what, until my illness, was the most traumatic and difficult time of my life. I didn't know it at the time but I was expanding at the start of the recession. Things started to go badly wrong from day one. I had plans of my shop approved and put the various building jobs out to tender. Some of the prices that came back were astronomical and would have made it a non-starter. I eventually plumped for a quote which was by far the cheapest but the local guy who gave me it - he shall remain nameless - was to let me down badly. Just as work was due to get underway, the builder-cum-electrician got a bigger job in Scotland and I found myself chasing him for three weeks to no avail while my deadline for completing the job quickly began to look extremely optimistic.

Whilst stocking my three successful shops, I had about £150,000 worth of further stock in boxes in the basement of my Stockton shop ready for business on Teesside Park. By the time I finally caught up with the builder we were way behind schedule and I told him that his priority was to complete the retail area of the shop and get up a partition wall to enable him to build the offices as and when he could. I was in a panic as I knew that if I hadn't opened the weekend I did, some three-and-a-half weeks behind my planned launch, I may well have gone under in terms of cashflow. The standard month's credit given by suppliers was almost at an end and the £150,000-worth of goods sat idle in unopened boxes was almost due for payment.

That Saturday I opened what was then the largest sports shop in the north-east. I was immensely proud of what I had built on a relatively small budget of £100,000 with all its fixtures and fittings but that day was one of the most nerve-wracking experiences of my life. I knew we had to achieve at least £6,000 on the day simply to break even. To my immense relief we took nearly £10,000. Nevertheless, the traumatic month in which I had played site foreman had really taken its toll and I was once again feeling the pressure of the job in a similar way to my experiences with Middlesbrough F.C.

Cashflow remained a problem over the ensuing months and I know many people believed I had made a mistake in opening at Teesside Park. In my view, that was not the case. It did hurt me, however, that for the first time in my life I was delaying paying my creditors by at least two months, though I know it is standard practice among many retailers. After about nine months, we finally started to see daylight in terms of getting our cashflow on track but I found that, while sales at Teesside Park were doing well, I seemed to be losing sales from my other three shops. So although turnover went up, profitability went down due to excess overheads, mainly the number of staff I was employing. Between the four shops I had over 40 employees. Turnover for the first 12 months on Teesside Park eventually exceeded £1.1 million and I anticipated that, although figures in the other three shops were disappointing, that figure would be approaching £2 million by the end of the second year.

Then came the sort of news I did not want to hear. In September 1992, another sports shop, Sports Division, opened for business just a few doors away from mine. Owning 20 shops in Scotland, Sports Division had huge buying power and the competition was fierce from the very start. My turnover, which had previously been steadily increasing, now levelled off and, once again, we began to fall behind with our cashflow. I found the months which followed both stressful and traumatic. Being a man of immense pride, stretching the goodwill that had existed between creditors and myself for many years got me down. I was robbing Peter to

Shop till I Drop

pay Paul and was constantly having to defer payments to creditors.

The pressure during this period was enormous. I was working from nine in the morning to nine at night, often seven days a week. I did all the buying over a wide spectrum of sports goods, served on the shop floor and even helped with the accounts, though I was now employing three full-time staff on that side of the business. The bank insisted I put in a computer system for stock control but refused to extend my overdraft to enable me to cover the cost of this expensive addition.

The stress and pressure mounted by the day until I reached the point where I was suffering digestion problems, couldn't sleep at night, had tightness in my chest and was short of breath. To this day I am convinced that 12-month period, combined with the previous pressure of football management, was the onset of my Motor Neurone Disease.

In order to break out of the vicious circle in which I was finding myself, I decided the best policy would be to sell the outlying shops and concentrate on my flagship outlet at Teesside Park. I felt that with only one shop on which to concentrate my efforts and staffed with all my best employees, I could possibly achieve a £2 million turnover without the aggravation of the other outlets. I duly put the other three shops on the market but was disappointed to find that I could get no-one remotely interested in any of them. It was a crazy situation whereby I had a £1.6 million turnover but was finding it hard to make any impact on either my overdraft or the amount of time it was taking me to pay the bills.

Having unsuccessfully tried to sell the smaller shops, the only alternative was to see if a multiple would be interested in buying my pride and joy at Teesside Park. I arranged for John Hornsby, a sports agent and close friend, to circulate around the right people news that I might be interested in selling the shop. Within three days, I received a call from a cash rich sports retailer from the south of England, Ashley Sport & Ski. Having flown into Teesside Airport the following Thursday morning, negotiations went on throughout the day until I was satisfied with their offer. I then left my solicitors - one of the top law firms on Teesside - and theirs to sort out the legal aspects of the deal, transactions which continued through Friday and into the early hours of Saturday morning. Ashley wanted to take over my limited company, to own Willie Maddren Sports Ltd and be open for business in time for that Saturday morning.

They had had a top solicitor flown in from London while one of their directors was very cunning to say the least. By way of contrast, my legal representation was

Extra Time – The Final Chapter

out of his depth. So much so in fact that I discovered the deal I had struck on the Thursday had been completely dissected by the late hours of Friday night and I found myself alone in terms of the ongoing negotiations which went on into the early hours of Saturday. As it turned out, if I'd had stronger representation I think I could have struck a far better deal than the one I got. But they sensed I was desperate to get out of the industry altogether. I'd had enough of working 12 hours a day and the mental trauma of playing about with figures into the early hours two and three times a week. The truth was I was physically and mentally exhausted.

As I left the office of my solicitors at five on the Saturday morning, I knew I had pretty much bailed out of the sports trade. Rumour and counter-rumour about how I had sold my business went around Teesside like wild fire in the weeks and months which followed. Some stories told the tale that the sale had made me a millionaire, others that I had been made bankrupt. Both were well wide of the mark. The truth was that I kept safe the jobs of every one of my staff, paid off every creditor and earned enough money on the deal not to have to work for about nine months.

Sport and Ski ran a closing down sale for well over 6 months. It concerned me that the public of Teesside may well have thought I was cashing in on it - nothing could be further from the truth as I had long since left the business.

I could have gone back into any of my remaining three outlets and continued to work in the sports trade but I was at a stage where I wanted out of it completely. For three months, I did absolutely nothing, spending my days simply recharging my batteries and regaining my zest for life. Finally, bored out of my brains, I began to look around for a new challenge.

During my years in the sports retail business, I had always expressed my envy of my close friend Geoff Stoker who had a successful car sales business in Hartlepool. He would tell me that he often sold four or five cars in a day and reveal how much net profit he made. I looked at the thousands of customers who had gone through my shops on that same day and realised they had produced nowhere near the same profit. For that reason I quite fancied the idea of owning my own garage and car sales room. However, I knew that first I would have to learn the job at a grass roots level. So, when one day Geoff revealed he could arrange an interview for me at the local Toyota and Mercedes dealership, Crofts, I readily agreed to go along. The interview was a success and I accepted a new job as a car salesman.

Shop till I Drop

I was initially unsure how well suited I would be for the job though it was my belief that a good salesman could sell anything. I knew I had that gift of selling. After attending a two-day training course at Toyota's Gatwick headquarters, I eased into the position quite comfortably and within three months was Crofts' third most successful salesman across their four outlets. The nine months I spent in car sales were the most pressure-free months I had enjoyed in a long, long time. Although the hours were long, for the first time in many years I was able to go home at the end of the day and forget all about work. There is no doubt I was enjoying life more than at any other time since my days as a professional footballer. Sadly, the good times weren't to last.

20

The Day that Changed My Life

FRIDAY, February 10th, 1995. That was the day my life changed. That was the day I was told I had Motor Neurone Disease. This may sound strange but I didn't feel devastated, not at least in the minutes after I had been told the news. I guess it took time to sink in. Being told you have a terminal illness isn't the sort of thing you can take in easily and I was in denial of the facts as I drove home from hospital. Only when I returned to the neurological ward with Hilary the following Friday did the awful truth strike home. And yet such unthinkable worries had been a million miles from my thoughts as I prepared to visit the hospital a week earlier.

Unless you have gone through it personally you cannot imagine what it is like to be told you are dying. Neither can you know how you will react unless you have the misfortune to face such an experience yourself. I, for one, surprised myself and have continued to do so ever since. And yet I could not have imagined the torment my family and I were to suffer when, in September 1994, I appeared to be in perfectly good health but for my troublesome right knee.

I did not know it then but the first physical sign that I was in the initial stages of Motor Neurone Disease was a slight weakness in my right hand, mainly between my thumb and forefinger when trying to unscrew bottle tops. Believing it to simply be a trapped nerve or other form of temporary weakness, I switched to twisting the top with my left hand, poured the drink and thought nothing more of it. Over the days which followed, however, I was frequently reminded of the weakness as I filled out paperwork at Crofts. My writing, which had never been particularly tidy, began to deteriorate.

By the end of November, the weakness had developed into a slight twitch in

The Day that Changed My Life

my right thumb. As I sat at my desk, I noticed my thumb twitching every few seconds. But even when over the next two or three weeks the quivers became constant I simply dismissed it as a trapped nerve and assured myself it was nothing to worry about.

Then, in mid-December, I was given reason to start feeling less assured. Enjoying a beer at home with my friend Geoff Stoker, I pointed out my thumb. "Have you seen that?" I said. Geoff asked me how long it had been going on, to which I replied that I had noticed it only a month earlier. "I don't want to alarm you, Willie, but maybe you ought to go and see a doctor and get it checked it out," he said, a look of concern on his face. "Why?" I asked. With some trepidation, Geoff explained: "Well, I've just read Ray Kennedy's autobiography and he stated that his Parkinson's Disease started with a twitch between his thumb and finger."

Before doing anything else, I felt I should read Kennedy's book and duly borrowed Geoff's copy. A former Arsenal, Liverpool and England star, Kennedy was a football adversary of mine for many years and a former team-mate at under-23 level but, at the age of just 35, he had been diagnosed as having Parkinson's Disease, a disorder of movement that also effects the personality, emotions and speech. As I read through his book, Ray of Hope, I started to draw comparisons with the onset of Parkinson's in his body and the minor symptoms I was experiencing. An initial quiver in his right index finger was the most

In action against Liverpool's Ray Kennedy during my playing days with Middlesbrough. It is a poignant picture now that Ray is suffering from a serious illness too - in his case Parkinson's Disease.

Extra Time – The Final Chapter

worrying similarity. More alarming was a reference to the former Rangers manager Jock Wallace who attributed his Parkinson's Disease to the stress of football management. Wallace was quoted as saying: "I'm fighting my illness and I'm winning. But I'm pretty convinced it was the pressures of managing Rangers during my second spell at the club which brought it on. Running a football club can be a great life, but as Kenny Dalglish and Graeme Souness have found, there is a price to pay." Although I could relate all too well with what both Kennedy and Wallace had experienced, I tried to dismiss negative thoughts from my mind. Nevertheless, I decided I should see a doctor to get the problem checked out.

I paid a visit to my general practitioner, Dr Jonathan Berry, in his surgery early in the new year and was relieved when after a 20-minute consultation he assured me I was not suffering from Parkinson's Disease. He felt that in his opinion my twitch might be the result of an old football injury, perhaps a disk trapping a nerve. To put my mind at rest, however, he arranged for me to see a neurological specialist, Dr Peter Newman, at Middlesbrough General Hospital.

A few days later, Dr Newman confirmed Dr Berry's belief that I did not have Parkinson's Disease. I was so relieved to be told what I didn't have, I never thought to ask what I might have and left without asking any further questions. On my arrival, Dr Newman had asked me to strip to the waist and for some minutes had inspected by arms and the top half of my torso. I had by now developed a slight flicker in my right bicep, albeit ever so feint, but he made no mention of it. Having closely examined me, however, he obviously suspected something was amiss and arranged for me to visit Newcastle General Hospital for a series of electrical tests to discover what was causing my twitches.

A week later I happily attended my appointment in Newcastle alone, convinced that there could be nothing seriously wrong with me. However, the tests carried out on me that day were quite unpleasant. The doctor stuck about 40 needles into the back of my hand, thumb, forearm, biceps, right thigh and left calf muscles, each time asking me to contract the muscle. Apparently, the needles were like an electronic monitoring system but it was an extremely painful exercise. The following experience, a series of electronic shocks to my right arm, right leg and the occasional one on my left leg, was equally unpleasant.

About a week later, a letter arrived on my doorstep confirming an appointment on February 10th back at Middlesbrough General's neurology ward with Dr Newman. Again, I did not feel the need to ask Hilary to accompany me on the

The Day that Changed My Life

appointment as I was still rather blasé about the whole affair. By this time, there was an obvious twitch in my right bicep and thumb and a slight flicker in my right fore-finger. It was quite annoying but no more than that and I certainly wasn't unduly worried about it. I wondered whether the symptoms might be indicative of a disk resting on a nerve in my neck, perhaps the result of heading countless footballs over my years as a professional footballer.

Strangely, as I walked from my car to the ward that day, I wondered what it must be like to be told you have a terminal illness. Not that I ever believed it would happen to me. Although that terrible prospect had crossed my mind on reading Ray Kennedy's book, I attended my appointment convinced that I was about to be told that an old football injury was back to haunt me.

Little did I know the all-encompassing impact that day would have on my life.

Unlike many rather formal and detached specialists I have come across, Dr Newman was relaxed and friendly as I sat in his surgery. But I could see from the look of concern on his face that my visit might not be as routine as I had expected it to be. Once again, he asked me to strip to the waist and stared at my upper torso for two or three minutes without saying a word. Then, for a second time, he ran through a series of tests. He asked me to lift my arms and elbows against the palm of his hand, to spread my fingers and push my hand against his and many other similar tests. He also studied the movement in the muscles of my right arm, thumb and forefinger. Having had X-rays taken, I asked Dr Newman if there was anything wrong with my neck or spinal cord with regards to old injuries.

"Surprisingly, Mr Maddren, your neck and vertebrae are in extremely good condition considering your former profession," he responded.

But a long, deep breath told me there was more to tell me. "However...as a result of the electronic tests, we have discovered neurological damage to your right arm and forefinger," he added.

"What do you mean by neurological?" I asked, stiffening with concern.

At that, he issued those immortal words: "Motor Neurone Disease."

I needed no explanation what Motor Neurone Disease was or what its onset meant. I knew it was a muscle-wasting illness as the wife of a friend of mine, a former Middlesbrough F.C. steward called Bob Robson, had died of it some 12 months earlier.

"That's a terminal illness, isn't it?" I said, more in confirmation than query.

"Yes, it is," he replied. "But I'm keeping my fingers crossed that yours might be a viral form of the disease that can be treated with drugs." For a few moments we discussed the possibility that I could have the viral condition and I was amazed how relaxed I remained. I can't say that I felt devastated because I don't think I had truly taken in what I had just been told.

The seriousness of the situation began to dawn on me only when Dr Newman asked: "Do you think your wife will want to come in and discuss your condition?" At that moment I knew that deep down he believed I had full blown MND and not the viral condition. I confirmed that Hilary would probably wish to speak to him and he agreed to see her as early as was convenient to us.

The painful truth took a long time to sink home. As I walked to my car, I thought: "Jeepers, I've just been told I've got a terminal illness." As I climbed in and began the drive home in an almost trance-like state, I even began to wonder if I had heard right or if it had all been some sort of mistake. It seemed inconceivable that I should have developed a serious illness. Since leaving behind the stresses and strains of the football and sports retail businesses, my health had been fine and my work at Crofts had helped me become more relaxed. Now this - it just didn't add up. "Can this really be true?" I asked myself. "No, it can't be right. I can't be dying." The truth is I was in denial.

The house was in darkness when I arrived home. It had gone half past five and Hilary hadn't arrived home after picking the kids up from school. I knew she might be another half an hour or so as, being a florist, it was a busy time of year for her, just four days before Valentine's Day. As I sat down alone in the dim light of the conservatory, I kept repeating over and over again: "It can't be true. It can't be true." I tried to rationalise the situation. Surely what the doctor had just told me couldn't really be happening to me, not when I had always been so fit. I was a professional footballer, for God's sake. How could an illness like this affect me? Then I remembered that Don Revie, the former Leeds and England manager who had played for Manchester City and a host of other top clubs, had died of Motor Neurone Disease. I tried to convince myself that I might just have the viral form of MND. But deep down I knew that wasn't the case. I don't know why, I just knew. The look in Dr Newman's eyes told me all I needed to know.

After about half an hour, Hilary arrived home with Laura and David. I expected her to come straight through the conservatory and ask how my appointment had gone but, as I had earlier, she had obviously dismissed it and had perhaps never given it much thought. No doubt she had a thousand other things on her mind - bouquet orders for Valentine's Day, the kids' tea, chores around the house. After a brief "hello" she began to potter around and prepare the tea.

I stayed silent until I could do so no more. Annoyed that I had to remind her, I snapped: "Aren't you going to ask me how I got on today?"

"Oh," she said, remembering my appointment. "I forgot you even had it. How did it go?"

"I didn't do very well, as it happens," I admitted before going on to tell her I had a strain of Motor Neurone Disease. As the words left my mouth I could hardly believe what I was saying. I deliberately avoided the word terminal as I didn't want to overly alarm Hilary if, God willing, it turned out I had the viral condition. Nevertheless, I stressed that my condition may be quite critical.

As soon as the words crossed my lips Hilary understood fully the seriousness of what I was saying. Like me, she knew what MND was. And, like me, she quickly went into a state of disbelief.

There were no tears that night. We both clung to the chance, the slight hope that I might not have full blown MND. No doubt Hilary prayed as hard as I did that I would just have the viral strain.

But within 24 hours I knew my luck was out. Dr Newman had revealed that the viral condition attacked only small areas of the body, often only one limb. As long as the twitch remained in my right hand and arm alone there was a chance that I might have it. Such hope vanished the moment a flicker began in my left arm. Now I knew what my fate was to be. I knew I would die of Motor Neurone Disease. I decided, however, to keep the truth to myself, for the time being at least.

That week never a minute passed by when the thought that I was dying did not enter my head. I wondered to myself why I hadn't broken down in tears. Why have I taken it so well? It can't be true. After several sleepless nights, I returned to the hospital to see Dr Newman on the Friday, accompanied by Hilary. On hearing the doctor's prognosis of my illness, Hilary became very tearful. Thankfully, I didn't break down. I was quite staggered, however, when Dr Newman revealed that some people die within six months of their first symptoms. At that moment the full impact of the situation hit us both like a sledge hammer. Now, not only did I have a terminal illness but I might not even live another six months. In an attempt to calm my fears, Dr Newman said there were odd exceptions where patients had lived up to 12 years after diagnosis and he made particular reference to Dr Stephen

Extra Time – The Final Chapter

Hawking, the famous author and astronomer, who had lived with the illness for nearly 20 years. He was an exception, however, as he suffered from a strain of the disease that did not affect his breathing muscles.

Dr Newman again asked me to strip to the waist. I told him that I had seen a flicker or two in my left arm. I think it was then that we all knew that my condition wasn't of the viral type. Gathering her senses, Hilary asked him to explain in greater detail the symptoms of MND and how it would develop. He gladly explained in laymen's terms that motor neurones are like electrodes that carry signals from the brain to the muscles. In patients with MND, the motor neurones are affected and eventually die. Therefore, all signals to the muscles cease, causing the muscles to waste. Naturally, the breathing muscles are the ones of the greatest importance as, once they go, death is inevitable. Another frequent cause of death is the inability to swallow, leading to problems of malnourishment and consequent weakness and inability to fight infection.

I asked Dr Newman what caused MND and was frustrated by his answer that its cause was still unknown. I revealed to him that I had been through prolonged periods of extreme stress during my time in football management and sports retail and I wondered if that had somehow brought it on. He said there was no scientific evidence to support such a theory. It is my belief, however, that those two stressful times in my life may well have caused some kind of imbalance in my health and the onset of the illness began then, though the symptoms had not started until a few years later. Another school of thought says that it could be caused by some sort of chemical poisoning but again there is no proof to support such a theory.

There were a few more tears from Hilary in Dr Newman's office, while I remained in shock. For the second time in my life I had been dealt a major blow. Just as my football career had been ended in its prime, now my life was to suffer the same fate. However, I was determined, even at that early stage, that I would remain positive and hoped that they might find a cure in my lifetime. I decided there and then that I was going to use what little time I had in a most positive manner. I was going to live with the disease rather than die with it. I am thankful that I have maintained that attitude from those early days.

I can honestly say that I wasn't angry. People often ask "Why me?" But my philosophy is the opposite - why not me? Why shouldn't it happen to someone with a high profile? MND can affect even the strongest, most capable of beings. There have been times when, in total frustration and despair, I have wondered why.

The Day that Changed My Life

But no-one is immortal, we all have to go some way. Hilary, naturally as my wife, has always asked why it had to be. "Why should it happen to someone as nice as you?" she would ask. "Why not the bad people in life?" There is no answer to those questions. However, Professor Pam Shaw, a leading researcher into MND, has since told me that she believes it is an illness that "nice people" suffer from and I do wonder if the fact that I have always cared enough to worry has actually been my downfall as far as my health is concerned.

Hilary and I wept as we lay in one another's arms that night. We said little. What was there to say? As we lay there, holding on to each other, my desperation for myself was overcome with a concern for those I had to tell. I wondered to myself how would I tell my 80-year-old parents that their youngest son would die before them? How could I tell my two youngest children, Laura and David, that I would not be around for them? What could I say to my eldest two, Lucy and Steven, who were in important last years of study? I had always assumed that I would be there to advise and protect my family. Suddenly this cruel illness would deprive me of all that.

I don't know how Hilary and I coped in those early weeks but somehow we found the strength to do so without giving the game away to our family or closest friends. Thankfully, we are both mentally strong and our love and support for one another got us through. We sat down and talked about it. We agreed that until such a time when I could no longer hide the illness, neither of us needed to burden our ageing parents or young family with the dreadful news. I was particularly conscious of my eldest two, knowing how devastated they would be. Such news might have had a disastrous effect on their studies which were so vital to their futures. At the time, Lucy was in her final year of a degree course while Steven was about to sit his A-levels. There was no way I could put their futures at risk to give them news that could wait a while longer.

In the first two months I shared the knowledge of my serious illness with only two people - my insurance broker and my lifelong friend Steve Smelt. Steve was working as physiotherapist for Sunderland Football Club and as I had an appointment in the city that day, I decided to go and see him. After keeping the dreadful truth a secret for two months, I just felt the need to talk to someone. Furthermore, Steve's medical knowledge meant he knew about the condition. Sharing the knowledge with someone else was a huge relief and I was glad to have made that visit to Roker Park, though Steve was understandably upset. Hilary later confided in her sister, Jean, and Christine, the manageress of her flower shop, and

Extra Time – The Final Chapter

I know she felt the same relief I had done.

Meanwhile, I made sure all my life policies were up-to-date and in order. My insurance broker, Malcolm Corking, was also a friend and he was understandably speechless when I told him what I had to say. He was staggered that I seemed so calm and appeared to be in such control of my emotions. My main concern was that everything was in order and that my wife and family would be well taken care of in the eventuality of my death. It was of no small comfort to me when those facts were confirmed by Malcolm.

In the meantime, I knew I had to get on with things and try to live as normal a life as was possible. I was grateful for the distraction of a new job. I had actually postponed my initial appointment with Dr Newman as it clashed with my first day with Heath Insurance. I had put my heart and soul into the job from day one and quickly felt at home in my new surroundings and began to feel that I had found my niche as a "new business" manager. Now, just a month into the job which had given me the satisfaction I had always craved, I was dying. Despite the illness and the secret I carried with me, I was able to get tremendous satisfaction from the job.

A fortnight after joining the company, my boss Brian Dunn sent me to London to take a look at Heath UK's national headquarters and arranged for me to visit Lloyd's of London the following day. My overnight stay was at the beautiful Tower Bridge Hotel but I struggled to fully enjoy my visit. Having been welcomed with such enthusiasm by my new colleagues in London, the question I kept turning over in my head was how long I would enjoy this working relationship.

Not a minute of my leisure time would pass by when I did not think about the fact that I was dying and wonder how long I had left. Even now, three years on, I am still asking that same question - thankfully.

At the end of April 1995, I was among many former Middlesbrough players and managers who were guests of the club at the last ever league match at Ayresome Park before Boro moved to a new stadium on the outskirts of the town. Before the match, each of the stars of the past conducted a lap of honour around the pitch and I had hoped to accompany my old team-mate Stuart Boam on the walk. However, he was taken aside for a TV interview and I was alone as I walked around the pitch, shaking hands with dozens of supporters and waving to thousands. Seeing the end of the old ground where I had enjoyed so many treasured moments was emotional enough but, deep down, I wondered if I would even be around four months later to see Boro playing at their new £16 million all-seater stadium which promised a bright new era for the club. I'm delighted to say that not only was I there to see the first ever match at the stadium but I have actually seen three full seasons of football there.

In those early months with Heath, there was fortunately no deterioration in the strength of my legs, though the muscle spasms in my right bicep and forearm were by now quite violent and I was beginning to suffer less severe spasms in my left arm. Indeed, the spasms were constant every minute of every day.

In May that year, I attended a meeting in Leeds but had to hold on to the boardroom table my colleagues and I were sat around in an attempt to control the tremors in my right arm. In the middle of the table was a large jug of water and, so violent were the spasms, that they transmitted through my arm to the jug, sending a ripple effect across the water. I immediately moved my arm before any of my workmates noticed. Throughout the remainder of the meeting I could clearly see my arm shaking under my shirt sleeve. I can only describe the spasms as being like a small fish moving under my skin. The more I moved my arms, the more violent the spasms would become. Thankfully, no-one seemed to notice.

In my third month in the job I attended a professional sales course in London along with two fellow staff and a professional tutor. By now my right hand had become quite limp and I began to wonder when someone would notice. That day-long sales course involved an enormous amount of writing, a task I found immensely difficult. It was becoming increasingly hard to grip a pen with any strength so my writing was pretty atrocious. How the hell I got through the day without anyone spotting my problem, I don't know. It was almost inconceivable that no-one noticed the difficulties I was having. But somehow I managed to keep my secret under wraps.

Meanwhile, sleeping became a big problem. The twitching in my fingers, shoulders and forearms was 24 hours a day. I often had to lay with my right hand between my legs in order to stop my fingers moving constantly. That tended to have the effect of transmitting the movements into the muscles in my forearm. I don't know which was more irritating. As time progressed, sleeping became all but impossible and I began to get maybe half an hour a night. As soon as I moved to turn over in bed, both legs would go into a cramp-like spasm and bend uncontrollably at right angles for five or six seconds before the grip of the spasm relaxed. Half an hour later, when I needed to turn over again, I would go through the same process, with the slightest movement sending my lower body into spasm with my legs locked straight. This would happen 15 or 16 times a night. I would lay there in a semi-conscious state, aware that my body could spasm any second.

My thoughts at that time were that I had to be brave for my family. Many times in those early weeks and months, with that dark shadow hanging over me, it would have been easy to have become depressed. I was thankful, therefore, for my job which was a wonderful distraction. It actually enabled Hilary and I to lead reasonably normal lives for the first six months after my condition was diagnosed. The day-to-day routine of work gave me less time to dwell on the negative aspects of my life.

It is quite possible that, but for the illness, I would have stayed in the insurance sales field. I was enjoying every minute of the challenge of selling commercial insurance, often in excess of £200,000, to top management within companies throughout Teesside. In my first nine months in the job, I generated hundreds of potential new clients and had converted a reasonable amount of new business. Although there had initially been a few doubting Thomases within the company who had perhaps wondered how the hell I, as a former footballer with no background in the field, thought I would be able to sell insurance. But I am a firm believer that with the right principles and techniques you can sell any product with a limited amount of background knowledge, and I had been proved right. In most cases, selling is the ability to get on and communicate with people and that was something which had always come easy to me.

It was my job to contact the top brass of Teesside's business fraternity to discuss with them insurance opportunities through the Heath Group. My name gave me a big advantage in simply getting to speak to those in charge. I would call the top management and mention that it was Willie Maddren on the phone and many people were naturally curious as to why I should be ringing them. However, I was very careful not to mention the dreaded word, insurance, in the opening dialogue. The conversation in the first two or three minutes would often be about football, with the talking usually done by them rather than me. That was a great advantage as it meant I didn't have to go into the hard sell without having broken the ice. Although I was slowing down, I probably had a 60 to 70 per cent success rate in making appointments with a view to Heath being given an opportunity to quote for the insurance needs of the commercial operations I contacted. In fact, such was my productivity that I became a little frustrated that Heath didn't seem to have the manpower to cope with the amount of new opportunities I was creating.

The Day that Changed My Life

Having been successful from the start, I didn't feel any pressure whatsoever. The job ideally suited my temperament and personality while, for the first time in my working life, the weekends were my own and I was able to spend more time than ever with my family. Meanwhile, I was being well paid for entertaining clients in the finest restaurants and on the best golf courses on Teesside. Indeed, my profile as a former footballer and manager resulted in me being invited to attend the golf day of one business as their guest when normally it would be the other way around! However, at the back of my mind I always knew that my illness would mean it would all come to a premature and disappointing end.

Given my lack of sleep and the energy-sapping effect of the illness, I did begin to find fatigue a real problem at work. I would be sat in my office, having phoned maybe 30 or 40 potential clients and done much dictation, thinking that I could do with a sleep. Indeed, in one or two important meetings I was frightened that I might actually fall asleep there and then.

In the August of that year, I attended another meeting in London, catching the 20 past six train from Darlington to King's Cross. As I made my way from King's Cross to the tube station, wearing a weighty overcoat, my legs felt so heavy that it was as if I had on a pair of diving boots. Having caught the tube to Liverpool Street station, I began the half-mile walk to Heath's HQ but quickly began to wonder if I would even make it. Several times over that short distance I was forced to stop and rest against a wall in an effort to catch my breath and recover some strength. Though I eventually completed the journey, it was a real shock to my system.

The prospect of losing my mobility was a frightening thought and I was fearful for my future. That day it began to hit home just how quickly the disease was progressing through my body. Part of the psychological torment of this cruel illness is the way it advances through your body, leaving you waiting helplessly for the next stage, for another part of your body to be affected. Indeed, if I was like that then, I wondered if I might even be in a wheelchair by Christmas.

The day after my exhausting trip to the capital, I decided to tell one of my bosses about my predicament. Concealing my illness from workmates had become a pressure in itself and I felt confiding in one of them might help alleviate the situation. I revealed my secret to my area manager Stuart Morley who, though naturally shocked by my revelation, was hugely sympathetic and supportive. I rarely took a lunch break but Stuart suggested that I should nip home for a cat nap during my dinner hour, as we lived only half a mile away from Heath's offices. It was a big comfort to know I had that option though only occasionally did I take him up on his offer.

I had spent much time in meetings with Stuart over the previous months but he admitted he had not had the slightest inclination about my illness. However, he did recall how he had dismissed the remarks of one of the office girls, Janice, who had commented on my "dead hand". I thought I had hidden my ailments quite well and didn't even think the hand was particularly limp at the time. But Stuart told me he had been quite happy with my level of performance and we agreed that, provided I could continue to work to the standards I had set myself, then there was no reason for my revelations to go any further.

Hilary and I felt that we should break the news in maybe October or November but certainly after August, by which time Lucy and Steven would have finished their exams. Time went by, however, and by November my illness still remained a secret. By then, I had lost much muscle bulk in my arms and shoulders but still felt reasonably fit and probably looked a lot better than I felt. That month, however, something happened that left Hilary and I in no doubt that we would not be able to keep things under our hat, for much longer. A good friend of mine, Pat Wayne, walked into Hilary's shop and quite tearfully announced: "Hilary, tell me it's not true. Someone has put a rumour about that Willie is terminally ill." Hilary's knees almost buckled as she heard those words but she managed to keep her composure sufficiently to convince Pat that there was no foundation in the gossip.

Pat had left the shop relieved but she later innocently revealed to Steven details of the rumour. That weekend, Steven, who lived with his mother, asked me if I was alright during his usual visit for Sunday lunch. "What do you mean, son?" I asked. "Oh, Auntie Pat has told me that someone has been going around saying you were dying." I could hardly look him in the eye but somehow I managed to bluff my way out of it, saying: "Don't be silly. Do I look like a man who is dying?"

That night, concerned that those close to us would discover my secret from someone else, I told Hilary that we would have to tell all the family in the near future, if not before Christmas, then certainly immediately after. I wanted to be the one to tell people. At the same time, I had to consider my eldest two. I felt I was protecting them from the truth but I knew it would be understandable if they felt I should have told them sooner. Christmas came and went without another word being uttered on the subject. I believed that Christmas would be my last and I did wonder if I should tell my children and family so we could all enjoy it together and

The Day that Changed My Life

make the most of it. But we decided against it, until the following February.

Before announcing the news to the world, I had the unenviable task of telling my children, brothers, sister and elderly parents. It was a prospect which sent a shiver down my spine. One evening I told Hilary I would tell my brothers, Dave and Chris, and my sister Claire that night while I was in the mood. However, I didn't want to tell them individually so began to make arrangements to get them together. I rang Claire to check if she would be in within the next hour as I would be popping around. I was hoping and praying that she wouldn't ask if it was anything important and was thankful that she didn't. The last thing I wanted was a flood of questions over the telephone. I then rang Dave to say I had something of importance to tell him but that I wanted him to go to Claire's house for seven o'clock prompt. Sadly, I couldn't get hold of Chris so decided I would have to tell him at a later date.

How difficult it was to tell my brother and sister in that emotional meeting. With a tear in my eye, my bottom lip trembling and an obvious tremor in my voice, I began to describe the fact that I had an illness called Motor Neurone Disease. No sooner had I uttered the words "terminal illness" than Claire stood up and ran out of the room. Perhaps she just could not even bear to hear those words. While Claire was out of the room, I continued talking to Dave and Claire's husband, Alex, who I had always been close to. Dave too was visibly taken aback and I could see he was fighting to hold back the tears. Alex was very constructive in his conversation and I was grateful that his intelligent questions helped me to keep my composure. Having regained her own composure, Claire returned to the room and we shared a cuddle and a few tears. In an attempt to be of some comfort, I told them I had had the illness for a year and that it did not appear to be progressing as quickly as it did in many people. The truth was I was trying to let them down softly as deep down I was unsure whether I would live even beyond the next six months. Ever since that day Dave, Claire and Chris have always been supportive. Indeed, initially Claire would ring me every night and I eventually had to tell her that there was no need to phone so often. My condition wasn't changing so rapidly and I knew how much she loved me. I have included two of Claire's poems in this book and I think anyone who reads them will know how close we are. I have also enjoyed a special relationship with Dave, spending many days out with him since that day.

Whilst getting the burden of that terrible secret off my chest was a great relief, it also released a great tidal wave of emotion that only Hilary and I had previously experienced. Indeed, the week in which we told those closest to us and others who

Extra Time – The Final Chapter

needed to know before we went public was one of the most challenging and emotional times of my life. One of the main symptoms of MND is that you become more emotional, so much so that it often becomes difficult to keep a lid on your feelings. Thankfully, I have found it hard to control my laughter rather than my tears. I often laugh hysterically, an uncontrollable belly laugh. I know many people cry with the condition but I have gone the other way. In fact, it has become a good way to let off steam.

I broke the news to Chris and his wife, Betty, the following evening and they were naturally sympathetic as they were immediately aware of the consequences on hearing of my condition. Betty's brother was very ill with Multiple Sclerosis and has sadly since died.

My next task was to tell Lucy and Steven. Having told them to be at our house for Sunday dinner for 12 prompt, I arranged for Hilary to be out of the house. In the minutes before their arrival I kept telling myself to keep my composure and to be strong for my children as I knew how upset they would be. On their arrival, I led them into the conservatory and asked them to sit down. I then began to explain that I had an illness call Motor Neurone Disease. Before I had the chance to blurt out the word terminal, they came towards me and we wrapped our arms around one another as we broke down in floods of tears. For some minutes there were no more words, just uncontrollable, emotion-charged tears. Somehow, eventually, I managed to get across that I would die of the illness and the three of us sat there hugging one another until the tears would temporarily subside. We would speak a few more words before the tears would kick in once again. I was disappointed with myself that I had broken down in front of them but, after 12 months of keeping it all in, I felt a sudden onrush of emotion that was impossible to hold back. Lucy and Steven asked why I hadn't told them sooner, to which I replied that I had tried to protect them during their important exam years. They accepted that but nevertheless wished I had told them earlier. In that unforgettable outpouring of emotion, they assured me that they would always be there for me. They have been true to their word.

On Hilary's return, there were more tears though I tried to reassure Lucy and Steven that I had lived a year with it and would be around for them for a long time still to come. Having regained my composure, I told them how some MND sufferers lived for a considerable number of years. What I didn't tell them, of course, was that the average life expectancy was between two-and-a-half and five years.

The Day that Changed My Life

Finally, at about six that evening, it was time for them to leave for their mother's home in Middleton St. George some miles away. My last words to them as they climbed into their cars were: "Be careful as you drive home. Concentrate and don't be thinking about what we've talked about today." Perhaps I'd had a premonition because their journey home wasn't a safe one.

An XR3 overtook Steven on the brow of a hill near Sedberge. Steven, already upset at the events of the day, beeped his horn at the lunatic, angry and dismayed at his wreckless driving. In response to Steven's rebuke, the mad man jammed on the breaks of his car, forcing Steven into an emergency stop to avoid running into the back of his car. The driver jumped out and confronted Steven. As the two of them stood arguing at the side of the road, Lucy's car came over the brow of the hill and crashed into the back of Steven's. Mercifully, Lucy was uninjured though there was considerable damage to both cars, while the idiot who had caused the accident jumped in his car and sped away from the scene. On top of the news they had heard about their father, it must have been terribly traumatic for both of them.

Later that evening, Hilary answered a telephone call but initially tried to conceal from me the fact that it was Lucy explaining what had happened. But I immediately knew something was wrong and insisted Hilary tell me. On hearing what had happened, I again broke down uncontrollably. I found it difficult to come to terms with the fact that not only had my children had to contend with hearing that their father was dying but they may well have been killed themselves. I couldn't help but consider the terrible injustice of it all. I think of myself as a Christian but that night I was asking certain questions.

The following morning, I drove Steven to Hull University, where he was studying for a degree, as I wanted to spend some time with him to reassure him. I brought up the subject of my illness several times during the journey but it was clear he was uncomfortable with the conversation and I had to make a conscious effort not to talk about it. That was obviously Steven's way of dealing with it. That night on my return from Hull, Lucy called round and it was typical of her loving nature to say: "Right Dad, I've cried all I can cry. I'm going to be there from now if you should need me." It was good to know I had her support at such a testing time. Later, Steven took a year out from his studies to enable him to spend more time with me and we both enjoyed our days out together immensely.

The next to be told were my elderly parents. Claire had initially been unsure about the wisdom of even telling them as she was concerned that the shock of it might kill our mother, who some years earlier, had undergone two major operations which she had done well to survive. But after reassurance from me that I would let them down lightly and a reminder that it would be much worse for them to read about it in the newspapers, Claire and Dave agreed to meet me at my parents' house the day after I had told Lucy and Steven. I wanted Claire and Dave to stay to comfort our parents after I had left the house but emphasised the need to keep things relaxed until I arrived as if they had simply popped in for a tea and a chat.

I didn't particularly want to address Dad because he is quite deaf and I didn't want to have to repeat myself constantly. However, just as I was about to tell Mum, Dad burst into the room and said that if there was anything important to be said then he needed to hear it too. Despite his hearing problem, he took in every word of what I had to say that day. I did try to let my parents down lightly, telling them that I had an illness and over many years it might become quite debilitating with the consequence that I might end up in a wheelchair. But I assured them: "I've had the illness a year but I'm feeling really well with it so there's no need to get upset. It's something I've come to terms with and I'm coping with it quite comfortably." Mum's bottom lip started to go quite visibly and she was clearly fighting to hold back the tears but she asked me to tell her more about the illness. I told her it was a muscle-wasting disease which had started in my right hand, at which she asked me to show her my hand. As she inspected it, she somehow managed to keep her emotions intact. I didn't feel the need to mention the terminal aspect of the illness as I felt it would be far easier for them to handle if they were left to piece it together in their own minds over time. Instead, I was relieved to have managed to tell them about my illness in such a calm and controlled manner.

Before I left, Dad put his arms around me and said that he would always be here for me but I was amazed how strong both my parents were. I know Mum had a cry after I left the house and quizzed Dave and Claire about the illness, but they had been briefed to keep the details to a minimum and to follow the same story line I had given.

By then, I had been around to see Hilary's parents, Edith and Arthur, as she had already given them the bad news. I wanted them both to see me looking reasonably fit and healthy to put their minds at rest. They were ever so pleased to see me and grateful I had gone round. I often think it must be terrible for them that they are not only thinking about me but coping with the idea that their youngest daughter, the apple of their eyes, may one day be left on her own to bring up two

The Day that Changed My Life

young children.

Is there a right way or a wrong way to tell your two young children that their Daddy is going to die? That was the dilemma Hilary and I faced and considered for many long hours before we finally decided to tell Laura and David. I was adamant that I did not want to risk breaking down in front of my 10-year-old daughter and six-year-old son so the unenviable task fell on Hilary's shoulders. However, we decided that she should only tell Laura first and that we would then ask her to explain it to David to see how much she had understood.

Sitting down one afternoon while I was out, Hilary told Laura, as sensitively as she could, that her Daddy had an illness, that he wouldn't get better from it and would one day end up in a wheelchair. Laura cried for some time though Hilary reassured her that although I was poorly, it might be a long, long time before I got really bad. To be honest, we wondered whether we had told her enough and had maybe been a little too protective with her. Looking back now, however, I'm sure we did the right thing as she must slowly have built a complete picture of what MND is all about through the many conversations she has overheard with family and friends over the last two years or so.

Having asked Laura to explain to David, Hilary sat down with them both that evening. Laura explained to her young brother that Daddy was poorly, that his muscles would get weak and that he musn't jump on him or pull his arms about in case he hurt him. There were more tears but after a wee bit of reassurance from his Mum, David suddenly stopped crying and asked: "Can I have a packet of crisps now?" When Hilary later told me that story I felt hugely comforted. Clearly enough of the message had got through but David was obviously able to deal with it in his own way.

Knowing we would go public with the news that week, we were also aware that the children might be bombarded with questions from schoolmates so Hilary paid a visit to Red House School to tell their headmaster and form teacher. We kept the kids off school the following day to enable the head to explain to their classmates that Laura's and David's Daddy was poorly and they would need plenty of kindness. As it happened, I think they had just about everyone in the school ask them if their Daddy was OK on their return to lessons the following day!

Of course, others who had to know were those at Heath Insurance though I was unsure what my employer's reaction would be as I had failed to tell them about my serious illness until a year into the job. Before telling my regional manager, I sought reassurance about how to go about things from my friend Brian Dunn, who had employed me for Heath Insurance but had since retired. Like myself, he had already been touched by MND as a friend of his, Brian Dixon, had died of the illness several years earlier. Brian helped to put everything in perspective for me, assuring me that Heath would look after me and that there would be provisions within my contract to ensure I was provided for throughout the rest of my life. I knew that, of course, but had wondered if that might be contested as I had known I had MND within a month of joining the Heath Group. I am pleased to say that the company has been magnificent in their support and they bent over backwards to help me after I went public. I will also be eternally grateful to Brian for employing me and giving me the opportunity to work for such a large and successful company who went on to look after me so wonderfully well.

That afternoon, I revealed the truth to my regional manager, Les Clarke, who was immediately supportive. He agreed to address all the staff and give them the dreadful news while I took a day off. Several colleagues were evidently devastated. Alan Tickner, who I had worked with closely, found it hard to believe that I had kept it under wraps for so long. But he was hugely supportive during what was a difficult time for me in the weeks which followed and I was grateful that he didn't swamp me with sympathy but remained very natural with me. Meanwhile, Gill Hutchinson, who did much of my secretarial work, was distraught. A friend of hers had already died of MND and she apparently cried on hearing my news. Strangely, there wasn't an awful lot said on my return to work. One or two colleagues did say how deeply sorry they were but several workmates continued as if nothing had happened. I guess it was their way of dealing with the situation.

I was concerned how potential clients might react once word spread that I was suffering from MND. I knew I would still have to ring around for new business and wondered if people might be reluctant to talk to me, perhaps out of embarrassment. Thankfully, I discovered that wasn't the case and it was very much business as usual. Indeed, one or two clients whose business I had won contacted me to say how sorry they were.

One of the more practical things I did before going public was to write to the committee of Eaglescliffe Golf Club to say I would not be renewing my subscriptions for the forthcoming year. I officially resigned my membership, saying that I would be unable to play golf that year due to work commitments. Neil Chamberlin, a friend and keen golfer, rang to ask me if I realised the significance of resigning. There was a 10-year waiting list to become a member and Neil reminded me that I had an option to put my membership on hold for a year for a smaller fee. I had a difficult time trying to wriggle out of that one, just as I did when Eaglescliffe secretary Leslie Still rang to reiterate Neil's advice.

Just before going public I gave the news to my ex-neighbour Alan Sowerby, whose wife Beryl had managed my sports shop for a while, and asked him to ring around friends and let them know. For some months after my diagnosis I had remained strong enough to enjoy the occasional round of golf at Eaglescliffe. But my game had inevitably deteriorated to the point where one day on the course my golf partner Leo Branaghan asked: "What the hell is the matter with your game, Willie? It has gone to pieces." Eventually, I had started to make excuses about why I couldn't play and he had found a new partner. Remembering how he had criticised my game, Leo was beside himself on hearing the news of my illness. He rang to apologise but I put him at ease by quipping: "You've only rang me because you want my three wood!" With that, I could hear the tone of his voice change and he became far more comfortable with the conversation. I'm pleased to say Leo remains a good friend to this day.

I spent many long hours deliberating over the best way to reveal to the world that I had Motor Neurone Disease. I did not want to have to deal with countless individual interviews so decided the best policy would be to make a statement through journalist Ray Robertson, my testimonial chairman and a former chief sports writer with the Northern Echo. Having known Ray for many years, I felt comfortable telling him and asked him to circulate the news to the rest of the media. Ray was naturally shocked. He couldn't believe I was able to tell him in such a controlled manner but took notes and agreed to have the story circulated to the local and national press for the following day.

Although Hilary and I wanted my illness to be common knowledge, I wasn't yet ready to speak to numerous different reporters so was rather upset when one particular guy became quite stroppy during a telephone call on the morning the story appeared in the Northern Echo. Several local radio and newspaper reporters contacted us on the day the story broke but all but this one accepted that I wasn't yet ready to add anything further to the statement I had made through Ray. This irritating chap rang from BBC Radio Cleveland very early that morning and persisted with his request for an interview, even when Hilary explained that we had nothing more to say. Without even once asking how I was, his only concern seemed to be about getting the scoop and he ended his conversation with Hilary by saying he hoped I would not give any of their competitors the exclusive interview "after all we have done for Willie over the years". If anything, it was the other way around and I had done them the favours in the past. I'm pleased to say that since that day Radio Cleveland have been most supportive in my campaign to raise the profile of MND.

Hilary and I were not prepared for the dramatic effect going public with my illness would have on our lives. Until then we had been able to continue to lead relatively normal lives but all that changed almost overnight. The two most obvious changes were that we were deluged by phone calls and letters from well-wishing friends, acquaintances and complete strangers and then I suddenly realised just how much good I could do in the battle against MND by lending my name to the fight.

All I Require

I often think God has been so unfair
To have burdened my brother with much more than his share

Seeing him in his wheelchair my thoughts multiply
I'm reminiscing his glory days, trying hard not to cry

I watch and admire the way he copes with handicapped life
And the adoring glances he gives to his children and devoted wife

I'm amazed at his tolerance and his ever genuine smile
He never shows bitterness, he's been blessed with heroic style

Some days he lacks energy, then miraculously finds drive
To raise more money for research to help fellow sufferers survive

He knows his charity efforts may not bring him personal gain
But he lives with the satisfaction his deeds are not in vain

They say God does everything for a reason and it's clear now to me
That he chose my remarkable brother for his charm and sincerity

God gave him the influence to inspire the timid and not so grand
Knowing Willie has great courage to face what life demands

My brother's determination releases the inner strength he does require
To see him fight and conquer his battle is all I desire

By Claire
(Willie's sister)

21

A Game I Can't Win

I'M LUCKY. That was how I felt on the day I told the people of Teesside that I was suffering from Motor Neurone Disease. Something truly heart-breaking happened that day to help me put my illness into perspective. That day we had hoped that a major news story might break to deflect some of the attention from my revelation, but I was to be left feeling rather guilty when the tragedy we had almost wished for actually occurred.

My story had appeared within the pages of the Northern Echo on the morning of March 13th, 1996. Having read the Echo early that morning, a photographer from another local newspaper, the Evening Gazette, paid a visit to our house to take pictures of me and my family before Laura and David left for school. We had hoped that my story would be kept relatively low key so were most surprised to see it emblazoned across the front page of the Gazette when its first edition hit the streets later that day. We found ourselves wishing that a big story would break to deflect attention from my plight. Our prayers were answered in a way we would never have wanted.

By the time the Gazette's second edition was in circulation, we were no longer front page news. Now the big story of the day told how Thomas Hamilton, a lunatic with a grudge, had walked into his local primary school and shot dead 16 young children and their teacher. That was the day of the Dunblane Tragedy.

I did not feel a terrible remorse for myself that day. Instead, I could only think of the heart-broken families of those poor children who had so sadly lost their lives in their infancy. I put myself in the position of those parents and imagined how I would have felt if my young son or daughter had been murdered. I know I would have been truly devastated.

A Game I Can't Win

Even now I still think I am lucky that it is me that is suffering from MND as I am not sure how I would have coped if any of my children had been diagnosed with a terminal illness. I do find it quite strange that throughout these past few years I have never felt particularly sorry for myself. I am only conscious of the hurt that I will cause my family and friends when I pass away. I can't help but hope that I won't die in too much pain and discomfort - that would only make it worse for my family.

I often think about the film 'Philadelphia' in which Tom Hanks plays a man dying of Aids who receives visits from those close to him in the hours before he passes away. I find that scene so moving as I naturally put myself in that position and wonder how long it will be before it is my family coming to see me, knowing it will be the last time they will ever speak to me.

Since my diagnosis, I have attended several funerals. One was for Jonathan Harrison, the husband of one of our children's nannies, who died at the age of just 24. I was heart-broken that one so young could be taken this way, especially as he was such a lovely person. At subsequent funerals, I would look at the coffin and wonder how long it would be before it was my turn. More recently, I was deeply saddened when my cousin Jack died at the age of 48, from lung cancer. I was left wondering whether I would surpass that tender age, as I am now in my 47th year.

Every date on the calendar - be it a wedding anniversary, birthday or whatever - eventually comes and goes. My big date with destiny is naturally not something I am looking forward to though I know, like everything else, it will come and go and life will go on for others long after I have gone.

I will fight this illness to the bitter end though I know the odds are not stacked in my favour. Late in 1997, Hilary and I asked my specialist, Dr Newman, the million dollar question - how long did I realistically have to live? The answer did not particularly surprise me, as I know the illness is tightening its grip on me and wearing down my defences, but Hilary was devastated with Dr Newman's words. After careful deliberation and what seemed like an eternity, he looked at me and admitted: "You will see this Christmas with your family but I think it is unlikely that you will make it through to Christmas '98." No doubt Dr Newman based his statement on his experience of witnessing the deterioration of many other MND sufferers over the years and I am sure he has great knowledge on the subject. But I have set myself a target of living and enjoying Christmas 1998 with my family. It will give me great pleasure in January of 1999 to say: "Hello, Doctor. I'm still here!"

Extra Time – The Final Chapter

I know ultimately my destiny is not in my hands but I firmly believe that by remaining positive I might just get there. Being positive is 50 per cent of the battle.

When, in February 1998, I was taken into hospital suffering from a virus, I did wonder if my time was up and that I might be in my final days or hours. My intake of breath was getting shorter and shorter, I was suffering great pain in my lungs and had much discomfort in my diaphragm. At the same time, I was running a high temperature and was worried that I might catch pneumonia as the MND had worn down my resistance against such things. When my doctor recommended me to spend a few days in hospital to ensure the infection didn't worsen, I wondered if this was it. Looking at Hilary and my brother Dave, I could see in their eyes that the thought had crossed their minds too as they had never previously witnessed me in such a state. Thankfully, I was back at home 24 hours later and within a week had recovered most of my strength. Clearly, I was still stronger than I believed as I had been able to fight off the infection. That incident did, however, give me an insight into what it might be like in the final moments of my life.

I have found much moral and mental strength through my belief in God. Soon after going public on my illness, I contacted Canon Bill Hall as I had many difficult questions to ask him about religion and the meaning of life. I suppose I wanted to be comforted and put at ease over my belief that eternal life follows death. Bill, a priest I had known well before Jack Charlton had invited him into Middlesbrough Football Club during the 1970's, spoke to me in such simplistic terms and I have drawn great comfort and strength each time I have met him. There is no doubt my regular chats with him have helped me to cope with my situation. Bill endorsed my lifelong faith and, before long, I decided the time was right to be confirmed as I wanted to commit myself to God. I was confirmed on the same wonderful evening as young David received his baptism. To this day I continue to pray every night, as I have always done. My prayers are usually for my parents, my family and for others less fortunate in the world. On the eve of a match during my playing days, I would never pray to win but for God to give me strength and keep me safe. It does concern me, however, that the world is in such rapid social decline. I hope and pray that one day the Church can once again be a shining light in helping to put people back on the right track. I do hope it is the Church rather than some kind of catastrophe that can help put things back into perspective for people who seem to be so consumed by personal gain.

What I have found since announcing my illness is that people react to such news in many different ways. Hilary and I weren't really prepared for the

A Game I Can't Win

outpouring of emotion which followed my announcement. Suddenly, the telephone was ringing constantly with friends and acquaintances wanting to come and see me. We did find it quite difficult. In fact, it reached the point whereby it was becoming an intrusion on our lives. Having learned to deal with the situation in my own mind over the previous year, I was suddenly dealing with other people's emotion. Ironically, I was having to comfort them! I would tell them: "Come on now, I don't need all this. As you can see, I'm fine at the moment, I'm dealing with it in a positive way and I want you to do that too."

Before going public, out of courtesy I had revealed details of my illness to George Smith, David Mills and many other close friends as I didn't want them to have the shock of learning about it from a newspaper story. I couldn't physically go to see everyone so, although not ideal, I had to tell some of them over the telephone, asking them to pop round in a few days once all the fuss had died down. Some people cried at the other end of the phone, while I remember ringing my old team-mate Bill Gates at his retirement retreat in the Cayman Islands. Bill had always been a single-minded person with a reputation as a football hard man but he could only mutter: "Willie, I don't know what to say." He couldn't take in what I had told him and he eventually had to hang up to compose himself. He rang back about an hour later and told me that, although he was not exactly on my doorstep, he and his wife Judith would always be there for me if I needed them. I do see Bill on his occasional visits back to the UK and we spend time reminiscing about the times we enjoyed in each other's company during our playing days.

Some people responded to my revelation with a stunned silence. What do you say when someone breaks news like that to you? It was several weeks before some were able to come to terms with it and pick up the phone or write to me. Others walked in the door and burst into tears. It was a natural reaction but I have to say it wasn't easy for Hilary and me as there was a temptation to join in. We had come a long way over the previous year and were determined not to take a step backwards and start to get overly emotional again.

Sunderland Football Club responded to news of my illness in a way which delighted me. Not only did they write to express their sorrow, as did Hartlepool, but I was invited by their manager Peter Reid to join the team on an away trip to Watford. Joining Steve Smelt, who was physio there at the time, I enjoyed the occasion immensely as it reminded me of my days as a player. It was good to know that someone with Peter's profile had time to stop and think of me when my morale was in need of a boost.

Extra Time – The Final Chapter

There were some people that I expected contact from who didn't initially get in touch. I was hurt that they didn't make an effort, though I'm pleased to say that after a considerable time that bridge has now been crossed and pretty much everyone I would have hoped for has expressed their sadness personally to me. If the situation was reversed I know I would have been the first person to pick up the phone but I know some people are embarrassed and don't know what to say in such a situation. But just a brief word over the phone would have been enough to show me they cared. Anyone suffering from a terminal illness or any major disability needs support and the knowledge that people are thinking about them. It is a great comfort to know that people you are, or have been, close to are there for you if you need them.

Soon after going public, I began to realise that I could use the media to raise the profile of Motor Neurone Disease. Right from the outset I had been surprised by just how little publicity MND received. More people die of MND than of Aids and yet the latter illness seems to get so much more publicity and many millions of pounds more funds for research. I was contacted by two members of the MND Research Fund's local branch, Luke Rutter and Bob Robson, who, although recognising I had plenty on my mind already, suggested I might put my name to a fund-raising effort. It would have been selfish of me not to use my profile to try and increase awareness of MND in the north east. I realised I was not a national figure but felt that, providing my health permitted, I could do an enormous amount of good for the fight against the illness. It excited me that I could perhaps be of some sort of inspiration not only to fellow MND sufferers, but to other terminally ill people too.

Having agreed to help out, I held an interview with Tyne-Tees Television as I recognised that TV was a more powerful medium than radio or the written word. Before being interviewed by reporter Duncan Wood in a stand of Ayresome Park, I was unsure whether I could go through with it as I was concerned that I might not be able to keep my emotions intact. I was pleased that I did keep myself under control despite talking about how the illness might affect me and my family but, more importantly, I got the message over loud and clear that Willie Maddren was starting a crusade to raise much-needed funding and publicity for the MND Research Fund.

The fund-raising snowballed from that day forward. We were contacted by people throughout Teesside and beyond expressing their wishes to hold fund-raising events in support of the Willie Maddren MND Fund. Two of my colleagues

A Game I Can't Win

from Heath Insurance, Janice and Graham Laverick, immediately agreed to take part in the Great North Run to raise funds but that was only the tip of the iceberg. Our friends, Geoff and Sandra Turnbull, joined forces with others to organise a gala evening in the grounds of their home in Elwick, raising some £5,500, while many more events followed.

Meanwhile, Angela Preston, whose father had sadly died with MND, joined forces with Lynn Dunning to organise a highly successful fashion show at the Tall Trees nightclub which raised over £4,000. I was delighted when two of my former players, Gary Pallister and Tony Mowbray, attended the evening along with another former Boro star, Paul Kerr. Addressing over 400 ladies and a smattering of male guests, I embarrassed Hilary in thanking God that at least there was one organ that MND definitely doesn't affect. As I went on, I could see Hilary making a sharp exit in the direction of the toilets. As she got up from her seat, however, I said: "There she is - the blonde lady with the rather tired look!" The ladies found my quip amusing but Hilary certainly didn't. In fact, all that year she kept telling me that I had to find a hobby for myself!

I found I was appearing at fund-raising events three or four nights a week. I made a point of making a personal speech at every function I attended, though sometimes I would be nervous that my voice might fail me as not only did I have to keep my emotions intact, but I was having great difficulty with my breathing. Occasionally my throat would suddenly dry up and I would not be able to make myself heard even in normal conversation. Fortunately, adrenaline ensured I never struggled when the moment came. There were times when I wondered if I really needed all the pressure when I was so ill. But I took enormous satisfaction from the work as I knew I was able to do so much good for other people. To be honest, all the hard work - the organising and fund-raising - was being done by others. I was simply putting my name to it.

I have to be honest and admit that my reasoning might in itself have been quite selfish. I gave so much time towards the campaign in the hope that the funds we raised might help to find a cure for the disease - or at least shine some light on the cause of the damn thing. Of course, I pray a cure might one day be found for MND though I fear it won't come in my lifetime. More realistically, I hope I might just have achieved enough to help others in years to come. If I knew what caused the onset of the illness, it might help me to come to terms with it.

One of the best occasions during my illness was undoubtedly a fund-raising

Extra Time – The Final Chapter

reunion at Middlesbrough's Ladle Hotel. The evening was organised by my former Boro skipper Gordon Jones and Ron Darby, a man I had met through the ex-Boro and England captain George Hardwick. Knowing that my former team-mates of the 60's and 70's would be seeing me in a wheelchair for the first time, I wasn't particularly looking forward to the evening. I was never comfortable being the centre of attention in my wheelchair and was apprehensive that old friends like Stuart Boam would be shocked to see me in my condition.

Fortunately, the night turned out to be a marvellous occasion, not just for me but for all those who attended. It was a night full of nostalgia and much emotion in which I re-newed acquaintances with many of my former team-mates. Each of the players were introduced and applauded into the room and it was difficult to keep my emotions under control as Stuart pushed me to my table. One special moment came when Jack Charlton approached me at the end of the evening to say how well I had done. Having witnessed a similar scenario with Don Revie many years earlier, he knew how hard it had been for me to put on a brave face.

Money came in from so many unexpected sources as the months went by. My Mum and Dad contributed £1,000 from their savings. I felt embarrassed over it but they said they would give all their life savings to make me well again. My brother Chris has done much fund-raising through Billingham Golf Club where he is a member. People would walk in off the street and hand in cheques at Hilary's shop, ranging from anything between £5 and £100. We even received a lovely little letter and a cheque from two young boys called Kevin Naylor and Martin Weatherley who had raised £37 from a raffle and jumble sale they had organised. What amused me was that they went to the trouble of asking us for a receipt - which we always gave - to prove to their friends that they had donated the money and not spent it on themselves!

Meanwhile, I was overwhelmed with the letters of condolence I received from all corners of the earth. One came from Australia. Tim Benson, who I had coached as a young lad at Hartlepool, wrote a very kind letter from his new home in Perth after hearing about my illness from his mother.

He wrote: "What I can say about you, Willie...is that you certainly reached great heights as a very talented soccer player indeed, but more importantly you have reached an even greater height as a human being and one that I have admired ever since the age of 18."

I found inspiration in his words as he continued: "One quality in you that I would like to think I have and understand something about is that you are a fighter and never quit. If there is one thing I know and have learnt throughout my life it is that no matter how many times life knocks you down, you get up, you look it in the eye, then you hit it with everything you've got. Life has thrown a hurdle in your way, Willie. Sure, it is bloody high and wide. So pick yourself up, look it fair and square in the eye, then give it everything you've got. They can sap the strength but they can never dim the light inside - and yours shines brightly."

The fund-raising had taken over our lives and it became almost a full-time job to answer every letter and to send receipts for every donation, no matter how small. Hilary and I were swept along on a tidal wave of emotion but I was starting to get very tired and knew I was overdoing it in terms of my commitment to the fund-raising. Of course, it was difficult to say no when people were being so generous with their money and time. I was beginning to move more slowly and deliberately and began to wonder how long I could keep up such a hectic calendar. As time went on, I gave up my job while Hilary reduced her input to her business to just one day a week, giving us more time to deal with the donations whilst allowing us to spend our days together. We are indebted to Christine and all her staff for allowing us that quality time together.

Eventually, as my health began to fail me, I had to take a back seat to the real heroes - the fund-raisers who were prepared to devote so much time to the MND cause. If I had needed confirmation that all the hard work was worth it, then it came with a visit to Newcastle to see research into MND being carried out by Professor Pam Shaw and her small team. We had been given much support and financial assistance in terms of equipment and support aids from the Cleveland branch of the MND Research Fund and the local health authority, but I always felt that I would want the majority of the money we had raised to go towards research into the disease. The centre, with its dozen or so laboratories, where Professor Shaw heads her scientific team is conducting more research programmes into the causes of MND and potential cures than anywhere else in the UK. Hilary and I came away from our visit there greatly encouraged. Pam and her staff were extremely positive and it was evident that they truly believe they would one day make a breakthrough.

However, it frustrates and disappoints me that so little funding goes into MND research, as we discovered on a visit to the Research Fund's national headquarters in Northampton. Over the previous year just £2 million had been raised, of which only £375,000 had gone into research. That figure has been upped to £700,000 this

Extra Time – The Final Chapter

year but it still pales into insignificance when it is compared with the vast sums of cash being thrown at the Aids problem. I feel sorry for people with Aids, especially those who have caught it through blood transfusions, but the imbalance in terms of the level of publicity and fund-raising when compared to MND does upset me. Both conditions are quite rare but Aids has received huge publicity as a result of its high profile victims in Hollywood. Perhaps the actor David Niven and former England boss Don Revie remain the most famous people to have had MND so its profile has never been so high. As it thankfully remains rare, few drugs companies are interested in spending time researching cures for the condition. The brutal truth is that there just aren't enough people suffering from MND to make detailed research a sound investment for the drugs companies.

Fortunately, the big-hearted efforts of those who have helped the Willie Maddren MND Fund enabled me to hand over a cheque to Professor Shaw of £40,000 late in 1997, a sum which was further boosted by a generous donation of £50,000 by the Oddfellows Trust. We have since raised a further £40,000 and no doubt the profits from sales of this book will considerably boost that figure.

I had initial concerns of my own about the future welfare of my family. After my diagnosis, my insurance broker Malcolm Corking had assured me that my life insurance policies meant my wife and children would be well taken care of after my death. Ironically, the future looked very healthy financially when I died, but whilst I was living there would be considerable uncertainty over our finances. We had a quite substantial mortgage on our property and I wondered what would happen when I had to give up my job. We panicked a little bit and put our house up for sale to enable us to reduce our mortgage commitments.

All my worries were washed away, however, thanks to a magnificent gesture by Middlesbrough chairman Steve Gibson. I was overwhelmed with Steve's generosity in offering to host a benefit game in my honour with all proceeds to go to my family. It would ensure I was able to enjoy life to the full with my family whilst I was still alive. He actually wanted to grant me a benefit year in which many social events could have been organised to raise funds but I told Steve that the match alone would be enough. I wanted to be able to enjoy the remainder of my life without another list of social events to attend.

A small committee was duly formed to organise the match and there were initial discussions about Middlesbrough's opposition being Juninho's former club, Sao Paulo, or even Celtic. With less than a month to go to the scheduled game,

A Game I Can't Win

With Middlesbrough chairman Steve Gibson (left) and my former defensive partner Stuart Boam at a fundraising get-together in 1997.

however, I was becoming a little bit concerned that no team of stature had been confirmed. Finally, about three weeks before the big day, Hilary received a phone call from the club's chief executive Keith Lamb, who asked her to tell me that the opposition for my benefit match would be Inter Milan. "Oh, is that good?" she asked. "Well, when you tell Willie I think you'll find he'll be rather pleased!" he replied. It was almost inconceivable that my game should involve not only one of the giants of world football but also a Boro team which would include new signings Fabrizio Ravanelli and Emerson who would be making their first appearances in front of the Teesside public. Apart from Steve Gibson, I was most grateful to Keith Lamb for securing such attractive opposition and to Graham Fordy of the club's commercial department for his work behind the scenes. In addition, I had to thank my committee of Ray Robertson, the club's bank manager Tony Ford and accountant Rob Barrigan of Coopers & Lybrand.

As the date of the game approached, I became nervous about being the centre of public attention. I desperately wanted to thank the supporters who turned out on the day by walking on to the pitch with a microphone but was worried that my deteriorating health might make such a gesture impossible. By that time I was having to be fed by Hilary as I was no longer able to grip cutlery properly, I had also had a couple of falls. With that concern in mind, I joked with Steven that if I did fall flat on my face that he should go full length too as if it was a Jurgen Klinsman-style dive we had planned! However, I felt it would be safer to simply walk so far on to the pitch, wave to the fans and then make my way back out of the limelight.

I was gripped by nerves before travelling to the Cellnet Riverside Stadium on the day of the match. Strangely, those nerves disappeared the moment I got sight of the stadium as we travelled over Harold Shepherdson Way that morning. It was as if I was back where I belonged. I was back at my beloved Boro.

Over 20,000 fans packed into the stadium for the game to create a fantastic atmosphere. The few moments I stood in the tunnel with my family waiting to be introduced to the crowd seemed like an eternity such were the butterflies in my stomach. When at last it was signalled for us to go on, I could hear the words of Tina Turner's "Simply the Best" bellowing out across the park and as we emerged from the tunnel, the ovation was quite deafening. My bottom lip began to tremble as we walked on to the pitch, Middlesbrough and Inter Milan players on either side of us. Desperately fighting to keep myself under control, I nodded a gesture of thanks to Boro manager Bryan Robson and his Inter counterpart Roy Hodgson. Holding the hands of Laura and David, and with Hilary, Lucy and Steven close behind, I somehow found the strength to curb my emotions as I waved to the crowds to show my appreciation for their wonderful support.

Having turned 360 degrees, I gave club presenter Mark Page the nod that I would be happy to address the crowd and he handed me the microphone. Though I had a lump in my throat, I was amazed how composed I became. The crowd fell silent as they realised I was about to speak. I started by thanking the fans for their support and Steve and the club for making the day possible. I went on to say that looking round at these magnificent surroundings, it was clear the club had really hit the big time and I hoped the new-look Boro side would go on to become the most successful team in Middlesbrough's history. Finally, I added a reference to that inspirational letter I had received from Australia. "On a personal note," I added. "I'm still in there fighting and will continue to do so. They might take my strength but they will never dim the light."

I was proud to have said thank you and farewell to the people of Teesside in such a dignified manner. I think I just about made it before being overcome by emotion. I handed back the microphone and embraced Hilary on the pitch, an action which was greeted by another wonderful ovation. As I walked back past the line of players I could see that many of them were moved by the occasion. I managed to make my way back to the tunnel and was thankfully out of view of the spectators when the tears exploded as Hilary and I hugged one another. At that moment, Bryan Robson walked by and offered the use of his office if I needed a few moments to compose myself. I couldn't help but wonder what he must have thought of me.

A Game I Can't Win

Soon after that memorable day, I received another inspirational letter, this time from a guy called Allan Wilson, a Boro fan who, though he now lived in Florida had managed to attend the game with his 10-year-old son, Ben. He wrote that before the match he had tried to explain to his son why, in his mind, Willie Maddren deserved such an accolade but acknowledged it was difficult to get this over to his son as I had never been a Juninho or a Ravanelli. But he added: "When you walked on to the Riverside pitch, Ben looked around him, turned to me and asked: 'Dad, why are all these guys crying?' I stood with tears in my eyes and a lump in my throat. I was floored by the composure that you demonstrated as I, and tens of thousands others, bade you farewell. I was left with the task of explaining to Ben how so many lives can be inspired by the actions of an individual and how actions speak so much louder than words - and that Willie Maddren was one who had just got the job done right!" Perhaps if I had known that there were grown men crying I might never have got through that speech.

Steve Gibson made another special gesture on the day of the benefit match when he handed me two tickets for life for the Directors' Box at the stadium. That gave me all the encouragement I needed to attend Boro's home games on a regular basis and, after a decade without football, I became one of the club's biggest fans again. Eventually, I could no longer cope with the steps up to the Directors' Box but the problem was overcome thanks to the kindness of SLP who allow me to watch games from my wheelchair sitting inside their executive box. Although my health doesn't permit me to attend every match, I always make a special effort to get to Boro's big games and looking forward to each game helps to keep my spirits up.

Boro fans really got value for money in that 1996-97 season. With Juninho fulfiling his potential to become one of the world's greatest players alongside Ravanelli and Emerson, I was able to see the best football in Middlesbrough's history. Sadly, Emerson became a shadow of the player we had seen in the first six weeks of the season while it was clear Ravanelli, although banging in the goals, was unpopular in the dressing room. It was obvious that the team spirit would suffer from Ravanelli's petulance and Emerson's AWOL sagas when he disappeared back to Brazil. Much was made at the time about the Italian's big pay packet but I don't think his team-mates would have given a damn about that if he had been a good bloke and a team player. I doubt very much whether he would have been tolerated by players in my day. People like Stuart Boam, Graeme Souness, Bobby Murdoch or myself would have brought him into line. At the same time, Emerson, although popular in the dressing room, did nothing for Teesside in

Extra Time – The Final Chapter

terms of his escapades, bringing much negative media coverage of the area and angering the club's fans.

I continued to watch Boro on a regular basis following their relegation and I have to say they fully deserved their promotion back to the Premier League a year later. Having lost Juninho, Ravanelli and Emerson, Bryan Robson brought in players of class who offered both determination and reliability. This new look team is capable of grinding out results in a way that their predecessors found impossible. Schwarzer is the type of goalkeeper who will win you games, Townsend has added balance to the team and the signings of Branca and Armstrong were timely. The player who has really impressed me, however, is Paul Merson. He is on a different planet in terms of his vision, control, touch and passing ability. It is my dream to see Boro win a major honour and, having come so close three times in the recent past, I still live in hope that I might witness that special day.

The football club and its staff have kept in regular contact with me during my illness and I was honoured when, early in 1998, they named their innovative educational unit in my name. The Willie Maddren Centre, based in the stadium's East Stand, boasts three purpose-built classrooms where thousands of 10 and 11 year olds take lessons based around national curriculum subjects such as Maths and Geography - but all with a football theme. The first of its kind in this country,

Two generations of Boro stars at a reunion in 1997. I'm pictured seated, second right, with former Middlesbrough chairman Mike McCullagh alongside me

the centre is proving a huge success in forging ever stronger links between the football club and the local community. It is of no small comfort to know that, through the centre, I will be remembered not only by fans from the past but by the children of the present and the future. Naming the centre in my name was the greatest tribute Middlesbrough Football club could have paid me.

With the funds raised through my benefit match, I have been able to enjoy many special moments with my family. Though my health has become progressively worse, I have been determined to spend much quality time with Hilary and the kids. But the extra time I began to spend with them did initially highlight to Lucy and Steven just how reliant I had become on Hilary. Just days after the benefit game, we all took a week's break in Majorca but I know my eldest two were shocked by my slow, deliberate movements. Returning from an evening out, I had one of my most extreme laughing fits and was doubled up on the pavement. Young David believed I was crying and was naturally concerned. Later, in the hotel room he was sharing with Steven, Lucy and Laura, he asked Steven: "Is my Daddy dying?" Upset at David's innocent question, Steven had to make a quick exit on to the balcony where he cried uncontrollable tears.

Later that year, I was delighted when my eldest two were able to join the rest of us on a magnificent holiday to California, taking in Disney World in Los Angeles and the Grand Canyon. It was there that I used a wheelchair for the first time. I had known since receiving the prognosis that I would one day become wheelchair-bound but I had been putting it off and putting it off. I had found it difficult to contemplate the idea of not being able to walk, especially as I had once been so fit. Going into a wheelchair was a huge psychological hurdle as I felt people would start to look at me in a different light. However, I realised our visit to the USA would be perfect as it was a place where no-one knew me. I found the transition surprisingly easy and it soon became obvious that it was quite a perk for the family, as anyone accompanying someone in a wheelchair was allowed to the front of the queue on all Disney rides!

After Disney, I achieved the ambition of a lifetime with a visit to the Grand Canyon and I wasn't disappointed. It was everything I imagined and more. However, during the journey from Los Angeles to Flagstaff, close to the Canyon, I suffered the psychological blow of realising I was no longer able to drive a car safely. Soon after setting off on a nine-hour journey, I was shocked how tired my arms were even on the monotonous straight roads and on occasions the car drifted too much for my liking. That was the last time I drove a motor vehicle as I gave up there and then in the interests of safety. Poor Hilary had to drive the majority of that 2,000-mile round trip. Realising I would never again experience the pleasure and freedom of driving a car hit me hard. It was beginning to dawn on me how events were stacking up against me in terms of my physical condition.

There are countless obstacles all disabled people have to get over every day - obstacles that healthy people would never even think of. However, I was horrified by the lack of consideration flight operators give disabled people like myself. Hilary requested seats with extra leg room in a no smoking area for the journey out to California, explaining that her husband was terminally ill and had respiratory problems. I was dismayed, therefore, to discover myself in a seat near the back of the aeroplane, just one row away from the smoking area. Our return flight, with a different company, was worse if anything. We again pre-booked seats with extra leg room, only to find on boarding the 'plane that we had been placed in normal seats whilst behind us, next to the emergency exit with plenty of leg room, were sat a group of youngsters with their legs stretched out before them. Hilary expressed her annoyance to a stewardess, who referred to me by saying: "People like *that* are a liability and could cause an obstruction in the event of an emergency evacuation." In other words, people like me should wait till the end and burn!

There is, however, an amazing array of equipment designed to help disabled people like myself, as I discovered on a visit to a place called the Disability Living Centre at the Freeman Hospital in Newcastle during the relatively early stages of my illness. I remember feeling horrified to see many of the appliances - electric wheelchairs, stairlifts and kitchen gadgets - as I realised that some time in the future I would have to use them. I hoped it would be a long way off but just three months later I could no longer cut up my own food and had to rely on Hilary to dress me every morning.

Being fed by Hilary did, however, result in one amusing incident when David brought home for tea a school friend, Joseph Harley. Hilary was feeding me when the door bell sounded so she left her seat to answer the door. At that moment, the telephone rang so Laura left the room to answer it, while David left the table to see who was at the door. I had never previously met young Joseph but he instinctively left his seat and proceeded to feed me my dinner. It was as if he had done it all his life. I found it both touching and amusing that one so young should be so lacking in inhibitions where an adult might have hesitated. David rarely offers to feed me but, on seeing his school pal doing the honours on his return to the room he grabbed the spoon off him and rather jealously said: "That's my job!"

A Game I Can't Win

It was during our visit to Newcastle that I saw the Closomat Loo, a piece of equipment I still regard as by far and away the best investment we have made as it has helped me to retain my dignity. Basically, it cleans and dries your bottom, making the hygiene side far more comfortable and bearable. I would firmly recommend it to anyone unable to use their hands and reliant on others to take them to the toilet. When we have been away on holiday and no longer have such an item at our service, I think it is a piece of equipment Hilary appreciates too!

Among the kitchen gadgets at the disability centre was a special carving knife for use by the disabled. Typically, Hilary looked at it and made the sarcastic comment: "You've never found reason to use one of them so far so I can't imagine why you would start worrying about calving up the Sunday roast now!"

During one potentially embarrassing, but ultimately amusing, episode, I received a visit from a district nurse who called to offer me a piece of apparatus to assist me in going to the toilet. The apparatus consisted of a bag at the end of a long tube which was designed to strap to your leg in case you got caught short. At the end of the tube was a condom-type fixture. I was hugely surprised when the nurse asked me to drop my trousers as he needed to see the size of my penis, for the fitting of the "condom". As I dropped my trousers in embarrassment, I was greatly relieved to hear him utter the word: "medium". I don't know what I would have said had he sighed: "small"!

During those relatively early stages of my illness, the thought that I would one day completely lose my independence and be totally reliant on Hilary was a frightening prospect. Being unable to feed, clothe or clean myself, go to the toilet on my own or even walk were all frightening. Indeed, I perished the thought of having to use a wheelchair and viewed the prospect as the end of the world. There is certainly no doubt that it was the biggest psychological hurdle I have had to overcome. And yet I now look on my electric wheelchair as a God-send as it has given me so much independence.

I have to admit that I do find it very difficult when I go to Middlebrough games and fans and friends I have known for many years see me approaching in a wheelchair. I can't help but think perhaps they are looking at me and recalling how fit I was in my footballing hey-day. I hope they don't feel sorry for me. Rather, I would hope there is a sense of admiration that I have overcome the embarrassment of being in a wheelchair. I would like to think I am proving to many others that life doesn't end just because you are forced into a wheelchair. No doubt thousands of people - perhaps some of whom are reading this book - are contemplating getting over just such a hurdle, whether it be accepting life in a wheelchair or a lesser quality of life in some other way. I would like to be an example to them. As I am readily recognised by so many people every time I leave my house, I believe the embarrassment for me is greater than it is for the average person. I can understand anyone who finds such a change hard to adapt to but I know that it is worth sticking with.

To anyone who thinks it is the end of the world because they are facing the rest of their life in a wheelchair, perhaps as the result of some sort of accident, I do have this to say - I would swap places with you tomorrow. Believe me, if I was given the option right now to live to my 70's in a wheelchair I would settle for that quite readily and think how lucky I was to have so many years ahead of me with my family and friends.

There are times, of course, when I do find it hard. It would have been so easy for me to stay at home when Middlesbrough played at Wembley in the 1997 Coca-Cola Cup final. I imagined the reaction of the supporters would be one of great sympathy but I made myself go, if only for my family, and was overwhelmed by the warmth of the fans as I was wheeled through a sea of red and white along Wembley Way. For fully five minutes, hordes of people separated like the Red Sea, many of them patting me on the back, shaking my hand and wishing me luck as a chorus of "There's only one Willie Maddren!" rang out. It was one of the most moving experiences of my life. What's more, I could see that the looks on the faces of those people were not of pity but of admiration. At that moment, I realised I had made quite an impression on them, not only as a footballer but as a good human being. That means more to me than being a great footballer can ever mean. I feel privileged to have enjoyed such a special bond with the people of Teesside and that day was typical of the love and warmth they have given me throughout my career and during these last few difficult years. Despite the disappointment of the result which followed, that incredible experience made the whole trip worthwhile. Indeed, my family and I experienced very similar scenes as we again made our way down the same walkway to the national stadium before the 1998 Coca-Cola Cup final.

Of course, all of this would have been impossible without Hilary's help. She has coped with looking after me with contemptible ease. Prior to my illness, she was the sort of person who would put her head on the pillow and be sound asleep within two minutes. Ever since the MND took hold of me, however, her routine has involved turning me over at least 15 to 20 times a night whilst I often wake her twice a night to use the toilet. Bless her heart, Hilary has never to this day complained. Never once has she even breathed a sigh of displeasure or shown a lack of patience with me. I think of myself as being reasonably eloquent but I do not have the words to fully describe the admiration I have for her. She picks up on my every mood and knows instinctively if I am troubled, always there with a loving, reassuring glance or words of encouragement. I doubt very much if I could have coped as well if this illness had been the other way round and Hilary was the one suffering from it.

Sometimes she has had to be cruel to be kind by restricting the number of visitors I have at our home in Norton. Each day, I get visits from a steady stream of family and friends but Hilary knows that if I talk too much - and I will, given the opportunity - then my diaphragm aches. Consequently, she has occasionally hung a sign at the front door reading "No visitors today, thank you." That might appear quite rude but Hilary knows I'm now at the stage where if I receive too many visitors it leaves me feeling exhausted and with no energy for the children.

It is in those times when I am at my weakest that I am thankful that I made the decision to have my troublesome left knee replaced about two years into my illness. I had doubted that I would need the knee operating on but it eventually reached the point where it was unable even to support my weight whilst transferring from my wheelchair into a car. At the same time, it was giving me horrendous pain and was making life increasingly difficult so I knew there was only one way forward. With the bottom half of my body anaesthetised, I sailed through the two-hour operation without any pain. But even the sounds of Dire Straits blasted into my ear at full volume through headphones could not drown the noise of the saw, chisel and hammer as surgeon Mr Montgomery separated my femur and tibia. I was still on the operating table waiting for my knee to be stitched up when the anaesthetist Mike Tremlett took the unprecedented step of phoning Hilary and letting me speak to her to tell her the operation had been a success. Hilary had been naturally concerned about me undergoing a relatively major operation in my condition but was hugely relieved to know all had gone well.

Despite my determination to remain upbeat, I am finding it harder and harder to be positive about life and negative thoughts are creeping in. I even find Hilary dressing me so much more of an aggravation than I did not so very long ago. One morning as she dressed me, I said to her: "Surely you can't get any pleasure out of seeing me like this." Hilary's response was typically upbeat as she insisted: "I'd rather have you around as you are now than not at all." To know that she would gladly look after me for the rest of her life gives me a huge lift. Such words keep me going when I am feeling down, reminding me that I am serving a purpose in someone's life. But I don't want my quality of life to become so bad that it pains my family to look at me suffering.

I do think myself very lucky to have someone as mentally strong and loving as Hilary. No doubt there are many people with illnesses or disabilities who don't have someone like her to look after them. She is a true mother hen in the way she looks after me. Of course, she plays down her role with words like: "Well, you would have done the same for me if the roles were reversed." Yes, I probably would but I doubt very much if I could have been as supportive as she is 24 hours a day.

It is when I recall just how close I came to never getting to know Hilary that I realise how fortunate I have been. I first saw her when I accompanied my friend Peter Binks to a pub after we had played a local cricket match for Preston. "We'll go down to the Masham pub in Hartburn," he announced. "There's a bird working there with about a 40 inch bust - she really is something to see!" Arriving in the bar, we discovered the lady in question wasn't working that night but a barmaid called Hilary was. Despite missing out on the big-busted lady, I was quite taken with Hilary, who worked at the pub in a part-time capacity. In future visits to the pub, I always found her attractive, though I did think she looked a bit stuck up! As she eventually stopped working there, it was not until a year later that I held my first conversation with her, in Trenches nightclub in Middlesbrough. Enjoying a meal, I kept looking across the room, trying to remember where I knew this attractive blonde from. She was with another guy but I kept catching her eye. Then, her male companion left the table to pay the bill and Hilary had stood up and was about to leave the room when I remembered where I had seen her.

"Do you still work at the pub?" I asked, knowing full well she didn't.

"Oh, no," she replied. "I have my own florist's business." With that, she threw her business card on the table - obviously playing hard to get!

"I'll pop in to buy some flowers when it's Mother's Day," I said, though I knew that was fully six months away.

"You don't have to wait until Mother's Day," she smiled. That was all the encouragement I needed. I paid a visit to her shop a few days later when I asked her if the arrangement with the young man I had seen her with was permanent. She

A Game I Can't Win

explained he was only an acquaintance. We never looked back.

Hilary and I have always been close but the bond between us has been strengthened two-fold over these last few years. We have been fortunate to have enjoyed so much quality time together and yet we can't help but feel cheated that we will be denied the opportunity to grow old with one another and share all those experiences that most people take for granted. We get particularly tearful when we see pension and life assurance advertisements on TV, showing an elderly couple walking together hand-in-hand along a beach. That is an experience we will be denied so we have tried to look upon these last few years as a form of early retirement.

I do try not to be negative in front of Hilary and certainly never in front of my children. Even in my blackest moments, I've never shown any weakness in the company of Laura or David and I pray to God he will keep me strong, even at the bitter end.

Sometimes I do find it so hard to look on the bright side. In certain situations, I am given painful reminders of my physical inadequacy, none more so than the night our intruder alarm began to sound at 1am. Imagine how I felt when Hilary and my 12-year-old daughter had to go downstairs to investigate while I lay there, half asleep on Temazepam and unable to offer any help whatsoever. The next morning I insisted we buy a good house dog and I'm pleased to say we now have a four-legged addition to the Maddren household. In fact, "Max" growls at Hilary, who feeds him, so God help anyone who makes the mistake of attempting to burgle our house!

Of course, I will also be denied the many years of pleasure I would have expected seeing my youngest two children growing up and my eldest two getting married and establishing themselves in life. To compensate, I have had to lower my sights and take my enjoyment from more simplistic pleasures.

It breaks my heart to see other people playing football in the garden with David. I do try to join in as best I can, even from my wheelchair, but the frustration as a former professional footballer at not being able to give David the benefit of my experience is very hard to take. As I sit and look on helplessly, it is then that this disease is truly cruel. At the same time, Laura is showing a talent for netball and I would love to be able to pass on to her my knowledge of ball games. Instead, I am forced to sit on the sidelines and watch.

I have been to one or two of Laura's rounders games for the school but I am always conscious that she might be a wee bit embarrassed when I turn up in my wheelchair. On one occasion, while out with my brother Dave, I noticed the kids were in the playground and sat looking through the fence. Laura noticed me and came over to the fence with three of her friends. I didn't stay long but, as I came away, I wondered if I had done the right thing even showing my face. When David came home from school that day, he was upset and later revealed that some of his classmates had teased him and laughed about his Dad. At that moment, I made my mind up that I would never repeat that action again.

Laura often asks such intelligent questions about my illness. On one occasion she asked: "Daddy, if they find a cure will you be as you are now for the rest of your life or, like a baby, will you grow new nerves and get stronger again?" I was amazed at the quality of the question from one so young. She often questions Hilary about how she will be able to pick me up like she does now when she is old. Of course, we have never actually told Laura about the terminal side of the illness but I think she has read between the lines and is simply trying to see what her Mum's reaction is when she asks that question.

To compensate for not being able to join in with Laura and David, I often find myself taking immense satisfaction and enjoyment from simply sitting and studying their faces and mannerisms. I look at the expressions on the face of my young son - the way he contorts his face always makes me smile. I see Laura turning into quite a young lady though it is when I look at her face that I hurt most inside. She is such a sensitive, emotional girl. I know it will hurt all my children when I die but I think she will find it the hardest.

It hurts too to know I won't get the opportunity to walk my eldest daughter Lucy down the aisle. As a father, it had always been something I had looked forward to but now I know I won't be around for her wedding day. But I am extremely proud of Lucy, who is such a beautiful girl.

It is hard to accept that I will be denied the simple pleasure of going out for a beer or to a sporting event with my elder son, Steven. Everyone says he is a model of me at a similar age though I think perhaps he is better looking than I was. I know my illness has affected Steven badly as he doesn't like to talk about it. That's not to say it hasn't affected Lucy, as I know she loves me dearly, but she is more relaxed discussing it. I'm immensely proud of both of them for their academic achievements and the way they have both grown into mature adults. And yet it worries me that I will leave my family in a world where there is so much social decay. With the increasing availability of drugs and rise in violence, it hurts me to know that I won't be around to protect and advise them. That responsibility will fall with Steven as the man of the house and we have already had a little discussion with regard to that. I'm comforted to know he has promised he will always come round to look after everyone, to take David to football and so on.

Over the past couple of years, the MND has began to affect the muscles in my voicebox and my speech has become progressively more slurred. Having always enjoyed a good conversation, it frustrates the life out of me that my energy levels are often so low that I only speak out of necessity. A time will come when I can no longer speak at all and I used to worry that in my final hours I might not be able to tell Hilary, my children and my family how much I loved them. To avoid such a possibility, Hilary and I have made sure we have said all the things we want to say to one another. Others, like our friend David Bingham who died in a car crash, never get the chance to even say goodbye to their loved ones so in that way we count ourselves fortunate.

I think my facial appearance sometimes camouflages the real deterioration in my physical condition. Many people genuinely, rather than sympathetically, say that I'm looking well. It is probably true to say that I don't have the harassed look that I did as a manager or shop owner but nothing could be further from the truth than me being well. As I complete this book, I feel the illness has got me on the ropes but as yet it hasn't backed me into a corner. Some nights I go to bed as early as six o'clock as my posture is so uncomfortable after another day sat in a wheelchair. I wonder to myself how much discomfort can the human body take?

Despite the deterioration in my physical condition, MND does not affect your mental condition so it is rather frustrating when occasionally people talk to me as if I've "lost my marbles".

More worryingly, I am starting to suffer lengthy periods of fatigue and I am concerned that my respiratory muscles might be failing me. Thankfully, I am still able to swallow reasonably well so have maintained a decent diet to stay fit and free from infections, but once the diaphragm goes I will not have long left.

It is difficult in times like that to be positive. I have to tell myself that today was a down day but it was only a blip and tomorrow I will feel better. I will still be alive to watch my family growing up and can still give them my love and devotion. At the same time, I take pleasure from the world around me and will often sit in the garden and take time to appreciate the things I would never previously have stopped to even consider. I look at the beauty and colour of flowers, the way the light reflects off the trees and different birds which fly into the garden. I have four call ducks which give me endless pleasure as they wander around the garden mimicking one another or dipping and diving around the pond. As the light catches the ripples of the water, it gives me a wonderful feeling. Of course, had I been fit, I would undoubtedly have been working or out on the golf course, never stopping to take in such simple pleasures. I only wish I'd had time to stop and smell the roses during that hurly burly lifestyle I led for so many years.

And yet when I look back on my life there are very few regrets. In times of despair, I comfort myself by recalling my achievements in professional football. I have been so lucky to have enjoyed a wonderful life in the game, being hero-worshipped by thousands, getting paid well for something I'd have almost done for nothing, travelling the world at the expense of Middlesbrough and England, seeing many of the world's greatest landmarks and eating in the finest hotels and restaurants.

My greatest joy in life, surpassing any of my sporting achievements, was being present at the birth of three of my four children. The miracle of life. I have a wonderful wife and family with whom I have spent many special moments. So why not me? Why shouldn't it be me who will die early? I have been privileged to have achieved more and got more pleasure in one lifetime than many would in 10 lifetimes. I have experienced so much in life that is good and I guess you can't have it all ways.

Don't get me wrong. I would love to have lived to an old age. To grow old with my wife. To see my children grow up. To see technology advance. Like anyone else, I can't help but wonder what the world might be like in 30 or 40 years' time. I love life and am determined to hang on to every last breath.

This is one game I can't win but I will go down fighting. I pray to God that he will give me more and more Extra Time. And yet even on the day they die many people look back upon their life and wonder what it was all for. When I go, I will do so in the knowledge that I lived life to the full and, through my wife and children, I found total happiness. No man could ask for more.

Extra Time – The Final Chapter

In memory of Willie
and all those who have fought a similar battle

Hilary

22

Hilary's Story

February 10th in any self-respecting florist's diary is one to remember. It's the day of no return. You have ordered mountains of very expensive red roses and a wonderful array of spring and exotic flowers Then all you can do is hope and pray that you have enough flowers to fill all those orders for romantic gestures of love. It's a worrying time, to say the least, but one of expectation and excitement too.

So why did he have to come home and spoil it? Why did he have to put the spanner in the works and tell me something that I could do nothing about but worry? I'd had a very long and tiring day, picked up the kids from their grandma's and got home to a dark and empty house. I knew Willie was home because his car was on the drive but I also knew he wouldn't have had the forethought to put something in the oven for tea. I could feel the temper rising inside me as I marched through the front door and into the kitchen.

In the madness and chaos of a working mum's day, I had completely forgotten where Willie had been in those previous hours. I had pushed to the back of my mind the fact he was due to get the results of the tests he had recently taken to get to the bottom of an irritating twitch in his hand and arm. Because - let's face it, girls - when a woman has a cold, a man's got pneumonia. When a girl's got a toothache, the guy's got a raging abscess. So, true to that form, this man should have had nothing more than a trapped nerve.

So why did he have to come home and tell me he was terminally ill? Why did he have to tell me he was going to die when I had to make the tea, get two young children off to bed and be up at 5am the next day? In my exhaustion, I was furious with him. Why couldn't he wait for the RIGHT time? But then there never is a right time to tell your wife you are going to die prematurely, is there?

That night, we talked quietly and softly about the fact that they may have got the diagnosis wrong. Maybe it was all just a big mistake. We didn't sleep much, just laid silently in each other's arms with 101 thoughts whizzing around our heads. But for the next few days it was business as usual. I had a florist's shop to run and life just had to go on. It wasn't until a week later when work had settled down, Valentine's Day had been and gone and I too had spoken to the specialist that I finally had an opportunity to take a day off. Willie was at work while our children, Laura and David, were at school. Home alone, with only my thoughts for company, the terrible truth sank in. The father of my children, my husband, my best friend was dying.

As I sat in the lounge, the tears I had held back for the sake of Willie and the children began to flow. Quickly, the sobs became uncontrollable, ear-splitting screams and howls of utter despair, pity and anger. My wails echoed through the house for hours. All those pent up emotions poured out inexorably. Why me? Why us? I felt my life had ended at 36. But I couldn't cry in front of Willie. Allowing him to see me cry would have been like admitting that I had accepted the diagnosis, it would have been showing a weakness, and I had to be strong. I knew Willie would have enough on his plate just coping with the knowledge that his body was going to deteriorate before his eyes. Strong I had to be and was going to be. And, as no-one else knew of our dreadful secret, life had to go on as normal. Eventually, I could go on crying no longer and I knew I had to stop, if only for fear the neighbours would think I was being murdered. Not that stopping was easy. In fact, I had to bite on a cushion to shut myself up.

In stark contrast to Willie's typically forgiving "Why not me?" approach, I was angry. Many times I did ask "Why me?" or, rather, "Why us?" I seemed to have spent all my life working hard and finally seemed to have got there, wherever there is. I had a great husband, two lovely children, my own successful business, a nice house and two cars. Coming from a very average middle class family, that was as much as I had ever dreamed of having. I had never aspired to anything more. Even the timing of this dreadful news seemed so cruel. Life had become so much simpler, less stressful and frenzied over the past year. The pandemonium of professional football and the financial worries that come with owning a large sports business were behind us. At last, our life was our own, revolving, as it should, around us as a family. It had been like that for 12 months and that is how I wanted it to stay. But now this horrible, black shadow had descended over our lives and things would never be the same again.

Of course, there is no answer to the question "Why me?" and yet I couldn't help asking what I had done to deserve this. I had been a good girl, or so I thought. I hadn't caused my parents too much grief, unless you count the time I was nearly expelled from college at 19, when I was found with a boy in my room in an all girls dormitory. Or the time when, at 21, I spent a year travelling across America on my own. Arriving alone in downtown Los Angeles late one night, clutching only a well-worn suitcase and a piece of paper scrawled with my cousin's telephone number, I walked two blocks in the dark before spotting a large group of tough-looking, young males standing on a street corner. "Could you tell me where the nearest telephone box is please?" I asked them politely, in what must have sounded like a typical English accent. I was well travelled and considered myself worldly wise, but I am perhaps fortunate to still be here to tell the tale of such stunning naivety. But those minor mishaps aside, what had I possibly done to deserve this terrible tragedy?

I never did get used to the idea that I would lose Willie, the man I thought I would spend the rest of my life with. But I did eventually come to accept it and we cherished the quality time we spent together. Typical of the man, he took all the blows and just got up and got on with it. But maybe I shouldn't have expected anything less of him. When, aged 24, I had told my parents that Willie and I were going to live together, my mother asked, "How do you know he's the right one?" I simply reminded her that she had spent her life telling me that I would know when I met the right one - and he was.

The ensuing years were to put so many obstacles in our way – some bigger than others – but we happily jumped them all together. During his illness, we grew so close. I can only describe it as a bond that simply could not be broken. There is a Celine Dion song in which she sings about her lover being her legs, voice and strength. That is how we felt. Willie wrote of the love we had being something that few in the world would experience. At the time, I thought he was wrong. Only experience and my advancing years have taught me that he was right. In my naivety, I believed most couples had to feel the way we did, at least when they get married, but I now accept that many do not.

How we ever got married is a wonder. Willie nobly asked my father's permission for my hand in marriage but sadly forgot to ever ask me. The closest

Hilary's Story

thing I got to the magic and romance of a marriage proposal was, "If you want to get married this year it will have to be May 12th." Of course, it was the only date free in his calendar of football, football and more football.

Ah yes, how can I forget those years when the ceaseless demands of the professional game threatened to engulf our very lives? Had we not been newly weds, still madly in love, our relationship may have come under unbearable pressure. As it was, those rose-tinted glasses of early married life were our saving grace. Back then, the fact that Willie was almost never home - and that when he was his mind was everywhere but with me - just didn't seem to matter. He was offered the job as Middlesbrough's manager on our return home from honeymoon – and it was unrelenting stress for the next 18 months. And let me explode the myth of *Footballers' Wives* here and now. Back then, at least, glitz and glamour didn't even come into it.

A mansion fit for a king and his queen? We weren't even the best off in our modest, middle class Eaglescliffe close. In fact, our new house was undoubtedly the least impressive on the street. Whilst our neighbours enjoyed the luxury of landscaped gardens and new patios, ours remained untouched bare earth until we could afford to pay for its transformation more than 12 months after we had moved in. Wall-to-wall interior design? Our hall, stairs and landing sported a natty roll of industrial ribbed carpet Willie got cheap from a dodgy door-to-door dealer, while the spare room boasted my mother's hand-me-down bedroom carpet, complete with disintegrating foam backing. His and hers Ferrari and Merc? Try Willie's club car, a dark blue Ford Sierra, and my work van! No, there were no flashy motors, dream holidays to sun-drenched beaches or expensive designer outfits in the life of this particular footballer's wife. I won't pretend we were poor, but we certainly were not rich. We were just normal. As normal, at least, as you can be when one of you is manager of Middlesbrough Football Club, a job I readily accept is beyond the wildest dreams of many of the club's supporters, regardless of Willie's meagre remuneration in comparison to his modern day successors.

Our only extravagance was to eat out at weekends, normally at The Kirk as it was just down the road from our house. Busy with my own formative business, I rarely attended Boro's games, but would keep my ears peeled for the score coming through on the radio to see if we were eating in or out that night. A win would mean a nice meal out, a loss and we would stay in with a Marks and Spencer special and a couple of bottles of wine.

Extra Time – The Final Chapter

It wasn't the done thing for Willie to be seen out enjoying himself after a defeat. But when we did go out, the nights were rarely our own. Spotting Boro's manager eating in the same restaurant, supporters would simply pull up a chair and talk football, oblivious to the fact that Willie was eating a meal with his wife. They didn't even look at me, it was as if I was invisible. And yet I just accepted that it came with the job and, as Boro manager, Willie was public property. I doubt very much I'd have been quite so understanding 10 years down the line but these were our blissful, early days of married life and I wasn't about to make a fuss over a few over-exuberant football fans. Willie, as always, was the perfect gentleman with our uninvited guests. He would always give them his time, showing patience and warmth as they quizzed him about his team selection, tactics or potential new signings.

February 1st 1986 was the last time our Saturday night dining experience was determined by 22 men kicking a bag of air around a pitch. That was the day Willie was sacked. And I was ecstatic! The situation at the club had become increasingly desperate over the previous months. With every disappointing result Willie became ever more determined to sort it all out himself, becoming increasingly distant from the rest of us. Lucy and Steven would spend their Sundays with us but even as Willie played with them in the local park it was clear his mind was at Ayresome Park, probably picking the team for next week's match or questioning his tactics for the previous day's fixture. Sunday mornings were inevitably spent with Willie's head buried in the morning newspapers, studying the league tables and working out how a win, draw or defeat might affect them. I could have given him anything to eat or drink because he would not have noticed. I doubt he would even have registered a flicker of interest had I served up a sheep's head for his lunch. It was clear he was under great pressure and yet not once did he take out his frustration on the children or I. I don't recall him ever even raising his voice or displaying anger with us. He was never moody or sullen. Perhaps those who said Willie was too nice to be a football manager were right. But for all Willie's commitment to the Boro cause it just wasn't to be.

Early afternoon on that fateful day I had booked a table for two at a local restaurant. But no sooner had the radio at the florist's brought news of Boro's defeat than I called the restaurant to cancel our table. Of course, such calls had previously been made more times than I cared to remember, but I knew this time it was different, that with this result Willie would lose his job. The girls at work were so disappointed for me. By contrast, I was elated. I was going to get my husband

Hilary's Story

back and was determined to celebrate. Publicly quaffing champagne on such a night was a non-starter, so I made plans for what proved to be a great night in. Naturally, Willie was gutted, but he was relieved too. He knew in different circumstances he would have made a success of the job but the odds had always been stacked against him. He had endured unbearable stress and pressure, and now a great weight had been lifted from his shoulders. As we drank and ate, the commiseration calls flooded in from well-meaning friends, but all I could think of was that we had our life back.

Willie being Willie, however, there was no putting his feet up for a much-needed rest. He always needed a challenge and quickly turned his attentions back to his sports retail business, which he had been able to devote only limited time to over the previous 18 months. Typical of the man, he quickly got the business back on an even keel before taking the brave and adventurous decision to move to the recently opened Teesside Retail Park. At a time when only the big multiples had taken the plunge to move to the shopping park, Willie displayed great foresight and vision to spot the massive potential that would, sadly, only be realised when it was too late for his own business.

He was a perfectionist to his detriment at times. But Willie only knew one way to work and that was to give the job in hand his absolute all. Sadly, that meant too often he didn't spend enough quality time with his family, a mistake he confesses to in this book. I well remember the day he took a rare afternoon off from his usual routine of working all the hours God sent. I was delighted we would be spending some time together, as I had taken to daydreaming about us having a family treat. But what did he do? He played golf. It was a stress buster, apparently. I guess I should have joined him. Instead, I played the dutiful wife and rarely complained, though I do confess I resorted to not cooking him any tea when he came home. He slowly got the hint. It's ironic, because in the years after his death I would have done anything, suffered any kind of life, if he had just been there to share it with me and the children. Hindsight is a wonderful thing.

Extra Time – The Final Chapter

My Kid Brother

I never thought I would experience the day
When my heart would be broken in two,
When my brother Willie had accomplished
All he could possibly do.

He's been my inspiration;
His loving memories will never go,
When I am down, I pick up my pen
And tearful thoughts will overflow.
I remember his first cry the night he was born,
Seeing his angelic little face so cute and forlorn.

I can picture him as a toddler kicking his first football,
He showed talent in his infancy superior to us all.
He played his heart and soul out on Young Street's common ground
With his little chubby legs, his freckled face, rosy and round.
Our brothers Dave and Chris encouraged and brought him on,
They too had football in their blood all were fit and strong.

Willie played for Port Clarence Juniors,
Where a scout spotted his potential.
He had a trial for Boro,
From then on his life was eventful.
My brother never got bigheaded, his modest nature would think that wrong,
But he remembered with pride his Haverton days
Where his roots once did belong.

R.I.P My Idol

by Claire
(Willie's Sister)

23

The Last "I Love You"

I was besotted with Willie but I don't think even I realised just how special he was until I saw how he coped with his illness. It brought out certain qualities in him that might never have surfaced had he been fortunate enough to live a long and healthy life.

My children will confirm that I do not have a single ounce of compassion when it comes to bumps and scrapes, aches and pains. I am not a good nurse and probably an even worse patient, as my dentist would no doubt agree. However, those years of nursing Willie were a pleasure, thanks to his incredible attitude. During his five-year battle with MND he went through immeasurable discomfort and periods of sustained frustration but never once did he complain. Never once did he say "I can't take this anymore". He had such a will to live and was determined to do so whatever the circumstances.

Perhaps I should have known that Willie would conduct himself with such dignity throughout his illness. Ever since I had known him he had suffered great pain in his knee from the injury that ended his football career. With the cartilage completely worn away, his knee crunched as he walked. The sound of that knee accompanied us on many an afternoon stroll, and he would limp in pain as he playfully chased the children around the garden. But not once did he complain. He simply got on with it.

It was with the same determined dignity that he confronted an illness that so engulfed our lives for so many years. He didn't want to become a burden to the family unit, and would sometimes sit uncomfortably in his wheelchair for hours if he believed I was too busy with the children to help him lie down for a rest. He never grumbled about the severe sleep deprivation he suffered, brought on by spasms and twitching. He simply never complained.

Extra Time – The Final Chapter

Remarkably, Willie never became bitter that his life would be cut short. He did, however, find it ironic when he read about people who were going to sue because they had been wrongly diagnosed with a terminal illness. He would joke how he wished someone would tell him it had all been a big mistake and he was going to be fine after all. In all seriousness, Willie knew that people had been through real trauma due to misdiagnosis but he would so love to have been given the chance to get on with the job of living.

During those years we grew increasingly closer, facing the ever more difficult challenges together. In the final years of Willie's life, as the MND took its toll, our lives were transformed to the point when it became hard to imagine a world outside our own front door. And yet the ensuing year that followed that fateful day when Willie revealed to me he had a terminal illness had proved that life could be relatively normal. As so few people initially knew of his illness, we were able to plod on in much the same way as we had before. Discussions with couples in similar situations to ours have also revealed that one particular response we had is an almost universal reaction when faced with such circumstances. When you are told you are going to die, it seems there is an urgency to get intimate with your partner on a more regular basis. In fact, Willie and I used every opportunity to get close. When, a few months later, he was still around and I was shattered, we agreed that the urgency had gone and we should get intimate a little less often!

As Willie's condition worsened, our social life naturally took a dramatic change. We rarely went out to parties or to dinner with friends. Night time was a no-go area for him. By the time it came to 7pm he was ready for his bed, not necessarily for sleep but for a change in posture. After sitting in his wheelchair all day he enjoyed stretching out on the bed and enjoying a little movement in his limbs. For a while at least I continued to accept invitations and would attend social events on my own. Invariably, within half an hour I would realise I didn't want to make small talk about the weather, babies, people's jobs or their fantastic holidays. I began to decline invitations and in time people stopped asking. I am sure friends understood it wasn't a snub, I would just rather be at home having a conversation with myself. And I do mean with myself. As Willie's voice deteriorated I became quite adept at holding a one-way conversation and winning an argument in double-quick time.

Unlike those relatively normal early months following his diagnosis, our new life could hardly have been more different from the one we had previously enjoyed.

The Last "I Love You"

It was as if we had we been transported to another planet. For Willie, there was no more rushing to business appointments, deadlines to meet or even strolls on the golf course. His days had become one great struggle just to cling on to some sense of normality.

In time, he required 24-hour-a-day care just to survive. He needed someone to dress him, wash him, feed him and read to him, someone to sit and keep him company, to make him smile and to make him laugh. And someone to be there for him when he cried through the dull ache and pain he suffered as a result of his wasting muscles and extreme lack of protection around his bones. To relieve his pain during his final months, I had to master the unenviable task of administering morphine directly into his spine via a tube. And yet these were not sad times. They were just 'life times', things we all have to go through and experience some time in our life, and perhaps they made me a better person.

It is difficult to make the best start to the day when your sleep is interrupted seven or eight times a night. And we are talking about me here. Fortunately, after some trial and error, Willie got his medication sorted, enabling us both to have a relatively restful night. There were the tablets to stop the twitching. Then one to stop the ache in his shoulders, for as he lost more and more muscle bulk his joints ached as he slept on them. There were more tablets to stop excessive salivation and a sleeping concoction to knock him out. And for every tablet he took, there would be more medication to counteract any detrimental side-affects.

As you do when you have a newborn baby in the room, I woke regularly to check Willie was still breathing. On numerous occasions each night I would wake to turn him over, from one side of the bed to the other, knowing he would be in pain if he stayed in one position all night. I would physically roll him to the other side of the bed, before slipping back in on the opposite side. This tiring procedure would be repeated over and over again throughout the night to the point where, after a year or two of doing so, I'm sure I was able to do it in my sleep.

Willie's resting was seldom deep and he would occasionally wake and ask to be put on the loo. This entailed a long and weary process, so I would often spend 20 minutes trying to talk him out of the idea. When I finally gave in I had to man-handle a 13-stone, six-foot man out of a bed, on to a chair with castors, wheel him to the bathroom, then very carefully position him on the loo. This whole, exhausting process would take up to 10 minutes. I would then lie on top of the bed, leaving him to his ablutions. I have to confess that on more than one occasion I drifted off into a deep sleep, waking with a start an hour or so later with poor Willie still sitting on the loo in some discomfort. His voice had become so weak that he couldn't make himself heard with a shout, and the truth is I was normally so tired I wouldn't have heard him anyway.

Even without my occasional unplanned naps, the subsequent journey back to bed meant the whole process would often take as long as 45 minutes. That is if there were no mishaps on the way, such as the time when I was putting Willie, sleepy with Temazepam, back into bed at three in the morning. In attempting to balance his large frame on the edge of the bed, I lost control and he started slipping through my hands. Experience had taught me there was little I could do to avoid the inevitable so, rather than risk hurting my back trying to catch him, the easiest thing to do was to let him fall slowly to the ground. Unfortunately, this meant he would end up in a heap on the floor, and lifting a dead weight from that position was beyond my strength or ability. This would, understandably, become quite distressing for Willie, so I would make him comfortable on the floor and cover him with a blanket while I went to get our 14-year-old daughter out of bed to help me lift him. Poor Laura never complained. It would take much effort and a great deal of ingenuity to lift him in stages from the floor on to, first, a little footstool, then, once he had recovered a little, on to a chair and then finally on to and into the bed. Each manoeuvre was perfectly practised to military precision. We would all then return to sleep, at least until the next roll-over.

It was usually around five in the morning when I would hear him fall into a very deep and comfortable sleep. With a little luck, he would remain in that restful state until eight or nine o'clock. This gave me a little time to get up and take the children to school. Both Laura and David had their own alarm clocks from a very early age and always got themselves up without a helping hand. They would wash, dress, eat their breakfasts and have their coats on ready to go before shouting me. Exhausted from the night's adventures, I would wearily roll out of bed and pull a tracksuit over my nightie before driving them to school. I often wondered what a sight I would have looked if the car had broken down while I was in that early-morning state. It's no exaggeration to say I normally looked like a tramp.

Back home from the school run, I could normally grab an hour to myself, taking the chance to eat breakfast and read the morning paper. Even if he did wake up, Willie would stay in bed to allow me that little bit of time to myself, for the real work was about to start. I would sometimes take him breakfast in bed.

The Last "I Love You"

Alternatively, it could be lunchtime before he had his porridge if he had to wait to get bathed and dressed first. He would eat a bowl of porridge slowly and determinedly, usually taking an hour out of the day to finish his breakfast. Having lifted each spoonful to his mouth, there was nothing else for me to do but sit and watch him savour each mouthful. Breakfast finally over, the next 90 minutes would be taken up washing and dressing Willie before he would finally arrive downstairs, via a chairlift, all spruced up and ready for lunch.

There are so many things we take for granted when we're fit and well. Willie's illness even affected the way he dressed and the clothes he wore. Style inevitably went out of the window, replaced by the necessity of practicality. Trousers now required an elasticated waist to make them easier to get on and off, and to make them more comfortable around his stomach. I also took to buying his trousers in a longer length to avoid them appearing half-mast when he was sitting in a wheelchair. Of course, it didn't matter that they were too long when he stood up, as he wasn't walking anywhere. Shirts and sweaters had to be big and roomy with a large neck opening to allow them to be pulled on and off easily without the risk of pulling at his weakened neck muscles. All of his clothes had to be of the sort that could be easily washed and tumble-dried as there were frequent spillages of food and drink while various different people fed him.

Coats had to have long sleeves to cover his hands while in the wheelchair. Even though Willie could drive the electric chair himself he couldn't wear a glove while doing so and therefore needed a long sleeve to protect his hand from the elements. All outdoor clothing required a hood to protect him from the biting wind, while footwear presented its own demands. Shoes had to be larger than necessary so they didn't restrict his feet as he sat all day. On the other hand – or should that be foot? – shoes that were too big made the little walking and transferring he did dangerous. We tried to avoid laces, while the soles of shoes had to be smooth enough to allow his feet to slide over carpet but have enough tread to stop him falling. Only when attending Boro games did Willie insist on retaining his former smart image, always preferring to wear a collar and tie. Shirts had to be bought a size bigger to allow plenty of room around the neck but, with some expert lessons on tie-fastening, I became a competent Windsor knot aficionado.

Most days were spent at home. We were fortunate to have a lovely, large garden and Willie would sit in the conservatory for hours on end, reading the daily paper - always starting from the back page and moving forwards, of course. Lunch would be long and leisurely, not from choice, because of the fabulous surroundings or the quality of the food, but because there was no other way. It would take him an hour just to eat a poached egg on toast followed by a bowl of custard, every mouthful graciously given by me or another member of the family.

After lunch, a visit from David Mills, George Smith, Bill Gates, Gordon Jones or another of his old teammates would make Willie's day. Even when his speech was at its worst, he revelled in listening to recollections of their playing days and the fun they'd had taking part in a sport they'd have done for nothing but actually got paid for doing. On the rare days when Willie was very down, I would try to deter people from coming in to see him. On answering the door I would warn them that he was not too well. Then, blow me if they didn't stick their head round the door and he would greet them with a huge smile and welcome. It made me sound so contrary. I am sure his friends thought I was just being dramatic and imagining he was not too well. And yet the minute they left he would sink back into gloom again. I think those moods were only ever witnessed by those very close to him, like Lucy, Steven, his brother Dave and I. He did not want the rest of the world to see he was feeling down.

Those regular visits from his few close friends were a blessing for me too. I would use the opportunity to sneak upstairs and finally get dressed, for the demands of time meant it was not uncommon to find me still in jogging pants and fleece – my nightie thankfully hidden beneath - at two in the afternoon. I recall on one occasion a friend very politely commenting on my appearance, that I always seemed to be wearing the same old clothes. I just grinned and silently thought: "If only she knew how hard it was to find the time to get dressed, let alone go shopping." In fact, the things that ladies love to do, such trivial niceties as a bit of retail therapy and lunching out, were but distant memories. If I needed something new to wear for a special occasion I would have to arrange for a sitter before sneaking out. But there was no time for browsing around the shops of Newcastle or the Gateshead MetroCentre. Instead, it was usually Middlesbrough and one-stop shopping in Binns for everything from clothes, shoes and face cream, then straight back home.

I never once thought of the 24-7 care Willie required as a chore. In fact I relished the time we were alone together. I just loved being with him, and would have spent the rest of my life looking after him if that had been God's wish. Even so, there were times when the situation got the better of me. One of these came when tackling the not inconsiderable challenge of an evening meal, another long and laborious routine which on this particular occasion resulted in me hitting the roof – or, rather, Willie's dinner hitting the ceiling.

Maybe I should explain. Willie's diet had gradually changed to accommodate the fact that his ever-weakening muscles meant even swallowing food had become a difficult and time-consuming task. His meals were therefore usually either soft - such as fish in sauce, rice pudding or custard-based dishes - or liquid, such as soups. Perhaps as a result of the extreme volumes of medication he was taking, his taste buds had unfortunately lost much of their sensation and he found food bland and tasteless. On this one particular evening, I was feeling very fatigued from a long day and was not impressed when he turned his nose up at the custard dessert I had prepared for him. In its place I offered him yoghurt, but within two spoonfuls he had made it clear he wasn't interested in that either. The night was now wearing on, the children were in bed and the world events of the day were being replayed on the evening news, but I wasn't giving up just yet.

Undeterred, I headed back to the kitchen and made him a bowl of semolina, returning with a determined belief that this time there would be success. Once again, I began the process of feeding Willie and it seemed to take an age for him to eat two very slow mouthfuls of semolina. Imagine then my despair when he dared to turn his nose up at my pudding once more. Letting out a loud, exasperated sigh I thrust my hands into the bowl, scooped out the now very cold and thick semolina, made it into a ball and threw it upwards. Incredibly, not only did this huge ball of semolina stick to our artexed ceiling but it actually blended in with the textured pattern. In fact, it is still there to this day! I was fuming, but Willie had the audacity to sit and giggle at my actions like some naughty schoolboy. How can you get mad with someone that does that?

After most evening meals Willie would listen to Laura and David read or help them with their homework. Having been very bright at school and still owning a good memory for fact, it would frustrate him to death when he knew he could help the kids with the homework but just couldn't make himself understood. Fortunately, I could understand him most of the time – in fact I had come to know his every mood and emotion without him usually needing to say a word – but his inability to communicate to others through words would sometimes get the better of him. He could become very frustrated when people simply couldn't understand what he was saying and would stamp his feet on the footboard of his wheelchair.

Extra Time – The Final Chapter

The rattling noise this made would make everyone sit up and take note. However, our dog, Max, always thought he was about to be scolded and would hotfoot it out of the room.

A device called a Lightwriter, which translated typed words into speech, helped overcome the communication to some degree, though once Willie lost mobility in his fingers it became an arduous task merely to say "Hello". He did, however, pre-set several sentences into the machine. "I would like a cup of tea", "I am tired" and "Hello, how are you?" were all frequently selected. Seldom heard but conveying a clear and concise message was the one he reserved for those who annoyed him – "F*** off!"

The day would come to a close with a mixture of warm drinks, medication and the continual buzz of Sky Sports in the background. He must have been the most well-informed person around as to what was going on in the world of sport. A Saturday morning ritual was to watch Sky's *Soccer AM* programme, which was coincidentally on air for the same length of time as it took Willie to have his breakfast and get dressed, so we both became hooked to the show's offbeat action. It's fair to say that Willie much preferred Saturday mornings to our Monday to Friday ritual, when he was subjected to watching several hours of *Richard and Judy*. Well a girl has to keep abreast of what's going on in the world too!

Throughout this time, the housework just piled up, along with the washing and ironing. Such tasks really didn't seem important any more and would always keep for another day. I had the rest of my life to do housework. My priorities lay with Willie's needs, except for the one day a week when I would spend time in my shop. That was where Willie's devoted brother Dave would step in. He was a tower of strength for Willie, frequently sitting with him to allow me to go to work or attend school activities with the children. They would quite often have a boys' adventure day out, which might be a trip to Whitby in our specially converted transit van, which allowed Willie to stay in his wheelchair and be driven lock, stock and barrel into the back of the vehicle. This negated the arduous task of manhandling him into a car seat before loading up his wheelchair and paraphernalia.

In time, it was no longer possible to leave Willie alone for any length of time as, sadly, he could do nothing for himself beyond moving around the house on his electric wheelchair. He didn't even have the strength to lift his hand back up if it slipped off the wheelchair's armrest. Willie decided we should advertise for a nurse to care for him at home one morning a week. He felt it would give Dave and I a rest and allow me to pop out on important errands without worrying over him. After we had interviewed several very nice ladies, in walked a ray of sunshine called Yvonne MacDonald. With her great personality and lovely, smiley face, Willie took to her immediately. We offered her the job there and then. It was only at this point, as we chatted, that Yvonne revealed that her husband was Gary MacDonald, a player Willie had released from Middlesbrough during his days at the club's manager.

When she had gone, Willie looked concerned and let out a big sigh. He would be reliant on this woman to look after him in my absence and couldn't help but wonder if, as an act of revenge for her husband's treatment, she would spit in his tea! Fortunately, we needn't have worried. Yvonne proved a first class carer, becoming a great member of our extended 'family' and helping out right until his passing.

The truth was it was hard to imagine there was another world outside our front door, a world where people ran and walked and rushed around, and where they didn't have their daily routine ruled by what hospital appointment they were due to attend or which healthcare professional was due to visit. Don't get me wrong, without the dedicated help of those people Willie's life would have been so much more difficult. The support and service we received from the local GP and hospital was second to none, while the daily visits from nurses and physiotherapists were a Godsend.

Then there were the regular short stays in the Butterwick Hospice, where Willie's medication would be reassessed, especially as it would sometimes take weeks or even months to get the right balance of his drugs concoction to avoid doing him as much harm as good. The staff came to know Willie and his mischievous ways as well as anyone. He always had a huge grin for all the nurses and staff who seemed to relish his visits. Following his death, I received the most wonderful card from some of them, saying it had been a pleasure to nurse him. That may seem like such a strange sentiment but it was one I shared. The few days he would spend at the hospice were also supposed to offer me some respite. Unfortunately, I couldn't stay away. All I wanted to do was be by his side. With communication an ever more difficult challenge for him, I wanted to be there in case he couldn't be understood. Of course, the hospice staff dealt with patients like Willie every day, but I just couldn't bring myself to let go, even when I desperately needed the rest.

Extra Time – The Final Chapter

Far from being a place of doom and gloom as those who have never experienced such an establishment might believe, the hospice was full of laughter and fun. Indeed, it was Willie's philosophy that people didn't go there to die but to help them live longer. He so enjoyed the daily baths and aromatherapy but the one particular place there he loved was its little chapel. When he attended services there I could see the frustration in his face that he couldn't belt out the hymns as he had always done. On other occasions it was calm, cool and reverent, and Willie loved just sitting in the stillness. Somehow he always took great strength from his visits there. Every year since his death I have placed flowers in the chapel, before taking a few moments to just sit and remember. I feel that he must be with me when I am there as that chapel was always so close to his heart.

It was at the hospice that Willie eventually lost his long, brave fight for life and passed away peacefully on the morning of August 29 2000. His wish had been that he would die in his own home, but when the time came I knew that it was better for us all if he stayed in the hospice. He was initially taken in for some respite care as he had been particularly unwell at home, but his condition worsened quickly. At first, he could still communicate via his eyes and gestures, but it became evident he required more medication to ease his discomfort.

I vividly remember the sadness in his eyes as I explained to him that the hospice staff would administer more painkillers but only at his request, as he had to be aware of the fact that they were likely to send him into a deep sleep that he may not wake from. It was only at this moment we both knew the time had come. He would not be going home this time. It seems strange now but until then I don't think I had realised he was about to leave us. In fact, I think it was only then that Willie realised he'd had enough, the time was right.

Once the extra medication had kicked in, he went into a deep sleep, never to open his eyes again. And yet he stayed with us a few more days, precious moments that will remain with the children and I forever. The wonderful nurses laughed and joked with him continually and, despite his deep slumber, his lips would curl at the edges and we knew he could hear us. Two days before his death, my brother John and his Brazilian wife Relindes made the long trip from the United States to bid their farewells. On entering the room, she addressed him in her usual broken English. Willie's face lit up, he knew she was there. He was always so fond of her that I sometimes think he hung on knowing they were on their way from the States.

I have special memories too of a Sainsbury's ready-made picnic the four

The Last "I Love You"

children and I enjoyed as Willie slept. Sunbeams shone into his room as we opened the French doors on to the patio outside and sat together on the floor. It was a surreal occasion, but certainly not sad or morbid. As the five of us laughed, joked and reminisced, I glanced at Willie and knew how happy he would be to have his family around him in such fine form. None of us can choose how we spend our final days but Willie's one big fear was that his loved ones would sit around his bed waiting for him to die. I think he would have been pleased with the way things worked out.

On the morning of his passing at 10.30, Steven and Lucy were called as it was feared he didn't have long. Later, as I asked them to leave the room, I knew he was ready to go. He would never leave us all while we were sitting around his bed. But he also knew I would not leave. As he had become increasingly more dependant on me for his every wish, I had always promised him I would never leave his side, and I wasn't going to break that promise. I slept at the hospice throughout those final days, refusing to go home for rest. The staff arranged for a bed for me next to his and we slept side by side, as we had done all our lives together. It wasn't going to change now.

And yet the all-consuming sadness that my amazing husband was about to die was combined with a sense of disappointment too. No-one tells you that the final hours are not packed with emotional farewells, loving glances and hugs, the sort of heartbreaking final farewells you see in TV dramas. No-one tells you that you'll spend hours listening to his breathing getting softer and softer until it finally stops. And no-one tells you he won't open his eyes one last time before that last breath and tell you he loves you. That is why it wasn't his passing that hurt the most but the last "I love you" that I didn't hear.

24

The Final Chapter?

They say the sun shines on the righteous. Well, the sun shone the day they buried Willie Maddren. To the melodic sound of a brass band, well-wishers lined the streets and mourners packed the church. He couldn't have asked for a better send-off.

Since Willie's passing six days earlier, we had been left to grieve quietly and privately. I thought I had prepared myself for his death, but nothing can truly prepare you. Apart from Willie's mum passing away a year earlier, I had not encountered the death of a close relative until shortly before Willie left us. My father, 86 and as fit as a fiddle, suffered a stroke, collapsed and died three days later in hospital. He loved life and lived it to the full. It was very sad but I couldn't grieve, for I had a truly heartbreaking situation at home. My husband of 49 was dying and I felt he should still have some living to do. Then, three weeks later, Willie was gone. Through the sadness, I tried to console myself with the knowledge that his life had been full and happy, his final years content and fulfilling.

From the hospice, I had gone home to tell Laura and David the bad news. I then made calls to those who needed to know and set about removing all signs of Willie's illness from our life. I called the company who had supplied his stairlift, told them my husband had just died and that I needed the equipment out of the house, insisting they came there and then. Our bed, which had been moved into our living room during his final months, was taken back upstairs, his wheelchair and walking frame were put away in the garage. Even the local chemist kindly granted my request to take away without delay the bottles of medication, needles and oxygen that had been such a large part of his daily routine for the previous five years.

The Final Chapter?

Don't get me wrong, we weren't forgetting Willie. We were terribly sad but we wanted to put behind us all those reminders of his illness. I only wanted memories of those carefree days before that dark cloud descended on us. We surrounded ourselves with smiling pictures of the times we shared with him before his illness, spending hours choosing special photographs and reminiscing about the good times.

In the days following Willie's passing I received many wonderful bouquets of flowers, but none touched me quite like one small bunch given to me by a relative stranger. Throughout his illness, Willie and I had always taken the dog for a walk at the same time each day. Along the way we would often pass a lady walking her dog, never extending our acquaintance beyond a nod and a polite "Hello". On the evening of the day Willie died, just when we would normally have been taking Max for a walk, the doorbell sounded. I opened the door and there stood our nodding acquaintance, her eyes full, her arms offering a bunch of flowers. Clearly choked, she didn't - couldn't - say anything, but I was truly touched by her kind gesture.

The day of Willie's funeral was a far from private affair. We had courted the media during his illness, as that was the one sure way of maximising the impact of the fund set up in his name. When he died, however, I wanted everyone to go away, to leave us alone and let us grieve in peace. The press respected that request until the day of the funeral. It was only natural that they should want closure to a story they had been running for the past five years. But the clicks and flashes of cameras as a barrage of press photographers took pictures of the coffin entering the church was too much. It was like the paparazzi. I had to bite my lip to stop myself from protesting in despair and anger.

And yet there was a saving grace to their attendance. I requested copies of the pictures they had taken. I must be the only widow on Teesside with 200 glossy photographs of her husband's funeral. Morbid? Not in the slightest. At a much later date I sat down and looked through them and was delighted to see the faces of many people I had not realised had attended. We have pictures of our births and marriages, so why not our funerals too? To this day I still get those pictures out and flick through them. Along with all those family and friends arriving to pay tribute to Willie, they show his coffin being carried solemnly and proudly by his two great friends and former teammates, George Smith and David Mills, his brother Chris and his eldest son Steven. The coffin is draped with red and lilac flowers. No, not red and white. As a florist, I had to use up what was in stock and that's all that was left. Willie wouldn't have wanted me to order anything in specially! The pallbearers carry his coffin between a guard of honour, studded with Middlesbrough football legends. Jack Charlton, Bryan Robson, Steve Gibson, Colin Cooper, Gary Pallister, Graeme Souness, Eric McMordie, Gordon Jones, Jim Platt, Mark Proctor, John Craggs and many more.

Among them too are faces I had not expected to see there that day. I had asked for close family and friends only to attend, but to my disappointment saw people who throughout Willie's illness hadn't once called to see him or picked up the phone to ask after his welfare. My blood boiled but I kept calm, remembering the occasion. These folks had obviously come to soothe their own souls alone and no one else's.

Two friends who were sadly unable to be there were Don Burluraux, one of Willie's Middlesbrough football contemporaries, and his wife, Jean. I was touched, however, by their own unique tribute to him, as they laid a bouquet of red and white flowers on the Cleveland Hills. Recalling their days as Boro teammates, Don picked a stunning spot on Cringle Moor, near Carlton Bank, where he and Willie had enjoyed and suffered frequent training runs on cold Monday mornings up those steep, rugged slopes. They later sent me photographs of the flowers overlooking a patchwork of fields with Roseberry Topping in the distant background. It was a view to die for. Willie could have asked for nothing more.

The church was packed for the service, although at one point I became concerned the vicar, Reverend Bill Hall, was about to draw a temporary halt to the proceedings. There were few things Willie hated more than church hymns being met with a muttering of voices rather than a cacophony of sound. He had therefore instructed Reverend Hall to stop the service if the mourners did not sing the hymns as they should be. So I fully expected the congregation to be silenced and made to start again when it became clear that one of Willie's favourite hymns, *Be Still, for the Presence of the Lord*, was rather less well known to many. Fortunately, the moment past. Then came a stirring rendition of *Love Changes Everything* by George Smith's daughter, Sara. Laura, at 14 showing maturity beyond her years, read out a poem she had written about her dad the night she discovered he had died, and Steven spoke proudly of his father's boundless courage, his unforgettable smile and his love of life.

We left the church, as we had entered it, to the sound of a brass band, now

The Final Chapter?

playing *The Day God Gavest Lord is Ended*. Our good friend Geoff Turnbull had kindly arranged for members of Peterlee Brass Band to perform. Just months before his passing, Willie and I had watched with great enjoyment *Brassed Off*, a humorous and poignant film on the struggles of a group of Yorkshire miners as they sought glory in the finals of a national brass band competition while facing the prospect of pit closures. With his great love of music, Willie had revelled in the wonderful sounds of that movie as we laughed and cried our way through its bittersweet tale. Now those brass sounds were accompanying more tears.

Then, as we waited for Willie's coffin to be placed into a hearse, ready for the journey to the cemetery, the clouds were lifted momentarily. With a typical display of the humour that forged such a close bond with Willie, David Mills complained about the weight of the coffin on his shoulder, adamant that his late friend had ordered Robert Crake, the funeral director, to fill it with bricks just to make him sweat. I felt a flash of guilt that I could smile as I stood behind my husband's coffin, but I knew Willie would be laughing with us.

It was to be a private burial, though again droves of extended family arrived. I so wanted to be on my own with him. So as people drifted away after the burial, I asked the funeral director to give me a minute, returning to the graveside alone for a moment's contemplation. I had to resist the urge to sit on the side of the hole and dangle my feet over the edge, just to be as close as possible for one final moment. After a short farewell, I looked up and saw the grave attendants waiting at a discreet distance and imagined them preparing to run to my rescue if I threw myself in. In truth, I was at peace and I knew that so too was Willie, at rest in 'Maddren's Corner', alongside his mother. The quiet moment over, I returned to the car for a trip to the football club, where the staff had kindly laid on a wonderful spread. Everyone laughed, joked and reminisced in a fitting end to a sad day.

The letters and cards of condolence came by the sackload; hundreds of them, each paying warm tribute to a great man. As with the books of remembrance, completed by family, friends and fans alike, they all mean so much. One remarked that with Wilf Mannion passing away just a few months earlier, it was some team God was assembling in heaven. With George Hardwick and Brian Clough having since joined them, he must be in charge of a world-beating Middlesbrough team by now. Many told of their respect for Willie as a player and as a man. "A great footballer but, more important, a great human being," said one. "Few could lace the boots of a great footballer, even less could lace the boots of a true gentleman,"

Extra Time – The Final Chapter

wrote another. "A Colossus of a man on and off the pitch. Greatness will live forever and Willie, you were great," said a touching tribute. Another spoke of his misfortune in management, saying: "You were the best manager the Boro ever had, you worked miracles with nothing to spend. You were simply the right person in the right place at the wrong time."

There were many more personal tributes too. "You were an inspiration while at the hospice, always with a smile despite the disease," wrote one hospice employee, a volunteer reflexologist called Kevin. "I learned a lot from this great man while I massaged his feet, which was a privilege." Then came a moving accolade from the Butterwick nurses, who wrote: "We all have some lovely memories of a truly great man. You were a pleasure to look after. Never angry, even when times were hard. We'll never forget your wink and your smile."

Then came the thoughts of one of his closest confidants, Steve Smelt. In a stirring letter to me, he wrote: "I do not feel sorry for Willie because I know he has gone to a much better place. I feel sorry for myself because I have lost a true friend. I was always truly amazed that whenever I visited he was always cheerful and showed no bitterness towards his situation. I always felt uplifted being in his company. I consider myself extremely fortunate to have known Willie. This in itself is special, but to have him as a friend was truly a privilege."

I drew strength and comfort too from the sentiment of a poem given to me by Barbara, wife of Willie's brother, Dave. I am sure the poem, *I Am Not There,* with its words of hope from death, has lifted the spirits of many who have grieved, like myself, for loved ones they have lost.

The funeral over and Willie at rest, we were left to get on with the rest of our lives. The children returned to school and I was home alone. For years the house had received a steady stream of callers - nurses, doctors, pharmacists, friends and family – but now the doorbell fell silent and the phone refused to ring. The house echoed with memories of Willie. Sadly, these were all memories of his illness, for we had only moved into the house following his diagnosis. People tried to support me by giving me the space they thought I needed. I visited the cemetery every day but there was never a day so warm as the day he was laid to rest.

What kept me sane were the children and my decision to return full-time to my florists' business. I threw myself back into my work, giving myself a purpose to each day. At the same time, I had to get up for the children and organise life for their sakes. Without this focus, I think I could and would have stayed in bed all day,

The Final Chapter?

never dressing or eating. I had lost all drive to get up and out, but the children's needs and the demands of work ensured I had neither the time nor the opportunity to submerge myself in grief and depression.

My darkest moments came when Laura and David were safely tucked up in their beds and I was alone with my thoughts. With Willie alongside me, I had been happy to sit and watch endless inane TV programmes. Now they all seemed so pointless. After five years of illness, I had wanted back the life that I thought I had missed. Without him, however, that life really didn't seem worth very much. People assumed I would want to be on my own and in a way they were right. Fortunately, I eventually took a friend's advice to accept any social invitations that came my way and gradually I began to piece my life together again.

It was ironic, however, that now we could do so many of the everyday things we had found impossible during Willie's long illness, none of them seemed so important after all. David had responded to his father's death in the typical fashion of a 10-year-old. "That means we can go to Pizza Hut now," he had announced. So to Pizza Hut we did go. Then there was ten-pin bowling, walks up Roseberry Topping, shopping trips that lasted more than an hour and the freedom to book foreign holidays without having to take into account wheelchair requirements. But the novelty soon wore off and we knew we would have foregone all of that newfound freedom just to have him back with us.

Initially, it seemed wrong to start laughing again. But we did – and Willie would have wanted it that way. We often recall stories about him and even make fun of the things he said and did. We're not being disrespectful to his memory. We know he would be laughing with us. He wouldn't want us to remember him with sombre faces but with happiness and humour. So I couldn't help myself when, during an open day at Laura's new school, a very polite sixth former asked my name, handed me a name badge and asked if Mr Maddren would be joining me. "I really hope not," I replied. "He died two years ago!" The poor girl was mortified. Laura scolded me for such wicked humour but we both thought it hilarious.

And yet those same proud days of achievement as the children receive certificates or medals have been tinged with sadness that Willie wasn't there for them at those special moments in time. It is sad too that the only memories Laura and David have of their father are of him in a wheelchair. I so wish they could remember his wicked cheerfulness with them as babies and his pride at watching them grow up and mature. One of the hardest things has been seeing TV footage

Extra Time – The Final Chapter

of Willie talking before he became sick and realising I had quite forgotten how his voice sounded before the effects of MND slowed it down. It saddens me that we were denied the opportunity to grow old together, a special and fulfilling experience that I will probably now share with someone else.

Willie's only dream never accomplished was to take me to Tahiti, somewhere he had been with the football club during his playing days. He longed for us to experience the romance of a walk along a sun-drenched South Pacific beach. Without planning, I found myself in Tahiti a year to the day of his passing. Never having been abroad for the few years before Willie's death, I booked Laura, David and I on a six-week dream holiday to New Zealand and the States, stopping off at Fiji, Bora Bora and Tahiti on the way home. Being in Tahiti on the anniversary of his death, we marked the day with a lovely meal out before strolling back to our magnificent hotel room overlooking the sea.

After settling the kids in the room, I had the urge to take a late-night walk. I picked a hibiscus flower, sat on the edge of the jetty and in the stillness of the night looked up to see a single star, brighter than any other, right above my head. With tears streaming down my cheeks, I sent the flower into the ocean and spoke with the man I had lost. As the stars shone, I asked Willie to help me through the challenges that lay before me, to make the right decisions, especially when it came to the children. I was finding the responsibility of always being the prime decision-maker difficult after all those years with him by my side. Despite the emotion, it was a special moment and yet I couldn't help but wonder what might have been. We had so wanted to share the experience of Tahiti but fate dealt that our two visits were separated by many years.

The first anniversary of his death was always going to be hard but I felt close to him on that emotion-charged evening. The first of everything in the initial year after the loss of someone special is always hard. On my birthday, friends took the children and I out for dinner. The first Christmas was difficult but we jetted off straight after the holiday period to visit my brother in Texas. Willie's birthday in January would have been his 50th and the children and I caught a flight from our base in Texas to see our good friends, Bill and Judith Gates, in the Cayman Islands. We celebrated his birthday under the Caribbean skies, eating exotic fish and drinking to his health. It would have been just perfect if he had been there to share it with us - and perhaps he was!

I so hoped he was there with us but I have to admit to never having felt his

The Final Chapter?

presence the way I thought I would. Willie and I had been so close that there were times when I knew what he was thinking and feeling without him even making a gesture. We had been as one and he had promised that after his death he would let me know he was okay on the other side. I know this may sound strange to some but I had always feared Willie would still be disabled and have no one to care for him in the after-life. Our conversations were always quite light-hearted, but he knew I was serious when I told him I had to know he didn't need looking after now that I was no longer there for him. We talked endlessly about a whole range of options for him to work on and he steadfastly believed he would be able to give me a sign that would allow me to get on with my life.

Sadly, there have been no signals, no hints, nothing – and it hasn't been for the want of trying on my part. When, after a year, I'd had no sign from Willie, I began making strenuous efforts to contact him. I began with a visit from a spiritualist. Using my middle name, Jane, to avoid giving him any obvious clues to my past, I arranged for him to visit me at home. As we sat in my front room, he talked of a tall, thin, grey man. He mentioned an Adam who had a problem with his arm. Despite my desperation to cling on to anything he said, he didn't get close to describing anyone that might have been Willie. The spiritualist accepted that we simply had not connected and refused to take money from me. I was terribly disappointed, but didn't give up hoping.

Since then I have had my palm read, my fortune told and tea leaves looked into but still there's been nothing. People have suggested that the reason I've had no success has been as a direct result of my own lack of belief in the routes I have taken. I have never believed in palm reading or the like but so wanted to believe, such was my desperation to contact Willie. He was deeply religious and never feared death as he knew he was going to a better place. Although I didn't share his strength of conviction, I was sure there was a heaven but now I don't know what to think. I feel cheated and, as a consequence, have given up trying to contact him. Of course, Willie might have given me a sign that I have missed, though he was never subtle!

The only time I feel there might perhaps have been a touch of the old Willie Maddren intervention was about three months after his death. Concerned that the two younger children wouldn't remember him, he had written letters to them and had left the documents in my safe keeping. When the day arrived that I felt they should read their father's words, disaster struck. Years earlier I had hidden the letters somewhere safe but when I went to retrieve them they were gone. I couldn't think where I might have moved them and, in a mood of increasing desperation, searched high and low without success. I was beside myself. Finally, I could search no more, sat down with a cup of tea and asked Willie to help me. In a flash, it came to me. I walked upstairs, into the bedroom, slipped my hand under a pile of underwear in the top drawer and pulled out the letters. It was obvious I must have put them there, moving them from their previous hiding place, but I had no recollection of doing so. Why would I have put them somewhere different and how did I know to look for them there? Some say that was Willie's sign to me but I want something more tangible.

Those letters, full of love and advice, remain precious to Laura and David. He felt that Lucy, Steven and I would remember him and would always know what we had meant to him, but he wanted his two youngest children to know how he felt about them. The letters explained that he had always loved them, had loved his life with them and would always be with them in spirit. He also gave them advice, insisting that they mustn't worry about the trivial things in life. I have always made a point of telling them what I think their father would have said in certain situations, but those words from him must mean so much more. The letters were a wonderful gesture, though I so wish he had left one for me too. He believed Steven, Lucy and I would have our memories and we do. But how I would love to be able to hold a piece of paper and to know these were his words and thoughts for me, just me and no-one else.

Willie showed me how to love and be loved, a legacy that has helped me move on. To share your life with someone special is a joy I believe few truly experience. I didn't think there could ever be another man in my life but I have learnt to move on and accept that life sometimes changes in ways you can't predict. I have found happiness in having someone else around and, while we both know he is not a replacement, it is a completely different and satisfying relationship. I will never stop remembering Willie, and it takes a man of great courage to take on a woman whose memories remain so close to her heart. But Willie taught me that life can be very short and you need to just grasp it with both hands and enjoy.

Letter or no letter, sign or no sign, Willie has continued to influence my life and actions. He is the reason why I now carry out regular work with the local branch of the Motor Neurone Disease Association, who were such a support to Willie and I during his illness. If, through my own experience of the disease, I can help in my own small way others whose lives are touched by the dark shadow of MND, then

The Final Chapter?

Willie's premature passing will have been a little less pointless.

While it is perhaps less surprising that he remains such an inspiration to me, how many in this world can move people in such a way that even three years after their death they can still be inspiring them? For it was Willie's remarkable ability to influence those whose lives he touched that resulted in more than 500 people attending an MND fundraising dinner in 2003. I was stirred into action after being contacted by a London-based Middlesbrough supporter called Colin Cooper. Having read Willie's book long after his death, Colin had been moved to set up a fundraising motorbike ride, collecting items of football memorabilia from every Premier League club along the way. When someone who didn't even know Willie was prepared to go to such lengths because of my late husband's words I knew I had to make that memorabilia work for the good of the charity.

I made a decision to hastily organise a fundraising dinner and was both surprised and delighted when tickets quickly sold out. Thanks to the support of former Boro captain Gordon Jones, Boro fan and local hotelier Ron Darby and many of Willie's old teammates who attended the dinner, the event was a great success. Indeed, it is no exaggeration to say there was a special feeling in the room that night. I had hoped we might raise £10,000 but in one memorable evening a further £25,000 was added to the Willie Maddren MND Fund. This was in no small part due to the generosity of Middlesbrough Football Club, who made a single donation of £10,000.

That night was a perfect example of how Willie continues to make a difference long after his death. It is that special ability which roused so many individuals to write to Willie and tell him how his biography had given them reason to reassess what was important in their lives. And it is that same priceless commodity that made me sit down and write these additional chapters to his life story – and you to buy and read it. The spirit of Willie Maddren lives on. I hope it touches your life in the same way it has touched so many before you. We might not have given him the Extra Time he so longed for, but it's not too late to try to give others the time that eluded him.

By purchasing this book you have helped contribute to the Willie Maddren MND Research Fund, in the hope that one day a cause and then a cure may be found. That will surely be a fitting final chapter for Willie Maddren.

And Willie, I am still waiting for that sign! x

Extra Time – The Final Chapter

I Am Not There

Do not stand at my grave and weep.
I am not there. I do not sleep.
I am a thousand winds that blow.
I am a diamond glints on snow.
I am the sunlight on ripened grain.
I am the gentle autumn rain.

When you awaken in the morning's hush
I am the swift uplifting rush
Of quiet birds in circled flight.
I am the soft stars that shine at night.

Do not stand at my grave and cry.
I am not there; I did not die.

Mary Elizabeth Frye

Lucy's Tribute

Father, Confidant and Entertainer!

It's been some time now since Dad's passing but I still think of him in some way every day. Above my desk at work, I have a picture of the two of us, and I often talk to him and ask his advice. This might seem silly to some people, but it wouldn't be to Dad. He strongly believed in life after death, just as I do. Talking to him brings me comfort. I often think of him on sunny days, knowing how much such weather lifted his spirits when he was confined to the house.

For some time after Dad passed away all I thought about was the pain he suffered and what the disease had done to him. I felt angry and disappointed at life. I was becoming bitter about it all. I know Dad would have hated to think of me reacting like that but it seemed so unfair and it hurt so much. It was almost intolerable seeing my younger brothers and sister so upset. I would watch the news and wonder why so many good people get taken away from their loved ones while so many criminals seem to get away scot-free.

Now, I very rarely allow my mind to drift back and think of things such as the day he told me he had MND or how he looked the day he died. Neither do I try to find the answer to the question "Why?" I find these memories and thoughts far too painful, as they always bring with them tears of deep sadness. I tend to push them out of my mind, replacing them with thoughts of a strong father who vehemently fought the disease and somehow managed to retain an amazing sense of humour and dignity throughout his struggle. I remember the times he made me laugh or his words of advice when we had one of our 'father-to-daughter chats'.

From the start, he made a decision to fight the disease with the best weapon he had – his strength of mind. Not having lived with him during his illness, I didn't witness his moments of real despair, but he always tried to remain positive in front of all of his children, putting on a brave face for all our sakes. I, for one, was grateful for that because it made coping with the situation so much easier and helped to bring us closer as a family.

Extra Time – The Final Chapter

Dad always displayed a caring nature for others, no matter what torment he was suffering. During the last two years of his life, I could hardly contain my emotions during some of my visits to see him, so evident was the struggle he was having. On one occasion he looked so dreadful that I could not hide my look of concern as I sat down beside him. But before I could say anything, he asked me how I was. I told him that he shouldn't be thinking about me, what mattered was how he was feeling. But he insisted that he wanted to know how I was doing. That was so typical of Dad. No matter how he felt, he always showed an interest in my life and needed to be sure I was still okay.

He once told me the things we take for granted are so much more important than we realise and it's the simple things in life that make a real difference, a lesson he had learnt the hard way. Recalling the stresses and strains that went hand-in-hand with his days as manager of Middlesbrough FC and with owning a business, he advised me to always put my happiness before any kind of status. He urged me to leave my job if it brought too much stress into my life and follow an easier career path, even if it meant a drop in salary. I knew he was right, and I have had cause to recall and heed those words of perspective many times over the last few years.

Speaking of simple things in life, during one of Dad's regular stays in the hospice, I recall tackling a crossword with him at a stage when, to make himself understood, he had to spell out words letter by letter. As we attempted to answer one of the clues, he spelt out to me what I believed was the answer, only to find he had spelt out, "I love you loads". It was a touching moment which meant a lot to me, though I have to admit it was swiftly followed by more letters, spelling out, "I want a cup of tea"!

I always enjoyed Dad's sense of humour. Before becoming ill, he loved to play practical jokes and generally act the fool. Even as a child, I recall his successful attempts to make me laugh with his little displays of temporary insanity. On one such occasion, with a tea towel on his head and front false teeth projecting from his mouth, he peered around the door resembling the Disney character, Goofy.

Whenever there was music – especially his favourites, Tom Jones and the Bee Gees – Dad couldn't resist singing along or having a boogie. I can still remember with crystal vision his impressive take-off of John Travolta in *Saturday Night Fever*. He was such a mover, but was rather less impressive when it came to remembering the lyrics to songs. He would often replace lines of lyrics in blissful ignorance. When enlightened with the correct ones, he would laugh, only to return to his original lyrics five minutes later. He clearly preferred the Willie Maddren version!

Even my 21st birthday was no exception as Dad's strange antics created another great moment. As guests enjoyed champagne in the afternoon sunshine, the music was suddenly turned up extra loud as he burst through the patio doors wearing a dress, wig and make-up. As he and his sister, Claire, danced, sang and laughed, I almost choked on the champagne at the ridiculous sight in front of me!

Even when Dad was really quite ill, he still made it his business to make me laugh. He definitely thought I was far too serious sometimes. As we sat reading the papers together one afternoon, he recalled how cold the winters had been when he was a young lad. By this point, his illness had weakened his voice to such an extent that understanding him had become quite difficult, but he explained to me that such was the bitter cold that his family would often huddle together around the fire for warmth. "And sometimes," he added, as he burst into laughter "Dad would light it."

Missing the joke, I couldn't understand why he was laughing, so I asked him to tell me it again in case I had missed something. He repeated the story, looked at my baffled face and once again bursting into laughter. I still didn't understand. After another failed attempt at making me understand the joke, he was laughing so hard that he was crying, resulting in Hilary rushing in, concerned there was a problem. I told her not to worry, that Dad was just having a good laugh at my expense. When I finally got the joke, I insisted it wasn't that funny anyway, which only served to ignite his hysteria once again. At least I managed to return the favour, Dad!

Lucy

Steven's Tribute

Putting Life in Perspective

I'm standing on the 18th green at Eaglescliffe Golf Club, the tension in the air is electric, and my heart sinks as Dad drains a six-foot putt to rob me at the last of a rare victory over him. We shake hands, he gives me a cheeky wink and we head off to the bar to share a couple of cold beers and a joke or two. I tease Dad that he's getting old, he's not hitting the ball far these days, and he'll soon be getting a regular thrashing on the golf course off his young lad. He takes my ribbing in the good humour it was intended, and ensures me he won't go down without a fight!

I was blissfully unaware that Dad had been suffering from MND for some time, and I didn't know that would be the last round I would ever enjoy with him. *He knew of course, but he was sparing me the pain of knowing what was to come.* That was typical of him, trying to save us all from worrying about him.

It was heartbreaking to watch that horrific illness slowly take its toll on Dad, and I remember feeling unbelievably helpless that I could do nothing to stop it. You feel angry that he's being robbed of the chance to do the simple things in life which we all take for granted. What amazed me was that he never moaned, never showed a hint of self pity, fought that illness for all he was worth, and all the while putting the family's feelings first. Throughout his illness his courage and ability to laugh, often at himself, was quite astounding.

On a family holiday to America, I was standing outside a shop along a jetty with Dad in his wheelchair while the family were shopping. He told me to take his hat off and pop it down on the ground in front of him to see how much money he could get. He sat there in his wheelchair, wearing huge dark shades, false teeth pushed out to look extra goofy, swaying side to side and humming Stevie Wonder's *I Just Called to Say I Love You* at passers by. He made me laugh so much I nearly fell off the other side of the jetty!

Outwardly I rarely spoke about Dad being ill, not because I didn't want to, but because I just couldn't do it. The way I saw it was that talking about it wasn't going

Steven's Tribute

to change anything anyway, so what was the point? Hilary was brilliant with my Dad, and I wanted to be strong for them both, Lucy, and especially Laura and David since they were so young. Getting teary in front of them just wasn't something I wanted to do if I could help it. I'm not ashamed to say that on my own I shed more than a tear, mainly due to the frustration that there was nothing anyone could do to stop the deterioration and that we were slowly losing him.

When Boro made it to the first Coca-Cola Cup final, I was pushing Dad up Wembley Way when a couple of Boro fans spotted him and shouted, "There's only one Willie Maddren." Suddenly the thousands lining the street erupted into that deafening chant as we moved through them all. It was one of the most moving things I have ever seen, and I felt a huge lump growing in my throat. Somehow I managed to fight back the tears as it would have seriously damaged Dad's street cred with him smiling away and trying to wave at these amazing fans, while his big, rugby-playing son was pushing him along crying like a five-year-old schoolgirl who's just dropped her toffee!

Dad very much believed in working hard for what you achieve, and while encouraging my sport, he always said that my studies should come first. He was always very keen to help us all with homework, especially if it was French as he fancied himself as a bit of a linguist. Unfortunately, Dad's French sounded more like Del Boy than Gerard Depardieu!

When I was too young to work on the shop floor at his store, but needed a new pair of football boots, he would often get me in to tidy up the stock room or unpack deliveries in return for the boots or a new shirt. It was just a token, but he was teaching me to earn what I get in life.

When I got older, I would work in his shop on Saturdays and during the holidays. He always expected me to work twice as hard as the other guys who worked there. I did longer hours and, in return, I got paid half as much! I thought enough was enough so I went into his office one day to ask for a pay rise, you know, just a couple of quid more. No big deal, right? Wrong! Dad's retort was to tell me that I was lucky he gave me anything, because if I loved him I should be working for free! I legged it out of there before I negotiated myself a substantial pay decrease.

On one occasion I was working there, he came over and asked if I wanted some lunch. He gave me a tenner and asked if I would get him a sandwich too. On our way home that night I asked him if I could have my wages for the day. He gave me

Steven's Tribute

a quizzical look, asked me what I thought that tenner was he gave me at lunchtime, then turned the stereo up! I felt seriously hard done by at the time, but such instances taught me a great deal. He got his own bloody lunch from that point on, that's for sure.

Dad may no longer be around, but I have many great memories of him as a father and as a friend, and he certainly has a great bearing on how I now live my life. I don't take myself too seriously, I have the ability to put the little things that aren't really too important into perspective and I have learnt that you have to go out and live your life and do the things you enjoy now, not later.

I don't think I ever step on to a golf course without thinking about Dad, and looking back I'm pleased he sank it, but hope that perhaps in another life, I get the chance to avenge that six-foot putt.

Steven

Laura's Tribute

My Dad, My Hero

I'm told my Dad would have been so proud of me, but how I wish I could hear it from him. I was just 14 when he passed away and so much has happened in my life in those years since. Words can't describe how much it would mean to hear what he thinks of me and how I have turned out, to share with him some of my achievements. It seems so unfair that he has missed, and will continue to miss, the major events in my life. In fact David has already asked me if he can walk me down the aisle. Sadly, there is no answer to the question "Why did it happen to such a lovely man as my Dad?"

Not a day goes by that I don't think of and miss my Dad. As I said in the eulogy I read out at his funeral, he was so much more than a loving father – he was my hero. I always knew I wanted to write a tribute to him and read it out at his funeral, so I went to bed and wrote a speech on the very day he died. As I discovered later, Mum didn't think I could get through the speech, but I'm proud to say I managed to read the whole thing without crying.

Despite losing him while I was still so young, I have many memories of him - some good and some not so good. I will always remember his smile, his wink, the love for his family and most of all his amazing attitude to life. But I also remember the things that I would rather forget - the terrible upset and frustration both Dad and Mum suffered. I can't even begin to imagine what they went through. I always tried to do my best to shine a light on sad situations, in an attempt to help in the best way I could, by bringing a smile to their faces. But sometimes my efforts were just not enough.

The day Mum told David and I that Dad wasn't very well and might not have long left remains vivid in my memory. We didn't see Dad much in the days before his death as Grandma looked after us at home while Mum spent long hours with him at the Butterwick Hospice. I don't mind admitting the anger I felt inside when Mum told us Dad had passed away. He knew David and I loved him but we never got to tell him before he died. I was a little angry that Lucy and Steven were able to be at his bedside and see him. Of course, Mum had our best intentions at heart, probably believing we were too young to say our final goodbyes, but I couldn't help thinking I was his daughter too. The devastating, sinking feeling when Mum, Lucy and Steven walked through the door is unforgettable. I just knew that he had gone. I didn't know what to do or say. I simply could not imagine life without him.

Nobody understood what David and I had to do at such a young age during Dad's long illness. I didn't have the life other people my age enjoyed and, I feel, took for granted. I had to grow up much faster than my school friends. And yet I am grateful rather than resentful. The whole experience made me who I am today. In particular, it gave me a greater understanding of disability.

When I think of my Dad, I sometimes picture him in his football glory days, wearing the red shirt and the curly perm. But they don't seem like the real him. I much prefer to see the more recent pictures which, despite his illness, show the welcoming smile of a loving man. Before he died, he wrote David and I letters. I read mine from time to time and receive great comfort from it. The things he wrote lay close to my heart and influence my life greatly. I think he wrote such a letter because he thought we would not remember him, but how could we forget such a wonderful person in our lives?

Laura

Eulogy for My Dad
Written and read out at her father's funeral, by Laura, aged 14

My Dad was a much loved husband, brother, father and friend. He knew he had so many people who loved him and who he loved back.
He was a very special person in many people's eyes, especially mine.

As you know, he lived life as best he could. He travelled the world, managed and played for the best team in the north-east, Middlesbrough, and inspired so many people, whether it was to love, to play football or to fight. And that is what he did for six years - battling from the muscle wasting disease, Motor Neurone. I will never forget my hero.

He gave me so many happy memories, whether they were when we laughed or special holidays, because he was always making the videos so we could look back in years to come and say "Did I honestly have that hair do?"

There are many beautiful stories we could tell of this wonderful and loving man - my Dad.

David's Tribute

Proud to be His Son

The ten short years that I had with Dad were just the best and will stay with me for a lifetime. But how I wish my memories were so less vague. My sadness at losing my Dad so young is at its most overwhelming when I see other kids getting picked up from school by their fathers. When my friends moan about their dads telling them off, I want to shout at them with anger and frustration. I want to tell them how happy they should be that they have a dad to fight and argue with, that they should just be glad they have someone there for them.

As a ten-year-old, I wanted to believe Dad would never die, that he would always be around, even if he was in a wheelchair. I never thought of him as disabled. He was just my Dad who happened to be in a wheelchair. If anything, it made me love him even more. Despite his illness and what I now know must have been hugely difficult times, he always seemed to be happy, always putting on a brave face in front of us. And yet I remember worrying that I would wake up to discover he had died, so each bedtime would always hug him and tell him I loved him.

No matter how vague, I treasure those memories I have of my Dad. From him coming home from work with a different car every day when he worked for Croft's garage to him teaching me how to toss a coin, they are all important. But, as his youngest son, it is perhaps no surprise that the majority of my recollections involving Dad revolve around the glorious game. I remember before his illness, being too young to join in as he and Laura played football. How I wish I had the chance to play footy with him now. He spent long hours watching me play the game and trying to make me a better player.

I clearly recall him sitting in his wheelchair watching me play football for Norton and wishing he wasn't there. I was never embarrassed that he was different to other dads, being in a wheelchair. I was embarrassed because I feared I wasn't good enough for him; that he, as an ex-professional footballer, wouldn't think I was good enough. On arrival back home, he would spend hours trying to pass on his football knowledge. Laura would be instructed to move coins and salt cellars around a table as he tried to explain to me the basics of tactics and positional play. We would also spend hours in the garden as he gave me lessons in kicking the ball properly. His fading speech meant it would take him hours to make himself understood with what would normally have taken a matter of minutes, but he wouldn't let me go in the house until I could do it right. The truth is I didn't want to know – I was tired and hungry. Now I so wish he was here to tell me and show me all that I need to know. He would have the most avid learner.

But the return home from football that most stands out in my mind is the day Lucy took Laura and I to the hospice. There, Mum took us to a private room and told us that it wouldn't be long before Dad died. The feeling was indescribable. I just felt an overwhelming sadness. Now, five years later, my one overwhelming feeling is pride at being his son.

David

MOTOR NEURONE DISEASE: AN INTRODUCTION

by Dr Peter Newman,
Consultant Neurologist at Middlesbrough General Hospital,
who treated Willie following his diagnosis.

Only 25 years ago, in the late 1970s, very few people had heard of Motor Neurone Disease (MND) but now the general public is much more aware of medical conditions and MND commonly features in newspaper and magazine articles. Well known people, including actor David Niven and football manager Don Revie, have had the condition. In the USA, MND is often known as Lou Gehrig Disease after the famous baseball player who suffered from the illness. Doctors sometimes use the term Charcot's Disease as it was this French neurologist who, with others, described the condition in the 1860s.

As is implied by the term Motor Neurone Disease, this is a disorder which affects the motor neurones. These are the nerves and nerve tracts that originate in the brain, traverse the spinal cord and send impulses through the peripheral nerves to stimulate activity in our muscles. If the motor neurones are damaged in any way, then the stimulation of the muscles fails and the muscles become weak and thin. Most of the muscles of the body can be weakened in this way but curiously MND does not involve the muscles which move the eyes. However, the limb and trunk muscles are affected, as are the muscles which support speech, swallowing and breathing.

MND is uncommon but in an area the size of Teesside and surrounding towns in which about two million people reside, there would probably be about 50 cases at any given time. Almost all cases are sporadic but with about five per cent there may be a family history of MND. The average age of onset of MND is 56 years and in a few instances, it can develop in people in their 30s or even younger. The elderly may also develop MND and thus it can be generally considered as a disorder of middle to old age. Whereas the life expectancy for MND sufferers is about three to five years from onset, some people have a much longer span while in others it is much shorter.

Extra Time – The Final Chapter

The first signs of muscle weakness appear in the arms in 40 per cent of cases, in the legs in 30 per cent and in the bulbar muscles of swallowing and speech in 25 per cent. As the disease progresses, then the muscle weakness and wasting which has begun in one limb will spread to the other limbs and then often begin to involve the bulbar functions. Mental processes are not, as a rule, affected but depression and anxiety are common. The terms progressive bulbar palsy (PBA), progressive muscular atrophy (PMA) and amyotrophic lateral sclerosis (ALS) are sometimes used to describe different facets of MND. Gradually, the patient with MND finds it harder and then impossible to use the affected muscles. This often leads to dependence on a wheelchair and/or on others to help with daily activites such as feeding and bathing.

The diagnosis of MND is usually made when the patient has been examined by a neurologist. Confirmation is obtained by means of electrical tests on the nerves and muscles (EMG). Sometimes other special tests like MR scanning or lumbar puncture are necessary to exclude other conditions. Once the diagnosis is certain then it is discussed with the patient and their family. As the condition is expected to progress, arrangements are usually made for the neurologist and the MND team of therapists to see the patient as frequently as is necessary. Not surprisingly, the diagnosis of MND comes as a terrible blow and the MND Association care adviser, GP and nurses all try to help as much as possible. No matter how much help is available, it is a very difficult time for the patient and family.

At present, the cause of MND is not fully understood. Many theories have been raised and disproven, including immunological explanations, heavy metal, mineral or other poisoning and virus or other infections. Environmental toxins may cause a condition similar to MND which is found in the Pacific island of Guam, but linking this with ordinary MND has not been possible. Much research has concentrated on the biochemical abnormalities which can be detected in the nerve cells affected by MND. Some naturally occurring chemicals are known to be potentially toxic to nerve cells, for instance the neurotransmitter substance glutamate, and many small pieces of the MND jigsaw are being provided by the laboratories which are working at these cellular and molecular levels.

So far, the cure for MND has been elusive. Drugs are being tested to see whether the motor nerve cell degeneration can be reduced or even reversed. One such drug is riluzole, which blocks the harmful effects of glutamate in the nerves. Although many people with MND take this drug, the evidence for any real benefit is not very good but there is every hope that subsequent drug developments will be more effective. Supportive interventions are very important in MND, particularly where the speech, swallowing or breathing muscles are failing, and, although the progression of the weakness cannot be stopped, its effects can be lessened substantially.

There is no escape from the fact that MND is a progressive neurological disorder which will eventually lead to the death of the patient. However, most people with the condition take the positive view that they are going to live with MND rather than die from it. They know that where there is life, there is hope - and that the breakthrough in MND will happen one of these days.

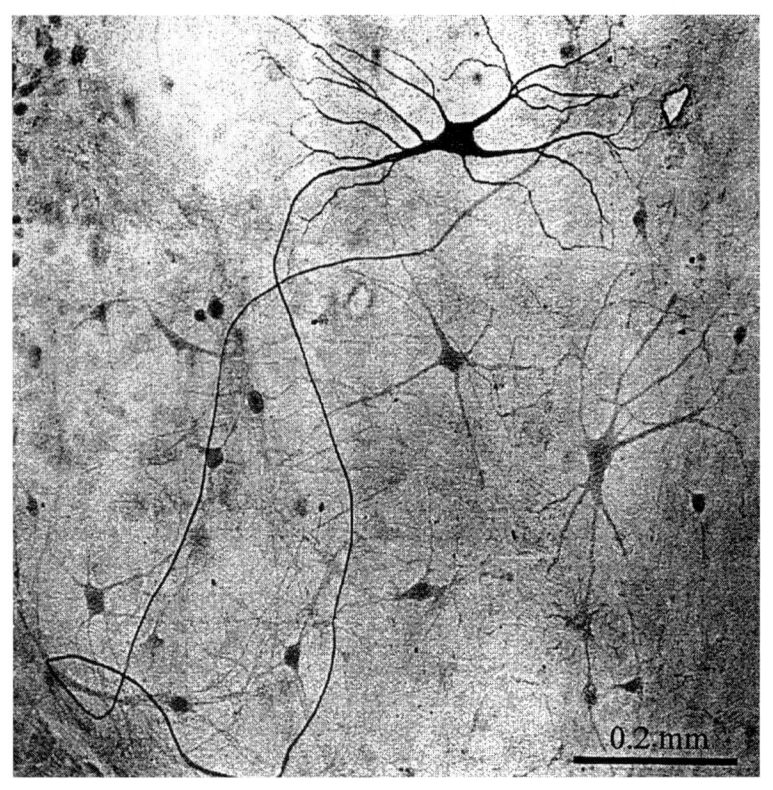

A magnified photograph of Motor Neurones.

NEURONES (Nerve Cells)
- **Sensory** (feeling) neurones: transmit sensations (touch, heat, pain, etc.) to brain
- **Motor** (movement) neurones: transmit electrical signals from brain to activate muscles.

STRUCTURE OF MOTOR NEURONE

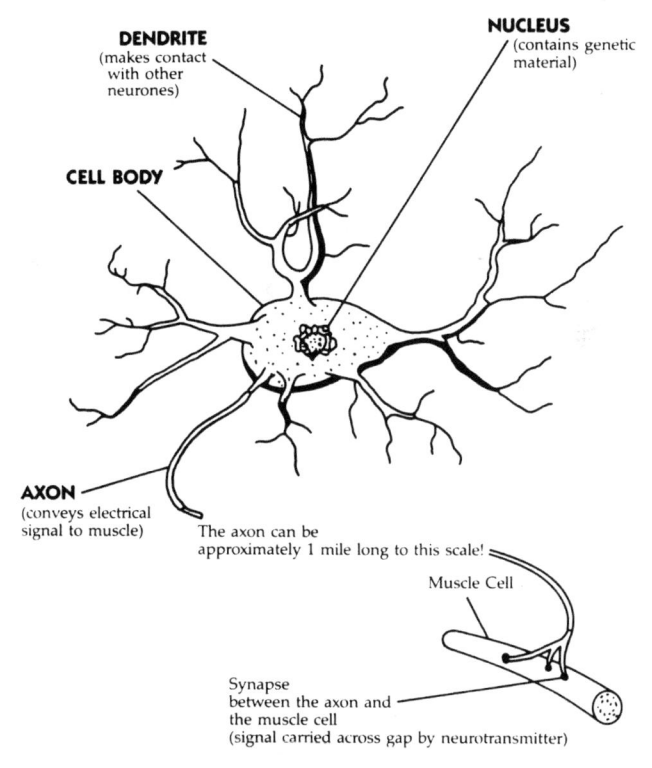

DENDRITE (makes contact with other neurones)

NUCLEUS (contains genetic material)

CELL BODY

AXON (conveys electrical signal to muscle)

The axon can be approximately 1 mile long to this scale!

Muscle Cell

Synapse between the axon and the muscle cell (signal carried across gap by neurotransmitter)

The axon, which varies from a few millimetres to a few metres in length, is rather like an insulated wire. In Multiple Sclerosis, the insulation (myelin sheath) degrades, allowing "leakage" of the electrical signal; in Motor Neurone Disease, the "wire" (core) itself degrades, weakening or interrupting the signal.

Extra Time – The Final Chapter

Celebrating my birthday in 2004 with Lucy, David, Steven and Laura.

Picture courtesy of Gary Walsh Photography

If you have enjoyed reading this book, recommend it to your friends but please don't lend it to them. Ask them to buy another copy. The extra sale may one day help to save someone's life if we can help find a cure for Motor Neurone Disease.

Thank You for your Support
Hilary Maddren

Willie Maddren   **Extra Time - The Final Chapter**

Guess who! Willie and I share a joke as we launch the original version of his book in 1998.

Willie Maddren   Extra Time - The Final Chapter

Willie shares a joke with Lucy, Laura, David and Steven in Majorca during the family's last holiday abroad together before Willie's passing.

Willie and I at our favourite restaurant, the Black Bull in Moulton. It was Willie's 49th birthday and proved to be the last time we would celebrate out.

Willie Maddren   Extra Time - The Final Chapter

Caught out! David sneakily shares a tub of ice-cream with his Dad.

Willie with his sister, Claire, and brothers, Dave (right) and Chris, on the wedding day of Claire's daughter, Alexander. It was to be one of the last times the four would be together.

Willie Maddren · Extra Time - The Final Chapter

Willie's good friends and former Boro teammates, David Mills and George Smith, were his pallbearers, together with his son, Steven, and brother, Chris.

Tribute: in Willie's memory, these red and white flowers were laid by Don and Jean Burluraux overlooking the beautiful Cleveland Hills.

BAKERS
TAILORING

Bakers Tailoring has been suiting the people of Middlesbrough since 1911. Starting off life as a merchant naval outfitter, Bakers have always been renowned for quality, service and style. Bakers Tailoring was relaunched on Middlesbrough's Linthorpe Road in March this year, opened by Middlesbrough's footballing legend Juninho. The interior has a 60s retro feel giving the ultimate shopping environment, a modern day gentleman's outfitters, carrying some of Europe's top quality collections, including Alfred Dunhill, Canali, Aquascutum, Cerruti 1881 and Pringle.

CUSTOM MADE TAILORING SPECIALISTS

CASUALWEAR

CONTEMPORARY CLASSICS

HOME & OFFICE VISITS AVAILABLE

FREE CUSTOMER PARKING

TEL: 01642 226358

194 LINTHORPE ROAD
MIDDLESBROUGH
TS1 3RF

www.bakerstailoring.com

We are grateful to the following organisations for supporting the publication of *Extra Time – The Final Chapter*. Their generosity may contribute to the discovery of a cure for Motor Neurone Disease...

BAKERS
TAILORING
Tel: 01642 226358

888.com — Main Sponsor

Middlesbrough Football Club
Tel: 0870 421 1986

Sunderland AFC
Tel: 0191 5515000

HILLPRINT MEDIA
Tel: 01325 245555

DEVEREUX TRANSPORT AND DISTRIBUTION
Tel: 01642 887700

The Prestige Group — CARING FOR THE ELDERLY
Tel: 01642 223334

MACKS Solicitors
Tel: 01642 252828

Middlesbrough Football Community Project
Tel: 01642 282128

North East TRUCK + VAN
Tel: 01642 370555

mmc — marske machine company
Tel: 01642 888999

GLAMAL
Tel: 01642 379700

Baines Jewitt Chartered Accountants
Tel: 01642 632032

DTW — Part of the pps plc group
Tel: 01287 610404

Middlesbrough Official Supporters Club
Tel: 01642 899412

ptarmigan SPORTS marketing
Tel: 0113 242 1155

THE CLINKARD GROUP LIMITED
Tel: 01642 606162

Rycroft — Mercedes-Benz
Tel: 01642 677877

WATSON WOODHOUSE SOLICITORS
Tel: 01642 247656

CP Waites chartered accountants
Tel: 01325 354440

Biffa Waste Services
Tel: 01642 458064

KEVIN LLOYD LTD. KLL Tel : 01642 226950	**Court Homemakers** Tel : 01642 891010	**THE LOAN shop** Tel : 01642 564569	**TRANSMORE van hire ltd** Tel : 01642 603732
WILTON ENGINEERING SERVICES LTD Tel : 01429 224000	**Jarreds** OFFICE EQUIPMENT GROUP Tel : 01642 217451	**Michael Poole** The Tees Valley Property Consultants Tel : 01642 254222	**HOME INTERNATIONAL** Tel : 01642 765421
DAVID FOX TRANSPORT Tel : 01642 469552	**CARTER STEEL LTD** Tel : 01642 679831	**GT GROUP** Tel : 0191 586 2366	**PARR GROUP** **Joseph Parr** *(Middlesbrough) Limited* Tel : 01642 679381
HEATPAC Tel : 01642 222248	**PROJECT SCAFFOLDING LTD.** Tel : 01642 222626	**A. BUCKLER (HAULAGE) LTD** Tel : 01642 243399	*Crake and Mallon* FUNERAL SERVICE Tel : 01642 611716
BARKER AND STONEHOUSE Tel : 01642 230988	**BORO JUNIOR LIONS** Tel : 0870 421 1986	**SembCorp Utilities UK** Tel : 01642 459955	**MIDDLESBROUGH FOOTBALL CLUB 1986** Former Players and Friends
D & J contracts FLOORING & CARPETING CONTRACTORS Tel : 01642 244253	**Day & Zimmerman** Tel : 01642 447940	**Hall & Co. Solicitors** Tel : 0191 384 3847	**the portland group (ne) ltd** Tel : 01388 747698
fmttm Tel : 01642 249696	**MSV** DIGITAL AUDIO-VIDEO SPECIALISTS Tel : 01642 676444	middlesbrough town centre company **re:generation** *creating investment confidence* Tel : 01642 226622	**Evening Gazette** Tel : 01642 245401